Bible Studies
Leviticus Numbers

Second Edition

James Malm

ISBN: 978-1-7753510-8-5

Copyright 2019 James Malm
All rights reserved

Dedication

This work is dedicated to the Great God whose house is eternity; the Father and Sovereign of all that exists, and the sum of all Truth, Wisdom, Love, Justice and Mercy.
May God's house be filled with children whose chief joy is to be like Him!

Visit our website
theshininglight.info

Table of Contents

Leviticus 7

    The Daily Sacrifice and Sacrificial System 8
    Leviticus Introduction 30
    Leviticus 1 32
    Leviticus 2 37
    Leviticus 3 44
    Leviticus 4 48
    Leviticus 5 55
    Leviticus 6 59
    Leviticus 7 65
    Leviticus 8 72
    Leviticus 9 78
    Leviticus 10 83
    The Clean and Unclean Explained 88
    Leviticus 11 99
    Leviticus 12 106
    Leviticus 13 109
    Leviticus 14 116
    Leviticus 15 124
    Leviticus 16 130
    Leviticus 17 139
    Leviticus 18 143
    Leviticus 19 148
    Leviticus 20 155
    Leviticus 21 160
    Leviticus 22 165
    Leviticus 23 171
    Leviticus 24 180
    Leviticus 25 184
    Leviticus 26 191
    Leviticus 27 198

Numbers 203

    Numbers Introduction 204

Numbers 1	208
Numbers 2	214
Numbers 3	218
Numbers 4	225
Numbers 5	233
Numbers 6	237
Numbers 7	244
Numbers 8	251
Numbers 9	256
Numbers 10	261
Numbers 11	266
Numbers 12	272
Numbers 13	274
Numbers 13	279
Numbers 14	284
Numbers 15	291
Numbers 16	297
Numbers 17	305
Numbers 18	308
Numbers 19	314
Numbers 20	319
Numbers 21	324
Numbers 22	328
Numbers 23	333
Numbers 24	336
Numbers 25	339
Numbers 26	345
Numbers 27	351
Numbers 28	354
Numbers 29	360
Numbers 30	365
Numbers 31	369
Numbers 32	376
Numbers 33	380

Numbers 34..385
Numbers 35..388
Numbers 36..392

Leviticus

The Daily Sacrifice and Sacrificial System

This is an overview of the Sacrificial System and the Daily as an introduction to the Leviticus study.

The Sacrificial System and Daily Sacrifice are anything but boring! They are solid spiritual meat which has not been understood or served in the Church of God for many, many, years.

The Daily Sacrifice is vital to understand in the context of prophecy; since the very last test before the tribulation will be on the false excuse that the Daily is not yet being offered.

Daniel 12:10 Many shall be purified, and made white, and tried; but the wicked [Sabbath polluters, idolaters of men and commandment breakers] shall do wickedly: and none of the wicked shall understand; but the wise shall understand.

The Vital Law of Sacrifice: Despised and Obscured by Satan; there are few things in the Bible more neglected or misunderstood than the Sacrificial System. Why? Satan hates the Sacrificial System; he does everything possible to cause men to do likewise. He seeks to conceal the glory of this system by getting men to think that it has been "done away" and is not worthy of notice or study. He wants men to think that it is bloody, hateful and repugnant; and that the God of Israel was a hateful and bloody God. In doing this he conceals the fact that the God of Israel was a

God of Love and the Sacrificial System was designed to teach about the great mercy and sacrifice of God.

The Purpose of the Sacrificial System

In the very ancient past Satan rebelled against God and one third of the angels followed him: **Revelation 12: 3** And there appeared another wonder in heaven; and behold a great red dragon, having seven heads and ten horns, and seven crowns upon his heads. 4: And his tail drew the third part of the stars of heaven, and did cast them to the earth:

During this rebellion, a great fight took place. Satan was trying to rise up and exalt himself over God; he did not want to be cast down!

Isaiah 14: 12: How art thou fallen from heaven, O Lucifer, son of the morning! How art thou cut down to the ground, which didst weaken the nations! **14:13**: For thou hast said in thine heart, I will ascend into heaven, I will exalt my throne above the stars of God: I will sit also upon the mount of the congregation, in the sides of the north: **14:14**: I will ascend above the heights of the clouds; I will be like the most High. **14:15**: Yet thou shalt be brought down to hell, to the sides of the pit.

Satan was cast down once before; and he shall be cast down yet again before the great tribulation,

Revelation 12: 9 And the great dragon was cast out, that old serpent, called the Devil, and Satan, which deceiveth the whole world: he was cast out into the earth, and his angels were cast out with him. 10: And I heard a loud voice saying in heaven: Now is come salvation, and strength, and the kingdom of our God, and the power of his Christ: for the accuser of our brethren is cast down, which accused them before our God day and night. See the remainder of Revelation 12.

We can see the evidence of this fight in the condition of the moon and planets. And since Satan was cast down to the earth; the earth must have been reduced to a similar condition: which would have required the Genesis recreating.

GOD DOES NOT WANT ANOTHER SUCH CONFLICT. Therefore, God has made men of flesh, so that they could learn the wages and consequences of sin; without destroying the universe!

And so that men, made of flesh would not have the power of angels or spirits to destroy; Man and his destructive abilities have been limited to the earth, until man learns the ways to peace.

God's law reveals the way to peace, harmony and prosperity. Breaking the principles revealed by that law; leads to decay, destruction, violence and death. Man MUST learn that lesson. He MUST learn through the bitter crucible of experience the TRUTH of the behaviors that bring peace and prosperity that God is trying to teach us in his Word.

To teach us these things: God have given us his Word.

He is now allowing us to experience the other side, so that people can learn by experience and can make an intelligent, informed decision after also experiencing God's ways in the future judgment.

For the past six thousand years some have been called out to God and learn by seeing the evils of this world and having their minds opened to the Word of God.

The Sacrificial System is the third part of the lesson.

The purpose of the Sacrificial System is to demonstrate over and over again, that sin brings death. What is sin?

1 John 3:4 Whosoever committeth sin transgresseth also the law: for sin is the transgression of the law [any transgression of the Word of God].

And the end result of sin is suffering, decay and death.

Romans 6:23 For the wages of sin is death; but the gift of God is eternal life through Jesus Christ our Lord.

The wages of sin must be paid! Almighty God could have just said; your sins are forgiven. Yet he required the death of his very; only begotten SON, to atone for our sins: WHY? To impress on us the vital importance of the fact that: SIN CAUSES DEATH; and that true repentance means that we are to go forward and "Sin No More."

We need to learn that God's Word and law defines the way to LIFE, and that breaking those principles leads to DEATH.

God the Father gave his SON to teach us that lesson; and God gave us the Sacrificial System: which is the legal framework for salvation under which the Lamb of God could legally die for us that we might be redeemed from being required to pay the wages of sin with our own lives.

The Law of Sacrifice allows the death of Christ to atone for the sincerely repented PAST sins of men! It teaches us that sin brings death; and it also provides an escape from past sins if they are sincerely repented of; and we Stop Sinning in future! Jesus Christ paid for our PAST sincerely repented sins and the indictment against us for our past sins was paid in full by his death.

Colossians 2:14 Blotting out the handwriting of ordinances that was against us [annulling the indictment or list of the laws which we had broken in the past before our sincere repentance], which was contrary to us, and took it out of the way [and removed the list of our past sins, by the application of his death to the sincerely repentant] , nailing it to his cross;

Christ died for all sinners, yet his sacrifice is only applied to those who sincerely repent and Stop Sinning, to go forward to live by EVERY WORD of GOD in future. It is the KEEPERS of God's Word who will be justified by the application of the sacrifice of Christ!

Romans 2:13 (For **not the hearers** of the law are just before God, but **the doers of the law shall be justified.**

Jesus taught:

Matthew 4:4 But he answered and said, It is written, **Man shall not live by bread alone, but by every word that proceedeth out of the mouth of God.**

Yes, EVERY WORD OF GOD! Jesus quoted directly from Deuteronomy 8:3

John the disciple taught by Christ tells us this:

1 John 2:3 And hereby we do know that **we know him, if we keep his commandments.**

2:4 He that saith, I know him, and keepeth not his commandments, is a liar, and the truth is not in him.

2:5 But **whoso keepeth his word, in him verily is the love of God perfected**: hereby know we that we are in him [We know that we are Christ's if we live by every Word of God the Father, and if we do not live by EVERY WORD of God like Christ did, we are not of Christ].

2:6 He that saith **he abideth in him ought himself also so to walk** [live], **even as he walked** [lived].

The law of sacrifice enables sincere repentance and forgiveness for past sins, so that people may receive the gift of the Holy Spirit and go forward to sin no more!

No wonder Satan hates it so much; Satan is the spiritual Pharaoh god king of this world and he does not want to lose his slaves; who are in bondage to sin and in bondage to him! Satan is loathe to give up his servants just as ancient Pharaoh was loathe to give up his slaves!

Is the Sacrificial System done away?

If that is true, there is no more sacrifice for sin! This system IS NOT DONE AWAY! Every single aspect of this system is a direct allegory to an aspect of the sacrifice of Jesus Christ.

When we sincerely repent and ask that the sacrifice of Christ be applied to us and that our sins be atoned for, we are offering: a sin offering, a trespass offering, a burnt offering, a peace offering, a drink offering, a meat [unleavened bread] offering, and a freewill offering.

Jesus Christ the Lamb of God fulfilled all the requirements of the Sacrificial System; an dour part is to STOP SINNING so that his sacrifice may be applied to us!

1 Corinthians 5:7 Purge out therefore the old leaven [of sin], that ye may be a new lump, as ye are unleavened [free from sin]. For even Christ our Passover is sacrificed for us:

Today we observe the Sacrificial System: by sincere repentance and going before God the Father with the Ultimate Sacrifice; of which all other sacrifices were merely a shadow. The Ultimate Sacrifice that truly atones for sin: the sacrifice of the Creator God.

We have a Special Reminder of this annually at the Passover. But, it is true that Christ fulfills the role of our sacrifice and High Priest EVERY TIME, we repent of sin and ask for the application of his sacrifice.

Being perfect, he needed to die only once: yet His Sacrifice needs to be APPLIED as often as we repent; therefore the Law of Sacrifice needs to be in place throughout history to be available for ALL humanity!

This does NOT justify habitual sin. To repent means: To STOP SINNING, however we may occasionally slip in our learning process, and all humanity does not repent at once; therefore the Law of sacrifice needs to be in place throughout history to be available for ALL humanity!

The Law of Sacrifice was given to us: as a reminder of the death that sin brings: and as a legal foundation for the Sacrifice of Christ: and as a demonstration of the various steps to salvation.

The sacrificial system reveals the various aspects of the ministry and actions of Jesus Christ in service to God and man: and finally it is an example that we should follow Christ in his service to God and man, by doing the will of God as expressed by the whole Word of God.

The Sacrificial System is: a Law of Love; given by a God of Love. To provide an atonement for and forgive our sincerely repented sins, and to teach mankind lessons that will bring peace, harmony and prosperity for all eternity!

The SACRIFICIAL SYSTEM can be divided into two categories, with seven different types of sacrifices. Every one of which typifies an important aspect of the Atoning Work of Jesus Christ as High Priest AND sacrifice.

The two different categories of sacrifices are:

1) **Sacrifices brought by and made by individuals, such as Passover and other personal sacrifices and offerings;** and

2) **The Sacrifices made by the High Priest on behalf of the WHOLE NATION.**

Each individual must make sacrifices in certain situations and may bring a Sacrifice at any time. These various sacrifices typify Christ's atoning sacrifice on behalf of the offering individual.

The High Priest must bring Sacrifices on behalf of the WHOLE NATION; on the annual Festivals (Numbers 28:16-31), the Sabbath (Numbers 28:9-10), the New Moons (Numbers 28:11) and also a Daily Offering (Numbers 28:1-8). It is these Sacrifices that consecrate these occasions.

These two categories reflect the fact that Jesus Christ acts on behalf of both individuals; and on behalf of the Spiritual Covenant Nation as a WHOLE.

The Mosaic Covenant ended with the death of the Husband and God the Father has called out scattered peoples from all nations, who were not themselves a nation; or a priesthood; and he has called them to be a spiritual people with a spiritual New Covenant which will soon be extended to all flesh (Jeremiah 31, Joel 2:28):

1 Peter 2:9 But ye are a chosen generation, a royal priesthood, an holy nation, a peculiar people; that ye should shew forth the praises of him who hath called you out of darkness into his marvellous light; **2:10** Which in time past were not a people, but are now the people of God: which had not obtained mercy, but now have obtained mercy.

Far from being done away, Jesus Christ himself will build a millennial Temple and restore these same physical sacrifices, which will again be made in Jerusalem (Ezekiel 40-48) .

The Seven Types of Sacrifices

The Trespass and the Sin Offerings are very closely related although differing slightly.

1) The Sin Offering is for sin against God and his commandments.

2) The Trespass Offering is for uncleanness or for sin requiring restitution, the modern equivalent would be that the Sin Offering was for breaking the law; while the Trespass Offering mainly pertained to civil matters like the breaking of promises and agreements.

The trespass offering was to atone for specific transgressions against others where restitution was possible, such as sins of ignorance, usually connected with fraud. For example, if a man had unwittingly cheated another, a ransom that was equal to the same value of the amount taken plus one-fifth would be repaid to the former property owner. If the offence is related to holy things, such as vows, tithes and first-fruits, then the worshiper must repay the amount owed plus one-fifth to the priest.

3) **The Burnt Offering** Leviticus 1: This animal is wholly burned and ascends as a sweet savour to God v 9, it atones (is accepted) for persons v 4, it represents a voluntary and wholehearted dedication to God which is a sweet odor to Him

4) **The Meat Offering** Leviticus 2: This is an awkward translation in the KJV from the age when all food was called "meat," and should be better translates as a Grain or Unleavened Bread Offering. This represents Jesus Christ the Word as the pure Unleavened Bread of Life, and it also directly represents Christ's BODY, presented and sacrificed in service to God.

5) **The Drink Offering** Exodus 29:40: The Drink Offering of wine poured out, pictures the shed blood of Christ, and His total willingness to serve the Father even to the death.

6) **The Peace Offering** Leviticus 7:28: The Peace Offering shows man now at peace and in harmony with God; after all sin has been atoned for and man willingly seeks to please God.

7) **The Freewill Offering** Deuteronomy 23;23: A Freewill Offering is given by anyone out of their abundance and joy. This is usually done at the Festivals.

The Sacrificial Animals

The BULL; is a picture of strength, patient service and power; representing Jesus Christ, loving and serving God the Father patiently and with strength; Showing by example that we are to patiently serve God will all our hearts and strength as well.

The LAMB; is a picture of meekness, trust and willingness to follow; showing that Jesus was willing to follow God the Father and to do His will, even to the point of giving up His life for His creation. And this as an example for us; that we should believe, trust and have absolute faith, humbly living by every Word of God the Father like little children, as Christ did.

The RAM; leads and protects the flock, thus revealing the leadership and loving protection that Jesus Christ provides for His Father's flock; The same kind of loving service that we should provide to God the Father and Christ in caring for HIS flock, who are our families and brethren.

The DOVE; is universally regarded as a symbol of harmlessness, peace and harmony; reflecting the nature of Jesus Christ which is without guile or animosity toward others; and the inner peace which is the ultimate fruit of true Godliness.

The GOAT; is a picture of sin being borne, for Christ shall divide the sheep from the goats, the holy from the profane. This animal shows Christ becoming sin for us and taking upon himself the sins of the whole world on that Day of Atonement.

An example of how to understand the scriptures through the Sacrificial System can be shown through the Wave Offering and the later First fruits Offering.

The Wave Offering

Leviticus 23:9-13; Here a LAMB is offered as a BURNT OFFERING; showing willing faithful wholehearted service to God, there is NO thought of sin.

The WAVE OFFERING is a MEAT (Grain) OFFERING which is mingled with OIL (a type of God's Spirit); all MEAT OFFERINGS are made without leaven (except the PENTECOST FIRST FRUITS OFFERING; showing Christ as the perfect Unleavened Bread of Life, the Word of God.

The grain is always the complete kernel of grain, stone ground fine; which in its perfection and purity is an appropriate symbol of the Bread of Life!

That is why it is so wrong and even sinful to use a white flour matzoth, devoid of nutritional value, purity and wholesomeness; as a symbol of

Christ at Passover. It is just an improper and false empty symbol devoid of anything Christ-like in its make up.

A DRINK OFFERING of wine is poured out, picturing shed blood, showing Christ giving His life in service to God; but still no thought of sin. This set of Offerings shows the perfection of Jesus Christ TO BE ACCEPTED FOR US (Leviticus 23:11) as our High Priest (Hebrews 5:10, 6:20). There is ABSOLUTELY; NO HINT OF SIN.

The Unleavened Bread and Wine of Passover were NOT new symbols by any means. They were basic symbols of the sacrificial system all along. Christ did not add new symbols at all, he merely brought to our attention the meaning of those symbols already codified in the law.

The FIRST FRUITS OFFERING on PENTECOST (Leviticus 23:15-21)

On the fiftieth day after the Wave Offering on Pentecost Sunday we have two loaves (showing an INCREASE over the one loaf at Wave Offering) and both of these FIRST FRUITS LOAVES are made WITH leaven v 17, a type of SIN.

These two loaves picture NOT Christ, but the increase and expansion of the first fruits to include all flesh in the millennium:

Joel 2:32 And it shall come to pass, that **whosoever shall call on the name of the Lord shall be delivered:** for in mount Zion and in Jerusalem shall be deliverance [Jesus Christ will rule all nations from Jerusalem and the remnant of humanity will be called to live by every Word of God all flesh (Joel 2:28)], as the Lord hath said, and in the remnant whom the Lord shall call.

Then with the First Fruits offering is a BURNT OFFERING of seven Lambs, showing all flesh now serving God the Father following the example of Christ's complete willingness to obey and meekly follow God the Father in humble obedience and faithful service to wholeheartedly live by every Word of God; which is sweet and acceptable to God our Father.

The rising smoke pictures wholehearted godly attitude and actions ascending up to God the Father and pleasing him. This on the Feast of First Fruits [Pentecost] also shows the first fruits following the example of Christ in service to God the Father.

Then one Bull showing Christ's powerful faithful service, together with the Unleavened Bread and Drink Offerings, showing Christ giving Himself and pouring out His life; totally for His Father and for His creation.

The Passover sacrifice on which either a lamb or a kid could be sacrificed, was offered for the called out only. At the start of the millennium when all flesh are called to God the kid has preeminence as the sin offering because of the expansion of the Passover offering to include the entire millennial harvest.

Then you shall sacrifice a GOAT for a SIN OFFERING, clearly showing Christ bearing the SIN of the first fruits.

Finally AFTER the SIN has been BORNE AND ATONED FOR (the sin represented by the leaven of the two loaves), comes a PEACE OFFERING of two Lambs; showing that the two loaves of first fruits are now at peace and in harmony with God.

The picture of the **WAVE OFFERING,** which is to be waved before God, to be accepted for us; is one of perfect service and the perfection of Christ, with no hint of sin anywhere.

The **PENTECOST FIRST FRUIT OFFERING** which is to be presented to God; is one of men being imperfect and polluted by SIN; thus requiring an atonement for SIN, before being brought into harmony with God the Father.

Brethren, some day the chosen shall become the Priests of God; The priests of the High Priesthood of Melchizedek [Jesus Christ]. We can develop a better understanding of the Word of God by learning of this SACRIFICIAL LAW which God has considered so necessary to enact and preserve for us. The Bible is full of much that is truly fascinating, if we would just take the time to consider it. How truly beautiful and intricate is the Word of God! This is only the simplest and most basic outline, given to encourage your studies.

The Job of the High Priest

First come the sacrifices commanded to be offered by the High Priest on behalf of the whole nation.

That includes the Festival offerings, the Sabbath and New Moon offerings; and the Evening and Morning or Daily Sacrifice.

The second group of sacrifices consists of those sacrifices offered by the people as their personal offerings.

It is the job of the High Priest to:

1) Intercede for the people with God, and offer the commanded sacrifices for the whole people as a group;

2) to offer the sacrifices of repentant individuals.

Jesus Christ has become OUR High Priest and Intercedes for us with God the Father, BOTH on an individual basis and on behalf of all the saints as a group.

Our spiritual High Priest Jesus Christ intercedes for us with God the Father applying his sacrifice to repentant individuals and to the body as a whole.

Today the overall assemblies, or body, or spiritual nation; has gone astray and removed itself from the protection of Christ, to be rejected by him (Rev 3:14-22).

Even when the overall spiritual body is rejected; those individuals who are repentant will be covered by Christ's sacrifice and cared for by him.

With the acceptance of Christ by God the Father, the Temple dwelling was officially changed fully from a building to a spiritual dwelling of God within men; and the sacrificial system was fully changed into a spiritual reality as well.

Jesus Christ was released from his marriage covenant to the nation of physical Israel by his death, and at his resurrection and ascension to God the Father he was accepted for us and was made a new High Priest replacing the high priesthood of Aaron. Yet God has made a promise to the descendants of Zadok that they would be called into the New Covenant and serve in the Millennial Temple

Jesus became espoused to a New Spiritual Nation in a New Spiritual Covenant: Today the whole Ekklesia is the Spiritual Nation of God, as each individual is a personal citizen of the Spiritual Nation of the New Covenant!

1 Peter 2:9 But ye are a chosen generation, a royal priesthood, an holy nation, a peculiar [special] people; that ye should shew forth the praises of him who hath called you out of darkness into his marvellous light;

In the Millennial Kingdom, a new Physical Temple will be built and physical sacrifices will again be presented, as a physical demonstration of that spiritual reality.

In this age there is NO such physical temple and therefore no physical sacrifices can be made!

Christ will come to his Temple: His people!

He is presently interceding for the called out Ekklesia as a group; and also intercedes on behalf of repentant individuals; on a daily basis with God the Father as our ONLY High Priest and Intercessor!

The Daily Sacrifice

Exodus 29:38 Now this is that which thou shalt offer upon the altar; two lambs of the first year day by day continually. **29:39** The one lamb thou shalt offer in the morning; and the other lamb thou shalt offer at even: **29:40** And with the one lamb a tenth deal of flour mingled with the fourth part of an hin of beaten oil; and the fourth part of an hin of wine for a drink offering.

29:41 And the other lamb thou shalt offer at even, and shalt do thereto according to the meat offering of the morning, and according to the drink offering thereof, for a sweet savour, an offering made by fire unto the LORD. **29:42** This shall be a continual burnt offering throughout your generations at the door of the tabernacle of the congregation before the LORD: where I will meet you, to speak there unto thee.

The Daily Sacrifice was:

    1) Offered twice a day; once in the evening at sunset and once in the morning at sun rise. Services and the process began some time earlier but the sacrifices were burned at sun rise and sun set.

    2) Was offered by the High Priest on behalf of the whole nation.

    3) Was a lamb.

    4) Was a Burnt Offering.

    5) Was offered at the door of the Tabernacle.

    6) The Daily was offered WITH the Meat [Unleavened Bread} and Drink [Wine] offerings.

The Daily was offered by the High Priest on behalf of the whole nation.

The High Priest is now Jesus Christ; and the whole Covenant Nation is now the spiritual Ekklesia of the called out. Those things of the Mosaic Covenant were mere shadows of the spiritual things of the New Covenant.

The lamb is offered twice each day, represented Jesus Christ as the Lamb of God, offering himself and working day and night to fulfill the two great principles of the law [service to God and to man], as the High Priest of God the Father and the High Priest of the Ekklesia; interceding between the two and reconciling the overall Ekklesia of the Called out, to God the Father, as well as reconciling individuals to God.

The Meat [Unleavened Bread] Offering accompanying the Daily Morning and Evening Sacrifice represents the pure perfect Word of God by which we are to live in Christ-like zeal.

The Daily Morning and Evening Offering, as an Offering by the High Priest; represents the work of Jesus Christ as the High Priest of the New Covenant on behalf of the whole body of the called out New Covenant nation.

Morning and evening picture a complete day (Gen 1); the lambs picture Christ as humbly serving the Father unto death and giving himself fully to God the Father as the Lamb of God; the Unleavened Bread picturing Jesus Christ as the Word, the Unleavened Bread of Life; who's nature of wholehearted loyalty to God the Father and of keeping all of the Father's Word, commandments and Will; is to be internalized by those Called into the New Covenant.

This offering began with the anointing of Aaron and is to be continued perpetually as an allegory of the eternal intercessional work of the New Covenant of Jesus Christ as the High Priest forever after the order of Melchizedek, and the High Priest of the New Covenant.

It is this daily offering that was stopped physically with the destruction of Jerusalem and the Temple in 70 A.D. (Dan 9:27).

It is NOT necessary for any physical Daily to be started and then stopped before the tribulation! It was already stopped at the end of the first half of the 70th week in 70 A.D., and was prophesied to remain stopped until the return of Christ.

Leviticus 6:19 And the LORD spake unto Moses, saying, **6:20** This is the offering of Aaron and of his sons, which they shall offer unto the LORD in the day when he is anointed; the tenth part of an ephah of fine flour **for a meat offering perpetual, half of it in the morning, and half thereof at night**.

6:21 In a pan it shall be made with oil [symbolizing the holy spirit]; and when it is baken, thou shalt bring it in: and the baken pieces of the meat offering shalt thou offer for a sweet savour [burned to smoke, rising to the Father a wonderful perfume of the intercessory work of our high Priest Jesus Christ] unto the LORD.

6:22 And the priest of his sons that is anointed in his stead shall offer it: it is a statute for ever unto the LORD; **it shall be wholly burnt**.

Every Unleavened Bread offering accompanying the Daily morning and evening sacrifice of the lambs shall be wholly burned.

6:23 For every meat offering for the priest shall be wholly burnt: it shall not be eaten.

The Burnt Offering represented this service of giving himself fully and totally [as the lamb was fully burnt] in service to God and man, as being very pleasing to the Father; the smoke ascending as a sweet odour and something pleasant to the Father.

The Unleavened Bread and Wine Offering attending: showing that Christ is fully dedicated and consumed with service; with body and life; the very Bread of Life and Blood of Life, symbolized by the Grain and Wine.

This sacrifice [like all sacrifices] was offered to help explain the service of Christ; and also as an example that we should also serve God the Father FIRST and then also our neighbour, as say the two great principles of the law.

This sacrifice was offered at the door of the tabernacle representing the very door of the hearts of the Ekklesia [who are now the Temple of God]; showing Christ standing at the door and knocking (Rev 3), interceding for us with God the Father if only we would be repentant and passionately love the Father, committing to keep the Father's commandments.

Today the Ekklesia [the church of God as a whole] have rejected any zeal to live by every Word of God the Father; still Jesus Christ is standing at the door knocking and willing to intercede for us, if we would only turn to our Father (Rev 3).

Those who will not open to godliness at this time will be rejected and spewed out; UNTIL they repent: That is the stopping of the daily (Dan 12:11) on behalf of the whole Ekklesia of the Nation (1 Pet 2:9) of the Called Out.

Christ's interceding work will continue on behalf of repentant individuals; which is the confirming of the New Covenant with the faithful individuals who will stand on God's Word and commandments.

NOTE: A new physical Temple will be built at Jerusalem during the Millennial Kingdom; and this sacrificial system will be restarted, Ezek 40-48; and NOT before!

These things will be school lessons to reveal the fullness of the service of God the Father and Christ for their people!

At that time the meaning and spirit behind the various sacrifices will be explained to the people in their fullness. That will be the job of the millennial priesthood!

The spiritual Daily Sacrifice in heaven will shortly be stopped for the whole nation of the Ekklesia, but the application of Christ's sacrifice on behalf of repentant individuals will continue.

A falling away means that there must first be a people who are faithful and who then later turn away. A continual falling away has always been in progress: Now that falling away is reaching its climax!

2 Thessalonians 2 Let no man deceive you by any means: for that day shall not come, except there come a falling away first, and that man of sin be revealed, the son of perdition;

Writing in a generality about the WHOLE Nation of the Called Out; many of those calling themselves God's people routinely pollute the Sabbath and Holy Days; they commit spiritual adultery by idolizing men and corporate churches as their ultimate moral authority instead of God's Word and commandments. They fudge in keeping the commandments, justifying compromise, which is rebellion against God; on an almost continual basis.

We rely on pagan writings and commentaries to support our positions and governance systems instead of on God's Word; committing spiritual fornication with Jezebel and her daughters. We rely on our false past traditions, refusing to correct error, or to accept the truth when it is revealed. We call evil, good; and good, evil; persecuting the faithful by calling them self-righteous or Pharisaic.

We do not cry aloud the message of REPENTANCE to specific sin, even within our own groups. We may say "repent" but of what specific sin? We cannot call to repentance because we ourselves refuse to repent and keep the commandments with zeal. We are full of deceitfulness, politicking and power grubbing, as well as elders who feed themselves and not the sheep.

I might go on about many living in adultery, divorcing and remarrying at will, in defiance of Jesus Christ, or about unequal marriages with unbelievers; the list is long.

In all this WE ARE ABSOLUTELY BLIND TO OUR WICKEDNESS.

Revelation 3:15 I know thy works, that thou art neither cold nor hot: I would thou wert cold or hot. **3:16** because thou art lukewarm, and neither cold nor hot, I will spue thee out of my mouth [the spiritual Daily will be stopped on behalf of the spiritual nation and these groups will be spued out of the body of Christ into great correction]. **3:17** Because thou sayest, I am rich, and increased with goods, and have need of nothing; and knowest not that thou art wretched, and miserable, and poor, and blind, and naked:

These sins and any breaking or compromise with any of God's commandments will result in our REJECTION by Jesus Christ and God the Father!

Daniel 9:27 And he shall confirm the covenant with many for one week: and in the midst of the week he shall cause the sacrifice and the oblation to cease, and for the overspreading of abominations he shall make it desolate, even until the consummation, and that determined shall be poured upon the desolate.

God allowed prince Titus to destroy Jerusalem and the Temple in 70 A.D. after the first half of the 70th week was fulfilled in the siege of Jerusalem and the flight of the faithful to Pella. That was at the end of the first half of the week and before the beginning of the second half of the week; i.e. in the midst of the week!

The physical Daily Sacrifice shall remain stopped and the physical temple will remain desolate until the coming of Christ to pour out what has been determined against the desolator which is the Scarlet Beast, ROME; the latter day heir of Babylon.

The New Covenant is a Covenant of espousal to marriage to the Lamb of God.

During the first Roman siege and destruction of Jerusalem, Jesus Christ confirmed that New Covenant with his people by preserving and caring for them in a refuge at Pella for 1,260 days (Rev 12:1-6).

In these latter days there will be war in heaven (Rev 12:7), to be quickly followed by a REJECTION of the Church of God groups by Jesus Christ into great tribulation!

After the overall group have been spewed out by God as per Revelation 3, Then those individuals who have repented and turned to the Eternal, will be removed to refuge for a second 1,260 days; while those who have been rejected are corrected.

Very many of these apostate people are full of love for their group and for the brethren and even for humanity. Many of these people are the finest people that one would care to meet; thoughtful, considerate kind, compassionate; yet there is a major problem. They have placed the second great commandment in front of the first great commandment in their focus and lost sight of any zeal for the Word and commandments of God.

It is heartrending to see some very wonderful people, so filled with love for others that they have become lukewarm for God's Word. God's commandments are just something that they go through the motions on, because they are more interested in the social aspects of the brotherhood.

When they are shocked into wakefulness by their correction, very many will repent and with a new found zeal will be transformed into Paul's. Our Father is so marvelous in his wisdom; he knows how to not only save, but how to perfect his people!

This world is full of abominations, and we are to be the salt of this earth, making it worth preserving by our God. We have LOST the salt of our savor to our God! This whole world; along with physical Israel and the Gentiles, including the majority of the spiritually called out today [Spiritual Israel]; the WHOLE WORLD: is to face God's wrath for its [and we for our own] wickedness and abominations.

Daniel 12:11 And from the time that the daily sacrifice [the heavenly spiritual intercession of Christ] shall be taken away, and the abomination that maketh desolate set up, there shall be a thousand two hundred and ninety days [to the resurrection to spirit].

Notice that the Daily Sacrifice of Christ's intercession is removed for the spiritual nation and Jesus will no longer intercede for the apostate Spiritual Ekklesia as corporate groups; thus ending the restraint and allowing the final abomination to be set up.

This is referred to by Paul as the restraining power that holds back the abomination until the appointed time.

2 Thessalonians 2:5 And now ye know what withholdeth that he might be revealed in his time. **2:6** For the mystery of iniquity doth already work: only he who now letteth [withholds, restrains] will let [withhold, restrains], until he [Christ's daily intervention for the nation] be taken out of the way.

This passage speaks of the abomination which I will get into in detail in another post; the point here is that this wickedness is restrained until the appointed time by he who withholds; which is: the daily intercession of Christ on behalf of the whole assembly of the called out.

Because the whole assembly of the called out, has become lukewarm for God's law and filled with abominations and unrepentant sin; it shall be rejected by Christ as per Revelation 3; then Christ shall confirm the New Covenant with the scattered faithful, by preserving them while the majority are corrected.

All sacrifices in this dispensation have been supplanted by the sacrifice of Jesus Christ! The Daily is also a spiritual application of the sacrifice of

Christ; just like the sacrifice of Christ can be applied personally to the individually repentant.

Christ's sacrifice is applied to us in a personal way upon repentance! Today the Daily is that sacrifice offered by the High Priest, Jesus Christ; on behalf of THE WHOLE SPIRITUAL NATION OR EKKLESIA OF THE CALLED OUT!

With the end of the Mosaic Covenant: the Aaronic high priesthood has ended and the new High Priest after the order of Melchizedek, is now Jesus Christ; who is restraining Satan and his wicked final false prophet until the appointed time, and who is fulfilling all the promises made to the ancients to bless the descendants of Jacob in the latter days.

At the appointed time the blessing and the restraint represented by the Daily Intercession of Christ for his called out spiritual nation WILL BE REMOVED, and the abomination will be set up as the miracle working false prophet in Rome. Then Christ will reject his called out collectively into great tribulation (Rev 3:16).

Details of the Morning and Evening Daily Sacrifice

The Daily Sacrifice was commanded to be offered every morning [dawn] and every evening [sunset]; The Daily was offered by the high priest as an allegory of Jesus Christ serving the Father night and day as our High Priest interceding for the people with God the Father.

In Genesis one we find that a 24 hour day is defined as an evening, or the dark portion beginning at sunset, and a morning, or the daylight portion of the 24 hours, ending at sunset. Logically then the Daily Sacrifice should be offered in the Morning and at sunset.

Yet we find Josephus and Philo both Hellenizers saying that the evening daily sacrifice was offered at the 9th hour, about 3 PM, not at sunset. (Ant. 14.4.3, Philo Special Laws I, XXXV (169).

How do we explain this difficulty? The answer lies in the fact that the Hour of Prayer at 3 PM BEGAN the ritual around the Daily Sacrifices, but it took several more hours before the lamb was killed, after which it was cleaned, skinned, washed, various rituals fulfilled and psalms recited and only at sunset was the lamb offered [burned] on the altar.

In fact the Hour [The Time] of Prayer [before the sacrifice] began at 3 PM and not the actual Evening Sacrifice. The Hour of Prayer was only a prelude to the Evening Sacrifice and not the sacrifice itself, and is mentioned in Josephus and Philo because the Hour of Prayer had come to be thought of as a part of the process of the Evening Offering. In fact the Hour of Prayer and all of these undertakings preceded the evening sacrifice which was offered [burned] at sunset.

The actual killing of the sacrifice did not take place until several hours after 3 PM and the actual offering of the sacrifice by burning was at sunset and before full darkness,

The daily morning and evening sacrifices were complex affairs which took several hours each to perform. The ritual involved a series of actions, prayers, the reciting of psalms and blessings, the actual killing followed by the cleaning and salting of the sacrifice and finally the offering of the sacrifice by burning which also took some time.

A lack of general understanding of these things has led to some confusion; when Josephus said that the evening sacrifice was at 3 in the afternoon, he meant that the whole process; that is the prayers before the sacrifice, BEGAN at 3 PM.

At 3 pm the hour of prayer began; the hour of prayer was not the hour of the actual offering of the sacrifice. Rather the afternoon hour of prayer **was the beginning of the prayers which preceded the actual sacrifice process** for offering [burning] the Daily immediately after sunset.

Remember that the sacrificial offering is the offering of the sacrifice on the altar not the actual killing. Animals were killed for food all the time, the difference is that the sacrificial animal is offered [burned] on the altar.

The killing of the offering took place earlier and the lamb was prepared, but the actual offering [burning] on the altar took place either immediately after dawn or immediately after sunset.

The Morning Sacrifice

The morning sacrifice was killed and then prepared and finally burned [offered] at dawn and the various prayers, blessings and Psalms lasted until about 9 AM. To accomplish the many rituals and prayers, they started the Morning Daily process well before sunrise.

The lamb was killed before dawn and then prepared after being killed, before it was burned as the offering at dawn, along with all of the various lots, preparations, prayers, Psalms etc.

In the morning they made sure to see the first appearance of the sun on the horizon before burning the lamb on the altar, and in the evening they made sure the sun was set before burning the sacrifice on the altar.

The morning sacrifice was killed before the sun rose and skinned, cleaned, salted and cut up before being burned [offered] just as the sun rose above the horizon, with various prayers, blessings and psalms to complete the sacrifice. To accomplish the many rituals and prayers, they started the Morning Daily process well before sunrise.

In the morning they made sure the sun was just rising before burning the lamb on the altar, and in the evening they made sure the sun was just setting before burning the sacrifice on the altar.

The order of the morning sacrifice was the same for the evening sacrifice; the only difference being that the morning sacrifice was offered [burned] on the altar after the sun rose and the evening sacrifice was burned on the altar after the sun set.

The Morning Sacrifice process began well before dawn, the lamb was killed and salted and then later burned [offered] at dawn and the full service with psalms, recitations and prayers lasted until almost 9 AM.

The idea that the Morning Sacrifice took place at 9 AM, is a misunderstanding; the whole Morning Sacrifice service took until about 9 AM, but the actual offering was burned just as the sun rose.

In the morning they made sure the sun was just rising before burning the lamb on the altar, and in the evening they made sure the sun was just setting before burning the sacrifice on the altar.

The order of the morning sacrifice was the same for the evening sacrifice; the only difference being that the morning sacrifice was offered [burned] on the altar after the sun rose and the evening sacrifice was burned on the altar after the sun set.

The Morning Sacrifice process began well before dawn, the lamb was killed and salted and then later burned [offered] at dawn and the full service with psalms, recitations and prayers lasted until almost 9 AM.

The idea that the Morning Sacrifice took place at 9 AM, is a misunderstanding; the whole Morning Sacrifice service took until about 9 AM, but the actual offering was burned just as the sun rose.

The Evening Sacrifice

At 3 PM the hour of prayer began; The hour of prayer was not the hour of the actual offering of the sacrifice. Rather the afternoon hour of prayer **was the beginning of the prayers which preceded the actual sacrifice process** for offering the Daily; which was burned [offered] at sunset.

The evening sacrifice began with the blessings and psalms and prayers at the Hour of Prayer before the killing of the lamb. The evening lamb was killed and was then skinned, cleaned, salted and cut up before being offered on the altar [burned] just after the sun set.

Blessings and psalms and prayers were offered before the killing of the lamb. The evening lamb was killed and then prepared and was offered on the altar when the sun had set.

The Evening Sacrifice WAS FIXED BY THE LAW (Numbers 28: 4,8) as "between the evenings" which is BETWEEN THE DARKNESS OF SUNSET AND THAT OF THE NIGHT

Such admonitions as "to show forth thy faithfulness every NIGHT upon an instrument of ten strings and on the psaltery" (Ps 92:2,3) and the call to those who "by NIGHT STAND IN THE HOUSE of the Lord," to "lift up their hands in the sanctuary and bless the Lord" (Ps. 134), indicating a sunset to full dark service - an impression confirmed by the appointment of Levitical singers for night service in 1 Chron 9:33; 23:30.

The Hour of Prayer which began at 3 PM, was not the actual sacrifice.

The temple gates were closed after the evening sacrifice except on Passover and Holy Days.

The Hellenic Pharisees taught that the meaning of evening and "between the two evenings" was from anytime after noon until dark.

The Mosaic Pharisees, Samaritans, Karaites, and Sadducees [the priests who actually performed the service], all taught that it was the time as AFTER sunset and BEFORE darkness (Interpreter's Bible, Ex.12:6; also The Jewish Encyclopedia, art. Passover, page 553).

In Numbers 28: 3-4 we read of the daily morning and evening sacrifices in the tabernacle. Here the word "evening" is in the Hebrew: "between the two evenings." That is, between sunset and full dark. Let us be clear; this is about what God had commanded; not about what they actually did!

The Sadducees [priests] did have this correct; and that it was the Rabbinic Hellenizers who either misunderstood or misrepresented the time of the Evening and Morning Daily for their own purposes.

In any case the Biblical command is clear and it is self evident from the Sabbath ending at sunset, that the evening refers to sunset and not to 3 in the afternoon. Therefore "Between the Evenings" refers to the period between sunset and full dark for the Daily Evening Sacrifice as well as the Passover.

The later writings of the Hellenized Rabbins that "Between the Evenings" was meaning anytime after noon and before darkness; was a misunderstanding from the fact that the Hour of Prayer began at 3 PM. The hour of prayer was not the actual sacrifice: But a prelude to the offering.

The Hour of Prayer began about 3 pm and the Evening Sacrifice preparations only began about an hour before sunset when the lamb was killed, prepared and salted and then offered by burning with prayers and psalms at sunset before it became fully dark.

The same process of looking out for the dawn was used in looking out for the sunset, at which time the lamb was burned [offered]. On Passover day as soon as the Evening Sacrifice was made the killing of the Passover lambs began.

Leviticus Introduction

The Book of Genesis was written as a general history up to Jacob; Exodus is about the calling out from Egypt as an allegory of a calling out from bondage to Satan and sin.

Leviticus is instructions for the priesthood and Levites and for the New Covenant faithful who are all called to become priests of Melchizedek [Jesus Christ]. Leviticus is a Book that we are to learn and take to heart, each sacrifice being an instructional allegory of an aspect of the ministry and sacrifice of Jesus Christ.

Numbers is a history of the wanderings of Israel in the wilderness and Deuteronomy is a recap of the history of Israel from the Exodus to the death of Moses and a warning that only those who learn and live by every Word of God may enter and remain in the physical Promised Land: as an instructional example that only those who are zealous to learn and to live by every Word of God will be resurrected into the spiritual Promised Land of eternal life.

What is the spiritual meaning behind the physical Levitical sacrifices and laws?

Every aspect of every offering is a picture of a part of the ministry and atoning work of Jesus Christ!

If we are to be priests of Christ it is important to understand everything about him and every aspect of his ministry. Indeed if we do not understand the sacrifices, we cannot understand much about Jesus Christ or prophecy.

Leviticus 1

The Personal Burnt Offering

All sacrifices are representative of the atoning sacrifice of Jesus Christ and must be the specified clean animals out of their own herds and flocks; signifying that Christ would come out from their own nation.

The specified animal must be without blemish; picturing the perfection and purity; the complete holiness and freedom from sin and any defilement or association with sin; of Jesus Christ!

We are to follow the lead of Jesus Christ and we are to diligently work to learn and to live by every Word of God and to be ONE in complete unity with God the Father and with the Son; and to be fully ONE in complete unity with the whole Word of God.

1 Peter 1:16 Because it is written, Be ye holy; for I am holy.

Leviticus 11:44 For I am the Lord your God: ye shall therefore sanctify yourselves, and ye shall be holy; for I am holy: neither shall ye defile yourselves with any manner of creeping thing that creepeth upon the earth.

11:45 For I am the Lord that bringeth you up out of the land of Egypt, to be your God: **ye shall therefore be holy, for I am holy.**

Leviticus 1 is about personal burnt offerings brought by individuals, and is not about national offerings brought by the high priest on behalf of the whole nation; hence the offering individual must place his hands on the offering and not the priest.

The burnt offering represents Jesus Christ the Lamb of God, giving himself voluntarily and wholly in service to God.

In addition the voluntary burnt offering brought by individuals, represents the voluntary wholehearted zeal of the individual bringing the offering to live by every Word of God as Jesus Christ does (Mat 4:4).

Leviticus 1:1 And the LORD called unto Moses, and spake unto him out of the tabernacle of the congregation, saying, **1:2** Speak unto the children of Israel, and say unto them, **If any man of you bring an offering unto the LORD,** ye shall bring your offering of the cattle, even of the herd, and of the flock.

The burnt offering is to be wholly consumed by the fire. This pictures Jesus Christ giving himself completely in service to God the Father. Just as the whole animal was consumed by the fire, so Jesus Christ was and is completely consumed with zeal for God the Father; which is an example that we are to follow.

The smoke of the Burnt Offering ascending upwards represented a sweet savor [odor, perfume] to God the Father, because it represents the wholehearted love and dedication to God of the offeror. The offering must be voluntary because it represents the voluntary Christ-like zeal of the individual bringing the offering.

1:3 If his offering be a burnt sacrifice of the herd, let him offer a male without blemish: he shall offer it **of his own voluntary will** at the door of the tabernacle of the congregation before the LORD.

The burnt offering was to be a male because it represented Jesus Christ. The offeror [not the priest] must place his hands on the head of the sacrifice and the Burnt Offering will be accepted as an example of the offerer's wholehearted Christ--like zeal to live by every Word of God.

1:4 And he shall put his hand upon the head of the burnt offering; and it shall be accepted for him to make atonement for him.

Notice that it is the offeror and not the priest who kills the Burnt Offering; thus plainly showing that Christ died for each one of us, and that the priest cannot atone for us. Only our own sincere repentance, the application of the sacrifice of Jesus Christ for repented sin and then our working diligently to go and sin no more in Christ-like zeal for God the Father and the whole Word of God, will reconcile us to God the Father.

Our relationship with our sacrifice [the Lamb of God] is a personal one, and we must follow men ONLY as they follow Christ to live by every Word of God like he does.

1:5 And he shall kill the bullock before the LORD: and the priests, Aaron's sons, shall bring the blood, and sprinkle the blood round about upon the altar that is by the door of the tabernacle of the congregation.

The blood of atonement is sprinkled on the altar. This is significant of ratifying a covenant with Messiah through his blood, signifying the blood of Messiah shed for all of us and for each of us; it signifies the sacrifice and work of Christ in reconciling men to God the Father.

1:6 And he shall flay the burnt offering, and cut it into his pieces. **1:7** And the sons of Aaron the priest shall put fire upon the altar, and lay the wood in order upon the fire: **1:8** And the priests, Aaron's sons, shall lay the parts, the head, and the fat, in order upon the wood that is on the fire which is upon the altar:

The inner parts and the legs are to be washed in water; which water is symbolic of the Holy Spirit and the Word of God, which we are to fully internalize into our innermost beings, and that we are to live [walk with our legs] as Christ walked being passionately faithful to live by every Word of God.

> **1 John 2:6** He that saith he abideth in him ought himself also so to walk [live], even as he walked [lived].

When the spear was thrust into Jesus and blood and water came out, it was a reminder of what he had taught in the Temple.

> **John 19:34** But one of the soldiers with a spear pierced his side, and forthwith came there out blood and water.

> **John 7:38** He that believeth on me, as the scripture hath said, out of his belly shall flow rivers of living water.

The smoke of the Burnt Offering which was entirely burned, rose up as a sweet savor [perfume] to God the Father, not because the Father likes the smell of burned flesh, but because the smoke represented the wholehearted dedication of Jesus Christ and His faithfulness to do the Father's will and to live by every Word of God.

Leviticus 1:9 But his inwards and his legs shall he wash in water: and the priest shall burn all on the altar, to be a burnt sacrifice, an offering made by fire, of a sweet savour unto the LORD.

The Burnt Offering of the "lesser cattle" [sheep and goats]

1:10 And if his offering be of the flocks, namely, of the sheep, or of the goats, for a burnt sacrifice; he shall bring it a male without blemish.

It was a pagan custom and it still is common today to face the east when worshiping, this comes from sun worship facing the sun rise. You will notice in every Masonic temple that the meeting is set up so that the people face the east [the sun rise] of the sun god. This is because the masons teach that they are the descendants of the Egyptian Mysteries.

God's Temple was set up to that the people worshiped facing the west with their backs to the rising sun.

The sacrifice being done in the NORTH was directly pointing to reconciliation to God the Father in his heavenly Temple.

1:11 And he shall kill it **on the side of the altar northward** before the LORD: and the priests, Aaron's sons, shall sprinkle his blood round about upon the altar.

The offering of any sheep or goats is done the same as for the bullock and the Burnt Offerings of the different animals have the same meaning, but the chosen animals represent different aspects of the Burnt Offering.

1:12 And he shall cut it into his pieces, with his head and his fat: and the priest shall lay them in order on the wood that is on the fire which is upon the altar: **1:13** But he shall wash the inwards and the legs with water: and the priest shall bring it all, and burn it upon the altar: it is a burnt sacrifice, an offering made by fire, of a sweet savour unto the LORD.

A Burnt Offering of doves or pigeons

This offering of birds enables even the very poor of the people who cannot afford to burn a whole bullock or lamb to bring a Burnt Offering.

1:14 And if the burnt sacrifice for his offering to the LORD be of fowls, then he shall bring his offering of turtledoves, or of young pigeons.

1:15 And the priest shall bring it unto the altar, and wring off his head, and burn it on the altar; and the blood thereof shall be wrung out at the side of the altar:

The crop is not to be burned because of the diet of these birds, the crop may contain some unclean insects; the feathers may also have unclean inhabitants.

1:16 And he shall pluck away his crop with his feathers, and cast it beside the altar on the east part [the offal is cast to the east, the place of the rising sun], by the place of the ashes:

The breast is to be split but not the back thereby exposing the birds internal cavity while keeping the bird whole.

1:17 And he shall cleave it with the wings thereof, but shall not divide it asunder: and the priest shall burn it upon the altar, upon the wood that is upon the fire: it is a burnt sacrifice, an offering made by fire, of a sweet savour unto the LORD.

The Burnt Offering represented the wholehearted voluntary Christ-like zeal of the offeror to serve God and to live by every Word of God the Father; it also represents the Christ-like wholehearted love and service that we are to have for God the Father and the whole Word of God.

It is a wholehearted zeal to learn and keep the whole Word of God that is a sweet perfume to God the Father; and it is the cooling of that zeal to live by every Word of God which quenches the Holy Spirit and separates us from God!

Is it really zeal for God to call his Sabbath holy and then to pollute it for our own pleasure?

Leviticus 2

The Meat [Unleavened Bread] Offering

In 1611 of King James all food was called meat, which is different from our modern definition of meat as flesh only. The Biblical Meat Offering was the offering of unleavened bread accompanying the drink [wine] and animal offerings.

All meat [unleavened bread] offerings are to be unleavened, picturing Jesus Christ as the Bread of Life, except one: The Pentecost Offering which pictures the spiritual brethren.

> **The Pentecost Offering-** Represents the first fruits still having sin, but having that sin covered by a sin offering. The Pentecost Offering was waved before God but was not burned on the altar.

> **Passover-** The flesh offering [the lamb] and the drink offering [the wine, representing the shed blood of Christ] of Passover, must be eaten with unleavened bread which is a special meat [unleavened bread] offering that is to be consumed by the people.

> Unleavened bread offerings [including the Passover symbol] are always to have pure olive oil [and salt] in it or to have that oil poured out upon it representative of God's Holy Spirit. Those who take unleavened bread for Passover which does not contain pure

olive oil are neglecting a very important component of salvation, the Holy Spirit! Salt is also an essential part of the Passover unleavened bread.

All unleavened bread for religious purposes must contain pure olive oil representing taking into ourselves the Holy Spirit of God, and salt [a preservative] symbolizing the eternal nature of our Covenant relationship with God.

This eating of unleavened bread during the Spring Feast and the unleavened bread accompanying the sacrifices pictures internalizing the Word of God, which is Jesus Christ as the Bread of Life.

On the Passover and every day of the Feast of Unleavened Bread we are to eat unleavened bread made with stone ground whole grain [symbolizing Jesus Christ], water [symbolizing the Word of God], pure olive oil [symbolizing the Holy Spirit] and salt [a preservative symbolizing the eternal nature of God and his New Covenant]. This eating pictures the eating or internalizing of the nature of God the Father and Jesus Christ and the whole Word and will of God.

Just as the sacrificial animals picture various aspects of the atoning death of Jesus Christ, the meat [unleavened bread] offerings picture Christ as the Bread of Life and must be eaten daily during the seven day Feast of Unleavened Bread. This pictures the need to internalize the nature of Jesus Christ [THE WORD] and God the Father through a diligent zeal to learn and live by every Word of God in Christ-like zeal.

Anyone who does not partake of the correctly made unleavened bread on Passover and every day of the Feast of Unleavened Bread is missing these important lessons and is sinning against the commandment of God; which is intended to teach us a zeal for the whole Word of God to learn it and to live by it.

Those who teach that it is not necessary to eat unleavened every day of the Feast are in rebellion against the Word of God.

The Meat Offering

Unleavened bread offerings [including the Passover symbol] are always to have pure olive oil in it or to have that oil poured out upon it, representative of God's Holy Spirit. The sacrificial unleavened bread is to also have the salt of the covenant in it and to have frankincense put on it. The oil being representative of the Holy Spirit and the frankincense picturing the sweet perfume of wholehearted service and UNITY with GOD and the WORD of God!

Unleavened bread made with salt and oil is to be offered; the salt picturing the everlasting nature of our Covenant to live by every Word of God, and the oil representing the enabling Holy Spirit of God.

> **Leviticus 2:13** And every oblation of thy meat offering shalt thou season with salt; neither shalt thou suffer the salt of the covenant of thy God to be lacking from thy meat offering: with all thine offerings thou shalt offer salt.

Wine is to be poured out as a "drink offering" picturing the pouring out of the life of Jesus Christ in sacrifice for sincerely repentant sinners, the wine being symbolic of the blood and the life is in the blood.

Leviticus 2:1 And when any will offer a meat [unleavened bread] offering unto the LORD, his offering shall be of fine flour [modern chemical fertilizers and milled flour has only existed a little over 100 years; this is a reference to what we would call organic stone ground whole grain flour, ground very fine]; and he shall pour oil upon it, and put frankincense thereon:

The meat [unleavened bread] offering which accompanies the animal offerings was burned on the altar; picturing Jesus Christ as the pure sinless the Bread of Life, the Word of God.

The entire written Word of God from Genesis to Revelation was inspired by Jesus Christ and is the nature of God the Father and Jesus Christ in print

The smoke of the burnt offering ascending upward, pictures the wholehearted dedication of Jesus Christ and his zeal for the whole Word of God; and is representative of the Christ-like zeal of the individual offeror to learn and live by every Word of God and so internalize the very nature of Jesus Christ and God the Father as a wonderful perfume of service to God the Father.

The unleavened bread Meat Offering with the Burnt Offering pictures the wholehearted dedication of the individual offeror to internalize every aspect of godliness and to live in Christ-like zeal to be at ONE and in TOTAL UNITY with God the Father.

Eating the unleavened bread at the Passover and through the Feast as God has commanded; pictures following the example of Jesus Christ and internalizing the very nature of God through a dedicated eating [study, keeping and fully internalizing] of every Word of God.

2:2 And he shall bring it to Aaron's sons the priests: and he shall take thereout his handful of the flour thereof, and of the oil thereof, with all the frankincense thereof; and the priest shall burn the memorial of it upon the altar, to be an offering made by fire, of a sweet savour unto the LORD:

2:3 And the remnant of the meat offering shall be Aaron's and his sons': it is a thing most holy of the offerings of the LORD made by fire.

Whether baked in the oven [like matzoth] or cooked in the pan [like flat pancakes], the Meat [unleavened bread] Offering accompanying the Burnt Offering is offered the same way.

2:4 And if thou bring an oblation of a meat offering baken in the oven, it shall be **unleavened cakes** of fine flour **mingled with oil**, or unleavened wafers **anointed with oil.**

2:5 And if thy oblation be a meat offering baken in a pan, it shall be of fine flour **unleavened, mingled with oil. 2:6** Thou shalt part it in pieces, and **pour oil thereon**: it is a meat offering.

2:7 And if thy oblation be a meat offering baken in the fryingpan, it shall be made of fine flour **with oil.**

2:8 And thou shalt bring the meat offering that is made of these things unto the LORD: and when it is presented unto the priest, he shall bring it unto the altar.

Some of the Meat Offering is to he burned as a MEMORIAL before God the Father of the dedicated loving service and faithful Christ-like voluntary zealous obedience of the offeror to faithfully consume [internalize] and to live by every Word of God.

The dedication of the Lamb of God to live by every Word of God is an example which we should be most diligent to follow.

2:9 And the priest shall take from the meat offering a memorial thereof, and shall burn it upon the altar: it is an offering made by fire, of a sweet savour unto the LORD.

2:10 And that which is left of the meat offering shall be Aaron's and his sons': **it is a thing most holy of the offerings of the LORD made by fire.**

Leaven represents the pride and vanity that sin brings causing us to think that we know best; and honey was used by the pagans as a symbol of knowledge that comes by the wisdom of man.

Today the Ekklesia is full of pride and vanity, thinking that they are the fountain of all wisdom and truth; while turning AWAY from the Word of God to keep our own ways (Rev 3:16).

2:11 No meat offering, which ye shall bring unto the LORD, **shall be made with leaven: for ye shall burn no leaven, nor any honey, in any offering of the LORD made by fire.**

2:12 As for the oblation of the firstfruits [Pentecost], ye shall offer them unto the LORD: but **they shall not be burnt on the altar** for a sweet savour [because the two Pentecost bread pieces are made with leaven].

Salt, which represents ZEAL for the whole Word of God, to learn and to keep it; must not be lacking in the meat [unleavened bread] offering: Just like Jesus Christ was consumed with zeal for God the Father, we should follow his example and also be filled with zeal for God the Father and every Word of God.

The recipe for the unleavened bread of Passover and the Feast of Unleavened Bread has all of these elements; except that frankincense is only to be poured out upon that offering which is to be burned.

See the Biblical Spring Festival book.

2:13 And every oblation of thy meat [unleavened bread] offering shalt thou season with salt; neither shalt thou suffer the salt of the covenant of thy God to be lacking from thy meat offering: with all thine offerings thou shalt offer salt.

All Unleavened Bread for Passover, the Feast of Unleavened Bread and the sacrifices is to be seasoned with salt as commanded in Leviticus 2:13.

Salt is a preservative which is added to indicate the eternal everlasting nature of our Covenant with God and our faithful everlasting abiding in that Covenant (Numbers 18:19).

The term "Covenant of Salt" in terms of adding salt to the unleavened bread of Passover and the sacrifices and then eating it, symbolizes that we are internalizing the nature of God within ourselves in an eternal Covenant with our LORD.

The salting of the unleavened bread of Passover and the sacrifices means that we are entering a "Covenant of Salt," an enduring everlasting covenant with our LORD.

In 2 Chronicles 13:5 God gave the kingship of Israel to David and his descendants forever through a "covenant of salt;" meaning an enduring everlasting covenant.

God is very specific and insistent that unleavened bread for religious purpose contain pure olive oil [Holy Spirit] and salt [representative of zeal]. Does your Passover and Feast of Unleavened Bread, unleavened bread, contain salt and pure olive oil?

How to Prepare the Wave Offering

2:14 And if thou offer a meat offering of thy firstfruits [the Wave Offering] unto the LORD, thou shalt offer for the meat offering of thy firstfruits green ears of corn [grain] dried by the fire, even corn beaten out of full ears. **2:15** And thou shalt put oil upon it, and lay frankincense thereon: it is a meat offering.

2:16 And the priest shall burn the memorial of it, part of the beaten corn [grain] thereof, and part of the oil thereof, with all the frankincense thereof: it is an offering made by fire unto the LORD.

Just before Passover Jesus brought up the subject of "bread" and explained to the people the spiritual meaning of the unleavened bread of the Passover, the Feast of Unleavened Bread, and the Meat [unleavened bread] Offerings.

> **John 6:32** Then Jesus said unto them, Verily, verily, I say unto you, **Moses gave you not that bread from heaven; but my Father giveth you the true bread from heaven. 6:33 For the bread of God is he which cometh down from heaven, and giveth life unto the world.**
>
> **6:34** Then said they unto him, Lord, evermore give us this bread.
>
> **6:35** And Jesus said unto them, **I am the bread of life: he that cometh to me shall never hunger; and he that believeth on me shall never thirst. 6:36** But I said unto you, That ye also have seen me, and believe not. **6:37** All that the Father giveth me shall come to me; and him that cometh to me I will in no wise cast out.
>
> **6:38 For I came down from heaven, not to do mine own will, but the will of him that sent me. 6:39** And this is the Father's will which hath sent me, that of all which he hath given me I should lose nothing, but should raise it up again at the last day. **6:40** And this is the will of him that sent me, that every one which seeth the Son, and believeth on him, may have everlasting life: and I will raise him up at the last day.
>
> **6:41** The Jews then murmured at him, because he said, I am the bread which came down from heaven. **6:42** And they said, Is not this Jesus, the son of Joseph, whose father and mother we know? how is it then that he saith, I came down from heaven?
>
> **6:43** Jesus therefore answered and said unto them, Murmur not among yourselves.

6:44 No man can come to me, except the Father which hath sent me draw him: and I will raise him up at the last day. **6:45** It is written in the prophets, And they shall be all taught of God. Every man therefore that hath heard, and hath learned of the Father, cometh unto me. **6:46** Not that any man hath seen the Father, save he which is of God, he hath seen the Father.

6:47 Verily, verily, I say unto you, He that believeth on me hath everlasting life. **6:48 I am that bread of life.** **6:49** Your fathers did eat manna in the wilderness, and are dead. **6:50** This is the bread which cometh down from heaven, that a man may eat thereof, and not die.

6:51 I am the living bread which came down from heaven: if any man eat of this bread, he shall live for ever: and the bread that I will give is my flesh, which I will give for the life of the world.

Brethren, we need to carefully study these things in order to better understand God the Father and Jesus Christ and the meaning of unleavened bread [Meat Offering] and the Passover Feast symbols

See the Biblical festivals books.

Anyone who internalizes the very nature of God the Father and Jesus Christ, internalizing the nature of God just as one would eat bread; being diligent to learn and to live by every Word of God - just as a starving person seeks to eat bread: Shall become like Jesus Christ and God the Father and shall inherit eternal life.

Leviticus 3

The Peace Offering

All offerings are to be without blemish because blemishes and imperfections are representative of the imperfection of sin. These offerings are to be without any blemish because the sacrificial animals represent the absolute purity from sin and all uncleanness of Jesus Christ the Lamb of God.

> **1 Peter 1: 18** Forasmuch as ye know that ye were not redeemed with corruptible things, as silver and gold, from your vain conversation received by tradition from your fathers; **1:19 But with the precious blood of Christ, as of a lamb without blemish and without spot:**

Just as Jesus Christ was pure from any blemish of sin; so we are to be free from the blemishes of sin. For us to become perfect as God the Father is perfect, we must be diligent and zealous to work hard to learn and to live by every Word of God, which Word defines the nature of God.

We must follow the Lamb whithersoever he goeth and we must NEVER follow any man contrary to the Word of God. We must be consumed the zeal for God the Father just as Jesus Christ was totally dedicated to God the Father and was in TOTAL UNITY with the Father and with the whole Word of God.

Living by every Word of God brings reconciliation and PEACE between us and God the Father; which is what the Peace Offering represents.

We are to be at one with, and at peace in total unity with God the Father; just as Jesus Christ was one with, and in total unity with God the Father.

Those who lack the zeal of Jesus Christ for God the Father and the whole Word of God; will not be among the chosen at the resurrection to spirit.

> **Matthew 5:48** Be ye therefore perfect, even as your Father which is in heaven is perfect
>
> **Ephesians 5:25** Husbands, love your wives, even as **Christ also loved the church, and gave himself for it; 5:26 That he might sanctify and cleanse it with the washing of water** by the word, **5:27 That he might present it to himself a glorious church, not having spot, or wrinkle, or any such thing; but that it should be holy and without blemish** [without any sin].

The Peace Offering of Cattle

Leviticus 3:1 And if his oblation be a sacrifice of peace offering, if he **offer it of the herd**; whether it be a male or female, **he shall offer it without blemish before the LORD.**

The laying on of hands sanctifies [sets apart to holy use] the sacrifice.

3:2 And he shall lay his hand upon the head of his offering, and kill it at the door of the tabernacle of the congregation: and Aaron's sons the priests shall sprinkle the blood upon the altar round about.

In the Peace Offering the fat on the innards and the kidneys must be removed and burned in the fire on the altar.

The fat symbolizes all of the energy and strength of Jesus Christ for God the Father! Jesus Christ was and is an example of dedication which we are to follow; being totally zealous for the will of God the Father to learn and to live by every Word of God in zealous energetic passionate enthusiasm for the Father and the whole Word of God.

The kidney's being the most sensitive part of the body, besides the genitals [which sensitivity is increased by circumcision as a type of spiritual circumcision of the heart (Jer 4:4)], represents a sensitivity to please God the Father by learning and keeping his Word and internalizing his nature to become LIKE God the Father: To grow into complete and total UNITY and ONENESS with God the Father just as Jesus Christ was and is ONE with God the Father!

We are NOT to seek spiritual unity with men: We are to seek spiritual UNITY with God the Father, and by doing so, we will be in UNITY will all those others who are also seeking ONENESS with God the Father!

The blood signifying the shed blood of Christ is cast on the sides of the altar.

3:3 And he shall offer of the sacrifice of the peace offering an offering made by fire unto the LORD; the fat that covereth the inwards, and all the fat that is upon the inwards, **3:4** And the two kidneys, and the fat that is on them, which is by the flanks, and the caul above the liver, with the kidneys, it shall he take away.

The kidneys and the fat on the internal organs is burned in the Peace Offering. The Peace Offering also rises to heaven in the smoke and represents complete Reconciliation and Peace between the offeror and God the Father and the Word, as a sweet savor acceptable and most pleasing to God the Father.

The Plan of Salvation in the Sacrifices

> **First,** the sin and trespass offerings represent the sacrifice of the Lamb of God atoning for all sincerely repented past sin, then

> **Second**, the burnt offering represents a passionate dedicated wholehearted living by every Word of God in passionate voluntary zeal, then

> **Third,** the peace and freewill offerings represent complete reconciliation of the offeror with God

3:5 And Aaron's sons shall burn it on the altar upon the burnt sacrifice, which is upon the wood that is on the fire: it is an offering made by fire, of a sweet savour unto the LORD.

3:6 And if his offering for a sacrifice of peace offering unto the LORD be of the flock; male or female, he shall offer it **without blemish.**

The Lamb Peace Offering

3:7 If he offer a lamb for his offering, then shall he offer it before the LORD. **3:8** And he shall lay his hand upon the head of his offering, and kill it before the tabernacle of the congregation: and Aaron's sons shall sprinkle the blood thereof round about upon the altar.

The rump of the lamb, the fat and the two kidneys are burned as the Peace Offering; the smoke ascending to heaven indicative of reconciliation and peace between the offeror and God.

3:9 And he shall offer of the sacrifice of the peace offering an offering made by fire unto the LORD; **the fat thereof, and the whole rump**, it shall he take off hard by the backbone; and the fat that covereth the inwards, and all the fat that is upon the inwards, **3:10 And the two kidneys, and the fat that is upon them**, which is by the flanks, and the caul above the liver, with the kidneys, it shall he take away.

3:11 And the priest shall burn it [the specified parts of the lamb] upon the altar: it is the food of the offering made by fire unto the LORD.

The Peace Offering of a Goat

3:12 And if his offering be a goat, then he shall offer it before the LORD. **3:13** And he shall lay his hand upon the head of it, and kill it before [the door or entry of] the tabernacle of the congregation: and the sons of Aaron shall sprinkle the blood thereof upon the altar round about.

3:14 And he shall offer thereof his offering, even an offering made by fire unto the LORD; **the fat that covereth the inwards, and all the fat that is upon the inwards, 3:15 And the two kidneys, and the fat that is upon them, which is by the flanks, and the caul above the liver, with the kidneys, it shall he take away.**

3:16 And the priest shall burn them upon the altar: it is the food of the offering made by fire for a sweet savour: all the fat is the LORD's.

The burning of the fat and kidneys in the Peace Offering indicates that the fat and kidneys belong to God. The eating of fat or blood is expressly forbidden for the people of God.

3:17 It shall be a **perpetual statute for your generations throughout all your dwellings, that ye eat neither fat nor blood.**

We need not work to remove every speck of marbling, however we should trim off obvious fat from meat and buy extra lean ground meat. The extra lean ground meat can be improved by adding an egg and bread crumbs, or a dash of olive oil and our favorite spice. It would also be proper to avoid deliberately high animal fat products like sausages.

We should wash our meat and remove all possible blood.

Leviticus 4

The Sin and Trespass Offerings

The Trespass and the Sin Offerings are very closely related although differing slightly.

The Sin Offering is for sin against God and any of his commandments.

The Trespass Offering is for uncleanness or for sin requiring restitution, the modern equivalent would be that the Sin Offering is for breaking the law; while the Trespass Offering mainly pertained to civil matters like the breaking of promises and agreements and required restitution to the victimized person.

The Trespass Offering was also prescribed in the cases of healed lepers in Leviticus 14:12, since leprosy [the term leprosy included all skin diseases and blemishes] was considered as an imperfection and as such was a type of sin.

The Sin and Trespass Offerings were the most important of all sacrifices, symbolizing the application of the sacrifice of Christ to those sincerely repenting of breaking any part of the Word of God.

The Sin Offering

The Sin Offering on behalf of a Priest, or for the whole congregation; is a male bull or bullock. This pictures the application of the sacrifice of Christ to atone for repented sin [sin is doing anything contrary to any part of the Word of God].

The offering for the ruler, judge or king was to offer a male goat, signifying his position as leader of the flock, but of lesser degree than a priest of God; and also showing that the congregation are to exalt God and the faithful priest above the king, judge or any other ruler.

Individuals are to offer FEMALE animals signifying their position as the wife of Christ.

> The highest kind of sin offering was to sacrifice a bullock when the High Priest had sinned, or if the whole congregation had sinned.
>
> The next kind would be a male goat for the ruler.
>
> The third kind consisted of a female goat for individual Israelites.
>
> The lowest grade was turtle-doves or young pigeons as a substitute for other sacrifices in case of poverty.
>
> The male for the ruler and the female for the ruled; has its obvious connotations

Both of these offerings speak to the sacrifice of Jesus Christ applied for our sincerely repented sins.

In addition to these, the Drink Offering of wine portrayed the pouring out of the blood of Christ in sacrifice for the sincerely repentant.

The Sin Offering for the priest

Leviticus 4:1 And the LORD spake unto Moses, saying, **4:2** Speak unto the children of Israel, saying, **If a soul shall sin through ignorance against any of the commandments of the LORD** concerning things which ought not to be done, and shall do against any of them: **4:3** If the priest that is anointed do sin according to the sin of the people; then let him bring for his sin, which he hath sinned, a young bullock without blemish unto the LORD for a sin offering.

The bullock as an animal pictures strength and the powerful dedicated patient service of Jesus Christ [including those called to the priesthood of Christ] to God the Father. The hands upon the head of the Offering represents the placing of the sin on the sacrifice and the bearing of that sin by the sacrifice, just as Jesus Christ bears the sins of the sincerely repentant.

The offender bringing the sacrificial animal in the sin and trespass offering, pictures sincere repentance and the application of the sacrifice of Jesus Christ to bear the sins of the repentant.

4:4 And he shall bring the bullock unto the door of the tabernacle of the congregation before the LORD; and shall lay his hand upon the bullock's head, and kill the bullock before the LORD.

The animal is to be killed before the Lord just as Jesus was killed before God the Father, and the blood was to be sprinkled seven times before God to demonstrate a complete bearing of sin.

4:5 And the priest that is anointed shall take of the bullock's blood, and bring it to the tabernacle of the congregation: **4:6** And the priest shall dip his finger in the blood, and sprinkle of the blood seven times before the LORD, before the vail of the sanctuary.

The blood was sprinkled on the altar of incense; the incense picturing the prayers of the people ascending up to God. The sprinkling of blood on the altar of incense indicated the rising up of the prayers of repentance.

In other words, atonement is made for sin in response to sincere repentance which this Sin Offering pointed to; this being an instructional example that the sacrifice of the Lamb of God removes sin and reconciles the sincerely repentant to God the Father.

The remaining blood was poured out at the base of the altar of Burnt Offering to signify that Christ had poured himself out to wholeheartedly serve God the Father unto death.

4:7 And the priest shall put some of the blood upon the horns of the altar of sweet incense before the LORD, which is in the tabernacle of the congregation; and shall pour all the blood of the bullock at the bottom of the altar of the burnt offering, which is at the door of the tabernacle of the congregation.

The fat and the kidneys were burned on the altar

4:8 And he shall take off from it all the fat of the bullock for the sin offering; the fat that covereth the inwards, and all the fat that is upon the inwards, **4:9** And the two kidneys, and the fat that is upon them, which is by the flanks, and the caul above the liver, with the kidneys, it shall he take away, **4:10 As it was taken off from the bullock of the sacrifice of peace offerings: and the priest shall burn them upon the altar of the burnt offering.**

The remainder of the Sin Offering must be burned outside the camp, or in later times outside the city of Jerusalem. Jesus Christ was killed outside the city gates as the perfect Sin Offering that these animals pointed to. This removal outside the camp represented the removal of sin from among the people.

4:11 And the skin of the bullock, and all his flesh, with his head, and with his legs, and his inwards, and his dung, **4:12 Even the whole bullock shall he carry forth without the camp unto a clean place, where the ashes are poured out, and burn him on the wood with fire: where the ashes are poured out shall he be burnt.**

The Sin Offering for the Whole Congregation

4:13 And if the whole congregation of Israel sin through ignorance, and the thing be hid from the eyes of the assembly, and they have done somewhat **against any of the commandments of the LORD** concerning things which should not be done, and are guilty; **4:14** When the sin, which they have sinned against it, is known, then the congregation shall offer a young bullock for the sin, and bring him before the tabernacle of the congregation. **4:15** And the elders of the congregation shall lay their hands upon the head of the bullock before the LORD: and the bullock shall be killed before the LORD.

Here the blood is to be sprinkled seven tine [symbolizing COMPLETE atonement for sin] before the Most Holy Place; This pictures Jesus Christ bringing his perfect atonement for the whole people into the holy throne room of God the Father.

In this case no blood is to be placed on the alter of incense.

4:16 And the priest that is anointed shall bring of the bullock's blood to the tabernacle of the congregation: **4:17** And the priest shall dip his finger in some of the blood, and sprinkle it seven times before the LORD, even before the vail.

4:18 And he shall put some of the blood upon the **horns of the altar which is before the LORD,** that is in the tabernacle of the congregation, and **shall pour out all the blood at the bottom of the altar of the burnt offering, which is at the door of the tabernacle** of the congregation.

The fat of the Sin Offering for the whole Assembly was burned on the altar and the remainder of the animal burned outside the city, just like the Sin and Trespass Offering for the priests.

4:19 And he shall take all his fat from him, and burn it upon the altar.

The Sin Offerings are to be burned outside the camp [city], only the fat and kidneys being burned on the altar.

4:20 And he shall do with the bullock as he did with the bullock for a sin offering, so shall he do with this: and the priest shall make an atonement for them, and it shall be forgiven them. **4:21 And he shall carry forth the bullock without the camp, and burn him as he burned the first bullock: it is a sin offering for the congregation.**

The Sin Offering for a Ruler

4:22 When a ruler [a judge or king] **hath sinned,** and done somewhat **through ignorance** against any of the commandments of the LORD his God concerning things which should not be done, and is guilty;

4:23 Or if his sin, wherein he hath sinned, come to his knowledge; he shall bring his offering, **a kid of the goats**, a male without blemish: **4:24** And he shall lay his hand upon the head of **the goat**, and kill it in the place where they kill the burnt offering before the LORD: **it is a sin offering. 4:25** And the priest shall take of the blood of the sin offering with his finger, and put it upon the horns of the altar of burnt offering, and shall pour out his blood at the bottom of the altar of burnt offering.

4:26 And **he shall burn all his fat upon the altar, as the fat of the sacrifice of peace offerings**: and the priest shall make an atonement for him as concerning his sin, and it shall be forgiven him.

The Sin Offering for Individuals

4:27 And if any one of the common people sin through ignorance, while he doeth somewhat against any of the commandments of the LORD concerning things which ought not to be done, and be guilty;

This offering is a **female** goat or lamb, which is distinct from the Passover where a **male** goat or lamb is killed.

The Goat Sin Offering for Individuals

4:28 Or if his sin, which he hath sinned, come to his knowledge: then he shall bring his offering, a **kid of the goats, a female without blemish, for his sin** which he hath sinned. **4:29** And he shall lay his hand upon the head of the sin offering, and slay the sin offering in the place of the burnt offering.

4:30 And the priest shall take of the blood thereof with his finger, and put it upon the horns of the altar of burnt offering, and shall pour out all the blood thereof at the bottom of the altar.

4:31 And he shall take away all the fat thereof, as the fat is taken away from off the sacrifice of peace offerings; and the priest shall burn it upon the altar for a sweet savour unto the LORD; and the priest shall make an atonement for him, and it shall be forgiven him.

The Lamb Sin Offering for Individuals

4:32 And if he **bring a lamb for a sin offering, he shall bring it a female without blemish.** **4:33** And he shall lay his hand upon the head of the sin offering, and slay it for a sin offering in the place where they kill the burnt offering.

4:34 And the priest shall take of the blood of the sin offering with his finger, and put it upon the horns of the altar of burnt offering, and shall pour out all the blood thereof at the bottom of the altar: **4:35** And he shall take away all the fat thereof, as the fat of the lamb is taken away from the sacrifice of the peace offerings; and the priest shall burn them upon the altar, according to the offerings made by fire unto the LORD: and the priest shall make an atonement for his sin that he hath committed, and it shall be forgiven him.

Hands were laid on the head of the sacrifice to sanctify [set apart] the sacrifice to bear the sins of the offeror. The sacrifice is a type of Jesus Christ bearing the sins of those who sincerely repent and commit to "go and sin no more".

The sin offerings have as their foundation the fact that the offeror comes admitting his/her sin and seeking atonement for his sin. The offering is for the sincerely repentant offeror.

Later this was perverted as people would make an offering, not to express repentance, but to FEEL righteous. They would offer and then continue or return to their sin, just as many today pray a prayer of repentance and feeling justified then rise up to continue in their sin.

This is a picture of many today who proclaim that the Word of God must be kept and then go their way to justify NOT keeping it with their reasoning's, just like the apostate Pharisees.

God will not be mocked and repentance must be wholeheartedly sincere; or Jesus Christ will NOT apply his sacrifice to the seeker.

> **Romans 2:13** (For not the hearers of the law are just before God, but the doers of the law shall be justified.

Repentance means a dedicated commitment to "go and sin no more!" It does not mean to pray and speak about God just to feel good about ourselves, which is self- righteousness; and then to go and do what we or some other person decides is right. We are to learn and live by the whole Word of God.

Ignorance is NO excuse for sin. It is our duty to study diligently and to learn the whole Word of God to keep it.

If we see sin; it is our duty to try to resolve it and if that is not possible to expose it to the brethren.

> **Leviticus 19:17** Thou shalt not hate thy brother in thine heart: thou shalt in any wise rebuke thy neighbour, and not suffer sin upon him.
>
> **Matthew 18:15** Moreover if thy brother shall trespass against thee, go and tell him his fault between thee and him alone: if he shall hear thee, thou hast gained thy brother.
>
> **18:16** But if he will not hear thee, then take with thee one or two more [witness to the facts], that in the mouth of two or three witnesses every word may be established.
>
> **18:17** And if he shall neglect to hear them, tell it unto the church [the assembly of the brethren]: but if he neglect to hear the church, let him be unto thee as an heathen man and a publican [and cast out of the assembly (1 Cor 5:11)].

Leviticus 5

Leviticus 5:1 And if a soul sin, and [someone] hear the voice of swearing, and is a witness, whether he hath seen or known of it [if a person witness evil he is to declare it and not to keep the thing secret]; if he do not utter it [refuses to rebuke the evil], **then he shall bear his iniquity.**

> **Leviticus 19:17** Thou shalt not hate thy brother in thine heart: thou shalt in any wise rebuke thy neighbour, and not suffer sin upon him.

When a person has their sin revealed to them, then they are convicted of guilt and must sincerely repent before God.

Uncleanness pictures any association with sin.

Leviticus 5:2 Or if a soul touch any unclean thing, whether it be a carcase of an unclean beast, or a carcase of unclean cattle [that which dies of itself or is killed by wild beasts], or the carcase of unclean creeping things, and if it be hidden from him; he also shall be unclean, and guilty.

If a person is defiled by any unclean creature he is unclean even if he is not aware of the problem.

5:3 Or if he touch the uncleanness of man, whatsoever uncleanness it be that a man shall be defiled withal, and it be hid from him; when he knoweth of it [when he finds out], then he shall be guilty.

If a person makes a vow and forgets it, when it is brought to his attention he must acknowledge the Trespass of not fulfilling that vow.

5:4 Or if a soul swear, pronouncing with his lips to do evil, or to do good, whatsoever it be that a man shall pronounce with an oath, and it be hid from him; when he knoweth of it, then he shall be guilty [repent of his guilt as soon as he knows the matter] in one of these.

When a person has his sin pointed out to him, he is to repent and to make an offering for his sin.

The physical sin and trespass offerings picture the atoning sacrifice of Jesus Christ covering our known and unknown sins and are intended to teach us that when we sin we are to sincerely repent and seek the application of the atoning sacrifice of the Lamb of God; and then STOP SINNING!

Leviticus 5:5 is the Sin Offering for individuals. We know this because the offering required is a *female* lamb or goat.

Here the previous Sin Offering instructions in Leviticus 4:27 are repeated and amplified by the instructions to add a Burnt Offering to the Sin Offering, and the addition of the turtle dove offering for the very poor.

5:5 And it shall be, when he shall be guilty in one of these things, that he shall confess [repent before God] that he hath sinned in that thing: **5:6** And he shall bring his trespass offering unto the LORD for his sin which he hath sinned, a female from the flock, a lamb or a kid of the goats, for a sin offering; and the priest shall make an atonement for him concerning his sin.

5:7 And if he be not able to bring a lamb, then he shall bring for his trespass, which he hath committed, two turtledoves, or two young pigeons, unto the LORD; one for a sin offering, and the other for a burnt offering.

The Sin or Trespass Offering pictures atonement for sin and the Burnt Offering pictures following the example of Christ in becoming filled with dedicated zeal to learn and wholeheartedly live by the Will and every Word of God.

5:8 And he shall bring them unto the priest, who shall offer that which is for the sin offering first, and wring off his head from his neck, but shall not divide it asunder: **5:9** And he shall sprinkle of the blood of the sin offering upon the side of the altar; and the rest of the blood shall be wrung out at the bottom of the altar: it is a sin offering.

We must first have our eyes opened to our sins and then we must sincerely repent before a sin or trespass offering [the sacrifice of Christ] can be applied to us in atonement for our sin thereby reconciling us with God the Father. Only then can the burnt offering be made since it represents a dedicated wholehearted zeal to live by every Word of God.

5:10 And he shall offer the second for a burnt offering, according to the manner: and the priest shall make an atonement for him for his sin which he hath sinned, and it shall be forgiven him.

If we are in a state of abject poverty, God in his tender mercy allows a person to bring a portion of flour as his Sin Offering. This is a Sin Offering and therefore does NOT have the oil representing the Holy Spirit, nor the frankincense representing the acceptable and sweet service of the offeror, which godly service does not come until after sincere repentance and the application of the sacrifice of Christ.

5:11 But if he be not able to bring two turtledoves, or two young pigeons, then he that sinned shall bring for his offering the tenth part of an ephah of fine flour for a sin offering; **he shall put no oil upon it, neither shall he put any frankincense thereon: for it is a sin offering.**

If we are in abject poverty, God will allow a handful of the flour is to be burnt on the altar as a memorial of the atoning sacrifice of Christ as the Unleavened Bread of Life, applied to the offeror.

5:12 Then shall he bring it to the priest, and the priest shall take his handful of it, even a memorial thereof, and burn it on the altar, according to the offerings made by fire unto the LORD: it is a sin offering.

5:13 And the priest shall make an atonement for him as touching his sin that he hath sinned in one of these, and it shall be forgiven him: and the remnant shall be the priest's, as a meat [unleavened bread] offering.

The Trespass Offering for Holy Things

The Trespass Offering for any trespass against holy things

The Trespass Offering is about wrongs such as uncleanness or inadvertently bringing harm.

5:14 And the LORD spake unto Moses, saying, **5:15** If a soul commit a trespass, and sin through ignorance, in the holy things of the LORD; then he shall bring for his trespass unto the LORD a ram without blemish out of the flocks, with thy estimation by shekels of silver, after the shekel of the sanctuary, for a trespass offering.

5:16 And he shall make amends for the harm that he hath done in the holy thing, and shall add the fifth part thereto, and give it unto the priest: and the priest shall make an atonement for him with the ram of the trespass offering, and it shall be forgiven him.

Ignorance of the commandments and the Word of God, comes from a lack of zeal for God and is itself a trespass against God the Father.

5:17 And if a soul sin, and commit any of these things which are forbidden to be done by the commandments of the LORD; **though he wist it not**, yet is he guilty, and shall bear his iniquity.

5:18 And he shall bring a ram without blemish out of the flock, with thy estimation, for a trespass offering, unto the priest: and the priest shall make an atonement for him **concerning his ignorance wherein he erred and wist it not,** and it shall be forgiven him.

5:19 It is a trespass offering: he hath certainly trespassed against the LORD.

Leviticus 6

A list of Trespasses

Leviticus 6:1 And the LORD spake unto Moses, saying, **6:2** If a soul sin, and commit a trespass against the LORD, and **lie unto his neighbour** in that which was delivered him to keep, or in fellowship, or in a thing taken away by violence, or hath deceived his neighbour; **6:3** Or have found that which was lost, and lieth concerning it, and sweareth falsely; in any of all these that a man doeth, sinning therein:

Those elders and leaders who have led the flock to follow themselves and not to be zealous to follow God the Father the owner of the flock; must quickly repent and shall surely be required to make amends.

6:4 Then it shall be, because he hath sinned, and is guilty, that he shall restore that which he took violently away, or the thing which he hath deceitfully gotten, or that which was delivered him to keep, or the lost thing which he found, **6:5** Or all that about which he hath sworn falsely; he shall even restore it in the principal, and shall add the fifth part more thereto, and give it unto him to whom it appertaineth, in the day of his trespass offering.

6:6 And he shall bring his trespass offering unto the LORD, a ram without blemish out of the flock, with thy estimation, for a trespass offering, unto the priest: **6:7** And the priest shall make an atonement for him before the

LORD: and it shall be forgiven him for any thing of all that he hath done in trespassing therein.

The Burnt Offering

6:8 And the LORD spake unto Moses, saying, **6:9** Command Aaron and his sons, saying, **This is the law of the burnt offering: It is the burnt offering, because of the burning upon the altar all night unto the morning, and the fire of the altar shall be burning in it.**

In the morning the priest must carry the ashes of the Burnt Offering which had burned all night to a place outside the camp. The selected priest did this in a very explicit manner, removing the ashes from the altar while wearing holy garments and then changing out of his holy garments to take the ashes outside the camp or city.

6:10 And the priest shall put on his linen garment, and his linen breeches shall he put upon his flesh, and take up the ashes which the fire hath consumed with the burnt offering on the altar, and he shall put them beside the altar.

6:11 And he shall put off his garments, and put on other garments, and carry forth the ashes without the camp unto a clean place.

In the morning after the ashes have been removed, more wood was placed under the altar before the morning sacrifice. The altar was built with a grate at the top for the sacrifice, this was above the fire box where the wood was placed, which fire box was above another grate covering the ash bin. In this way the fire could be kept continually burning as the ashes fell through the grate into an ash bin for removal.

The Daily Sacrifice pictured the continual Intercession by the Lamb of God for the whole nation of the Called Out of Egypt, and in spiritual terms represents his dedicated service as Mediator and High Priest for Spiritual Israel.

Understanding this is vital as very many think that a physical sacrifice must be started before the tribulation can begin. That is NOT true, because the Daily in this dispensation is the daily work of Jesus Christ at the throne of God the Father in heaven, interceding for his espoused bride; and it is the rejection of the Laodicean's by Christ for their departure from zeal for the whole Word of God (Rev 3:14-22), which is the stopping of the spiritual daily sacrifice at the end time.

6:12 And the fire upon the altar shall be burning in it; it shall not be put out: and the priest shall burn wood on it every morning, and lay the burnt offering in order upon it; and he shall burn thereon the fat of the peace offerings.

The fire on the altar was to be continual and never put out.

That fire represents the consuming zeal of Jesus Christ for God the Father and the whole Word of God; while the offering of the lamb itself pictures the Lamb of God giving himself willingly and FULLY in service to God the Father.

The Offering in the evening and the morning, pictures a 24 hour day [Gen 1, the evening and the morning are a complete day] and the CONTINUAL service by Jesus Christ to God the Father in all things and in particular interceding and covering the sincerely repented sins of the Called Out.

It is because today's Ekklesia [Laodicea] will not repent as organized groups, thinking that they are spiritually rich and in need of nothing, that they will be rejected by Jesus Christ into the correction of great tribulation (Rev 3:16).

6:13 The fire shall ever be burning upon the altar; it shall never go out.

The Meat [Unleavened Bread] Offering

6:14 And this is the law of the meat [unleavened bread] offering: the sons of Aaron shall offer it before the LORD, before the altar.

The unleavened flour represents Jesus Christ as the pure unleavened "Bread of Life" for the repentant; the salt represents the enduring nature of the Covenant and the love of God, the oil represents the presence of the Holy Spirit; the frankincense represents the sweet perfume of zeal for God the Father; and each of these burned on the altar and rising up as smoke into the sky, represents a sweet lovely perfume of Christ-like zeal to live by every Word of God, of the offeror.

6:15 And he shall take of it his handful, of the flour of the meat offering, and of the oil thereof, and all the frankincense which is upon the meat offering, and shall burn it upon the altar for a sweet savour, even the memorial of it, unto the LORD.

No leaven is permitted; showing the purity and sinlessness of Jesus Christ the Lamb of God: Because all leaven was a type of sin in the sacrificial system.

The unleavened flour or bread in this sacrifice represents Jesus Christ and is holy to God the Father; it is to be eaten by those consecrated in the priesthood and represents internalizing the very nature of Jesus Christ and God the Father.

6:16 And the remainder thereof shall Aaron and his sons eat: with unleavened bread shall it be eaten in the holy place; in the court of the tabernacle of the congregation they shall eat it.

This next verse reveals that the flour is not to remain as simple flour but is baked into unleavened bread; this **unleavened bread** symbolizing the purity from all sin and uncleanness, of Jesus Christ.

6:17 It shall not be baken with leaven. I have given it unto them for their portion of my offerings made by fire; it is most holy, as is the sin offering, and as the trespass offering.

This bread offering is to be eaten by males only, meaning that it is the priests who eat the unleavened bread of the Meat Offerings. Spiritually this refers to all those Called Out to become priests of Jesus Christ after the order of Melchizedek internalizing the sinless nature of Jesus Christ through internalizing the whole perfect Word of God.

The sacrificial offerings "Made by Fire" [burned on the altar] are holy; and the New Covenant Called Out are to be holy, sinless and with out any blemish of sin.

1 Peter 1;16 Because it is written, **Be ye holy; for I am holy**.

Leviticus 6:18 All the males among the children of Aaron shall eat of it. It shall be a statute for ever in your generations concerning the offerings of the LORD made by fire: every one that toucheth them shall be holy.

The Daily Sacrifice Meat Offering [Grain, Unleavened Bread]

This identifies the Daily morning and evening Offering as an Offering made by the High Priest; and represents the work of Jesus Christ as the High Priest of the New Covenant.

The morning and evening picturing a complete day (Gen 1); the lambs picture Jesus Christ as humbly serving God the Father unto death and giving himself fully to the Father as the Lamb of God; the Unleavened Bread picture Jesus Christ as the Bread of Life who's nature of wholehearted loyalty to God the Father and of living by every Word of God is to be internalized by all those who have been Called Out into the New Covenant.

This Daily Offering began with the anointing of Aaron as high priest and was to be continued perpetually as an allegory of the eternal work of Jesus Christ as the High Priest of the New Covenant after of the order of Melchizedek.

It is this spiritual daily offering intercessory work of Jesus Christ on behalf of the whole Ekklesia [today's Laodicea] that is to be stopped to set up the abomination.

It is this spiritual work of Christ which restrains Satan and the final abomination (2 Thess 2).

Christ's intercession for the whole of today's Laodicean Ekklesia will be stopped because of our overspreading wickedness in losing our zeal to live by every Word of God and replacing our zeal for God with a zeal for idols of men and organizations (Rev 3:16).

It is NOT necessary for any physical Daily Sacrifice to be started and then stopped before the tribulation!

6:19 And the LORD spake unto Moses, saying, **6:20** This is the offering of Aaron and of his sons, which they shall offer unto the LORD in the day when he is anointed; the tenth part of an ephah of fine flour **for a meat offering perpetual, half of it in the morning, and half thereof at night**.

6:21 In a pan it shall be made with oil [symbolizing the Holy Spirit]; and when it is baken, thou shalt bring it in: and the baken pieces of the meat [grain, unleavened bread] offering shalt thou offer for a sweet savour [burned to smoke which rises up to God the Father, a wonderful perfume of the Intercessory Work of our spirit High Priest, Jesus Christ] unto the LORD.

6:22 And the priest of his sons that is anointed in his stead shall offer it: it is a statute for ever unto the LORD; **it shall be wholly burnt.**

Every unleavened bread offering accompanying the Daily Morning and Evening Sacrifice of the lambs was wholly burned.

6:23 For every meat offering for the priest shall be wholly burnt: it shall not be eaten.

Further instructions on the Sin Offering

6:24 And the LORD spake unto Moses, saying, **6:25** Speak unto Aaron and to his sons, saying, This is the law of the sin offering: In the place where the burnt offering is killed shall the sin offering be killed before the LORD: it is most holy.

No part of a sin offering for a priest or for the general congregation could be eaten;

A portion of a sin offering for a ruler or an individual could be eaten by the priests.

6:26 The priest that offereth it for sin shall eat it: in the holy place shall it be eaten, in the court of the tabernacle of the congregation.

The sin offering pictures the atoning sacrifice of the Lamb of God, Jesus Christ; therefore whoever touches it becomes holy as Christ is holy. This pictures the blood of Christ covering and atoning for sin; and the repentant person to whom that sacrifice is applied becoming holy as Christ is holy, through his sacrifice being applied to the sincerely repentant person.

Just as Jesus Christ continues in sinless holiness; we must also continue in sinless holiness; going forward to learn and keep the whole Word of God in Christ-like zeal for God the Father to live by every Word of God.

6:27 Whatsoever shall touch the flesh thereof shall be holy: and when there is sprinkled of the blood thereof upon any garment, thou shalt wash that whereon it was sprinkled in the holy place.

Even the vessels and utensils touching any part of this sacrifice are holy and are not to be put to any other purpose.

6:28 But the earthen vessel wherein it is sodden shall be broken: and if it be sodden in a brasen pot, it shall be both scoured, and rinsed in water.

A portion of a sin offering for a ruler [who is an individual] or any individual could be eaten by the priests, but only males may eat of this sacrifice; spiritually this refers to all those Called Out to become priests of Jesus Christ after the order of Melchizedek internalizing the sinless nature of Jesus Christ through internalizing the whole perfect Word of God.

6:29 All the males among the priests shall eat thereof: it is most holy.

NO Sin Offering to atone for a priest or for the congregation as a whole; may be eaten by anyone.

6:30 And no sin offering, whereof any of the blood is brought into the tabernacle of the congregation to reconcile withal in the holy place, shall be eaten: it shall be burnt in the fire.

Leviticus 7

Leviticus 7:1 Likewise this is the law of the trespass offering: it is most holy. **7:2** In the place where they kill the burnt offering shall they kill the trespass offering: and the blood thereof shall he sprinkle round about upon the altar. **7:3** And he shall offer of it all the fat thereof; the rump, and the fat that covereth the inwards, **7:4** And the two kidneys, and the fat that is on them, which is by the flanks, and the caul that is above the liver, with the kidneys, it shall he take away: **7:5** And the priest shall burn them upon the altar for an offering made by fire unto the LORD: it is a trespass offering.

The fat covering the inner parts; tail fat, kidneys, lobe of the liver, and the two kidneys are to be burned on the altar, the remaining flesh is to be eaten by the priests in the Holy Place. The individual offeror may not eat any part of the offering

7:6 Every male among the priests shall eat thereof: it shall be eaten in the holy place: it is most holy.

In the case of a sin offering for the high priest or the whole congregation: none of the offering may be eaten. The fat covering inner parts; fat tail, kidneys, lobe of the liver, and the two kidneys are to be burned on the altar and the remainder of the animal is to be taken and burned completely outside the camp or city.

The priest that conducts the Sin and Trespass sacrifices for individuals and for the ruler [judge or king] shall have all that which is not burned on the altar.

> **1 Corinthians 9:13** Do ye not know that they which minister about holy things live of the things of the temple? and they which wait at the altar are partakers with the altar? **9:14 Even so hath the Lord ordained that they which preach the gospel should live of the gospel.**

Leviticus 7:7 As the sin offering is, so is the trespass offering: there is one law for them: the priest that maketh atonement therewith shall have it.

When someone offers a Burnt Offering which is wholly consumed on the altar the officiating priest shall have the hide as his wages. Otherwise the entire animal is to be burned to ashes.

7:8 And the priest that offereth any man's burnt offering, even **the priest shall have to himself the skin of the burnt offering which he hath offered.**

The priest that prepares a Meat [Unleavened Bread] offering shall have the part that is not burned.

7:9 And **all the meat** [unleavened bread] **offering** that is baken in the oven, and all that is dressed in the fryingpan, and in the pan, **shall be the priest's that offereth it.**

7:10 And every meat offering, mingled with oil, and dry, shall all the sons of Aaron have, one as much as another.

Peace Offerings

In addition please see: Leviticus 3: The Peace Offering

7:11 And this is the law of the sacrifice of peace offerings, which he shall offer unto the LORD.

7:12 If he offer it for a thanksgiving [in gratitude and rejoicing over having the atonement of the Sin Offering of Christ applied to him and being reconciled to God], then he shall offer with the [animal] sacrifice of thanksgiving **unleavened cakes mingled with oil, and unleavened wafers anointed with oil, and cakes mingled with oil, of fine flour, fried.**

The unleavened bread pictures the sinlessness of Christ and leavening pictures the sin and imperfection of the offeror which requires a Sin Offering.

7:13 Besides the [unleavened] cakes, **he shall offer for his offering leavened bread** with the sacrifice of thanksgiving of his peace offerings.

The leavened bread shall be lifted up towards God by the priest and then brought back down: It shall NOT be burned on the altar as holy, because the leaven represents the imperfection of sin in the offeror; it shall be eaten by the priest.

7:14 And of it he shall offer one [cake of unleavened bread] out of the whole [one cake from the several cakes of the offering] oblation for an heave offering unto the LORD, and it shall be [belong to] the priest's that sprinkleth the blood of the peace offerings.

The Peace Offering may be eaten on the first day only.

7:15 And the flesh of the sacrifice of his peace offerings for thanksgiving **shall be eaten the same day that it is offered; he shall not leave any of it until the morning.**

The sacrifice of a vow is to be eaten on the first and second days only anything remaining until the third day must be burned.

7:16 But if the sacrifice of his offering be a vow, or a voluntary offering, it shall be eaten the same day that he offereth his sacrifice: **and on the morrow also the remainder of it shall be eaten: 7:17** But the remainder of the flesh of the sacrifice **on the third day shall be burnt with fire.**

7:18 And **if any of the flesh of the sacrifice of his peace offerings be eaten at all on the third day, it shall not be accepted, neither shall it be imputed unto him that offereth it: it shall be an abomination, and the soul that eateth of it shall bear his iniquity.**

If a part of the sacrifice becomes unclean it must be destroyed in the fire; however any clean person may eat of the Peace Offering and the offeror may eat and rejoice with his family. This speaks of the eternal community among the faithful zealous godly, and their ONENESS and UNITY with God.

7:19 And the flesh that toucheth any unclean thing shall not be eaten; it shall be burnt with fire: and as for the flesh, **all that be clean** shall eat thereof.

Any person who eats of the peace offering while having sin or being unclean and polluted shall be utterly rejected, thus picturing the sinful being rejected by Christ on the spiritual level.

In spiritual terms this means that any person willfully sinning, or equating loyalty to men and organizations as loyalty to God and obeying them and not being zealous to wash themselves clean from sin by internalizing the whole Word of God: Cannot be at peace with Jesus Christ or with God the Father!

Today the Ekklesia is unclean through their idolatry in being zealous in following men and their organizations, and not being zealous to learn and to live by every Word of God. Those blemishes on the bride, that uncleanness and sin: Have separated us from our God!

Therefore we cannot have a peaceable harmonious relationship with our God or his zealous servants!

This is a very serious matter: We have rejected any zeal for our God and his Word to follow whatever men say. That behavior has separated us from Jesus Christ our espoused Husband and from God our Father in heaven. It is for this reason that today's Ekklesia is being rejected by God:

> **Revelation 3:16** So then because thou art lukewarm, and neither cold nor hot, [we are hot for our own ways, and cold for the ways of God.] I will spue thee out of my mouth.

The latter day Ekklesia which is overwhelmingly Laodicean, is being forcefully rejected by Jesus Christ, who will no longer intercede for us with God the Father.

The Daily Sacrificial work of our High Priest Jesus Christ is going to be stopped for Laodicea; who has lost any zeal to learn and keep the whole Word of God: Preferring instead to idolize men and organizations as little gods instead of being faithful to the Mighty One of Jacob!

We have turned away from any zeal for the whole Word of God and we have become an unclean thing to be rejected by the Eternal

> **1 Corinthians 3:17** Know ye not that ye are the temple of God, and that the Spirit of God dwelleth in you? **3:17** If any man defile the temple of God, him shall God destroy; for the temple of God is holy, which temple ye are.

> **Revelation 3:17** Because [we are proud and think we are the source of all wisdom and truth] thou sayest, I am rich, and increased with goods, and have need of nothing; and knowest not that thou art [spiritually] wretched, and miserable, and poor, and blind, and naked:

> **3:18** I counsel thee to buy of me gold tried in the fire [in the correction of great tribulation], that thou mayest be rich [in spiritual things]; and white raiment [which is the righteousness that comes from internalizing and keeping the whole Word of God], that thou

mayest be clothed, and that the shame of thy nakedness [that our sins are not revealed] do not appear; and anoint thine eyes with eyesalve [seek understanding from the Holy Spirit which is given to the repentant who are zealous to learn and live by every Word of God], that thou mayest see.

The tribulation is now imminent to correct today's apostate Ekklesia

3:19 As many as I love, I rebuke and chasten: be zealous therefore, and repent.

Leviticus 7:20 But the soul that eateth of the flesh of the sacrifice of peace offerings, that pertain unto the LORD, having his uncleanness upon him, even that soul shall be cut off from his people.

7:21 Moreover the soul that shall touch any unclean thing, as the uncleanness of man, or any unclean beast, or any abominable unclean thing, and eat of the flesh of the sacrifice of peace offerings, which pertain unto the LORD, even that soul shall be cut off from his people.

We cannot be at ONE in unity with Jesus Christ and with God the Father, while teaching compromise with the Word of God.

Those who claim to be at One with God and justify sin [like polluting the Sabbath] are false teachers and wolves among the flock.

General Laws of the Sacrifice

We must not eat any animal fat, but if the animal is not killed in sacrifice it can be used for other purposes like greasing things or making soap.

7:22 And the LORD spake unto Moses, saying, **7:23** Speak unto the children of Israel, saying, Ye shall eat no manner of fat, of ox, or of sheep, or of goat. **7:24** And the fat of the beast that dieth of itself, and the fat of that which is torn with beasts, may be used in any other use: but ye shall in no wise eat of it.

This is not some light thing to God and is the same as if one refused to fast on the Fast of Atonement.

7:25 For whosoever eateth the fat of the beast, of which men offer an offering made by fire unto the LORD, even the soul that eateth it **shall be cut off from his people.**

The same is true of eating any blood

7:26 Moreover ye shall eat no manner of blood, whether it be of fowl or of beast, in any of your dwellings. **7:27 Whatsoever soul it be that eateth any manner of blood, even that soul shall be cut off from his people.**

7:28 And the LORD spake unto Moses, saying, **7:29** Speak unto the children of Israel, saying, He that offereth the sacrifice of his peace offerings unto the LORD shall bring his oblation unto the LORD of the sacrifice of his peace offerings.

The offeror of the Peace Offering must give the breast, fat and kidneys to the priest so that he may "wave" them; lifting them up and down to be accepted by God for the offeror. This speaks to the resurrection and rising to heaven of the Lamb of God to be accepted for us like the Wave Offering, reconciling us to peace with God the Father.

7:30 His own hands shall bring the offerings of the LORD made by fire, the fat with the breast, it shall he bring, that the breast may be waved for a wave offering before the LORD. **7:31** And the priest shall burn the fat upon the altar: but the breast shall be Aaron's and his sons'.

The breast is to be given to the priest for the wave offering, to be lifted and brought back down and then to belong to the priest, the fatty parts are to be burned on the altar and the right foreleg given to the officiating priest (heave offering) and the rump and ribs are for the offeror.

7:32 And the right shoulder shall ye give unto the priest for an heave offering of the sacrifices of your peace offerings. **7:33 He among the sons of Aaron, that offereth the blood of the peace offerings, and the fat, shall have the right shoulder for his part.**

7:34 For the wave breast and the heave shoulder have I taken of the children of Israel from off the sacrifices of their peace offerings, and have given them unto Aaron the priest and unto his sons by a statute for ever from among the children of Israel.

Please notice that these parts of the sacrifices were in addition to the tithes, which is another subject.

The granting of these parts to the priests was much more than physical sustenance; it was an admonition that the priests [the Aaronic priesthood has now been replaced by the High Priesthood of Jesus Christ] MUST be partakers of the offerings; that the ministry must consume the sacrifices as an allegory that they must fully internalize the nature of Jesus Christ, which the eating of the sacrifices represents.

7:35 This is the portion of the anointing of Aaron, and of the anointing of his sons, out of the offerings of the LORD made by fire, in the day when he presented them to minister unto the LORD in the priest's office; **7:36** Which the LORD commanded to be given them of the children of Israel, in the day that he anointed them [when the priesthood was established], by a statute for ever throughout their generations.

The sacrificial system sums up the work of Jesus Christ and the example of service that we are to follow!

The job of the ministry and brethren of Jesus Christ today is to internalize the whole Word of God; and to bring ourselves and the people into a peaceful reconciled relationship with God the Father by rebuking sin and teaching true sincere repentance, and by teaching a passionate zeal to learn and to live by every Word of God!

We are to internalize the very nature of God the Father and Jesus Christ into ourselves, and then we are to teach others to do likewise: We are to serve and teach others to serve God the Father and Jesus Christ with patient Christ-like dedicated wholehearted living by every Word of God.

7:37 This is the law of the burnt offering, of the meat offering, and of the sin offering, and of the trespass offering, and of the consecrations, and of the sacrifice of the peace offerings; **7:38** Which the LORD commanded Moses in mount Sinai, in the day that he commanded the children of Israel to offer their oblations unto the LORD, in the wilderness of Sinai.

Leviticus 8

The Consecration of the Priesthood and Tabernacle

Leviticus 8:1 And the LORD spake unto Moses, saying, **8:2 Take Aaron and his sons with him, and the garments, and the anointing oil, and a bullock for the sin offering, and two rams, and a basket of unleavened bread; 8:3 And gather thou all the congregation together unto the door of the tabernacle of the congregation.**

8:4 And Moses did as the LORD commanded him; and the assembly was gathered together unto the door of the tabernacle of the congregation. **8:5** And Moses said unto the congregation, This is the thing which the LORD commanded to be done.

This event is the initial consecration of the priesthood of Aaron and the Tabernacle of God at Sinai.

The priesthood of Aaron was an instructional allegory of the priesthood of Jesus Christ; ALL of the first fruits are called into the priesthood of Jesus Christ [Melchizedek].

We must first repent and be baptized, committing to "go and sin no more;" then the blood of the sacrifice is applied to cover our sins, and then being washed clean [so that no blemish of sin exist] by the water of the whole Word of God, we can be sanctified by the anointing of the Holy Spirit.

8:6 And Moses brought Aaron and his sons, and washed them with water.

Then, just as the priesthood of Aaron was dressed in priestly garments, the priesthood of Melchizedek [Jesus Christ] can be dressed in the royal robes of righteousness; which is the whole Word of God.

> **Revelation 19:8** And to her was granted that she should be arrayed in fine linen, clean and white: for the fine linen is the righteousness of saints.

Leviticus 8:7 And he put upon him the coat, and girded him with the girdle, and clothed him with the robe, and put the ephod upon him, and he girded him with the curious girdle of the ephod, and bound it unto him therewith. **8:8** And he put the breastplate upon him: also he put in the breastplate the Urim and the Thummim.

8:9 And he put the mitre [crown] upon his head; also **upon the mitre, even upon his forefront, did he put the golden plate, the holy crown;** as the LORD commanded Moses.

The olive oil representing the Holy Spirit was used to sanctify the tabernacle and all the holy things.

The pure olive oil used to sanctify the physical Aaronic priesthood and tabernacle set them apart to serve God in the Mosaic Covenant: This was an allegory representing the Holy Spirit and the very nature of God the Father in heaven being placed on and in the New Covenant spiritual priesthood of Melchizedek, and setting them apart to the service of God the Father in heaven.

8:10 And Moses took the anointing oil, and anointed the tabernacle and all that was therein, and sanctified them. **8:11** And he sprinkled thereof upon the altar seven times, and anointed the altar and all his vessels, both the laver and his foot, to sanctify them.

Aaron and the Mosaic priesthood were sanctified and set apart to the Aaronic priesthood by the oil; which is an instructional allegory that the New Covenant spiritual priesthood of Melchizedek is set apart to God by the Holy Spirit

8:12 And he poured of the anointing oil upon Aaron's head, and anointed him, to sanctify him [to set him apart for the service of God].

8:13 And Moses brought Aaron's sons, and put coats upon them, and girded them with girdles, and put bonnets [bonnets or "lesser crowns" the high priest having the High Crown, this being an allegory of the spiritual High Priest Jesus Christ [Melchizedek] as King over all the resurrected first fruits who will be kings and priests under him, wearing lessor crowns] upon them; as the LORD commanded Moses.

The sin offering covering the sins of the priesthood is offered

8:14 And he brought the bullock for the sin offering: and Aaron and his sons laid their hands upon the head of the bullock for the sin offering.

The blood of the Sin Offering for the priests was poured out to purify them in the Mosaic Covenant; which was an instructional allegory of the sacrifice of the Lamb of God our Sin Offering, being applied to the sincerely repentant and reconciling them to God the Father in heaven. This speaks of Jesus Christ in his capacity as the Sin Offering for the called out to his eternal priesthood.

8:15 And he slew it; and Moses took the blood, and put it upon the horns of the altar round about with his finger, and purified the altar, and poured the blood at the bottom of the altar, and sanctified it, to make reconciliation upon it.

The fat of the Sin Offering was burned on the altar for the priests, picturing the energy and strength of Jesus Christ in atoning for sin and reconciling the repentant to God the Father in heaven.

8:16 And he took all the fat that was upon the inwards, and the caul above the liver, and the two kidneys, and their fat, and Moses burned it upon the altar.

The remainder of the bullock was taken and burned completely, outside the camp; according to the instructions for a Sin Offering for the priests.

8:17 But the bullock, and his hide, his flesh, and his dung, he burnt with fire without the camp; as the LORD commanded Moses.

The Burnt Offering

Sin having been atoned for, a Burnt Offering was then offered for the priests, picturing the complete dedicated wholehearted service of Messiah to God the Father; which example the Aaronic priests and ALL of the New Covenant first fruits called to be priests of Jesus Christ Melchizedek are to follow.

The Ram pictures leadership of the flock in the strong power of dedicated godliness and zeal for the whole Word of God

8:18 And he brought the ram for the burnt offering: and Aaron and his sons laid their hands upon the head of the ram. **8:19** And he killed it; and

Moses sprinkled the blood upon the altar round about. **8:20** And he cut the ram into pieces; and Moses burnt the head, and the pieces, and the fat.

Washing the inward parts of the ram was still another indication that we are to wash away all sin by fully internalizing the Word and nature of God into the very heart of our beings.

> **Ephesians 5:25** . . . . even as Christ also loved the church, and gave himself for it; **5:26 That he might sanctify and cleanse it with the washing of water by the word, 5:27 That he might present it to himself a glorious church, not having spot, or wrinkle,** [any uncleanness or sin] **or any such thing; but that it should be holy and without blemish.**

Leviticus 8:21 And he washed the inwards and the legs in water; and Moses burnt the whole ram upon the altar: it was a burnt sacrifice for a sweet savour, and an offering made by fire unto the LORD; as the LORD commanded Moses.

The Ram of Consecration for the priests: This appears to be a kind of Peace Offering

8:22 And he brought the other ram, the ram of consecration: and Aaron and his sons laid their hands upon the head of the ram. **8:23** And he slew it; and Moses took of the blood of it, and put it upon the tip of Aaron's right ear [representing that he should always be attentive to HEAR the Word of God], and upon the thumb of his right hand [representing that he should always be attentive to keep and live by every Word of God with all the strength of his hand], and upon the great toe of his right foot [representing that he should be attentive to walk (live) by every Word of God]. **8:24** And he brought Aaron's sons, and Moses put of the blood upon the tip of their right ear, and upon the thumbs of their right hands, and upon the great toes of their right feet: and Moses sprinkled the blood upon the altar round about.

The fat, kidneys, the right foreleg and a piece of unleavened bread were then waved to God the Father; being lifted up and then brought back down by the priests.

8:25 And he took the fat, and the rump, and all the fat that was upon the inwards, and the caul above the liver, and the two kidneys, and their fat, and the right shoulder: **8:26** And out of the basket of unleavened bread, that was before the LORD, he took one unleavened cake, and a cake of **oiled** [unleavened] bread, and one [unleavened] wafer, and put them on the fat, and upon the right shoulder: **8:27** And he put all upon Aaron's hands, and upon his sons' hands, and waved them for a wave offering before the LORD.

These parts were then burned on the altar; the smoke rising up into the air as a demonstration that these men had been reconciled to God the Father through the Sin Offering and had internalized the unleavened bread of the nature of God so that peace now reigned between God and the consecrated priesthood.

This being an allegory that we are reconciled to God the Father by sincere repentance, the application of the Sin Offering of Jesus Christ, and the washing of the water of the whole Word of God gained by diligently learning and zealously living by every Word of God; and we will then receive the gift of the Holy Spirit to empower us to live by every Word of God.

8:28 And Moses took them from off their hands, and burnt them on the altar upon the burnt offering: they were consecrations for a sweet savour: it is an offering made by fire unto the LORD.

Moses as the mediator of the Mosaic Covenant was given the breast of the Ram of the Peace Offering from the priests consecration.

Jesus Christ is the Mediator of the New Covenant and his part is the leadership of the called out as pictured by the breast of the ram given to Moses. The Ram is symbolic of leadership of the flock.

8:29 And Moses took the breast, and waved it for a wave offering before the LORD: for of the ram of consecration it was Moses' part; as the LORD commanded Moses.

The blood was sprinkled on the priests, indicating that the called out and chosen New Covenant priesthood will be consecrated and covered by the blood of Jesus Christ. The olive oil was also sprinkled on then as representative that the called out and chosen resurrected priests of the order of [Melchizedek] Jesus Christ will be filled with the Holy Spirit of Jesus Christ and God the Father.

Many have been called to become priests of Jesus Christ, but most will fail to overcome and only a very small number will be Chosen (Mat 20:16, 22:14).

8:30 And Moses took of the anointing oil, and of the blood which was upon the altar, and sprinkled it upon Aaron, and upon his garments, and upon his sons, and upon his sons' garments with him; and sanctified Aaron, and his garments, and his sons, and his sons' garments with him.

The Ram of Consecration of the priests with its unleavened bread offering is to be eaten by the priests being sanctified. This is a reference to the fact that the called out priests of the order of Jesus Christ must internalize the Ram [Jesus Christ the head of the Ekklesia (1 Cor 11:3)] and the Bread of Life [Jesus Christ the Word of God (John 6:35)].

8:31 And Moses said unto Aaron and to his sons, Boil the flesh at the door of the tabernacle of the congregation: and there eat it with the bread that is in the basket of consecrations, as I commanded, saying, Aaron and his sons shall eat it. **8:32** And that which remaineth of the flesh and of the bread [until morning] shall ye burn with fire.

The priests being sanctified were to remain in the tabernacle for seven days. These seven days picture completeness, and the New Covenant Chosen for the priesthood of Jesus Christ will consist of only those who have proved their complete devotion to God and the whole Word of God.

8:33 And ye shall not go out of the door of the tabernacle of the congregation in seven days, until the days of your consecration be at an end: for seven days shall he consecrate you.

8:34 As he hath done this day, so the LORD hath commanded to do, to make an atonement for you.

8:35 Therefore shall ye abide at [inside of] the door of the tabernacle of the congregation day and night seven days, and keep the charge of the LORD, **that ye die not:** for so I am commanded.

8:36 So Aaron and his sons did all things which the LORD commanded by the hand of Moses.

Leviticus 9

After their seven days of consecration in the tabernacle the priests were brought out on the Eighth Day. The Eighth Day always represents a new beginning and the newly consecrated high priest was presented to the people on the Eighth Day, beginning the Mosaic Aaronic priesthood.

The new priesthood then offered a Sin Offering because they were physical and although priests of God they were flesh and capable of sin. A Burnt Offering was then made to once again impress upon the Called Out priests that they were to be wholeheartedly zealous for learning, keeping and teaching the whole Word of God; just as Jesus Christ dedicated himself to teach and keep God the Father's Word and Will and to live by every Word of God the Father (Mat 4:4).

Leviticus 9:1 And it came to pass on the eighth day, that Moses called Aaron and his sons, and the elders of Israel; **9:2** And he said unto Aaron, Take thee a young calf for a sin offering, and a ram for a burnt offering, without blemish, and offer them before the LORD.

Aaron was to make Sin and Burnt Offerings on the Eighth Day when the priests were fully consecrated.

Following the offerings for the priests, a Sin and Burnt Offering were to be made for the entire congregation, followed by a peace offering for the entire congregation; to indicate that they had been reconciled to God.

This was another allegory that once the Sin and trespass Offering of the Lamb of God is applied to the sincerely repentant we are reconciled to and at peace with God the Father.

The work and priesthood of Aaron was an allegory of the work and priesthood of the High Priest of the New Covenant, Jesus Christ; who gave himself as our Sin Offering to reconcile us with God the Father.

The people were to bring a Peace Offering showing that: Through the application of the Sin Offering and the High Priest's mediation, the people could enter into a state of peace with God.

This signifies that spiritually our sincere repentance to turn from sin to zealously live by every Word of God and the application of the sacrifice of Jesus Christ the Lamb of God the spiritual High Priest of the New Covenant; reconciles us to God to become fully UNITED and of ONE mind and totally at Peace with God the Father and with the Son.

9:3 And unto the children of Israel thou shalt speak, saying, Take ye a kid of the goats for a sin offering; and a calf and a lamb, both of the first year, without blemish, for a burnt offering; **9:4** Also a bullock and a ram for peace offerings, to sacrifice before the LORD; and a meat [unleavened bread] offering mingled with oil: for to day the LORD will appear unto you.

9:5 And they brought that which Moses commanded before the tabernacle of the congregation: and all the congregation drew near and stood before the LORD.

If we repent of sin and the Sin Offering of Jesus Christ is applied to us and we commit ourselves to go and sin no more by the power of the Holy Spirit [represented by the oil], and if we commit ourselves to learn and to live by every Word of God with dedicated zeal, which is represented by the Burnt Offering: then we are reconciled and at Peace with God the Father, as pictured by the Peace Offering.

The Holy Spirit of God will dwell in us and among all those who live by every Word of God with passionate love and dedicated zeal! Then we will be the spiritual children of God!

9:6 And Moses said, This is the thing which the LORD commanded that ye should do: and the glory of the LORD shall appear unto you.

Aaron being a fallible man had to make atonement for himself and for the people, but we have a perfect High Priest who was without sin and had no need to atone for himself, and therefore able to offer himself to atone for the sins of the sincerely repentant (Heb 7).

The Mosaic high priest was an allegory to teach us about the eternal High Priesthood of Jesus Christ [Melchizedek]; see the entire book of Hebrews.

9:7 And Moses said unto Aaron, Go unto the altar, and offer thy sin offering, and thy burnt offering, and make an atonement for thyself, and for the people: and offer the offering of the people, and make an atonement for them; as the LORD commanded.

Aaron then offered the Sin Offering for himself

9:8 Aaron therefore went unto the altar, and slew the calf of the sin offering, **which was for himself.**

9:9 And the sons of Aaron brought the blood unto him: and he dipped his finger in the blood, and put it upon the horns of the altar, and poured out the blood at the bottom of the altar: **9:10** But **the fat, and the kidneys, and the caul above the liver of the sin offering, he burnt upon the altar;** as the LORD commanded Moses.

9:11 And the flesh and the hide he burnt with fire without the camp.

This burning of the Sin Offering outside the camp, symbolized the total removal of all sin from the congregation of believers.

After the Sin Offering for himself Aaron then presented the Burnt Offering symbolizing a Christ-like dedicated zeal to wholeheartedly learn and keep the whole Word of God as Jesus Christ did.

After Aaron had killed the Burnt Offering his sons assisted him with the details of the Offering. Even so, we are called out to become priests of Melchizedek and to assist our High Priest Jesus Christ to teach and bring humanity into a proper relationship with God the Father.

9:12 And he slew the burnt offering; and Aaron's sons presented unto him the blood, which he sprinkled round about upon the altar.

9:13 And they presented the burnt offering unto him, with the pieces thereof, and the head: and he burnt them upon the altar. **9:14** And he did wash the inwards and the legs, and burnt them upon the burnt offering on the altar.

Aaron offered the Sin and Burnt Offerings for himself, because he was a high priest subject to sin; but a Sin Offering was not required to be offered for our sinless sacrifice and High Priest, Jesus Christ, because he had no sin.

The atoning offerings were then made by the physical high priest on behalf of the people called out of Egypt; picturing the Passover sacrifice of Jesus Christ for the repentant Called Out from the spiritual Egypt of bondage to Satan and sin.

9:15 And he brought the people's offering, and took the goat, which **was the sin offering for the people, and slew it, and offered it for sin**, as the first.

After the sacrifice of Jesus Christ is applied to atone for the sins of the sincerely repentant, they are then to dedicate themselves to Christ-like wholehearted service to God the Father as pictured by the Burnt Offering.

9:16 And he brought the burnt offering, and offered it according to the manner.

The Unleavened Bread Offering pictures Jesus Christ as the Pure Sinless Bread of Life. The handful burned on the altar picturing Christ as the Bread of Life, consecrated and accepted by God the Father; and the remainder to be eaten, picturing the internalizing of the very nature of Christ by the repentant called out (John 6).

9:17 And he brought the meat offering, and took an handful thereof, and burnt it upon the altar, beside the burnt sacrifice of the morning.

Then with sin sincerely repented of and atoned for and the repentant being zealous to learn and to live by every Word of God which is to internalize the very nature of Jesus Christ and God the Father as revealed in the whole Word of God: We are reconciled to peace with God the Father and with the Son Jesus Christ!

The Peace Offerings are then made according to the commandments previously studied

9:18 He slew also the bullock and the ram for a sacrifice of **peace offerings**, which was for the people: and Aaron's sons presented unto him the blood, which he sprinkled upon the altar round about, **9:19** And the fat of the bullock and of the ram, the rump, and that which covereth the inwards, and the kidneys, and the caul above the liver: **9:20** And they put the fat upon the breasts, and he burnt the fat upon the altar: **9:21** And the breasts and the right shoulder Aaron waved for a wave offering before the LORD; as Moses commanded.

9:22 And Aaron lifted up his hand toward the people, and blessed them, and came down from offering of the sin offering, and the burnt offering, and peace offerings.

When all these things were done according to the instructions of Messiah as delivered to Moses; the glory of the presence of God fell on the tabernacle in the sight of all the people, and the fire of God consumed the offerings. Thus demonstrating that God will be present through his Holy Spirit, in his spiritual Temple of the sincerely repentant Called Out of Sin!

At the Feast of Pentecost in 31 A.D. God officially moved from the physical Temple to dwell in a Temple of his faithful.

> **Acts 2:3** And there appeared unto them cloven tongues like as of fire, and it sat upon each of them.

Repentance [represented by the obedience of bringing the offerings] and the application of atonement for sin; followed by a dedicated zeal to serve God and to learn and keep God's Word and to "go and sin no more," reconciles us to God the Father and brings the gift of forgiveness and the Holy Spirit which will lead us into godliness!

God is not divided against himself and God's Spirit will NEVER lead anyone to go against or to compromise with the Word of God! That is how we discern the Spirit of God from every counterfeit spirit; by consistency with the Word of God!

Leviticus 9:23 And Moses and Aaron went into the tabernacle of the congregation, and came out, and blessed the people: and the glory of the LORD appeared unto all the people. **9:24** And there came a fire out from before the LORD, and consumed upon the altar the burnt offering and the fat: which when all the people saw, they shouted, and fell on their faces.

Leviticus 10

This chapter concerns events on the Eighth Day after the seven days of the Consecration of the priests in Chapter 9. This concerns the sacrifices of the Eighth Day and the event of the sin of Nadab and Abihu in placing strange fire on the altar in defiance to the command of God.

The fire of God represents the Holy Spirit [see Acts 2) and the strange fire represented any false spirit. Therefore Nadab and Abihu were killed for our example; teaching us that being of any other spirit than the Spirit of God brings death. It is God alone who gives the fire of the Holy Spirit to the sincerely repentant, who have been covered by the Sin Offering of the Lamb of God.

God's Holy Spirit will not coexist with the false spirit of sin and rebellion against the Word of God. What these two men did was contrary to the commandments of God. Even though well intentioned they did what they thought was right, instead of living by every Word of God and doing what God had commanded.

Anyone who teaches anything different from the Word of God or compromises with God's Word in any way, is not being led by the Holy Spirit; no matter what they claim.

Today, many claim that God's Spirit has led them to do this or to believe that when it is contrary to God's Word; such people are deceived not understanding that God's Spirit is in full unity with the Word of God.

Leviticus 10:1 And Nadab and Abihu, the sons of Aaron, took either of them his censer, and put fire therein, and put incense thereon, and offered strange fire before the LORD, which he commanded them not. **10:2** And there went out fire from the LORD, and devoured them, and they died before the LORD.

Moses pointed out to his brother Aaron that his two sons had rebelled against the Word of God and had brought this upon themselves, by NOT glorifying God through obedience to the Word of God.

It is for this very same reason, of deciding our own ways for ourselves and not being zealous to obey the whole Word of God, that today's Ekklesia, their leaders and elders and the people who follow them in place of following God; are being rejected by Jesus Christ and cast into division, disarray and great tribulation in the hope that by afflicting the flesh the spirit might be saved.

Those who seek to learn and live by every Word of God in repentant zeal, will be sanctified [Set Apart to godliness] by God; while those who are not zealous to learn and keep the whole Word of God will be rejected by him; they will NOT be among the chosen.

10:3 Then Moses said unto Aaron, This is it that the LORD spake, saying, I will be sanctified in them that come nigh me, and before all the people I will be glorified. And Aaron held his peace.

The difference between priests and Levites

Aaron and his descendants were to be the priesthood, while all other descendants of Levi were called to be Levites. The function of the Levites was the same as the function of today's Deacons; to support the priesthood, by performing the needed physical duties, and thereby allowing the priests/ministry to focus on spiritual things unhindered by physical chores.

The Levites were tasked with removing the bodies of the two offenders so that the priests would not become unclean by a dead body. The two offenders were carried outside the camp, symbolizing that sinners against obeying the whole Word of God are to be rejected out of the assembly of believers who do live by every Word of God.

In today's spiritual terms this refers to the rejection by Christ of all those who obey and follow men and organizations [or any other] and being zealous for a man or "church;" instead of being zealous to live by every Word of God.

A few years ago someone wrote to me saying "I love [a church] so much," and that is the problem: People loving corporations or men more than they love the Word of God to learn and to live by it, instead they love and make idols of men and their organizations.

10:4 And Moses called Mishael and Elzaphan, the sons of Uzziel the uncle of Aaron [not of the Aaronic priesthood but still Levites], and said unto them, Come near, carry your [dead] brethren from before the sanctuary out of the camp. **10:5** So they went near, and carried them in their coats out of the camp; as Moses had said.

Aaron is told NOT to mourn publicly for his sons, because they had died by the hand of God for their sin of rebellion and disobedience; and to publicly mourn for sinners was not consistent with the office of the priests. Yet the congregation could mourn for these men which pictures a mourning over the sin that brought their deaths.

Shaving the beard [most often the whole head] and rending clothes was a demonstration of being in mourning in those days.

10:6 And Moses said unto Aaron, and unto Eleazar and unto Ithamar, his sons, Uncover [shave] not your heads [for the two dead men], neither rend your clothes; lest ye die, and lest wrath come upon all the people: but **let your brethren, the whole house of Israel, bewail the burning which the LORD hath kindled** [to kill the two men].

The priests [spiritually we are ALL called to be priests of the New Covenant High Priesthood of Jesus Christ] are not to turn to the right or left, and they are not to blemish their calling to the priesthood and anointing with the Holy Spirit, for ANY reason!

We, as people called out to become priests of the New Covenant priesthood of Jesus Christ [Melchizedek] are to be passionately zealous for our calling to learn and live by and teach every Word of God; at ALL tines FOREVER!

Those who are zealous for their own ways and who are not zealous to live by every Word of God, and those who equate loyalty to some man or organization as loyalty to God: will be rejected by Jesus Christ and God the Father!

Once we have committed ourselves to godliness at baptism we are to continually grow towards complete total UNITY with God the Father, turning AWAY from what we think is right to do what GOD says is right!

10:7 And ye shall not go out from the door of the tabernacle of the congregation, lest ye die: for the anointing oil of the LORD is upon you. And they did according to the word of Moses.

The priests were forbidden to drink alcohol when they were serving in their offices, lest the alcohol pervert their judgment.

The elders and brotherhood of today's Called Out are not to be given to wine or alcohol, lest their judgment be perverted and they forget the differences between the holy and the profane, between the Word of God and the ways of men. There is far too much alcohol use and alcoholism in the Ekklesia today.

Many brethren and very many elders need to repent of excessive alcohol consumption. I challenge you to record every time you drink and how many hours you waste doing so, and compare that with how much time you spend studying and thinking on the Word of God. Let's get back to the correct focus in our lives!

10:8 And the LORD spake unto Aaron, saying, **10:9** Do not drink wine nor strong drink, thou, nor thy sons with thee, when ye go into the tabernacle of the congregation, lest ye die: it shall be a statute for ever throughout your generations:

Intoxicants including but not limited to alcohol, often pervert sound judgment and lead us away from a good understanding of the whole Word of God.

10:10 And **that ye may put difference between holy and unholy, and between unclean and clean; 10:11 And that ye may teach the children of Israel all the statutes which the LORD hath spoken unto them by the hand of Moses.**

Aaron and his remaining sons were to eat the unleavened bread of the offerings continually [not just during the Feast of Unleavened Bread] while in active service at the Tabernacle/Temple. This typifying the internalizing of the Bread of Life, the Logos, Jesus Christ in print; the whole Word of God.

10:12 And Moses spake unto Aaron, and unto Eleazar and unto Ithamar, his sons that were left, Take the meat [unleavened bread] offering that remaineth of the offerings of the LORD made by fire, and eat it **without leaven** beside the altar: for it is most holy: **10:13** And ye shall eat it in the holy place, because it is thy due, and thy sons' due, of the sacrifices of the LORD made by fire: for so I am commanded.

10:14 And the wave breast and heave shoulder shall ye eat in a clean place; thou, and thy sons, and thy daughters with thee: for they be thy due, and thy sons' due, which are given out of the sacrifices of peace offerings of the children of Israel.

The priests were to eat a part of the sacrifices, symbolizing that they must also internalize the nature of God and the Lamb of God along with the offeror's.

10:15 The heave shoulder and the wave breast shall they bring with the offerings made by fire of the fat, to wave it for a wave offering before the LORD; and it shall be thine, and thy sons' with thee, by a statute for ever; as the LORD hath commanded.

The goat Sin Offering on behalf of the people was burned by Aaron instead of being eaten by the priests, for Aaron could not eat of it when his two sons had died.

10:16 And Moses diligently sought the goat of the sin offering, and, behold, it was burnt: and he was angry with Eleazar and Ithamar, the sons of Aaron which were left alive, saying, **10:17** Wherefore have ye not eaten the sin offering in the holy place, seeing it is most holy, and God hath given it you to bear the iniquity of the congregation, to make atonement for them before the LORD? **10:18** Behold, the blood of it was not brought in within the holy place: ye should indeed have eaten it in the holy place, as I commanded.

Aaron explained that he held himself responsible for the sin of his sons and therefore he had not eaten the Sin Offering of the people, but had burnt the Sin Offering outside the camp **as was to be done for the sin of a priest.**

It is a true thing that the priests/ministry are responsible for teaching and correcting the sins of the people. The elders of today's spiritual Ekklesia are held responsible by Almighty God for the sins of the brethren, because our elders have neither taught us to live by every Word of God, nor have they rebuked much of the sin in today's assemblies.

> **James 3:1** My brethren, be not many masters, knowing that we shall receive the greater condemnation.

Leviticus 10:19 And Aaron said unto Moses, Behold, this day have they offered their sin offering and their burnt offering before the LORD; and such things have befallen me: and if I had eaten the sin offering to day, should it have been accepted in the sight of the LORD? **10:20** And when Moses heard that, he was content.

The Clean and Unclean Explained

All nations, governments and even organizations have laws and rules. Such laws and rules are essential for the smooth running of any organization or society. The government of the Kingdom of God is no exception and has its own constitution which is the whole Word of God contained in Holy Scripture.

- The Ten Commandments are the basic constitution of God's Kingdom distilled down to the basic principles for godly living.

- The term "law" is a general reference to the entire five books of Moses and all of the instructions therein. There are really very few laws, with the Ten Commandments and the Sabbath and Festivals, the law of the unclean, the law of marriage, and a few other various laws.

- The Statutes are those ordinances [laws] which expand upon the basic Ten Commandments and further reveal how they are to be kept. The word ordinance is actually a synonym for statutes.

- Judgments refer to precedents set by making a judgment based on the Commandments or the Law.

- The word "precept" means instruction or wisdom and refers to the wise instructions of God. A precept would be: **Deuteronomy 11:18**

> Therefore shall ye lay up these my words in your heart and in your soul, and bind them for a sign upon your hand, that they may be as frontlets between your eyes.

Before we speak of the ten basic commandments and other laws we must understand that it is necessary to learn to discern between good and evil and between right and wrong, and to choose to do what is right by the Word of God.

The commandments and law of God were taught to Adam and Eve and Cain and Abel, for they knew and understood a basic law of sacrifice. Later Noah saved seven pairs of every clean animal and one pair of every unclean animal showing that he understood the law of clean and unclean.

Noah also offered sacrifices as did Abraham and others, while Pharaoh knew better than to take Abram's wife and Joseph respected his master and refused to take his master's wife.

Indeed God destroyed all flesh except for those on the ark for their sins and also destroyed Sodom. All of these things show that the Commandments and law of God were in effect since creation, since if there had not been a law there would have been no breaking of a non existent law and therefore no sin.

Yet if anyone chooses to argue with these facts let them read the very words of God himself.

Speaking to Isaac God said **Genesis 26:4** And I will make thy seed to multiply as the stars of heaven, and will give unto thy seed all these countries; and in thy seed shall all the nations of the earth be blessed; **26:5** Because that **Abraham obeyed my voice**, and **kept my charge, my commandments, my statutes, and my laws.**

God's basic laws were in effect since creation and the sacrificial law came into effect as soon as humanity sinned and needed a sacrifice. Then when Israel was delivered from bondage in Egypt she entered into a marriage covenant with her Maker at Sinai.

Isaiah 54:5 For **thy Maker is thine husband**; the Lord of hosts is his name; and thy Redeemer the Holy One of Israel; The God of the whole earth shall he be called.

At Sinai God commanded Israel to "remember' his Sabbath" and proclaimed his commandments anew.

At that time God also added the Aaronic priesthood to teach the people and expanded the Sacrificial System into various different parts; both of these things as an instructional allegory to teach us God's plan of salvation.

Annual Festivals were also added for the same reason, to teach us about God's plan of salvation, but the basic core of God's law including the moral laws, the laws of clean and unclean and the law of sacrifice have existed since man has existed.

The Law of the Clean and the Unclean

The law of the Clean and the Unclean is to teach us the difference between the holy and the profane, and to teach us that God will NOT tolerate any breaking or compromise with his commandments. Anyone who claims that the law of clean and unclean is merely a health matter is very much mistaken, in fact this law has nothing to do with health issues.

God commands us not to consume or even to touch the unclean thing. This is an object lesson and a TEST. Will we obey God, or will we do what we or some man decides is right?

We may consume or use ONLY the dead bodies of creatures that have been sanctified by the word of God.

1 Timothy 4:4 For every creature of God is good, and nothing to be refused, if it be received with thanksgiving: **4:5** For [if] it is sanctified by the Word of God and prayer.

Many spend a lot of time avoiding pork, other unclean creatures, furs, and the skins of unclean creatures, and that is good; yet we have failed to learn the spiritual lesson of this law. The law of the clean and the unclean is a spiritual law as well as a physical law, meaning in its spiritual context that we are to avoid all sin.

2 Corinthians 6:17 Wherefore come out from among them, and be ye separate, saith the Lord, and **touch not the unclean thing**; and I will receive you.

The New Covenant is a spiritual Covenant involving the presence of the Holy Spirit of Almighty God. The major lesson of the clean and the unclean law is that God will not tolerate even the slightest presence of sin.

It is the physical unclean thing which defiles the physical body, which is a lesson that any sin will defile us spiritually.

We are commanded in the New Testament to avoid defiling our bodies with any unclean thing, because through the indwelling of the Holy Spirit we are the Temple of God and God will NOT coexist with any physical or spiritual defilement.

1 Corinthians 3:17 If any man defile the temple of God, him shall God destroy; for the temple of God is holy, which temple ye are.

We are commanded to become holy as God is holy, and holiness means that we are to be pure from the defilement of sin like God is pure from sin.

1 Peter 1:15 But as he which hath called you is holy, so be ye holy in all manner of conversation [conduct; in thought, words and deeds]; **1:16** Because it is written, Be ye holy; for I am holy.

The laws of clean and unclean are about far more than mere physical health as those who lack spiritual understanding teach.

We MUST keep BOTH the physical law and its spiritual purpose and intent, in order to learn fully the intended lessons. Those who compromise with the physical law will never learn its spiritual lessons.

By compromising with many laws on the physical plane; many have cut themselves off from learning the spiritual intent of those laws and quenched God's Spirit, driving it out of the Temple of their hearts. For God will NOT co-dwell with wilful unrepentant sin!

The basics are

> 1) That whatever a man eats [internalizes] either physically or spiritually he becomes; either turning to godliness by spiritually internalizing Christ as the Bread of Life; or internalizing wickedness.

> 2) That what is touched physically corresponds to what we tolerate in our midst spiritually. Do we tolerate and allow the presence of unrepentant sin, compromise with God's commandments and do we make excuses for and justify sin; instead of strongly condemning sin and correcting the breaking of God's Word?

Do we reject the repeated and wilful sinner from our midst, or do we tolerate his example infecting the whole body?

Titus 3:10 A man that is an heretick after the first and second admonition reject; **3:11** Knowing that he that is such is subverted, and sinneth, being condemned of himself.

Knowing that a little leaven [sin in the assemblies], leavens the whole body of believers.

1 Corinthians 5:6 Your glorying [in tolerating sin, mistakenly thinking that you are loving the sinner by tolerating his sin] is not good. Know ye not that a little leaven leaveneth the whole lump? **5:7** Purge out therefore the old leaven, that ye may be a new lump, as ye are unleavened. For even Christ our passover is sacrificed for us:

Let me interject here that this refers the Word of God; and not to man-made traditions.

The law of clean and unclean is also far more than just what you eat, or touch, however I will begin with the law of clean and unclean meats.

This law is found in Leviticus 11 and Deuteronomy 14 where God clearly defines what is clean and unclean in the nature of dead animals. Anyone who even as much as touches the dead unclean animal must wash and be unclean until the evening [the sun has set].

Leviticus 11:24 And for these ye shall be unclean: whosoever toucheth the carcase of them shall be unclean until the even.

We are not to consume or even to touch the dead body of any unclean creature. That includes skins and furs.

The hair or wool sheared from LIVING animals may be used, as the operative concept is DEATH, with the dead unclean creature picturing the person who dies in wickedness remaining polluted by sin.

The dead clean creature pictures the righteous godly person, and the dead unclean creature pictures the person who is spiritually unclean before God and therefore consigned to eternal death.

The dead bodies of the clean animals picture those persons clean from sin, through their faithfulness to God and awaiting their resurrection to eternal life as Christ the Lamb of God was resurrected to eternal life; the dead bodies of the unclean creatures picture persons who are polluted by sin and condemned to destruction.

The purpose of the law of the clean and the unclean is NOT health and this is not "just physical." Like all the other laws it is a physical law intended to teach us spiritual principles.

The purpose of the law of the clean and unclean is to teach us to discern between the holy and the profane.

The priesthood is to teach the people the difference between the holy and the profane, the clean and the unclean.

Ezekiel 44:23 And they shall teach my people the difference between the holy and profane, and cause them to discern between the unclean and the clean.

Speaking of today's apostate Ekklesia and its leaders, who have led the brethren astray from God to follow themselves, God says:

Ezekiel 22:25 There is a conspiracy of her prophets in the midst thereof, like a roaring lion ravening the prey; they have devoured souls; they have taken the treasure and precious things; they have made her many widows in the midst thereof.

22:26 Her priests have violated my law, and have profaned mine holy things: they have put no difference between the holy and profane, neither have they shewed difference between the unclean and the clean, and have hid their eyes from my sabbaths, and I am profaned among them.

What does this mean?

The law of the clean and unclean is an analogy of spiritual cleanness; or the spiritual uncleanness of exposure to sin and compromising with God's Word.

To eat the unclean thing is the same as internalizing wickedness, instead of internalizing the nature of God the Father and Jesus Christ; and to touch the unclean thing is to tolerate and consort with sin, to permit sin to remain uncorrected within the collective body.

Like all good housekeepers my mother would roar if we tracked dirt into her home; yet in a spiritual sense we think nothing of tracking the filth of sin into the very Temple of Almighty God; our minds.

To tolerate sin without rebuking it is to tolerate spiritual uncleanness among us! To compromise with the Sabbath and pay others to work for us in restaurants is to not only tolerate sin, it encourages the sin of polluting the Sabbath and it is active participation in other men's sins.

1 Timothy 5:22 Lay hands suddenly on no man, neither be partaker of other men's sins: keep thyself pure [from sin and all spiritual and physical uncleanness].

When we eat, we internalize what we eat and it becomes a part of us, and when we touch filth we become polluted with that filth.

If you put your hand in sewage; would you not then wash it to cleanse it?

The lesson is the same, and God uses certain animals to teach us about eating and internalizing evil. He uses the very touching of the unclean dead body to teach us that dipping our hand in the wickedness of spiritual sewage will make us unclean and detestable to God.

If we have been exposed and touched evil, we are contaminated with that evil and need to be cleansed; just like a person handling sewage begins to stink of that sewage. And if we actually eat the physical unclean thing which is representative of internalizing spiritual sewage; how much more do we stink of sin before our God?

Brethren, the idea of the clean and the unclean is to teach us to put a difference between the spiritually holy and the profane things [sin]!

This is an analogy, just like circumcision is an analogy of true repentance and the removing of the covering veil of our sins.

Let me be very clear: AS God would tolerate NO unclean thing in his physical temple and commanded all Israel to avoid uncleanness: he will remove all spiritual uncleanness OUT of his spiritual Temple.

Why do you think that Jesus cast the sinners out of the Temple? To correct them and that sin YES! but also as an example for us that if we wilfully sin or even tolerate sin in our assemblies we will also be rejected and cast out of the presence of God Almighty God will NOT TOLERATE any hint of sin in his Temple; which is his PEOPLE!

Let's get this clear: Almighty God will NOT tolerate anyone who compromises with HIS commandments or who breaks his laws; they will be rejected from being his Spiritual Temple!

Let's make this even clearer: Almighty God will NOT dwell in a filthy sinful environment!

God's Spirit will NOT remain in a wilfully sinful person! And we become wilfully sinful the minute we begin to make excuses for sin; when we say that we are only weak flesh and that he will forgive, and then use that as an excuse to avoid any serious effort to overcome.

If we justify working on Sabbath [sunset Friday to sunset Saturday] by saying that God is love and he would not want us to lose our jobs: WE ARE SINNERS and God's spirit will leave us if we do not quickly and sincerely REPENT!

Today apostate religion is FULL of tolerance and compromise; full of reasoning and excuses to not obey God and to do what we want regardless of what God has commanded; full of sin! We are carnal and worldly and we cannot distinguish between the holy and the profane, between spiritual cleanness and spiritual uncleanness.

We have quenched God's Spirit and have become filled with faith in our own righteousness; which is spiritual FILTH and UNCLEANNESS in the eyes or our God.

1 Corinthians 3:16 Know ye not that ye are the temple of God, and that the Spirit of God dwelleth in you? **3:17** If any man defile the temple of God, him shall God destroy; for the temple of God is holy, which temple ye are.

It is past time to repent and regain our lost passionate love and zeal for our Father and his commandments.

We have fallen away from our God and we know it not, because we cannot discern between what is holy and what is profane, between the spiritual cleanness of keeping all of God's commandments with uncompromising zeal; and the sin of a shoddy, lukewarm, spiritually lazy form of love for God, fearing and loving the things of this wicked world more than the things of Almighty God.

James 4:7 Submit yourselves therefore to God. Resist the devil, and he will flee from you. **4:8** Draw nigh to God, and he will draw nigh to you. Cleanse your hands [purify your thoughts and actions], ye sinners; and purify your hearts, ye double minded.

2 Corinthians 7:1 Having therefore these promises, dearly beloved, let us cleanse ourselves from all filthiness of the flesh and spirit, perfecting holiness in the fear of God.

Other Forms of Uncleanness

Bodily discharges involve a loss of strength and are representative of the wages of sin [death], most especially blood is representative of death, for no higher life form can live without its blood, and sin requires the shedding of blood and the death of the sinner.

Menstruation is a continual reminder that by woman, sin and death came into the world and by a woman's bearing of the Son of God to die for the sins of the world, sins are removed and humanity is reconciled to God.

1 Timothy 2:14 And Adam was not deceived, but the woman being deceived was in the transgression. **2:15** Notwithstanding she shall be saved in childbearing, if they continue in faith and charity and holiness with sobriety.

Blood is about death which is the result of sin.

To tolerate sin without serious condemnation of that sin and serious correction; is to lead those sinners to their death. Presented as love, this attitude is the exact opposite of love!

The other forms of uncleanness involve **disfigurement, and disease**; which is physical imperfection and is analogous to spiritual imperfection.

Matthew 5:48 Be ye therefore perfect, even as your Father which is in heaven is perfect.

This is also a part of the sacrificial law, in that a sacrificial animal must be perfect because it represents the perfection of Jesus Christ.

Paul speaking to the vegetarians about eating meat, tell us that these creatures which are sanctified by the Word of God may be eaten.

1 Timothy 4:4 For every creature of God is good, and nothing to be refused, if it be received with thanksgiving: **4:5** For it is sanctified by the word of God [sanctified in in Lev 11 and Deu 14] and prayer.

The lesson about Peter's vision of the sheet of unclean things in Acts, was as Peter himself said; a lesson that the Gentiles could be called to God like the Jews.

Acts 10:28 And he said unto them, Ye know how that it is an unlawful thing for a man that is a Jew to keep company, or come unto one of another nation; but **God hath shewed me that I should not call any man common or unclean.**

Therefore brethren, do not believe those who say that the unclean law was only an ancient health law.

The law of the clean and the unclean is about holiness, and it is a law from God to keep our physical bodies pure from the unclean thing, and to keep our minds, thoughts and deeds clean from all sin and impurity.

Consider how many brethren are full of vicarious sin! How many of us imagine some sin which we would very much like to do themselves but dare not, so we fill our minds with wicked thoughts or seek to live out our sinful fantasies vicariously by watching others do what we would like to do but dare not do!

Brethren, this is the sin of tempting ourselves, it is the sin of defiling our minds with sin even if we do not actually do the deeds, and it is the sin of lust and coveting to do the unlawful thing!

God will not hold us guiltless if we defile our minds, His House; with sinful imaginations and secret desires to sin!

Warning: Kosher certifying agencies go by their sect's traditions and not by the scriptures. For instance many will permit the use of unclean bones and skins in the making of gelatine, and nearly all permit the use of unclean skins and furs for wearing even though we are commanded not to even touch the dead bodies of unclean creatures. It is absolutely forbidden by God to use unclean skins and furs even as clothing.

Islam [Halal] also relies on the traditions of its various branches, allowing the eating of the camel for instance.

If you want gelatine the simplest way to get a clean product is to buy from a vegetarian outlet, which would sell Agar made from sea weed. Before I begin Leviticus 11, I want to point out that the modern Rabbinic movement is an outgrowth of the Hellenic Pharisees of Babylon and

Egypt. These folks have used their own reasoning to create their own traditions which often make the commandments of God of no effect.

A classic example of this is their views on the clean and the unclean.

We are commanded to not even touch a dead unclean animal, yet many sects claim that the commandment is only concerned with eating the flesh. Using that false premise they say that any other products from dead unclean creatures may be used at will. Some Orthodox sects insist on wearing hats made of dog skin/fur for their members, yet they will not walk on the same side of the street with a woman lest she be unclean.

All kosher certifying agencies are not the same. There are several different Kosher certifying organizations and some will certify as kosher any product of dead unclean animals except the actual flesh. they will accept anything made from skin and bone such as gelatin, soap etc and label it kosher.

The word kosher means fit or proper and blessed by a Christ rejecting Rabbi.

Do NOT assume that a kosher mark means that the product is clean by biblical standards unless you know the agency doing the certifying. Such things as kosher marshmallow only mean that it was blessed by a Rabbi; it may contain gelatine from biblically unclean sources. When looking for products of this kind it is best to shop at a Vegan outlet, then you can be sure that the product contains no animal based products..

As far as source labelling, buy gelatine made from sea weed like Agar gelatine. Vegan vegetarian labelling is far more credible than kosher such matters.

God separated certain animals as clean and others as unclean to teach us the object lesson that there is a difference between the holy and the profane.

Living "unclean" animals are not unclean to touch and neither is the hair or wool sheared from living animals; it is the DEAD animals that are unclean and not to be eaten or even touched. That means that the skin and furs of dead unclean animals are not to be touched.

Paul admonished the New Covenant faithful to obey the laws of clean and unclean, and to eat only those things sanctified by scripture; which sanctification is listed in Leviticus 11.

We may eat or use with thanks for God's provision to us, the dead bodies of those creatures SANCTIFIED by the Word of God ONLY! We are to avoid contact with those dead creatures not sanctified by our use by the Word of God.

1 Timothy 4:4 For every creature of God is good, and nothing to be refused, if it be received with thanksgiving: **4:5** For [or IF it is] it is [it must be] **sanctified by the word of God and prayer.**

Leviticus 11

God established the laws of clean and unclean as an object lesson to teach us that there is a difference between the holy and the profane.

Living "unclean" animals are not unclean to touch and neither is the hair or wool sheared from living animals; it is the DEAD animals that are unclean and not to be eaten or even touched. That means that the skin and furs of dead unclean animals are not to be touched.

Paul admonished the New Covenant faithful to obey the laws of clean and unclean, and to eat only those things sanctified by scripture; which sanctification is listed in Leviticus 11.

We may eat or use with thanks to God the dead bodies of those creatures SANCTIFIED by the Word of God ONLY! We are to avoid contact with those dead creatures not sanctified for our use by the Word of God.

> **1 Timothy 4:4** For every creature of God is good, and nothing to be refused, if it be received with thanksgiving: **4:5** For [IF] it is [it must be] **sanctified by the word of God and prayer.**

Leviticus 11:1 And the LORD spake unto Moses and to Aaron, saying unto them, **11:2** Speak unto the children of Israel, saying, These are **the beasts which ye shall eat among all the beasts that are on the earth. 11:3 Whatsoever parteth the hoof, and is clovenfooted, and cheweth the cud [both], among the beasts, that shall ye eat.**

We may not eat, use or touch the dead body of any creature that does not BOTH chew the cud and split the hoof among animals, or any underwater creature that does not have BOTH fins and scales at the time that we take it. We may not eat, use or touch the dead body of any bird that does not have a crop and is not able to fly, nor can we eat any insect that does not have both legs for leaping and wings for flying.

We must also be very careful to properly clean fish, fowl and land animals to remove the gut and crop intact so as to prevent any unclean thing which they may have eaten from contaminating the flesh. For example a salmon may have bits of shrimp etc. in its gut and fowl may have insects in their gut or crop.

11:4 Nevertheless these shall ye not eat of them that chew the cud, or of them that divide the hoof: as the camel, because he cheweth the cud, but divideth not the hoof; he is unclean unto you.

11:5 And the coney, because he cheweth the cud, but divideth not the hoof; he is unclean unto you. **11:6** And the hare, because he cheweth the cud, but divideth not the hoof; he is unclean unto you.

11:7 And the swine, though he divide the hoof, and be clovenfooted, yet he cheweth not the cud; he is unclean to you.

11:8 Of **their flesh shall ye not eat, and their carcase shall ye not touch;** they are unclean to you.

Things in the waters

11:9 These shall ye eat of all that are in the waters: whatsoever hath fins and scales in the waters, in the seas, and in the rivers, them shall ye eat. **11:10** And all that have not fins and scales in the seas, and in the rivers, of all that move in the waters, and of any living thing which is in the waters, they shall be an abomination unto you: **11:11** They shall be even an abomination unto you; ye shall not eat of their flesh, but ye shall have their carcases in abomination.

11:12 Whatsoever hath no fins nor scales in the waters, that shall be an abomination unto you.

Birds

11:13 And these are they which ye shall have in abomination among the fowls; they shall not be eaten, they are an abomination: the eagle, and the ossifrage, and the ospray, **11:14** And the vulture, and the kite after his kind; **11:15** Every raven after his kind; **11:16** And the owl, and the night hawk, and the cuckow, and the hawk after his kind, **11:17** And the little owl, and the cormorant, and the great owl, **11:18** And the swan, and the pelican, and the gier eagle, **11:19** And the stork, the heron after her kind, and the lapwing, and the bat.

The characteristics and features of clean birds can be determined from the scripturally known clean birds; namely the dove (turtledove), pigeon, and quail (Leviticus 1:14-17, 12:8, 14:22, 15:14-15; Psalm 105:40; Matthew 3:16, 21:12; Mark 1:10, 11:15; Luke 2:24, 3:22; John 1:32, 2:14-16).

The turtledove and pigeon are clean birds as they were used in sacrifices and only clean birds could be used for sacrifices (Leviticus 1:14-17, 12:8, 14:22, 15:14-15). A dove (the Holy Spirit) descended upon Yeshua (Jesus), illustrating that doves are clean birds (Matthew 3:16; Mark 1:10; Luke 3:22; John 1:32). Doves were sold along with oxen and sheep in the Israeli
marketplace, further indicating that doves are clean birds (Matthew 21:12; Mark 11:15; John 2:14-16). Quails are clean birds as the Lord provided them to the Hebrews for food after the Hebrew exodus from Egypt (Psalm 105:40).

Clean birds have all of the following characteristics:

- they are foragers and are not birds of prey or scavengers
- they have craws or crops
- they have a gizzard with a double lining which can easily be separated
- they have three front toes with an elongated middle front toe and a hind toe
- they spread three front toes on one side of a perch and their hind toe on the other side
- they do not eat in flight, landing to eat.

Unclean birds lack one or more of the characteristics of clean birds. The characteristics and features of unclean birds can be determined from the list of unclean birds listed in Scripture.

Unclean birds include those that are:
- birds of prey
- carrion-eating scavenger birds
- ratite birds
- web-footed, and zygodactyl-footed [two front and two back toes] birds
- waterfowl
- flying mammals (bats)

The pelican and the seagull are listed in Scripture among the unclean birds.

The pelican and seagull possess webbed feet, as do ducks, geese, and swans. Ducks, geese, and swans are unclean because they lack some of the characteristics and features of clean birds – they do not have crops, they have different body structures than clean birds do, their body fat is intertwined with their flesh and they have webbed feet.

Insects

11:20 All fowls that creep, going upon all four, shall be an abomination unto you.

11:21 Yet **these may ye eat** of every flying creeping thing that goeth upon all four, which have legs above their feet, to leap withal upon the earth; **11:22** Even these of them ye may eat; the locust after his kind, and the bald locust after his kind, and the beetle ["Beetle" is a poor translation, the Hebrew word #2728 חַרְגֹּל chargol {khar-gole'} meaning a leaping locust. —Brown-Driver-Briggs (Old Testament Hebrew-English Lexicon)] after his kind, and the grasshopper after his kind. **11:23** But all other flying creeping things, which have four feet [but do not have legs to leap with], shall be an abomination unto you.

To prepare locusts, grasp the body between thumb and forefinger and grasp the head between the other thumb and forefinger and pull, the head will come off taking the internal viscera with it. Then pull off the small front legs and the wings and cook with your favourite recipe. Don't have a recipe? Try Google!

The Law of the Unclean

To even touch the carcass [dead body] of an unclean creature makes one unclean and they cannot enter a holy place (the tabernacle or temple) and must bathe and be unclean until the sun is set. This is symbolic that any person who is spiritually unclean by reason of sin cannot enter the presence of God.

11:24 And for these ye shall be unclean: whosoever toucheth the carcase of them shall be unclean until the even. **11:25** And whosoever beareth ought of the carcase of them shall wash his clothes, and be unclean until the even.

11:26 The carcases of every beast which divideth the hoof, and is not clovenfooted, nor cheweth the cud, are unclean unto you: every one that toucheth them shall be unclean. **11:27** And whatsoever goeth upon his paws, among all manner of beasts that go on all four, those are unclean unto you: whoso toucheth their carcase shall be unclean until the even.

To touch the dead body makes one unclean and if we wear skins and furs from dead unclean creatures it is as if we have eaten them; for both acts make us unclean.

11:28 And he that beareth the carcase of them **shall wash** [himself and] **his clothes, and be unclean until the even**: they are unclean unto you.

The operative word here is carcase and refers to a dead body. Touching a living animal or using the hair or wool taken from a living animal is not unclean.

11:29 These also shall be unclean unto you among the creeping things that creep upon the earth; the weasel, and the mouse, and the tortoise after his kind, **11:30** And the ferret, and the chameleon, and the lizard, and the snail, and the mole. **11:31** These are unclean to you among all that creep: whosoever doth touch them, when they be dead, shall be unclean until the even.

11:32 And **upon whatsoever any of them, *when they are dead*, doth fall, it shall be unclean; whether it be any vessel of wood, or raiment, or skin, or sack, whatsoever vessel it be, wherein any work is done, it must be put into water, and it shall be unclean until the even;** so it shall be cleansed.

11:33 And **every earthen vessel,** whereinto any of them falleth, whatsoever is in it shall be unclean; and **ye shall break it.**

11:34 Of all meat [food] which may be eaten, that on which such water cometh shall be unclean: and all drink that may be drunk in every such vessel shall be unclean.

11:35 And **every thing whereupon any part of their carcase falleth shall be unclean; whether it be oven, or ranges for pots, they shall be broken down: for they are unclean and shall be unclean unto you.**

11:36 Nevertheless a fountain or pit, wherein there is plenty of water, shall be clean: but that which toucheth their carcase shall be unclean.

11:37 And if any part of their carcase fall upon any sowing seed [which is dry and not germinating] which is to be sown, it shall be clean.

11:38 But if any water be put upon the seed [because it would cause the grain to begin germinating I.E. come to life], and any part of their carcase fall thereon, it shall be unclean unto you.

11:39 And if any beast, of which ye may eat, die [of itself]; he that toucheth the carcase thereof shall be unclean until the even. **11:40** And he that eateth of the carcase of it shall wash his clothes, and be unclean until the even: he also that beareth the carcase of it shall wash his clothes, and be unclean until the even.

11:41 And every creeping thing that creepeth upon the earth shall be an abomination; it shall not be eaten. **11:42** Whatsoever goeth upon the belly, and whatsoever goeth upon all four, or whatsoever hath more feet among all creeping things that creep upon the earth, them ye shall not eat; for they are an abomination.

Those who make themselves unclean are an abomination to God. WHY? To teach us the difference between spiritually holy things and spiritually profane things.

The dead physically unclean thing is a picture of sin and the death of the wicked in their unrepented sin, of those who are not in UNITY and AT ONE in holiness with God the Father!

The clean thing that is killed by man is a picture of the perfection, purity and sinlessness of godliness!

11:43 Ye shall not make yourselves abominable with any creeping thing that creepeth, neither shall ye make yourselves unclean with them, that ye should be defiled thereby.

11:44 For I am the LORD your God: ye shall therefore sanctify yourselves, and ye shall be holy; for I am holy: neither shall ye defile yourselves with any manner of creeping thing that creepeth upon the earth.

Physical defilement is a picture of spiritual defilement by association with and partaking in the sins of others.

In other words avoiding the physically unclean thing teaches us that we are to avoid contact with all spiritual uncleanness [sin].

If we love to vicariously participate in sin by enjoying watching others sin [porn s a classic in this], of if we participate in others sins by hiring catered meals or patronizing restaurants on the Sabbath; we have become spiritually unclean and we have separated ourselves from God!

> **1 Timothy 5:22** Lay hands suddenly on no man, **neither be partaker of other men's sins: keep thyself pure.**

Leviticus 11:45 For I am the LORD that bringeth you up out of the land of Egypt, to be your God: ye shall therefore **be holy, for I am holy**.

This is the kind of priests, the kind of ministry of the High Priesthood of Jesus Christ; that God wants:

Ezekiel 44:23 And **they shall teach my people the difference between the holy and profane, and cause them to discern between the** [physically and spiritually] **unclean and the clean. 44:24** And in controversy they shall stand in judgment; and they shall **judge it according to my judgments: and they shall keep my laws and my statutes in all mine assemblies; and they shall hallow my sabbaths.**

We should be zealous to be physically clean, in this overwhelmingly unclean world and we should go forward to be zealous to become spiritually clean, without any spot, blemish or wrinkle of spiritual uncleanness or sin.

We should be as shocked, disgusted and appalled at the very idea of eating some scripturally unclean thing, or for some spiritual uncleanness and sin like calling the Sabbath holy and then paying others to serve us; as we would be if we were served a bowl of sewage.

Leviticus 11:46 This is the law of the beasts, and of the fowl, and of every living creature that moveth in the waters, and of every creature that creepeth upon the earth: **11:47** To make a difference between the unclean and the clean, and between the beast that may be eaten and the beast that may not be eaten.

See the parallel description of clean and unclean meats in Deuteronomy 14

Leviticus 12

Leviticus 12 is about things associated with childbirth

Leviticus 12:1 And the LORD spake unto Moses, saying, **12:2** Speak unto the children of Israel, saying, If a woman have conceived seed, and born a man child: then she shall be unclean seven days; according to the days of the separation for her infirmity shall she be unclean.

We are commanded to circumcise our sons on the eighth day of their life. The eighth day represents a new beginning.

Circumcision removes a piece of skin covering a most sensitive area and is an allegory of the removal of the sin that separates people from God thereby making people sensitive to the whole Word of God.

Physical circumcision is an allegory of the spiritual circumcision of the heart which is sincere repentance

> **Jeremiah 4:4** Circumcise yourselves to the Lord [sincerely repent], and take away the foreskins of your heart [remove the sin which separates us from God], ye men of Judah and inhabitants of Jerusalem: lest my fury come forth like fire, and burn that none can quench it, because of the evil of your doings.
>
> **Isaiah 59:1** Behold, the Lord's hand is not shortened, that it cannot save; neither his ear heavy, that it cannot hear: **59:2** But your

iniquities have separated between you and your God, and your sins have hid his face from you, that he will not hear.

Circumcision of the flesh is an allegory of circumcision of the heart which is sincere repentance and the application of the sacrifice of Christ which truly reconciles all humanity to God the Father.

Leviticus 12:3 And in the eighth day the flesh of his foreskin shall be circumcised.

Paul tells us that adult converts need not be circumcised in the flesh for they are already circumcised in heart; that in no way obviates the command to circumcise our male children on the eighth day; since they are not circumcised in heart. We are to circumcise all of our male children on their eighth day of life.

After Jesus Christ comes all human males will be circumcised in both the heart and in the flesh, for ALL nations will go up to Jerusalem to worship the Eternal

> **Ezekiel 44:9** Thus saith the Lord God; **No stranger, uncircumcised in heart, nor uncircumcised in flesh, shall enter into my sanctuary, of any stranger that is among the children of Israel.**
>
> **Zechariah 14:16** And it shall come to pass, that **every one that is left of all the nations** which came against Jerusalem **shall even go up from year to year to worship the King, the Lord of hosts,** and to keep the feast of tabernacles.

Seclusion of mother and child

After the first seven days of seclusion the mother must remain in seclusion for another 33 days making a total of 40 days in seclusion. The forty days is the period of purifying before entering the tabernacle, temple or any holy place.

Let me also say that such a seclusion is of great benefit to the mother and child; giving them time in a close family home environment to bond and to recover from the birth and develop immunity to disease. Breast feeding is highly important for this bonding and natural immunization process.

One should never allow the child to be artificially immunized by physicians since the mercury preservatives often used are known to cause autism and a variety of other issues like SIDS; and baby formulas should be avoided unless the mother cannot nurse; even then whenever possible the first choice should be a converted wet nurse [with a biblical diet] and not formula.

Commercially prepared baby foods which are high in starch and preservatives [a ticking time bomb for future diabetes] should also be avoided. Simply mash your own soft food for the child.

Leviticus 12:4 And she shall then continue in the blood of her purifying three and thirty days; she shall touch no hallowed thing, nor come into the sanctuary, until the days of her purifying be fulfilled.

If the child is female the mother's separation is double that of a male child

12:5 But if she bear a maid child, then she shall be unclean two weeks, as in her separation: and she shall continue in the blood of her purifying threescore and six [66] days.

66 days plus two weeks is 80 days. My wife and I practiced this by mutual consent for our three sons and one daughter.

We make these specified sacrificial offerings today by going to God the Father in prayer and asking that the sacrifice of Christ be applied to us and to the child, setting the child apart through our faithfulness, and asking for an understanding of these things.

The sin offering for the mother, being the application of Christ's sacrifice for the repentant obedient woman: And a burnt offering to demonstrate wholehearted faithful service to God the Father and Jesus Christ.

The woman is commanded to reproduce and childbearing is a great service to God the Father, because a woman gave birth to Messiah the Christ, the Deliverer of humanity.

12:6 And when the days of her purifying are fulfilled, for a son, or for a daughter, she shall bring a lamb of the first year for a burnt offering, and a young pigeon, or a turtledove, for a sin offering, unto the door of the tabernacle of the congregation, unto the priest: **12:7** Who shall offer it before the LORD, and make an atonement for her; and she shall be cleansed from the issue of her blood. This is the law for her that hath born a male or a female.

12:8 And if she be not able to bring a lamb, then she shall bring two turtles [turtle doves], or two young pigeons; the one for the burnt offering, and the other for a sin offering: and the priest shall make an atonement for her, and she shall be clean.

Leviticus 13

The leper was unclean and could not enter the tabernacle / temple or be touched by anyone until he / she was made clean.

Biblical leprosy is not the same as today's disease called leprosy, but any disfiguring disease of the skin was lumped together under the general heading of leprosy.

The main issue of the various skin diseases lumped together under the title "leprosy" was disfigurement [which includes tattoos and other deliberate disfigurement], which prevented a clean and pure appearance; rather than contagion.

The issue of leprosy was the same as that of any sacrificial animal being required to be without blemish; the blemish and imperfect appearance being symbolic of being spotted by sin.

Persons with such blemishes could not enter the tabernacle/temple, as an instructional allegory that no one having any sin would be accepted into the presence of God.

The issue of clean unclean was an instructional allegory for us that God will have absolutely NOTHING to do with sin: and that NO uncleansed sinner [not made clean by sincere repentance and the application of the sacrifice of Christ and going forward to live by every Word of God] can inherit eternal life.

Jesus cleansed lepers to demonstrate that he could remove the blemishes of the flesh, as an instructional example that he could remove the blemishes of sin as well. He healed the physically sick to reveal that he would heal the spiritually sick and he opened the eyes and ears of the blind and deaf to demonstrate that he would open the eyes and ears of spiritual understanding

> **Ephesians 5:25** . . . . even as Christ also loved the church, and gave himself for it; **5:26** That he might sanctify and cleanse it with the washing of water by the word [to learn and keep the whole Word of God thus removing the spots and blemishes of sin], **5:27** That he might present it to himself a glorious church, not having spot, or wrinkle, or any such thing; but that it should be holy and without blemish.

The wicked who lack zeal to make themselves perfect, as Jesus Christ and God the Father are perfect, through the diligent study and keeping of every Word of God; are likened to spots and blemishes [of sin] on the garments of righteousness.

> **2 Peter 2** And shall receive the reward of unrighteousness, as they that count it pleasure to riot in the day time. Spots they are and blemishes, sporting themselves with their own deceivings while they feast with you;

The law of the uncleanness of disfiguring skin diseases, is an allegory of the need to be healed of the spotting and blemishes of sin.

Just as any sacrificial animal must be without blemish, because it represents the purity, perfection and sinlessness of Jesus Christ the Lamb of God; so the law of uncleanness from disfiguring skin diseases is an allegory that those people who enter into the presence of God must also be pure, perfect and free from every blemish of sin.

Perfection [and the removal of all spots and blemishes of sin] comes through the internalizing of the whole Word of God to learn it and to live by it.

> **2 Timothy 3:16** All scripture is given by inspiration of God, and is profitable for doctrine, for reproof, for correction, for instruction in righteousness: **13:7** That the man of God may be perfect, thoroughly furnished unto all good works.

There are many different skin diseases labeled as leprosy, which is why Leviticus 13 is so long, it identifies the symptoms of many such diseases. I am not going to go into the symptoms of every disfiguring skin disease except the occasional comment.

The big picture is the meaning of assigning the status of uncleanness to those who are not physically perfect in the Mosaic dispensation; this being an allegory of those who are not clean spiritually and are spotted by the blemishes of sin in the New Covenant.

Those who are not diligent to learn, to live by and to teach the whole Word of God, and instead rely on their own ways and follow idols of men and organizations contrary to scripture; are full of the spiritual leprosy of the spots and blemishes of sin.

Leviticus 13:1 And the LORD spake unto Moses and Aaron, saying, **13:2** When a man shall have in the skin of his flesh a rising, a scab, or bright spot, and it be in the skin of his flesh like the plague of leprosy; then he shall be brought unto Aaron the priest, or unto one of his sons the priests: **13:3** And the priest shall look on the plague in the skin of the flesh: and when the hair in the plague is turned white, and the plague in sight be deeper than the skin of his flesh, it is a plague of leprosy: and the priest shall look on him, and pronounce him unclean.

13:4 If the bright spot be white in the skin of his flesh, and in sight be not deeper than the skin, and the hair thereof be not turned white; then the priest shall shut up him that hath the plague seven days: **13:5** And the priest shall look on him the seventh day: and, behold, if the plague in his sight be at a stay, and the plague spread not in the skin; then the priest shall shut him up seven days more: **13:6** And the priest shall look on him again the seventh day: and, behold, if the plague be somewhat dark, and the plague spread not in the skin, the priest shall pronounce him clean: it is but a scab: and he shall wash his clothes, and be clean.

Scabs that grow to cover injury do not make anyone unclean since they are a healing process and will fall away when the wound heals; only a genuine disfiguring disease makes one unclean.

13:7 But if the scab spread much abroad in the skin, after that he hath been seen of the priest for his cleansing, he shall be seen of the priest again. **13:8** And if the priest see that, behold, the scab spreadeth in the skin, then the priest shall pronounce him unclean: it is a leprosy.

The spreading and growth of any encrustment on the skin indicates that it is more than a simple healing scab.

13:9 When the plague of leprosy is in a man, then he shall be brought unto the priest; **13:10** And the priest shall see him: and, behold, if the rising be white in the skin, and it have turned the hair white, and there be quick raw flesh in the rising; **13:11** It is an old leprosy in the skin of his flesh, and the priest shall pronounce him unclean, and shall not shut him up [for examination after a period of time]: for he is unclean.

Here we have a key that it is the spotting and blemishes that make the person unclean, for a person completely covered with every part looking the same and having no standout spots or blemishes; is considered clean even if he has a disease.

13:12 And if a leprosy break out abroad in the skin, and the leprosy cover all the skin of him that hath the plague from his head even to his foot, wheresoever the priest looketh; **13:13** Then the priest shall consider: and, behold, if the leprosy have covered all his flesh, he shall pronounce him clean that hath the plague: it is all turned white: he is clean.

It is the spots and blemishes that make a person unclean, because they are analogous of the spotting, blemishes and the imperfection of sin.

13:14 But when raw flesh appeareth in him, he shall be unclean. **13:15** And the priest shall see the raw flesh, and pronounce him to be unclean: for the raw flesh is unclean: it is a leprosy.

13:16 Or if the raw flesh turn again, and be changed unto white, he shall come unto the priest; **13:17** And the priest shall see him: and, behold, if the plague be turned into white; then the priest shall pronounce him clean [if his whole body is white and not spotted] that hath the plague: he is clean.

13:18 The flesh also, in which, even in the skin thereof, was a boil, and is healed, **13:19** And in the place of the boil there be a white rising, or a bright spot, white, and somewhat reddish, and it be shewed to the priest; **13:20** And if, when the priest seeth it, behold, it be in sight lower than the skin, and the hair thereof be turned white; the priest shall pronounce him unclean: it is a plague of leprosy broken out of the boil.

13:21 But if the priest look on it, and, behold, there be no white hairs therein, and if it be not lower than the skin, but be somewhat dark; then the priest shall shut him up seven days: **13:22** And if it spread much abroad in the skin, then the priest shall pronounce him unclean: it is a plague.

Healed boils do not make one unclean unless they become infected and spread; like sin grows and spreads.

13:23 But if the bright spot stay in his place, and spread not, it is a burning boil; and the priest shall pronounce him clean.

13:24 Or if there be any flesh, in the skin whereof there is a hot burning, and the quick flesh that burneth have a white bright spot, somewhat reddish, or white; **13:25** Then the priest shall look upon it: and, behold, if the hair in the bright spot be turned white, and it be in sight deeper than the skin; it is a leprosy broken out of the burning: wherefore the priest shall pronounce him unclean: it is the plague of leprosy.

13:26 But if the priest look on it, and, behold, there be no white hair in the bright spot, and it be no lower than the other skin, but be somewhat dark; then the priest shall shut him up seven days: **13:27** And the priest shall look upon him the seventh day: and if it be spread much abroad in the skin, then the priest shall pronounce him unclean: it is the plague of leprosy.

13:28 And if the bright spot stay in his place, and spread not in the skin, but it be somewhat dark; it is a rising of the burning, and the priest shall pronounce him clean: for it is an inflammation of the burning.

Diseases of the hair and scalp

13:29 If a man or woman have a plague upon the head or the beard; **13:30** Then the priest shall see the plague: and, behold, if it be in sight deeper than the skin; and there be in it a yellow thin hair; then the priest shall pronounce him unclean: it is a dry scall, even a leprosy upon the head or beard.

13:31 And if the priest look on the plague of the scall, and, behold, it be not in sight deeper than the skin, and that there is no black hair in it; then the priest shall shut up him that hath the plague of the scall seven days: **13:32** And in the seventh day the priest shall look on the plague: and, behold, if the scall spread not, and there be in it no yellow hair, and the scall be not in sight deeper than the skin; **13:33** He shall be shaven, but the scall shall he not shave; and the priest shall shut up him that hath the scall seven days more: **13:34** And in the seventh day the priest shall look on the scall: and, behold, if the scall be not spread in the skin, nor be in sight deeper than the skin; then the priest shall pronounce him clean: and he shall wash his clothes, and be clean.

13:35 But if the scall spread much in the skin after his cleansing; **13:36** Then the priest shall look on him: and, behold, if the scall be spread in the skin, the priest shall not seek for yellow hair; he is unclean.

13:37 But if the scall be in his sight at a stay [stopped from spreading], and that there is black hair grown up therein; the scall is healed, he is clean: and the priest shall pronounce him clean.

Freckles do not make one unclean since they are natural

13:38 If a man also or a woman have in the skin of their flesh bright spots, even white bright spots; **13:39** Then the priest shall look: and, behold, if the bright spots in the skin of their flesh be darkish white; it is a freckled spot that groweth in the skin; he is clean.

Balding does not make one unclean, it is natural and not a disease

13:40 And the man whose hair is fallen off his head, he is bald; yet is he clean. **13:41** And he that hath his hair fallen off from the part of his head toward his face, he is forehead bald: yet is he clean.

If the baldness be caused by a disease, the balding person is unclean

13:42 And if there be in the bald head, or bald forehead, a white reddish sore; it is a leprosy sprung up in his bald head, or his bald forehead. **13:43** Then the priest shall look upon it: and, behold, if the rising of the sore be white reddish in his bald head, or in his bald forehead, as the leprosy appeareth in the skin of the flesh; **13:44** He is a leprous man, he is unclean: the priest shall pronounce him utterly unclean; his plague is in his head.

The unclean by reason of a skin disease [a spot, blemish, skin cancer etc] shall be kept outside the congregation until he is healed. This pictures the truth that a person having been spotted by the blemish of sin cannot enter the Body of Christ and is not to be accepted into the congregation (1 Cor 5:11).

Spiritually this means that without the cleansing of sincere repentance and the application of the atoning sacrifice of Jesus Christ to remove the uncleanness of sin which disfigures and blemishes the unrepentant sinner; one cannot enter the presence of God or receive the Holy Spirit.

> **1 Corinthians 3:16** Know ye not that **ye are the temple of God, and that the Spirit of God dwelleth in you? 3:17 If any man defile the temple of God, him shall God destroy**; for the temple of God is holy, which temple ye are.

Leviticus 13:45 And the leper in whom the plague is, his clothes shall be rent, and his head bare, and he shall put a covering upon his upper lip, and shall cry, Unclean, unclean.

13:46 All the days wherein the plague shall be in him he shall be defiled; he is unclean: he shall dwell alone; without the camp shall his habitation be.

Cloth and leather which are spotted by an infection are unclean and are to be destroyed if the piece cannot be cleansed.

13:47 The garment also that the plague of leprosy is in, whether it be a woollen garment, or a linen garment; **13:48** Whether it be in the warp, or woof; of linen, or of woollen; whether in a skin, or in any thing made of skin; **13:49** And if the plague be greenish or reddish in the garment, or in the skin, either in the warp, or in the woof, or in any thing of skin; it is a plague of leprosy, and shall be shewed unto the priest: **13:50** And the priest shall look upon the plague, and shut up it that hath the plague seven days: **13:51** And he shall look on the plague on the seventh day: if the plague be spread in the garment, either in the warp, or in the woof, or in a skin, or in any work that is made of skin; the plague is a fretting leprosy; it is unclean.

13:52 He shall therefore burn that garment, whether warp or woof, in woollen or in linen, or any thing of skin, wherein the plague is: for it is a fretting leprosy; it shall be burnt in the fire.

13:53 And if the priest shall look, and, **behold, the plague be not spread in the garment**, either in the warp, or in the woof, or in any thing of skin; **13:54** Then the priest shall command that **they wash the thing** wherein the plague is, and he shall shut it up seven days more: **13:55** And the priest shall look on the plague, after that it is washed: and, behold, if the **plague have not changed** his colour, and the plague be not spread; it is unclean; thou shalt burn it in the fire; it is fret inward, whether it be bare within or without.

13:56 And if the priest look, and, behold, the plague be somewhat dark after the washing of it; then he shall rend it out of the garment, or out of the skin, or out of the warp, or out of the woof: **13:57** And if it appear still in the garment, either in the warp, or in the woof, or in any thing of skin; it is a spreading plague: thou shalt burn that wherein the plague is with fire.

13:58 And the garment, either warp, or woof, or whatsoever thing of skin it be, which thou shalt wash, **if the plague be departed from them, then it shall be washed the second time, and shall be clean.**

13:59 This is the law of the plague of leprosy in a garment of woollen or linen, either in the warp, or woof, or any thing of skins, to pronounce it clean, or to pronounce it unclean.

Leviticus 14

The cleansing of lepers

Hyssop and two clean birds, pigeons or turtle doves [as the sacrificial birds for the poor] are to be brought to the priest by the healed leper.

Hyssop a plant associated with soap and therefore was considered a cleansing agent. Scarlet is the colour of blood, representative of the application of the blood of the Lamb of God, cleansing from sin.

Leviticus 14:1 And the LORD spake unto Moses, saying, **14:2** This shall be the law of the leper in the day of his cleansing: He shall be brought unto the priest: **14:3** And the priest shall go forth out of the camp; and the priest shall look, and, behold, if the plague of leprosy be healed in the leper; **14:4** Then shall the priest command to take for him that is to be cleansed two birds alive and clean, and cedar wood, and scarlet, and hyssop:

One bird is to be killed so that its blood falls down into running water; picturing the sacrificial blood of Christ and the living water of the Holy Spirit and the whole Word of God.

The healed leper and the living bird were to be sprinkled with the blood and water mixture; after which the person would go forth cleansed: This symbolized the cleansing of the repentant by the blood of Jesus Christ and going on to live by every Word of God through the power of the holy Spirit.

The living bird flying away is a picture of the uncleanness leaving the man or house and is akin to the removal of the Satan-goat on Atonement Day.

14:5 And the priest shall command that one of the birds be killed in an earthen vessel over running water: **14:6** As for the living bird, he shall take it, and the cedar wood, and the scarlet, and the hyssop, and shall dip them and the living bird in the blood of the bird that was killed over the running water: **14:7** And he shall sprinkle upon him that is to be cleansed from the leprosy seven times, and shall pronounce him clean, and shall let the living bird loose into the open field.

The cleansed leper must then wash himself and his clothes and shave off his hair and remain outside his house for seven days

14:8 And he that is to be cleansed shall wash his clothes, and shave off all his hair, and wash himself in water, that he may be clean: and after that he shall come into the camp, and shall tarry abroad out of his tent seven days.

On the seventh day the afflicted person must again shave off his hair and wash himself and then he shall be clean when that day ends and a new day begins at sun set (Lev 17:5).

14:9 But it shall be on the seventh day, that he shall shave all his hair off his head and his beard and his eyebrows, even all his hair he shall shave off: and he shall wash his clothes, also he shall wash his flesh in water, and he shall be clean [when the sun sets].

The eighth day represents a new beginning; and now being made clean a Trespass Offering was to be made.

14:10 And on the eighth day he shall take **two he lambs** without blemish, and **one ewe lamb** of the first year without blemish, and three tenth deals of fine flour for a meat offering, mingled with oil, and one log of oil.

14:11 And the priest that maketh him clean shall present the man that is to be made clean, and those things, before the LORD, at the door of the tabernacle of the congregation: **14:12** And the priest shall take one he lamb, and offer him for **a trespass offering**, and the log of oil, and wave them for a wave offering before the LORD: **14:13** And he shall slay the lamb in the place where he shall kill the sin offering and the burnt offering, in the holy place: for as the sin offering is the priest's, so is the trespass offering: it is most holy:

- The blood placed on the tip of the right ear is a reference to opening the ear and mind of people to the Word of God through the atoning sacrifice of Christ.
- The right thumb of the right hand refers to the cleansing of our deeds and works of trespass and sin.
- The great toe of the right foot refers to our walk [life] through this world being cleansed from past sin and going forward to sin no more; living [walking] as Christ lived [walked] (1 John 2:6).

14:14 And the priest shall take some of the blood of the trespass offering, and the priest shall put it upon the tip of the right ear of him that is to be cleansed, and upon the thumb of his right hand, and upon the great toe of his right foot:

The sprinkling of the [olive] oil representing the Holy Spirit, seven times, pictures complete cleansing from uncleanness and sin and a full reconciliation and unity with God through the Holy Spirit.

14:15 And the priest shall take some of the log of oil, and pour it into the palm of his own left hand: **14:16** And the priest shall dip his right finger in the oil that is in his left hand, and shall sprinkle of the oil with his finger seven times before the LORD:

The oil represents the Holy Spirit which is given to the person cleansed by the Sin and Trespass offerings [representing Jesus Christ the ultimate Sin and Trespass Offering].

Oil applied to the right ear is a reference to the Holy Spirit opening the ear and mind [the understanding] of man to the Word of God through the atoning sacrifice of Jesus Christ for sincerely repented past sin and trespass.

The oil applied to the right thumb of the right hand refers to the cleansing of our deeds and works of trespass and sin.

The oil applied to the great toe of the right foot refers to our walk through this world being cleansed from past sin and trespass, and going forward to live by every Word of God and sin no more.

14:17 And of the rest of the oil that is in his hand shall the priest put upon the tip of the right ear of him that is to be cleansed, and upon the thumb of his right hand, and upon the great toe of his right foot, upon the blood of the trespass offering:

The remainder of the oil was to be poured out on the head of the supplicant; representing the pouring out of the Holy Spirit on the sincerely repentant and his/her cleansing from all uncleanness and sin.

14:18 And the remnant of the oil that is in the priest's hand he shall pour upon the head of him that is to be cleansed: and the priest shall make an atonement for him before the LORD.

After the Trespass Offering, a Sin and a Burnt Offering along with their Meat [unleavened bread] Offerings was then to be made.

14:19 And the priest shall **offer the sin offering**, and make an atonement for him that is to be cleansed from his uncleanness; and afterward he shall kill the burnt offering: **14:20** And the priest shall offer the burnt offering and the [the accompanying unleavened bread] meat offering upon the altar: and the priest shall make an atonement for him, and he shall be clean.

The poor person's offering

14:21 And if he be poor, and cannot get so much; then he shall take **one lamb for a trespass offering** to be waved, to make an atonement for him, and **one tenth deal of fine flour mingled with oil for a meat offering, and a log of oil; 14:22 And two turtledoves, or two young pigeons, such as he is able to get; and the one shall be a sin offering, and the other a burnt offering.**

The poor man shall also bring his offerings on the Eighth Day [which represents new beginnings]: Alluding to the Feast of The Eighth Day.

14:23 And he shall bring them **on the eighth day** for his cleansing unto the priest, unto the door of the tabernacle of the congregation, before the LORD.

The offering of the poor is made in place of the offering by the more solvent leper, and the Holy Spirit is poured out upon the poor as well as on the better off.

14:24 And the priest shall take the lamb of the trespass offering, and the log of oil, and the priest shall wave them for a wave offering before the LORD: **14:25** And he shall kill the lamb of the trespass offering, and the priest shall take some of the blood of the trespass offering, and put it upon the tip of the right ear of him that is to be cleansed, and upon the thumb of his right hand, and upon the great toe of his right foot:

14:26 And the priest shall pour of the oil into the palm of his own left hand: **14:27** And the priest shall sprinkle with his right finger some of the oil that is in his left hand seven times before the LORD: **14:28** And the priest shall put of the oil that is in his hand upon the tip of the right ear of him that is to be cleansed, and upon the thumb of his right hand, and upon the great toe of his right foot, upon the place of the blood of the trespass offering: **14:29** And the rest of the oil that is in the priest's hand he shall put upon the head of him that is to be cleansed, to make an atonement for him before the LORD.

14:30 And he shall offer the one of the turtledoves, or of the young pigeons, such as he can get; **14:31** Even such as he is able to get, the one for a sin offering, and the other for a burnt offering, with the meat offering: and the priest shall make an atonement for him that is to be cleansed before the LORD.

This law for the poor shows the mercy of God for the destitute who do not have the commanded offerings to bring.

14:32 This is the law of him in whom is the plague of leprosy, whose hand is not able to get that which pertaineth to his cleansing.

Why does God require all this offering because a person has had a skin disease? Because it represents the spotting of uncleanness and sin in the spiritual sense. Such blemishes and imperfection and impurity in the flesh represents spiritual imperfections and sin.

This is an object lesson that we are to be filled with the Word of God by the Holy Spirit, and to remain unspotted by sin.

The uncleanness of leprosy was an example and object lesson that when we lose sight of our zeal for the whole Word of God, we become spotted with the spiritual blemishes of sin or association with sin.

When we are not being diligent to learn and live by the whole Word of God: We become imperfect and filled with the blemishes of sin and trespass; and we are NOT fit to be a part of the Chosen Bride of Christ, and the Holy Spirit will no longer dwell in us.

We are to work to remove all spots and blemishes of sin and trespass and to make ourselves a fit place for God's Spirit to dwell; ready to have a place in the collective Bride of Christ.

> **James 1:27** Pure religion and undefiled before God and the Father is this, To visit the fatherless and widows in their affliction, and to **keep himself unspotted from the world**.
>
> **2 Corinthians 7:1** Having therefore these promises [from God as a reward for repentance and learning and keeping his Word], dearly beloved, let us cleanse ourselves from all filthiness of the flesh and spirit, perfecting holiness [becoming LIKE God through internalizing the very nature of God, by learning and living by every Word of God] in the fear of God.
>
> **James 4:7** Submit yourselves therefore to God. Resist the devil, and he will flee from you. **4:8** Draw nigh to God, and he will draw nigh

to you. Cleanse your hands, ye sinners; and purify your hearts, ye double minded. **4:9** Be afflicted [fast], and mourn, and weep [in heartfelt repentance]: let your [proud haughty joy and zeal in your own ways be brought to contrition] laughter be turned to mourning, and your joy to heaviness [regret and sincere repentance over sin]. **4:10** Humble yourselves in the sight of the Lord [repent of your own worldly ways and turn to learn and keep the whole Word of God], and he shall lift you up.

Mildew, rot and fungus in a building as a kind of leprosy

This is another indication that the leprosy is the disfigurement and not a case of modern leprosy.

Leviticus 14:33 And the LORD spake unto Moses and unto Aaron, saying, **14:34** When ye be come into the land of Canaan, which I give to you for a possession, and I put the plague of leprosy in a house of the land of your possession; **14:35** And he that owneth the house shall come and tell the priest, saying, It seemeth to me there is as it were a plague in the house:

The building is to be evacuated and then inspected

14:36 Then the priest shall command that they empty the house, before the priest go into it to see the plague, that all that is in the house be not made unclean: and afterward the priest shall go in to see the house:

14:37 And he shall look on the plague, and, behold, if the plague be in the walls of the house with hollow strakes [thin streaks], greenish or reddish, which in sight are lower [penetrate deep into the wall] than the wall;

The infected building must be closed up for seven days to see if the leprosy disappears or spreads.

14:38 Then the priest shall go out of the house to the door of the house, and shut up the house seven days: **14:39** And the priest shall come again the seventh day, and shall look: and, behold, if the plague be spread in the walls of the house;

If the building remains infected, the infected areas must be removed and the building cleaned thoroughly.

14:40 Then the priest shall command that they take away the stones in which the plague is, and they shall cast them into an unclean place without the city: **14:41** And he shall cause the house to be scraped within round about, and they shall pour out the dust that they scrape off without the city into an unclean place: **14:42** And they shall take other stones, and put them in the place of those stones; and he shall take other morter, and shall plaister the house.

If the plague returns the building must be destroyed

14:43 And if the plague come again, and break out in the house, after that he hath taken away the stones, and after he hath scraped the house, and after it is plaistered; **14:44** Then the priest shall come and look, and, behold, if the plague be spread in the house, it is a fretting leprosy in the house; it is unclean.

14:45 And he shall break down the house, the stones of it, and the timber thereof, and all the morter of the house; and he shall carry them forth out of the city into an unclean place.

All persons who have entered the polluted house are unclean.

14:46 Moreover he that goeth into the house all the while that it is shut up shall be unclean until the even. **14:47** And he that lieth in the house shall wash his clothes; and he that eateth in the house shall wash his clothes.

If the plague is healed the house will be pronounced clean.

14:48 And if the priest shall come in, and look upon it, and, behold, the plague hath not spread in the house, after the house was plaistered: then the priest shall pronounce the house clean, because the plague is healed.

The house is to be cleansed in similar fashion to the cleansing of a leper.

14:49 And he shall take to cleanse the house two birds, and cedar wood, and scarlet, and hyssop: **14:50** And he shall kill the one of the birds in an earthen vessel over running water: **14:51** And he shall take the cedar wood, and the hyssop, and the scarlet, and the living bird, and dip them in the blood of the slain bird, and in the running water, and sprinkle the house seven times: **14:52** And he shall cleanse the house with the blood of the bird, and with the running water, and with the living bird, and with the cedar wood, and with the hyssop, and with the scarlet: **14:53** But he shall let go the living bird out of the city into the open fields, and make an atonement for the house: and it shall be clean.

The bird sacrificed and its blood mixed with water is an allegory of spiritually being made clean from repented association with sin and being spotted by worldliness; through the shed blood of Jesus Christ and the cleansing of water of [keeping] the Word of God by the Holy Spirit, through diligent study to learn and to live by every Word of God.

The "water" of the Word cleanses through the understanding given by the Holy Spirit (John 7:38-39); which comes through sincere repentance and the application of the sacrifice of Christ.

As we learn and keep the Word of God, the Holy Spirit causes the very nature of God to grow within us.

Our sincere repentance and the application of the sacrifice of Christ cleanses us from all sincerely repented past sin; and the diligent learning and keeping of the whole Word of God, to go and sin no more, enables us to remain clean from future sin.

> **Ephesians 5:25** . . . . even as Christ also loved the church, and gave himself for it; **5:26** That he might sanctify and cleanse it with the washing of water by the word,

The bird flying away is a picture of the uncleanness leaving the man or house; akin to the removal of the Satan-goat on Atonement Day.

Leviticus 14:54 This is the law for all manner of plague of leprosy, and scall, **14:55** And for the leprosy of a garment, and of a house, **14:56** And for a rising, and for a scab, and for a bright spot: **14:57** To teach when it is unclean, and when it is clean: this is the law of leprosy.

Leviticus 15

Various types of uncleanness

A drainage from the skin

Physical imperfection and impurity is an instructional example of SPIRITUAL imperfection and impurity.

Any person with a draining from his body [including seed of copulation and menstruation (Lev 15:16-24)] is physically imperfect and unclean. Such drainage indicates a weakening of the body, representative of a weakening of the spiritual body that sin brings.

A person who is spiritually impure and imperfect cannot come into the presence of God the Father; except through the cleansing of the spiritual uncleanness of trespass or sin through the process of sincere repentance and the application of the blood sacrifice of Jesus Christ the Lamb of God.

Leviticus 15:1 And the LORD spake unto Moses and to Aaron, saying, **15:2** Speak unto the children of Israel, and say unto them, When any man hath a running issue out of his flesh, because of his issue he is unclean.

Whether the drainage is continual or intermittent, the person is unclean

15:3 And this shall be his uncleanness in his issue: whether his flesh run with his issue, or his flesh be stopped from his issue, it is his uncleanness. **15:4** Every bed, whereon he lieth that hath the issue, is unclean: and every thing, whereon he sitteth, shall be unclean.

Any person coming in contact with the uncleanness must wash and remain unclean until the evening [sunset]: Thus pictures the uncleanness remaining until the end of the day, and a New Beginning of purity after the sun has set to begin the new day.

15:5 And whosoever toucheth his bed shall wash his clothes, and bathe himself in water, and be unclean until the even.

It is not just the affected person who is unclean, but all who are in close contact with him or her. This is a picture of the command of Paul:

> **1 Timothy 5:22** . . . . . **neither be partaker of other men's sins: keep thyself pure**.

This point of uncleanness by association, particularly refers to sinning vicariously through associating with the sins of others.

Classic examples would include buying food and drink in restaurants and bars on the Sabbath or Holy Days; with the outrageous excuse that these folks are going to sin anyway, so we may participate in their sins; of course that excuse opens the way to participate in every sin that men do.

Another example is our tolerance for open apostates and false teachings among us. If we permit doctrine that has been proven false to be taught among us, we have made ourselves and our groups spiritually unclean, we have allowed the temple of God which is the body of the faithful to be polluted by doctrinal uncleanness and we will be rejected by God if we do not quickly repent.

> **Titus 3:10** A man that is an heretick [from the sound doctrine of the whole Word of God] after the first and second admonition reject; **3:11** Knowing that he that is such is subverted, and sinneth, being condemned of himself.

Leviticus 15:6 And he that sitteth on any thing whereon he sat that hath the issue shall wash his clothes, and bathe himself in water, and be unclean until the even. **15:7** And he that toucheth the flesh of him that hath the issue shall wash his clothes, and bathe himself in water, and be unclean until the even. **15:8** And if he that hath the issue spit [spatter the water] upon him that is clean; then he [the clean person who had been in contact with the unclean fluid] shall wash his clothes, and bathe himself in water, and be unclean until the even.

15:9 And what saddle soever he rideth upon that hath the issue shall be unclean.

15:10 And whosoever toucheth any thing that was under him [the unclean person] shall be unclean until the even: and he that beareth any of those things shall wash his clothes, and bathe himself in water, and be unclean until the even.

15:11 And whomsoever he toucheth that hath the issue, and hath not rinsed his hands in water, he shall wash his clothes, and bathe himself in water, and be unclean until the even. **15:12** And the vessel of earth, that he toucheth which hath the issue, shall be broken: and every vessel of wood shall be rinsed in water.

Do we see how that Jesus Christ who taught this avoiding of any physical uncleanness, was providing a physical example to teach us that we are to avoid any spiritual uncleanness; because no one who is spiritually unclean or has any sort of spiritual blemish of uncleanness, trespass or sin, may enter the presence of God the Father in heaven (1 Thess 4)?

We are to avoid the unclean thing both physically and spiritually.

> **Romans 6:19** I speak after the manner of men because of the infirmity of your flesh: for as ye have yielded your members servants to uncleanness and to iniquity unto iniquity; even so now yield your members servants to righteousness unto holiness.

Spiritually we are to wash away all spiritual uncleanness and pollution by sincere repentance and the application of the sacrifice of the Lamb of God empowered by the Holy Spirit to a passionate zeal to learn and live by every Word of God. Then the Holy Spirit by the washing of the water of the Word of God, which if we keep it teaches up to become holy and pure from all uncleanness and every blemish of sin.

> **Ephesians 5:26** That he **might sanctify and cleanse it with the washing of water by the word,**

The collective bride is to remove all blemishes of uncleanness and sin to make herself pure, holy and ready for her marriage to the Holy Husband Jesus Christ, and to enter the Holy Family of God the Father.

We are to work diligently to learn sound doctrine and to excise all error!

We are not to associate with any unclean thing and that means far more than avoiding vicarious sin: It also means that we are to turn away from proven false doctrine [teachings], which are spiritual pollution and are an uncleanness of sin which separates us from God!

> **2 Corinthians 6:14** Be ye not unequally yoked together with unbelievers: for what fellowship hath righteousness with unrighteousness? and what communion hath light with darkness? **6:15** And what concord hath Christ with Belial? or what part hath he that believeth with an infidel? **6:16** And what agreement hath the

temple of God with idols? for ye are the temple of the living God; as God hath said, I will dwell in them, and walk in them; and I will be their God, and they shall be my people.

6:17 Wherefore come out from among them [those polluted by the uncleanness of commandment breaking], and be ye separate [from the uncleanness of exposure to sin], saith the Lord, and **touch not** [the false teachings of spiritually unclean men] **the unclean thing; and I will receive you. 6:18 And will be a Father unto you, and ye shall be my sons and daughters, saith the Lord Almighty.**

Leviticus 15:13 And when he that hath an issue is cleansed of his issue; then he shall number to himself seven days for his cleansing, and wash his clothes, and bathe his flesh in running water, and shall be clean.

15:14 And on the eighth day he shall take to him **two turtledoves, or two young pigeons,** and come before the LORD unto the door of the tabernacle of the congregation, and give them unto the priest: **15:15** And the priest shall offer them, **the one for a sin offering, and the other for a burnt offering;** and the priest shall make an atonement for him before the LORD for his issue.

The copulatory seed of men is considered unclean because it is an issue from the man and after the act he and his wife are to wash and be unclean until the sun sets.

15:16 And if any man's seed of copulation go out from him, then he shall wash all his flesh in water, and be unclean until the even. **15:17** And every garment, and every skin, whereon is the seed of copulation, shall be washed with water, and be unclean until the even. **15:18** The woman also with whom man shall lie with seed of copulation, they shall both bathe themselves in water, and be unclean until the even.

The drainage of the menses makes a woman unclean for a full seven days after onset. At the end of the seventh full day she is to wash and be unclean until the evening.

Even if flow stops intercourse is not to take place until after the seventh day ends. This is one of the sins in today's Ekklesia, that men are not willing to wait the whole seven days for their women.

Ezekiel 18:5 But if a man be just, and do that which is lawful and right, **18:6** And hath not eaten upon the mountains [eaten things that belong to idols; that is, learning the false doctrines of worldliness], neither hath lifted up his eyes to the idols of the house of Israel, neither hath defiled his neighbour's wife, neither hath come near to a menstruous woman,

Leviticus 15:19 And if a woman have an issue, and her issue in her flesh be blood, she shall be put apart seven days: and whosoever toucheth her shall be unclean until the even. **15:20** And every thing that she lieth upon in her separation shall be unclean: every thing also that she sitteth upon shall be unclean. **15:21** And whosoever toucheth her bed shall wash his clothes, and bathe himself in water, and be unclean until the even.

15:22 And whosoever toucheth any thing that she sat upon shall wash his clothes, and bathe himself in water, and be unclean until the even. **15:23** And if it be on her bed, or on any thing whereon she sitteth, when he toucheth it, he shall be unclean until the even.

15:24 And if any man lie with her at all, and her flowers be upon him, he shall be unclean seven days; and all the bed whereon he lieth shall be unclean.

An extended issue of blood

15:25 And if a woman have an issue of her blood many days out of the time of her separation, or **if it run beyond the time of her separation**; all the days of the issue of her uncleanness shall be as the days of her separation: she shall be unclean.

15:26 Every bed whereon she lieth all the days of her issue shall be unto her as the bed of her separation: and whatsoever she sitteth upon shall be unclean, as the uncleanness of her separation. **15:27** And whosoever toucheth those things shall be unclean, and shall wash his clothes, and bathe himself in water, and be unclean until the even.

In the case of an extended issue of blood, she shall count seven days after the issue was healed and shall wash that day, and on the Eighth Day she shall bring an offering. The Eighth Day is a new beginning.

15:28 But if she be cleansed of her issue, then she shall number to herself seven days, and after that she shall be clean.

15:29 And **on the eighth day** she shall take unto her **two turtles** [turtle doves], **or two young pigeons,** and bring them unto the priest, to the door of the tabernacle of the congregation. **15:30** And the priest shall offer the **one for a sin offering, and the other for a burnt offering**; and the priest shall make an atonement for her before the LORD for the issue of her uncleanness.

This is all about entering the holy place, the tabernacle or temple, which is symbolic of entering the presence of God.

To enter into the presence of holiness, those of the Mosaic Covenant were required to be pure and free from all physical impurity and uncleanness and sin; which is an example that those in the New Covenant must be spiritually pure and free from all uncleanness, impurity and sin in order to be reconciled to and enter the presence of God the Father in heaven.

That process, is to be called out to God the Father through Jesus Christ, then adding to that belief the works of sincere repentance, a baptismal commitment to go and sin no more, and then we will receive the application of the atoning sacrifice of Jesus Christ. Only then, when all uncleanness and sin has been removed, are we reconciled to God the Father and he will dwell in us through his Holy Spirit.

My friends, today the Spiritual Ekklesia is filled with all manner of spiritual uncleanness and sin; idolizing men and exalting idols of men and organizations above their zeal to live by every Word of God.

To make ourselves ready to have a part in the resurrected collective bride, every blemish of uncleanness and sin must be removed.

> **1 Corinthians 3:17 If any man defile the temple of God** [with any sin or spiritual uncleanness], **him shall God destroy; for the temple of God is holy, which temple ye are.**

We must repent quickly of all of our spiritual uncleanness and sin, lest we fall into the strong correction of God the Father in heaven.

Leviticus 15:31 Thus shall ye separate the children of Israel from their uncleanness; that they die not in their uncleanness, when they defile my tabernacle that is among them.

15:32 This is the law of him that hath an issue, and of him whose seed goeth from him, and is defiled therewith; **15:33** And of her that is sick of her flowers, and of him that hath an issue, of the man, and of the woman, and of him that lieth with her that is unclean.

Leviticus 16

The Fast of Atonement

For more on this subject please see "The Biblical Fall Festivals" book.

The tabernacle and later the temple were to be made according to the pattern provided by God. The scriptures even give us detailed instructions on the plan of the millennial temple to be built by Christ (Eze 40 - 48).

All scripture was given for our instruction, and the tabernacle, priesthood and the Holy Days are no exception.

Inside the tabernacle in the far west was the Most Holy Place, which represents the throne room of God the Father. All those coming to God the Father had to turn their backs on the east [the rising sun as the symbol of Lucifer [Satan] for sun worshipers] and seek God the Father in the west.

Between the Most Holy Place and the priesthood and people, was a heavy curtain [drapery] that represented the barrier of sin that separates the people from God the Father.

The physical Aaronic high priest was an allegory of Jesus Christ who became the spiritual High Priest between God the Father and the people forever, on Wave Offering Sunday in 31 A.D. It is Jesus Christ who intercedes for us with God the Father and applies his reconciling sacrifice to the repentant.

At the death of Christ for the repentant, the veil representing the sin that separates us from God the Father was torn in two, revealing that the barrier of sin could be removed and the way for access by people to God the Father was through sincere repentance and the application of the sacrifice of Christ.

Jesus Christ died ONCE, yet the Passover [in the first month] represents the atoning sacrifice of Jesus Christ applied to the sins of the repentant Called Out of physical and spiritual Egypt; and the Day of Atonement [in the seventh month] represents the atoning sacrifice being applied to the repentant of the main harvest of humanity.

Instructions for the Day of Atonement

The physical High Priest may not enter the Most Holy Place when or as he wished; lest he die. This means that anyone tainted by sin cannot enter into the presence of God the Father

Leviticus 16:1 And the LORD spake unto Moses after the death of the two sons of Aaron, when they offered before the LORD, and died; **16:2** And the LORD said unto Moses, Speak unto Aaron thy brother, that he come not at all times into the holy place within the vail before the mercy seat, which is upon the ark; that he die not: for I will appear in the cloud upon the mercy seat.

To enter the Most Holy Place, and that only once a year; the physical high priest must present a sin offering and a burnt offering for himself. The sin offering to cover his own sins and the burnt offering to picture wholehearted dedication to the Father and his Word.

16:3 Thus shall Aaron come into the holy place: with a young bullock for a sin offering, and a ram for a burnt offering.

To enter the Most Holy Place the physical high priest must wash himself, picturing the washing away of all sin and being washed clean from all sin by sincere repentance and the application of the sacrifice of Christ; followed by baptism and going forward to live by every Word of God in future.

The Word of God teaches us to discern between good and evil, and to reject the evil and accept the good thereby keeping us from future sins.

> **Ephesians 5:25** Husbands, love your wives, even **as Christ also loved the church, and gave himself for it; 5:26 That he might sanctify and cleanse it with the washing of water by the word, 5:27 That he might present it to himself a glorious church, not having spot, or wrinkle, or any such thing; but that it should be holy and without blemish.**

The high priest is then to put on pure priestly linen garments, linen being a type of purity and righteousness of keeping the Word of God.

> **Revelation 19:7** Let us be glad and rejoice, and give honour to him: for the marriage of the Lamb is come, and his wife hath made herself ready. **19:8** And to her was granted that she should be arrayed in fine linen, clean and white: for **the fine linen is the righteousness of saints.**

Leviticus 16:4 He shall put on the holy linen coat, and he shall have the linen breeches upon his flesh, and shall be girded with a linen girdle, and with the linen mitre shall he be attired: these are holy garments; therefore shall he wash his flesh in water, and so put them on.

The physical high priest must offer the sin offering and the burnt offering for himself; and also take two kids of goats for a sin offering, and a ram for a burnt offering for the assembly of people.

16:5 And he shall take of the congregation of the children of Israel **two kids of the goats for a sin offering, and one ram for a burnt offering.**

Verse six is only an explanation of what the bullock was for; the order of offering is laid out further on.

16:6 And Aaron shall offer his bullock of the sin offering, which is for himself, and make an atonement for himself, and for his house.

Instructions for The Two Goats.

Both goats are to be presented at the door of the tabernacle where the lots were to be cast.

16:7 And he shall take the two goats for the sin offering, and present them before the LORD at the door of the tabernacle of the congregation.

One lot was cast for sacrifice representing Christ, and another lot for the scapegoat. It is God who decides the fall of the lot, to demonstrate that God decides between good and evil as the ultimate judge of humanity

"Azazel" is translated as "scapegoat" in the KJV. This is misleading, since the word scapegoat has connotations of wrongful accusation in modern English. "Azazel" actually means "appointed for complete removal" and refers to this goat representing Satan the original source of sin being entirely removed.

16:8 And Aaron shall cast lots upon the two goats; one lot for the LORD, and the other lot for the scapegoat.

The lot of Christ identifies the goat to be sacrificed as representative of the sacrifice of Jesus Christ to atone for sin.

The sacrificial lamb or goat of Passover represented the application of the sacrifice of Christ to the early harvest of the Called Out; and the sacrificial goat of the Day of Atonement represents the sacrifice of Christ being applied to the rest of humanity in the fall main harvest.

16:9 And Aaron shall bring the goat upon which the LORD's lot fell, and offer him for a sin offering.

The scapegoat was to carry uncleanness and sin away from the main fall harvest of humanity. This represents the removal of all uncleanness and sin so that the repentant of the main harvest can be reconciled to God the Father. The scapegoat represents Satan being removed from influencing humanity forever more.

16:10 But the goat, on which the lot fell to be the scapegoat, shall be presented alive before the LORD, to make an atonement with him, and to let him go for a scapegoat [To be completely removed from among the people forever.] into the wilderness.

The Sin Offering

Then the Sin Offering was made [after the lots, but before the two goats ceremony] for the physical high priest. Please bear in mind that the physical high priest was a physical man who must have his own sins atoned for, before he could enter the Most Holy Place [The Hebrews study is key here.].

Yet we now have a High Priest who has entered the Most Holy Place in heaven without any sacrifice for his own sins, because he was free from all sin and perfect before God the Father, being the sacrifice and sin bearer for both the Called Out of the early harvest [and once these things happen in their full fulfillment] for main fall harvest of humanity.

16:11 And Aaron shall bring the bullock of the sin offering, which is for himself, and shall make an atonement for himself, and for his house, and shall kill the bullock of the sin offering which is for himself:

After sacrificing the bullock for himself, the physical high priest entered the Most Holy Place on the Day of Atonement, with the censor filled with the holy fire and the incense of the prayers and praise of the repentant faithful.

The incense was to be be placed before the Mercy Seat which is the name of the throne of God the Father, figurative that God's throne is covered in the prayers and praise of those who come to him in sincere repentance, petitioning him for reconciliation through the blood of the Sin Offering [Jesus Christ].

The fire that came from heaven and burned perpetually on the altar in the temple was a symbol of the Shekinah [glory of the presence of God, which came down from heaven in the form of fire] or Holy Spirit.

The sweet incense represented the rising of prayers and praise, offered to God the Father in heaven.

The glory of God the Father is so great that a cloud of incense picturing prayers of sincere repentance from sin; must come between the Father and the petitioner; demonstrating that the Father will not tolerate any sin at all, not even the appearance of sin, to pollute His Holy presence.

Just as God will not tolerate sin, neither should we. Those who compromise with God's Word will NEVER be reconciled to God; for the sacrifice of Christ is ONLY applied to the sincerely repentant!

> **Romans 2:13** (For not the hearers of the law are just before God, **but the doers of the law shall be justified.**

The incense pictures the prayers of repentance of those seeking to be reconciled to God the Father in heaven; and without that complete wholehearted repentance, we CANNOT be reconciled to God the Father and we DO NOT have access to God.

Any organization that teaches tolerance for sin and compromise with any part of God's Word is cut off from God!

On this Day of Atonement, let us fast the fast of true repentance and renew our zeal to live by every Word of God!

16:12 And he shall take a censer full of burning coals of fire from off the altar before the LORD, and his hands full of sweet incense beaten small, and bring it within the vail: **16:13** And he shall put the incense upon the fire before the LORD, that the cloud of the incense may cover the mercy seat that is upon the testimony, that he die not: **16:14** And he shall take of the blood of the bullock, and sprinkle it with his finger upon the mercy seat eastward; and before the mercy seat shall he sprinkle of the blood with his finger seven times.

The seven times sprinkling pictures the complete acceptance by God the Father of the atoning sacrifice of Christ [who is the spirit High Priest being illustrated by the Aaronic high priest] for all of humanity; first for the early harvest and now on Atonement for the main harvest of humanity.

Now the goat of the Sin Offering for the multitude is sacrificed, and its blood is also brought into the Most Holy Place and sprinkled on and before the throne of God the Father. This offering atones for the people of the fall main harvest of humanity..

Then the First Goat Representing Christ is Sacrificed [Like the Passover Lamb] For The Sins of the Main Harvest

16:15 Then shall he kill the goat of the sin offering, that is for the people, and bring his blood within the vail, and do with that blood as he did with the blood of the bullock, and sprinkle it upon the mercy seat, and before the mercy seat: **16:16** And he shall make an atonement for the holy place, because of the uncleanness of the children of Israel, and because of their transgressions in all their sins: and so shall he do for the tabernacle of the congregation, that remaineth among them in the midst of their uncleanness.

No person may enter the tabernacle/temple during the entire ceremony while the physical high priest is moving between the Most Holy Place and the altar of sacrifice.

16:17 And there shall be no man in the tabernacle of the congregation when he goeth in to make an atonement in the holy place, until he [the high priest] come out [of the tabernacle / temple after completing the ceremony], and have made an atonement for himself, and for his household, and for all the congregation of Israel.

16:18 And he [the high priest] shall go out [of the Most Holy Place] unto the altar that is before the LORD, and make an atonement for it [an atonement to cleanse the altar]; and shall take of the blood of the bullock, and of the blood of the goat, and put it upon the horns of the altar round about. **16:19** And he shall sprinkle of the blood upon it with his finger seven times, and cleanse it, and hallow it from the uncleanness of the children of Israel.

After this ceremony of entry into the Most Holy Place and the reconciliation of the people to the Father; the sins of the nations were be laid on the head of the ScapeGoat.

The Live Azazel Goat

After the sacrificial goat is killed as a Sin Offering for all the people; the scapegoat is removed from among the people. This was an instructional allegory that all humanity of the latter main harvest could only enter the presence of God the Father only after the removal of sin [by the removal of

Satan and sincere repentance] and the application of the sacrifice of Christ the Lamb of God.

16:20 And when he hath made an end of reconciling the holy place, and the tabernacle of the congregation, and the altar, he shall bring the live goat: [outside the Most Holy Place]

16:21 And Aaron shall lay both his hands upon the head of the live goat, and confess over him all the iniquities of the children of Israel [In future all nations shall be grafted into Israel], and all their transgressions in all their sins, putting them upon the head of the goat, and shall send him away by the hand of a fit man into the wilderness: **16:22** And the goat shall bear upon him all their iniquities unto a land not inhabited: and he shall let go the goat in the wilderness.

The "Azazel" goat [representing Satan] does not bear the sins of the people like Christ bears and atones for sin; rather the goat representing Satan bears **responsibility** for the sins of the whole main harvest of humanity who had died in their sins. The removal of this goat symbolizes the removal of Satan the source of the sins of the people, freeing the people of the main fall harvest from their bondage to Satan, sin and death.

Then with the Fast of Atonement removal of Satan, the ultimate fountainhead of sin, and the people repenting with fasting; the sacrifice of Christ can be expanded from the Passover sacrifice for a few, to redeem the entire [repentant] main harvest of humanity from all sin.

The high priest must leave the tabernacle after having touched the goat of sin, and he must remove the holy garments and wash himself from his contact with the Satan goat.

Then the holy garments must be washed after contact with sin because they picture the total purity from sin and the complete righteousness of Jesus Christ the High Priest of the New Covenant.

16:23 And Aaron [and subsequent high priests] shall come into the tabernacle of the congregation, and shall put off the linen garments, which he put on when he went into the holy place, and shall leave them there: **16:24** And he shall wash his flesh with water in the holy place, and put on his garments, and come forth,

Once the Satan goat is removed, the people have sincerely repented and sin having been atoned for by the Sin Offerings [which represent the application of Christ's sacrifice], the main fall harvest of humanity can be reconciled to God the Father as they are resurrected in their courses through the seven thousand year main harvest of the Feast of the Ingathering of Nations [Tabernacles].

The burnt offerings representing a reconciled people serving the Father in wholehearted completeness, just as Jesus Christ also serves God the Father in total passionate wholehearted loving faithful obedience and zeal to do the whole will of God the Father!

. . . and offer his burnt offering, and the burnt offering of the people, and make an atonement for himself, and for the people. **16:25** And the fat of the sin offering shall he burn upon the altar.

The fit [strong] man who took the goat into the wilderness, must wash himself and his clothes before coming back among the people. This to cleanse even the uncleanness incurred by touching the goat, which was bearing the sins out from among the people.

16:26 And he that let go the goat for the scapegoat shall wash his clothes, and bathe his flesh in water, and afterward come into the camp.

Then the bodies of the goat and bull sin offerings, are to be removed from the camp and burned outside the congregation, according to the law of the Sin Offerings.

16:27 And the bullock for the sin offering, and the goat for the sin offering, whose blood was brought in to make atonement in the holy place, shall one carry forth without the camp; and they shall burn in the fire their skins, and their flesh, and their dung.

The men who carried the bodies of the Sin Offerings outside the camp must also wash themselves and their clothes from the uncleanness of being associated with the sin being borne by the sacrifices.

16:28 And he that burneth them shall wash his clothes, and bathe his flesh in water, and afterward he shall come into the camp.

The Command for a Complete Fast on the Tenth Day of the Seventh Month

This is not just some ritual fast; it is to be a fast of repentance from all sin, and a commitment to go forward and sin no more; so that the sin offering of Jesus Christ may be applied to us personally.

16:29 And this shall be a statute for ever unto you: that **in the seventh month, on the tenth day of the month, ye shall afflict your souls, and do no work at all**, whether it be one of your own country, **or a stranger that sojourneth among you**: **16:30** For on that day shall the priest make an atonement for you, to cleanse you, that ye may be clean from all your sins before the LORD. **16:31** It shall be a sabbath of rest unto you, and ye shall afflict your souls, by a statute for ever.

The ceremony began with Aaron, and was to be carried on by his successors in the high priesthood. Jesus Christ has now replaced the high priesthood of Aaron as the spiritual High Priest of the New Covenant, removing our sins and reconciling us to God the Father in heaven.

16:32 And the priest, whom he shall anoint, and whom he shall consecrate to minister in the priest's office in his father's stead, shall make the atonement, and shall put on the linen clothes, even the holy garments: **16:33** And he shall make an atonement for the holy sanctuary, and he shall make an atonement for the tabernacle of the congregation, and for the altar, and he shall make an atonement for the priests, and for all the people of the congregation.

All humanity is to be grafted into spiritual Israel in the millennial kingdom of God; after which all humanity that has ever lived and died and not had a part in the resurrection to spirit, will be resurrected in their courses and also grafted into spiritual Israel.

The spring Holy Days picture the early spiritual harvest, and the fall Holy Days of the Seventh Month picture the main harvest of humanity.

The Passover lamb pictures the sacrifice for the early spiritual harvest of the Called Out, and the goat Atonement Sin Offering pictures the sacrifice of Christ as applied to the main fall harvest.

Israel, called out of Egypt, is a type of the spiritual called out from sin for the first six thousand years, and a type of the early harvest!

Israel in the main fall harvest festivals is a type of the main harvest of all humanity to be reconciled to the Father and brought into the family of God.

16:34 And this shall be an everlasting statute unto you, to make an atonement for the children of Israel for all their sins once a year. And he did as the LORD commanded Moses.

Leviticus 17

Leviticus 17:1 And the LORD spake unto Moses, saying, **17:2** Speak unto Aaron, and unto his sons, and unto all the children of Israel, and say unto them; This is the thing which the LORD hath commanded, saying, **17:3** What man soever there be of the house of Israel, that killeth an ox, or lamb, or goat [for a sacrifice to God], in the camp, or that killeth it out of the camp,

One may kill and eat anywhere, but any offering or sacrifice must be killed at the tabernacle / temple. This is about killing in sacrifice and is forbidding sacrifices in other places except at the tabernacle / temple.

This is a command against sacrificing in the High Places where the heathen sacrificed to their gods. Finally this is a command to come before God and serve him, and forbids us from worshiping God in our own ways; and not in the specific manner which God has commanded.

No sacrificial animal including the Passover lamb may be killed at any place excerpt at the temple in Jerusalem.

It is because there is no physical Temple today that no physical sacrifices may be offered at this time. The physical sacrifices were only physical teaching tools to teach the various aspects of the work and atonement of the Lamb of God. The Daily Sacrifice and all other sacrifices are now fulfilled in the spiritual sense by the work of Christ in heaven as our ONLY Mediator.

In the millennium a new physical Temple will be built by Jesus Christ, and the physical sacrifices will be renewed again [Eze 40 - 48) as instructional tools to teach mankind the various aspects of the work and atonement of Christ.

17:4 And bringeth it not [alive] unto the door of the tabernacle of the congregation, to offer an offering unto the LORD before the tabernacle of the LORD; blood shall be imputed unto that man; he hath shed blood; and that man shall be cut off from among his people:

The people were to no longer offer sacrifices where WE CHOOSE, but were to offer all sacrifices before God at HIS Tabernacle/Temple, for God dwelt in his Tabernacle/Temple.

17:5 To the end that the children of Israel may bring their sacrifices [bring them alive to kill before God], which they [had before times offered] offer in the open field, even that they may bring them [alive] unto the LORD, unto the door of the tabernacle of the congregation, unto the priest, and offer them for peace offerings unto the LORD.

All sacrifices must be killed at the tabernacle / temple, from this commandment forward, and the fullness of the commandments regarding each sacrifice must be carried out completely, so that men might learn the lessons intended by that particular type of sacrifice.

17:6 And the priest shall sprinkle the blood upon the altar of the LORD at the door of the tabernacle of the congregation, and burn the fat for a sweet savour unto the LORD.

All sacrifices must now be offered to God at HIS Temple, in the manner prescribed by God. To sacrifice in any other way or at any other place is to sacrifice to demons, for it is rebellion against the commandments and Word of God.

We are to be diligent to learn and to keep the whole Word of God with zeal. In terms of the physical sacrifices we are to learn the lessons and intended meanings of the sacrifices in the spiritual sense, so that we can comprehend the work and atoning sacrifice of Jesus Christ.

17:7 And they shall no more offer their sacrifices unto devils, after whom they have gone a whoring. This shall be a statute for ever unto them throughout their generations.

Leviticus 17 has two meanings

1. We must worship God according to God's Word and not according to what we decide for ourselves, and second,

2. We are to worship God alone and not any idol or foreign [strange] god; and an idol is ANYTHING or ANY PERSON that comes between us and God.

17:8 And thou shalt say unto them, Whatsoever man there be of the house of Israel, or of the strangers which sojourn among you, that offereth a burnt offering or sacrifice, **17:9** And bringeth it not unto the door of the tabernacle of the congregation, to offer it unto the LORD; even that man shall be cut off from among his people.

Here we are forbidden to eat any blood for the life is in the blood, and the blood represents the shed blood of Jesus Christ atoning for our sins. Be very careful to avoid eating any blood, even to the point of making your soup stock and then straining it before adding your other ingredients.

Jesus Christ has given us the wine offering to drink at Passover as a picture of his shed blood. In the sacrificial system, wherever wine is poured out as a part of the sacrifice it pictures the shed blood of Jesus Christ.

17:10 And whatsoever man there be of the house of Israel, or of the strangers that sojourn among you, that eateth any manner of blood; I will even set my face against that soul that eateth blood, and will cut him off from among his people. **17:11 For the life of the flesh is in the blood: and I have given it to you upon the altar to make an atonement for your souls: for it is the blood that maketh an atonement for the soul.** **17:12** Therefore I said unto the children of Israel, No soul of you shall eat blood, neither shall any stranger that sojourneth among you eat blood.

The Word of God which was inspired by Jesus Christ is very clear and emphatic on this point. If we must fast on the day of Atonement then we must also avoid eating blood, for the penalty of failure to obey in either case is the same.

17:13 And whatsoever man there be of the children of Israel, or of the strangers that sojourn among you, which hunteth and catcheth any beast or fowl that may be eaten; he shall even pour out the blood thereof, and cover it with dust. **17:14 For it is the life of all flesh; the blood of it is for the life thereof: therefore I said unto the children of Israel, Ye shall eat the blood of no manner of flesh: for the life of all flesh is the blood thereof: whosoever eateth it shall be cut off.**

Of all animals including the CLEAN creatures; if it dies naturally of itself, or is killed by other animals it is unclean to us and eating it is no different than eating any other unclean thing.

This is a physical allegory of the spiritual person becoming unclean by any sin or by learning any false doctrine, false teaching or false way. That person can only be, and must be made clean by sincere repentance and the application of the sacrifice of Jesus Christ and the washing of water of the Word of TRUTH, the whole Word of God.

17:15 And every soul that eateth that which died of itself, or that which was torn with beasts, whether it be one of your own country, or a stranger, he shall both wash his clothes, and bathe himself in water, and be unclean until the even: then shall he be clean.

If we do not wash ourselves spiritually, removing the uncleanness of any association with sin with the water of the whole Word of God through living by every Word of God; and if we do not cleanse our garments [our garments are representative of either wickedness or righteousness]: We are not God's people.

> **Revelation 7:14** And I said unto him, Sir, thou knowest. And he said to me, These are they which came out of great tribulation, and **have washed their robes, and made them white in the blood of the Lamb.**
>
> **Revelation 19:7** Let us be glad and rejoice, and give honour to him: for the marriage of the Lamb is come, and his wife hath made herself ready. **19:8 And to her was granted that she should be arrayed in fine linen, clean and white: for the fine linen is the righteousness of saints.**

If we will not cleanse ourselves from sin by sincere repentance we must pay the price for our sins.

Leviticus 17:16 But if he wash them [his clothes] not, nor bathe his flesh; then he shall bear his iniquity.

Leviticus 18

Leviticus 18:1 And the LORD spake unto Moses, saying, **18:2** Speak unto the children of Israel, and say unto them, I am the LORD your God.

Egypt was a type of bondage to sin and Canaan was a type of the unrepentant wicked who will ultimately be destroyed for their unrepented sins; and as such this is a warning to the spiritual Israel of today's Ekklesia to avoid any association with sin and worldliness.

18:3 After the doings of the land of Egypt, wherein ye dwelt, shall ye not do: and after the doings of the land of Canaan, whither I bring you, shall ye not do: neither shall ye walk in their ordinances.

This specifically forbids observing Sunday or participating in Christmas and Easter as well as all other pagan rooted non biblical festivals. We are NOT to learn false doctrines and teachings to keep them; we are to worship God in the way that our God commands us and not in any other way.

Just like physical Israel was to be faithful to live by every Word of God in the letter; so spiritual Israel is to be faithful to live by every Word of God in BOTH the letter and the spiritual intent of the letter.

18:4 Ye shall do my judgments, and keep mine ordinances, to walk therein: I am the LORD your God.

The Mosaic Covenant blessings promised for being zealous to learn and keep the whole Word of God were physical prosperity; and the New Covenant blessings promised for being zealous to learn and live by every Word of God is eternal life with peace and prosperity!

18:5 Ye shall therefore keep my statutes, and my judgments: **which if a man do, he shall live in them: I am the LORD.**

Laws concerning marriages with near of kin

The term "uncover their nakedness" is a euphemism for sex.

18:6 None of you shall approach to any that is near of kin to him, to uncover their nakedness: I am the LORD.

18:7 The nakedness of thy father, or the nakedness of thy mother, shalt thou not uncover: she is thy mother; thou shalt not uncover her nakedness.

18:8 The nakedness of thy father's wife [referring to our father's wife whether she is or is not our mother] shalt thou not uncover: it is thy father's nakedness.

This was a new law concerning sisters, or Abraham would have been condemned in his day.

18:9 The nakedness of thy sister, the daughter of thy father, or daughter of thy mother, whether she be born at home, or born abroad, even their nakedness thou shalt not uncover.

18:10 The nakedness of thy son's daughter, or of thy daughter's daughter, even their nakedness thou shalt not uncover: for theirs is thine own nakedness.

18:11 The nakedness of thy father's wife's daughter, begotten of thy father, she is thy sister, thou shalt not uncover her nakedness.

18:12 Thou shalt not uncover the nakedness of thy father's sister [an aunt]: she is thy father's near kinswoman.

18:13 Thou shalt not uncover the nakedness of thy mother's sister [an aunt]: for she is thy mother's near kinswoman.

18:14 Thou shalt not uncover the nakedness of thy father's brother, thou shalt not approach to his wife: she is thine aunt.

18:15 Thou shalt not uncover the nakedness of thy daughter in law: she is thy son's wife; thou shalt not uncover her nakedness.

18:16 Thou shalt not uncover the nakedness of thy brother's wife: it is thy brother's nakedness.

18:17 Thou shalt not uncover the nakedness of a woman and her daughter [Whether she is our own daughter or our wife's daughter by another marriage, the taking of a woman and her daughter is absolutely forbidden.], neither shalt thou take her son's daughter, or her daughter's daughter, to uncover her nakedness; for they are her near kinswomen: it is wickedness.

The following seems to have sprung from Jacob's marriages.

18:18 Neither shalt thou take a wife to her sister, to vex her, to uncover her nakedness, beside the other in her life time.

Here is a specific command to avoid lying with a woman in her menses.

18:19 Also thou shalt not approach unto a woman to uncover her nakedness, as long as she is put apart for her uncleanness.

God repeats his command against adultery.

18:20 Moreover thou shalt not lie carnally with thy neighbour's wife, to defile thyself with her.

Below is a command against idolatry and sacrificing our children to idols. This referred to the ancient practice of throwing children into the fire as a sacrifice to false gods.

In the spiritual sense this refers to failing to diligently teach our children about God and his ways and to willfully allowing them to be filled with the idolatry of false doctrine [teachings].

18:21 And thou shalt not let any of thy seed pass through the fire to Molech, neither shalt thou profane the name of thy God: I am the LORD.

Homosexuality is declared an abomination by God; and God will ultimately destroy all abominations and unrepentant practitioners of abominations. In fact God regards all of these sins as abominations.

18:22 Thou shalt not lie with mankind, as with womankind: it is abomination.

Inter species sexuality is a great abomination to God, yet in our modern world so called scientists are working at bastardizing species of animals etc by intermingling their genes.

18:23 Neither shalt thou lie with any beast to defile thyself therewith: neither shall any woman stand before a beast to lie down thereto: it is confusion.

Here God reveals why he is commanding Israel to utterly destroy the Canaanites. It is because of all these things and all their wickedness that they were made a type of sin and were to be utterly destroyed as an example for us, so that we may learn that we will also likewise be destroyed if we do not repent of sin like Rahab did.

With God this was an act of great mercy on the Canaanites for they were made an example of the end of the unrepentant sinner, yet they will still be raised up in their time and they will remember what came upon them for their sins and then they will quickly and sincerely repent.

18:24 Defile not ye yourselves in any of these things: for in all these the nations are defiled which I cast out before you: **18:25** And the land is defiled: therefore I do visit the iniquity thereof upon it, and the land itself vomiteth out her inhabitants.

Entry into and possession of the promised land [both physical and spiritual] is contingent on NOT committing any of these abominations. This was commanded to physical Israel and is also applicable on both the physical and spiritual plane to spiritual Israel.

Becoming one flesh in an unlawful way is symbolic of committing spiritual adultery by allowing anything to come between us or loving and following any other above our espoused spirit husband Jesus Christ.

We are espoused to Jesus Christ and we are to be totally faithful to HIM and to God the Father: Never turning aside to false gods and the false teachings of false religions, nor to any of their abominations. For if we seek after the abominations of false gods we will be utterly rejected and spewed out by Jesus Christ (Rev 3:16).

18:26 Ye shall therefore keep my statutes and my judgments, and shall not commit any of these abominations; neither any of your own nation, nor any stranger that sojourneth among you: **18:27** (For all these abominations have the men of the land done, which were before you, and the land is defiled;) **18:28** That the land spue not you out also, when ye defile it, as it spued out the nations that were before you. **18:29** For whosoever shall commit any of these abominations, even the souls that commit them shall be cut off from among their people.

We are to be absolutely faithful and full of zeal to learn and live by every Word of God, to wholeheartedly seek to please God our Father in heaven and our espoused Husband Jesus Christ.

Under God's law the closest kin that may marry are cousins, any relationship closer than that is forbidden. Any relationship with idols and false religions and their false teachings, is also forbidden; which includes obeying men or the false traditions of men above obeying the Holy Scriptures.

18:30 Therefore shall ye keep mine ordinance, that ye commit not any one of these abominable customs, which were committed before you, and that ye defile not yourselves therein: I am the LORD your God.

Leviticus 19

Leviticus 19:1 And the LORD spake unto Moses, saying, **19:2 Speak unto all the congregation of the children of Israel, and say unto them, Ye shall be holy: for I the LORD your God am holy.**

Physical Israel was to be pure from all sin, and Spiritual Israel is to be pure and free from all sin just as God is pure from all sin. We are to be zealous to learn and to keep the whole Word of God in BOTH letter and spirit; internalizing the very nature of God our Father in heaven and to become just like him!

We now come to a series of commandments concerning general conduct.

The very first commandment is to fear [respect] our parents.

The spiritual context, is that we are to fear [respect] God our Father in heaven and we are to be faithfully obedient to ALL that he teaches and requires; that we are to wholeheartedly work to please him at all times and that we are to respect and sanctify God's Sabbaths! The plural usage for Sabbath, refers to both the weekly Sabbath and the annual Sabbaths.

Today the Ekklesia pays lip service to the Sabbath, calling it holy time; and then they routinely defile God's time by buying, selling, cooking, working and otherwise defiling God's HOLY TIME. In doing this they condemn themselves with their own mouths and worse, adding sin to sin; they condemn those who ARE zealous for God's Holy Sabbaths.

By acknowledging God's Holy Sabbath and then polluting it, and persecuting those who do sanctify the Sabbaths of God; they defy God their Father in heaven breaking the commandment to honor our father as well.

How can such men escape the righteous correction of God?

19:3 Ye **shall fear every man his mother, and his father, and keep my sabbaths: I am the LORD your God**.

An idol is anything that separates us from God.

Today many brethren make idols out of worldly wealth, pleasures, corporate churches, men; and false traditions; loving their organization, elder, leader or traditions above any love for living by every Word of God: As for the elders, many love their positions and pay cheques and the adulation of the brethren above the truth of God.

We exalt all these things above the Word of God! We do not put God and his Word FIRST in our lives, but follow the words of men blindly as they lead us away from any zeal for the Word of God.

19:4 Turn ye not unto idols, nor make to yourselves molten gods: I am the LORD your God.

A reminder of the law concerning Peace Offerings

19:5 And if ye offer a sacrifice of peace offerings unto the LORD, ye shall offer it at your own will. **19:6** It shall be eaten the same day ye offer it, and on the morrow: and if ought remain until the third day, it shall be burnt in the fire. **19:7** And if it be eaten at all on the third day, it is abominable; it shall not be accepted. **19:8** Therefore every one that eateth it shall bear his iniquity, because he hath profaned the hallowed thing of the LORD: and that soul shall be cut off from among his people.

The law of gleaning and concern for the needy

19:9 And when ye reap the harvest of your land, thou shalt not wholly reap the corners of thy field, neither shalt thou gather the gleanings of thy harvest. **19:10** And thou shalt not glean thy vineyard, neither shalt thou gather every grape of thy vineyard; thou shalt leave them for the poor and stranger: I am the LORD your God.

It is sin to knowingly make a false statement. It is also a great sin to use and twist an out of context fragment of truth to deceive about the whole truth. Making a mistake is not lying if we correct the matter as soon as possible after discovering our error.

19:11 Ye shall not steal, neither deal falsely, neither lie one to another.

To swear falsely is to take the name of God in vain.

19:12 And ye shall not swear by my name falsely, neither shalt thou profane the name of thy God: I am the LORD.

We are not to steal either directly or by defrauding.

Do you begin to see that the Ten Commandments are a summation of these basic laws!?

19:13 Thou shalt not defraud thy neighbour, neither rob him: the wages of him that is hired shall not abide with thee all night until the morning.

We are to be positively concerned for the needy and the handicapped.

19:14 Thou shalt not curse the deaf, nor put a stumblingblock before the blind, but shalt fear thy God: I am the LORD.

We are to be fair and just in all our ways; not being partial to persons because of riches or poverty.

In the spiritual sense this command is broken by all those who love the rich or demean the poor; and most especially by all those who exalt men and organizations as their idols; being respecters of persons.

We are to always test all things by the Word of God and to hold fast to God's Word while rejecting anything that is contrary to the Word of God; regardless of what title anyone may claim for themselves or how much we respect the man; WE MUST RESPECT AND LOVE GOD MORE!

19:15 Ye shall do no unrighteousness in judgment: thou shalt not respect the person of the poor, nor honor the person of the mighty: but in righteousness shalt thou judge thy neighbour.

We are not to spread unsubstantiated rumor which is gossip and tale bearing, nor are we to knowingly falsely accuse others.

19:16 Thou shalt not go up and down as a talebearer among thy people: neither shalt thou stand against the blood of thy neighbour; I am the LORD.

We are not to hate our neighbour by allowing him to continue in unrebuked sin! We are to warn our neighbour and we are to rebuke sin, so that perchance we might save our neighbour!

Many are backwards in thinking that love is to overlook false teachings and sins, and not to rebuke the error that is leading our brethren to their own destruction. Truly if we truly loved them, we would warn them and openly rebuke the sin in the hope that they might possibly be turned back to God and be saved.

19:17 Thou shalt not hate thy brother in thine heart: thou shalt in any wise rebuke thy neighbour, and not suffer [allow him commit sin without giving a warning] sin upon him.

We are not to hate any person. Remember the words of John in 1, 2 and 3 John? The God of the so called Old Testament has not changed! He is a God of LOVE and has a deep concern for all humanity!

19:18 Thou shalt not avenge, nor bear any grudge against the children of thy people, but thou shalt love thy neighbour as thyself: I am the LORD.

We are not to mix seed or fibers in cloth, or to mix kinds of animals. The focus on this is PURITY.

The spiritual lesson is to keep ourselves PURE and unspotted by the false doctrines and prophecies of false religions. We are not to allow our white linen garments of righteousness to become blemished by the unrighteousness of error and sin, or by trying to mix truth and righteousness with the impurity and defilement of false ways.

This is a great sin that began with the Nicolaitane form of church governance, placing men between the brethren and God.

Today many groups have been deceived into believing false teachings and follow these false teachings and false prophecies rather than the Word of God.

Many will fall at this stumbling block of trying to mix truth with error, ending up with an abominable mixture of a little truth polluted and defiled by much error so that the leaven of error pollutes the whole doctrine.

19:19 Ye shall keep my statutes. Thou shalt not let thy cattle gender with a diverse kind: thou shalt not sow thy field with mingled seed: neither shall a garment mingled of linen and woollen come upon thee.

In those days excessive debt that could not be paid off was dealt with by indentured servitude.

In other words the debtor signed a contract for himself or a member of his family to work off the debt and the contracted person became the bond servant of the creditor for the required period of time.

This law is about such a creditor taking advantage of someone under his direct authority and control. If he was male and his servant was a female and he took advantage of that situation abusing his power and control over the person, it was considered to be forcing the lady and an act of sin, and he was to make a sin offering for his sin.

The offering was to be a ram which was a very expensive price and in another place, he was required to marry the lass and forfeit the possibility of any future divorce, and also to pay an expensive price to her father for her; with the lady's father having the right to refuse the marriage and still require the payment.

> **Deuteronomy 22:28** If a man find a damsel that is a virgin, which is not betrothed, and lay hold on her, and lie with her, and they be found; **22:29** Then the man that lay with **her shall give unto the damsel's father fifty shekels of silver, and she shall be his wife; because he hath humbled her, he may not put her away all his days.**

As for the lady, we must understand that what was meant by scourging in Lev 19:20 was far different than the Roman scourging.

Scourging

> Christ suffered an exceptional scourging [punishment] by the Roman method, designed to punish and weaken him for his execution.
>
> The Hebrew word "scourge" as used in Lev 19:20, would be better translated as "thoroughly investigated" the original Hebrew word "biqqoreth" expressing the idea of investigation.
>
> H1244 biqqoreth bik·kō·reth meaning to thoroughly investigate: translated as scourged in reference to the Middle Ages practice of investigation by trial or afflicting. This is a cultural translation word issue.
>
> Strong's Number H1244 matches the Hebrew בִּקֹּרֶת (biqqoreth), which occurs 1 time in 1 verse in the Hebrew concordance of the KJV

This also has its spiritual application!

Leviticus 19:20 And whosoever lieth carnally with a woman, that is a bondmaid, betrothed to an husband, and not at all redeemed, nor freedom given her; she shall be scourged [investigated]; they shall not be put to death, because she was not free. **19:21** And he shall bring his trespass offering unto the LORD, unto the door of the tabernacle of the congregation, even a ram for a trespass offering. **19:22** And the priest shall make an atonement for him with the ram of the trespass offering before the LORD for his sin which he hath done: and the sin which he hath done shall be forgiven him.

The fruit of the trees you plant cannot be harvested for the first three years; then that which is harvested in the fourth year belongs to God as the first fruits to rejoice before God with at the Festivals, and the fruit harvested in the fifth year is ours.

19:23 And when ye shall come into the land, and shall have planted all manner of trees for food, then ye shall count the fruit thereof as uncircumcised: three years shall it be as uncircumcised unto you: it shall not be eaten of. **19:24** But in **the fourth year all the fruit thereof shall be holy to praise the LORD withal. 19:25** And in the fifth year shall ye eat of the fruit thereof, that it may yield unto you the increase thereof: I am the LORD your God.

Again we are not to eat any blood. We are not to use enchantments or spells, and we are not to observe times [astrology]. To our shame the observing of times and horoscopes which is forbidden as an abomination by God, is commonly practiced in the Ekklesia especially by ladies. This is a grave sin which will keep you out of the resurrection to spirit.

19:26 Ye shall not eat any thing with the blood: neither shall ye use enchantment, nor observe times.

19:27 Ye shall not round the corners of your heads, neither shalt thou mar the corners of thy beard. **19:28** Ye shall not make any cuttings in your flesh for the dead, nor print any marks upon you: I am the LORD.

Sexual morality is very important to God; it is the backbone of a successful society; and the sanctity of marriage is meant to teach us that our marriage to Christ must be one of the utmost fidelity, forever.

19:29 Do not prostitute thy daughter, to cause her to be a whore; lest the land fall to whoredom, and the land become full of wickedness.

All of the annual and weekly Sabbaths are to be kept faithfully, for they represent our faithfulness to our God. If we are not interested in pleasing and spending time with our Creator now, why would we do so for all eternity? Our zeal for the Sabbaths of God now, reveals to our Lord the extent of our zeal to be with him in eternity.

If we are not zealous for God's Sabbaths now; we show God that we will not be zealous for him in eternity.

19:30 Ye shall keep my sabbaths, and reverence my sanctuary: I am the LORD.

Do NOT seek out occult persons and things, no NEVER; let us always depend on our God and not on the great liar who is the enemy of God! There are many in today's Ekklesia who seek out the words of false prophets rather than sincerely seeking God's Word. Such persons will fall into the correction that they fear, and as they follow the spiritually blind they will end up in the same pit as the wicked.

19:31 Regard not them that have familiar spirits, neither seek after wizards, to be defiled by them: I am the LORD your God.

We should have respect for the elderly and especially for the elderly in the faith.

19:32 Thou shalt rise up before the hoary head, and honour the face of the old man, and fear thy God: I am the LORD.

Be hospitable to the stranger, without compromising with the Word of God.

19:33 And if a stranger sojourn with thee in your land, ye shall not vex him. **19:34** But the stranger that dwelleth with you shall be unto you as one born among you, and thou shalt love him as thyself; for ye were strangers in the land of Egypt: I am the LORD your God.

Be just and fair in all our doings; for justice is of God.

19:35 Ye shall do no unrighteousness in judgment, in meteyard, in weight, or in measure. **19:36** Just balances, just weights, a just ephah, and a just hin, shall ye have: I am the LORD your God, which brought you out of the land of Egypt.

When we commit to the spiritual New Covenant with God at baptism, we are committing to learn and to live by every Word of God; to internalize the very nature of God and to become at one in complete unity with and totally like our righteous Father in Heaven!

19:37 Therefore shall ye observe all my statutes, and all my judgments, and do them: I am the LORD.

Leviticus 20

In certain seasons of the year wicked people seeking to please their false gods sacrificed their children and threw them into a blazing fire before the idol of Moloch and various other idols.

The modern version of this practice of sacrificing our children is called abortion. God expressly forbids this barbaric practice.

There is a spiritual facet of this situation, because when we teach our children to live contrary to the Word of God and we teach them to serve idols of men, organizations, or worldly pleasures; when we do these things we are teaching our children to serve our idols just like the Canaanites did, only in a slightly different way.

When we do not diligently teach our children the way of eternal life, and we teach them to exalt anything, including corporate churches and leaders; above the whole Word of God, to follow them and turn away from any zeal to live by every Word of God; we are sacrificing our own children by leading them into the lake of fire, as the Canaanites threw their children into the fire of Molech.

ALL idolaters will be destroyed and that includes those who idolize corporate churches and religious leaders and organizations to follow them contrary to living by every Word of God.

Leviticus 20:1 And the LORD spake unto Moses, saying, **20:2** Again, thou shalt say to the children of Israel, Whosoever he be of the children of Israel, or of the strangers that sojourn in Israel, that giveth any of his seed unto Molech; he shall surely be put to death: the people of the land shall stone him with stones. **20:3** And I will set my face against that man, and will cut him off from among his people; because he hath given of his seed unto Molech, to defile my sanctuary, and to profane my holy name.

Those who say that we must understand the Bible as some man interprets it, are idolaters! We are to test the words of men against the Word of God and we are to hold fast to God's Word! Not the other way around!

20:4 And if the people of the land do any ways hide their eyes from the man, when he giveth of his seed unto Molech, and kill him not: **20:5** Then I will set my face against that man, and against his family, and will cut him off, and all that go a whoring after him, to commit whoredom with Molech, from among their people.

God is AGAINST any person who allows anyone or anything to come between them and God, which is idolatry!

God will destroy the person who idolizes anything at all! We are to worship Almighty God alone and with a sincere whole heart; we are not to allow any person or thing to come between us and Almighty God; for such persons or things then become our IDOLS!

Those who read the scriptures as interpreted by men and do not test the words of men by the scriptures and follow men ONLY as they are faithful to live by every Word of God; have made that man their idol and will be destroyed by God for their idolatry unless they sincerely repent.

Those who teach their children to follow men as being the same as following God; are leading their children to destruction and they are speeding on to their own destruction.

20:6 And the soul that turneth after such as have familiar spirits, and after wizards, to go a whoring after them, I will even set my face against that soul, and will cut him off from among his people.

It is the Eternal who sets us apart to holiness [sanctifies us]; the deceitful words of false and unconverted teachers who would lead us away from the whole Word of God to follow themselves will only lead us into the same destruction that they are falling into.

20:7 Sanctify yourselves therefore, and be ye holy: for I am the LORD your God. 20:8 And ye shall keep my statutes, and do them: I am the LORD which sanctify you.

God repeats these things over and over to Moses, to impress on us the importance of keeping these things in both the physical and spiritual sense. We are to be faithful to learn and to live by every Word of, and by the whole will of God our Father in heaven.

20:9 For every one that curseth his father or his mother shall be surely put to death: he hath cursed his father or his mother; his blood shall be upon him.

God emphasizes the sanctity of marriage to teach us that our marriage to Jesus Christ is to be sanctified in faithfulness for ALL ETERNITY; with NO departure from zeal and passionate cleaving to our eternal Husband Jesus Christ.

20:10 And the man that committeth adultery with another man's wife, even he that committeth adultery with his neighbour's wife, the adulterer and the adulteress shall surely be put to death.

Laws Governing Sexual Conduct

20:11 And the man that lieth with his father's wife hath uncovered his father's nakedness: both of them shall surely be put to death; their blood shall be upon them. **20:12** And if a man lie with his daughter in law, both of them shall surely be put to death: they have wrought confusion; their blood shall be upon them.

God loves the homosexual, therefore the deeds of homosexuals are an abomination to God; and the homosexual person is to be killed so that his example does not infect others. Today there are millions who not only commit this wickedness; they loudly proclaim pride in their sin, so that their sin exceeds that of Sodom.

Exacting the death penalty is the duty of governments and no individual is to take it upon himself to attack anyone.

20:13 If a man also lie with mankind, as he lieth with a woman, both of them have committed an abomination: they shall surely be put to death; their blood shall be upon them.

20:14 And if a man take a wife and her mother, it is wickedness: they shall be burnt with fire, both he and they; that there be no wickedness among you.

20:15 And if a man lie with a beast, he shall surely be put to death: and ye shall slay the beast.

20:16 And if a woman approach unto any beast, and lie down thereto, thou shalt kill the woman, and the beast: they shall surely be put to death; their blood shall be upon them.

20:17 And if a man shall take his sister, his father's daughter, or his mother's daughter, and see her nakedness, and she see his nakedness; it is a wicked thing; and they shall be cut off in the sight of their people: he hath uncovered his sister's nakedness; he shall bear his iniquity.

Any man and women who have intercourse during her seven days of uncleanness from the onset of menses will be cut off from the congregation of God, just as surely as those who will not fast on the Day of Atonement.

This is a physical law having the spiritual application that this blood curse was given as an allegory of sin coming into the world and teaching the need to eschew, abhor and avoid all defilement of sin.

All couples must abstain for the full commanded seven days from the onset of menses to the sunset ending the seventh day. This is an allegory that we are to avoid any and all contamination by sin no matter how strong the temptation.

20:18 And **if a man shall lie with a woman having her sickness** [menses]**, and shall uncover her nakedness; he hath discovered her fountain, and she hath uncovered the fountain of her blood: and both of them shall be cut off from among their people.**

A repeat of certain commandments regarding sexual matters

20:19 And thou shalt not uncover the nakedness of thy mother's sister, nor of thy father's sister: for he uncovereth his near kin: they shall bear their iniquity.

20:20 And if a man shall lie with his uncle's wife, he hath uncovered his uncle's nakedness: they shall bear their sin; they shall die childless.

20:21 And if a man shall take his brother's wife, it is an unclean thing: he hath uncovered his brother's nakedness; they shall be childless.

The only exception being a levirate marriage to the wife of a childless brother (Deu 25).

Entry into the physical and spiritual Promised Land is fully contingent on learning and zealously living by every Word of God.

20:22 Ye shall therefore keep all my statutes, and all my judgments, and do them: that the land, whither I bring you to dwell therein, spue you not out.

We are not to commit these sins like the Canaanites did, for which God commanded their destruction; or we will likewise be destroyed.

The history of Israel in Egypt and afterwards right up to the advent of the physical Christ, was recorded for our instruction and our example to teach us spiritual lessons.

- Physical Israel is an instructional allegory of the New Covenant (of Jeremiah 31) and the spiritually called out to God the Father through Jesus Christ the Lamb of God.
- Bondage in Egypt is an instructional example of bondage to sin.
- The physical promised land is a type of the spiritual Promised Land of eternal life with God.
- The Canaanites were a type of the unrepentant sinner and the end of the unrepentant sinner; which is to be excluded form the Promised Land of eternal life and to be destroyed for their unrepented sin.

20:23 And ye shall not walk in the manners of the nation, which I cast out before you: for they committed all these things, and therefore I abhorred them.

20:24 But I have said unto you, Ye shall inherit their land, and I will give it unto you to possess it, a land that floweth with milk and honey: I am the LORD your God, which have separated you from other people.

We are to learn about the physically clean and unclean from these laws and to learn to discern between the spiritually clean [the purity of God] and the spiritually unclean [all sin].

20:25 Ye shall therefore put difference between clean beasts and unclean, and between unclean fowls and clean: and ye shall not make your souls abominable by beast, or by fowl, or by any manner of living thing that creepeth on the ground, which I have separated from you as unclean.

20:26 And ye shall be holy unto me: for I the LORD am holy, and have severed you from other people, that ye should be mine.

This is in reference to anyone seeking guidance from spirits either directly or through others; which is idolatry, and spiritual adultery, and rebellion against our LORD.

20:27 A man also or woman that hath a familiar spirit, or that is a wizard, shall surely be put to death: they shall stone them with stones: their blood shall be upon them.

Leviticus 21

The early called out are not and will not be priests of God until after the resurrection. We are all now called to BECOME priests of God at the resurrection and we are to be hearers and learners of godliness until every blemish of sin is overcome.

It is when Christ resurrects the faithful that God's chosen will fully become the priests of God of the order of Jesus Christ. During this physical life the early first fruits are in training to become priests and kings under Jesus Christ, but we are not kings and priests until we have been judged and chosen and resurrected to that office.

No priest of God may touch any dead body, except that God in his mercy allows the touching of those immediately near of kin to himself. This is a physical instruction to convey the spiritual lesson that all priests are to remain undefiled by association with the wages of sin which is death.

All of the early called out to the New Covenant are called to become priests of God under our High Priest Jesus Christ [Melchizedek], and are to remain unpolluted by sin and the wages of sin, which is death.

Leviticus 21:1 And the LORD said unto Moses, Speak unto the priests the sons of Aaron, and say unto them, There shall none be defiled for the dead among his people: **21:2** But for his kin, that is near unto him, that is, for his mother, and for his father, and for his son, and for his daughter, and for his brother. **21:3** And for his sister a virgin, that is nigh unto him, which hath had no husband; for her may he be defiled. **21:4** But he shall not defile himself, being a chief man among his people, to profane himself.

The called out must not mourn for the dead by afflicting themselves physically, so that they abase themselves before the public.

Public asceticism [self abuse] is not humility before God, it is a fraud designed to make people think that such men are humble, when they actually reject God's ways and do this to impress the spiritually ignorant.

Public shows of mourning for those not of near kin or fraudulent shows of fake put on humility, are designed to impress and deceive the public.

We are to follow the whole Word of God and not to follow any man who lives in rebellion against God while putting on a public show of false humility.

21:5 They shall not make baldness upon their head, neither shall they shave off the corner of their beard, nor make any cuttings in their flesh [this was a common practice of other nations in morning for the dead].

We are to be holy as God is holy, teaching the righteousness of the TRUTH of the whole Word of God, not making grand public gestures to deceive people into turning away from God to follow the traditions of men.

21:6 They shall be holy unto their God, and not profane the name of their God: for the offerings of the LORD made by fire, and the bread of their God, they do offer: therefore they shall be holy.

The called out are to be holy in their household, and are forbidden to marry an immoral or a divorced woman [an unconverted spouse]. Just as this was a law for the priesthood in physical Mosaic Israel, it is a binding law in Spiritual Israel today. We are all called to be priests of of God after the order of Melchizedek and we must not intermarry with unconverted persons.

If a man is married to a woman and they divorce "while remaining in the faith," they may not marry any other.

If a man or woman is divorced for pornea [disloyalty] which is the only lawful reason for divorce; then he/she is to be rejected from the assembly as unconverted.

> **Matthew 5:32** But I say unto you, That whosoever shall put away his wife, saving for the cause of fornication [pornea, disloyalty especially sexual], causeth her to commit adultery: [and] whosoever shall marry her that is divorced committeth adultery.

Leviticus 21:7 They shall not take a wife that is a whore, or profane; neither shall they take a woman put away [divorced] from her husband: for he is holy unto his God.

The early harvest Called Out brethren are absolutely forbidden to divorce and then remarry "within the faith." Jesus Christ said that those who do so are living in adultery.

There are many in today's assemblies including elders who are living in the sin of adultery; for which cause they have been separated from God and their prayers are not heard.

Yet, if one's spouse turns away and hates the faith leaving it and leaves the faithful spouse; the faithful are then free to remarry, only within the faith.

21:8 Thou shalt sanctify him [the priests are to be set apart to godliness] therefore; for he offereth the bread of thy God: he [Spiritually those that teach the unleavened bread of the Word of God are holy to God and must not be joined with unbelievers] shall be holy unto thee: for I the LORD, which sanctify you, am holy.

Our offspring who reject this way will face judgment if they do not repent: Therefore we must diligently teach them to be faithful to the whole Word of God.

21:9 And the daughter of any priest, if she profane herself by playing the whore, she profaneth her father: she shall be burnt with fire.

The physical high priests were the mediators of the Mosaic Covenant and a type of Jesus Christ the Mediator of the New Covenant; and as such they must not mourn for any dead person, even his nearest kin; by damaging his body, or degrading himself before the people.

21:10 And he that is the high priest among his brethren, upon whose head the anointing oil was poured, and that is consecrated to put on the garments, shall not uncover his head, nor rend his clothes; **21:11** Neither shall he go in to any dead body, nor defile himself for his father, or for his mother; **21:12** Neither shall he go out of the sanctuary, nor profane the sanctuary of his God; for the crown of the anointing oil of his God is upon him: I am the LORD.

The High Priest must take a virgin to wife! What marvelous and complete symbolism; because the bride of the physical High Priest is representative of the bride of the spiritual High Priest Jesus Christ!

The bride of Christ has been made pure as a virgin through sincere repentance and the atoning sacrifice of her Husband and her zeal to be faithful to HIM ALONE, above ALL others!

21:13 And he shall take a wife in her virginity. **21:14** A widow, or a divorced woman, or profane, or an harlot, these shall he not take: but he shall take a virgin of his own people to wife.

> **Revelation 14:4** These are they which were not defiled with women [false religions, gods and false doctrines]; for they are virgins [They are faithful to God the Father and to their spiritual husband Jesus Christ.]. These are they which follow the Lamb whithersoever he goeth. These were redeemed from among men, being the firstfruits unto God and to the Lamb. **14:5** And in their mouth was found no guile: for they are without fault before the throne of God.

Leviticus 21:15 Neither shall he profane his seed among his people: for I the LORD do sanctify him.

The physical high priest of Aaron, if he is faithful; is sanctified as a type of the eternal spiritual High Priest of the New Covenant, Jesus Christ!

Just as no person with any blemish out of the sons of Aaron may approach to serve in the Temple; so NO person with any spiritual blemish may be changed to spirit to serve in the eternal spiritual priesthood of Melchizedek [Jesus Christ]!

Just as physical Israel was to be holy as God is holy; how much more should the New Covenant spiritual Israel be free from all sin and defilement and be holy as God is Holy?

> **Ephesians 5:25** . . . . Christ also loved the church, and gave himself for it; **5:26 That he might sanctify and cleanse it with the washing of water by the word, 5:27 That he might present it to himself a glorious church, not having spot, or wrinkle, or any such thing; but that it should be holy and without blemish.**

Leviticus 21:16 And the LORD spake unto Moses, saying, **21:17** Speak unto Aaron, saying, **Whosoever he be of thy seed in their generations that hath any blemish, let him not approach to offer the bread of his God.**

> **Jude 1:23** And others save with fear, pulling them out of the fire [with warnings and by rebuking sin]; hating even the garment spotted by the flesh [blemished with worldliness and the sins of the flesh, or any defilement of sin and all uncleanness].

All these physical blemishes are types of the spiritual blemishes and defilement's of sin and uncleanness that will keep us OUT of the resurrection to spirit. We are to be spiritually clean and free from all sin and from all uncleanness if we want to enter into the resurrection to spirit.

We must NEVER compromise with zeal to learn, understand and live by every Word of God, fully internalizing godliness as our very own nature! In that way God's nature which is contained in his Word, will become our nature; and we will become like him and at one with God our Father in heaven!

Leviticus 21:18 For whatsoever man he be that hath a blemish, he shall not approach: a blind man, or a lame, or he that hath a flat nose, or any thing superfluous, **21:19** Or a man that is brokenfooted, or brokenhanded, **21:20** Or crookbackt, or a dwarf, or that hath a blemish in his eye, or be scurvy, or scabbed, or hath his stones broken; **21:21** No man that hath a blemish of the seed of Aaron the priest shall come nigh to offer the offerings of the LORD made by fire: he hath a blemish; he shall not come nigh to offer the bread of his God.

This is a lesson that the spiritually imperfect who are blemished by sin cannot enter the presence of God, unless they are healed from their sin by sincere repentance and the application of the atoning sacrifice of the Lamb of God.

21:22 He shall eat the bread of his God, both of the most holy, and of the holy. **21:23** Only he shall not go in unto the vail, nor come nigh unto the altar, because he hath a blemish; that he profane not my sanctuaries: for I the LORD do sanctify them.

21:24 And Moses told it [taught these commands of God] unto Aaron, and to his sons, and unto all the children of Israel.

Leviticus 22

The priests of the Mosaic and the New Covenant may not approach holy things in a state of defilement. In the spiritual New Covenant application this means that no person who is defiled by sin may have a part in the resurrection to eternal life, unless they have their sin atoned for by sincere repentance and the application of the sacrifice of Christ.

Jesus Christ will only apply his sacrifice to the sincerely repentant who commit to go and sin no more.

The false teaching that Jesus is love and forgives automatically being full of mercy, so we need not be zealous to learn and live by every Word of God, is from Satan.

Leviticus 22:1 And the LORD spake unto Moses, saying, **22:2** Speak unto Aaron and to his sons, that they separate themselves from the holy things of the children of Israel, and that they profane not my holy name in those things which they hallow unto me: I am the LORD. **22:3** Say unto them, Whosoever he be of all your seed among your generations, that goeth unto the holy things, which the children of Israel hallow unto the LORD, having his uncleanness upon him, [The unrepentant sinner who is defiled by sin, is cut off from God.] that soul shall be cut off from my presence: I am the LORD.

Physical uncleanness is a type of spiritual uncleanness and the pollution of sin.

Notice here that sunset and evening are used synonymously; proving that evening truly means sunset. Yes you CAN prove that evening means literal sunset from the Bible.

22:4 What man soever of the seed of Aaron is a leper, or hath a running issue; he shall not eat of the holy things, until he be clean. And whoso toucheth any thing that is unclean by the dead, or a man whose seed goeth from him; **22:5** Or whosoever toucheth any creeping thing, whereby he may be made unclean, or a man of whom he may take uncleanness, whatsoever uncleanness he hath; **22:6** The soul which hath touched any such shall be unclean **until even**, and shall not eat of the holy things, unless he wash his flesh with water. **22:7** And **when the sun is down**, he shall be clean, and shall afterward eat of the holy things; because it is his food.

Besides the unclean dead creatures, anything that is not killed by human hand is unclean for us.

22:8 That which dieth of itself, or is torn with beasts, he shall not eat to defile himself therewith; I am the LORD.

No unrepentant sinner can enter the spiritual family of God

> **2 Corinthians 7:1** Having therefore these promises, dearly beloved, let us cleanse ourselves from all filthiness [sin] of the flesh and spirit, perfecting holiness in the fear of God.

We are to be spiritually pure from all sin and from all teachings contrary to the whole Word of God; and if we want to enter the resurrection of the just we are to be pure and clean from all compromising with any part of the whole Word of God.

> **2 Corinthians 6:14** Be ye not unequally yoked together with unbelievers: for what fellowship hath righteousness with unrighteousness? and what communion hath light with darkness? **6:15** And what concord hath Christ with Belial? or what part hath he that believeth with an infidel? **6:16** And what agreement hath the temple of God with idols? for ye are the temple of the living God; as God hath said, I will dwell in them, and walk in them; and I will be their God, and they shall be my people.

God will not dwell in any person who is unclean being polluted by sin! We must sincerely repent and then go on to SIN NO MORE, through the indwelling strength of the Spirit of God!

> **6:17** Wherefore come out from among them [We must reject all willful sinners and those who teach that God's love is a license to continue in sin and compromise with the Word of God.], and be ye

separate, saith the Lord, and touch not the unclean thing; and I will receive you.

Leviticus 22:9 They shall therefore keep mine ordinance, lest they bear sin for it, and die therefore, if they profane it: I the LORD do sanctify them.

Just as only those of the Mosaic priesthood under the Mosaic Covenant may approach the physical holy things; Only those called out to become priests of the New Covenant, and who sincerely repent and make a baptismal commitment TO GO AND SIN NO MORE: may be given the Holy Spirit.

22:10 There shall no stranger [unconverted person] eat of the holy thing: a sojourner [someone visiting a priest and eating at his table] of the priest, or an hired servant, shall not eat of the holy thing.

In the Mosaic covenant those who are purchased possessions may eat the holy things; this symbolizing that those called into the New Covenant have been bought with a great price, the life of Jesus Christ their Creator.

The children of the FAITHFUL Called Out, are sanctified by their FAITHFUL parents, **as long as they are subject to their FAITHFUL parents**.

22:11 But if the priest buy any soul with his money, he shall eat of it, and he that is born in his house: they shall eat of his meat [food].

A priest's daughter who takes a husband is to be subject to her husband and is no longer sanctified by her father since she has left his house: But, if she return to her father's family childless and is subject to her father again, she is to be sanctified by her obedience to her father, if he is a faithful priest of God.

22:12 If the priest's daughter also be married unto a stranger, she may not eat of an offering of the holy things. **22:13** But if the priest's daughter be a widow, or divorced, and have no child, and is returned unto her father's house, as in her youth, she shall eat of her father's meat: but there shall be no stranger eat thereof.

A penalty for sinning by ignorance, concerning eating holy things

22:14 And if a man eat of the holy thing unwittingly, then he shall put the fifth part thereof unto it, and shall give it unto the priest with the holy thing.

We are not to remain in sin and then continue to partake of holy things.

This applies particularly to those modern elders who draw tithes from the brethren while remaining in a sinful state; teaching false things, failing to strongly rebuke sin and failing to set an example of enthusiastic zeal to live by every Word of God.

Such men by not doing their job are stealing unearned wages from God.

22:15 And they shall not profane the holy things of the children of Israel, which they offer unto the LORD; **22:16** Or suffer them to bear the iniquity of trespass, when they eat their holy things: for I the LORD do sanctify them.

The burnt offerings of the people must be made of their free will and not extorted from them by words or pressure. This is an instruction that the money offerings of the brethren today must never be coerced.

22:17 And the LORD spake unto Moses, saying, **22:18** Speak unto Aaron, and to his sons, and unto all the children of Israel, and say unto them, Whatsoever he be of the house of Israel, or of the strangers in Israel, **that will offer his oblation for all his vows, and for all his freewill offerings, which they will offer unto the LORD for a burnt offering**; **22:19** Ye shall offer at your own will a male without blemish, of the beeves, of the sheep, or of the goats.

The animal offerings made to God must be from the free will of the person and must be without blemish for they represent the Lamb of God, Jesus Christ; who was without any blemish of sin.

22:20 But whatsoever hath a blemish, that shall ye not offer: for it shall not be acceptable for you. **22:21** And whosoever offereth a sacrifice of peace offerings unto the LORD to accomplish his vow, or a freewill offering in beeves or sheep, it shall be perfect to be accepted; there shall be no blemish therein. **22:22** Blind, or broken, or maimed, or having a wen, or scurvy, or scabbed, ye shall not offer these unto the LORD, nor make an offering by fire of them upon the altar unto the LORD.

An offering made to God must be a perfect and complete sacrifice, but a freewill offering shared with others [usually during the Festivals] could have a part missing [for example lacking a tail] as long as there are no blemishes on the remaining parts of the animal.

> **Deuteronomy 16:10** And thou shalt keep the feast of weeks unto the LORD thy God with a tribute of a freewill offering of thine hand, which thou shalt give unto [share with the Levites and eat in the presence of] the LORD thy God, according as the LORD thy God hath blessed thee: **16:11** And **thou shalt rejoice before the LORD thy God, thou, and thy son, and thy daughter, and thy manservant, and thy maidservant, and the Levite that is within thy gates, and the stranger, and the fatherless, and the widow,**

that are among you, in the place which the LORD thy God hath chosen to place his name there.

Leviticus 22:23 Either a bullock or a lamb that hath any thing **superfluous or lacking in his parts,** that mayest thou offer **for a freewill offering; but for a vow it shall not be accepted**.

Back to the rule for sacrifices to God

22:24 Ye shall not offer unto the LORD that which is bruised, or crushed, or broken, or cut; neither shall ye make any offering thereof in your land.

The various animal and unleavened bread offerings represent the work and sacrifice of Jesus Christ for the sincerely repentant, therefore the unrepentant stranger may not offer any animal or unleavened bread offering in sacrifice.

> **Exodus 12:48** And when a stranger shall sojourn with thee, and will keep the passover to the Lord, let all his males be circumcised [Spiritually in the New Covenant they must be converted in heart (Jer 31).], and then let him come near and keep it; and he shall be as one that is born in the land: for no uncircumcised [unconverted person] person shall eat thereof.

Leviticus 22:25 Neither from a stranger's [from the unrepentant] hand shall ye offer the bread of your God of any of these; because their corruption is in them, and blemishes be in them: they shall not be accepted for you.

Animals from eight days old and older may be accepted as offerings. This is because the eighth day represents a new beginning, as does circumcision on the eighth day and the Eighth Day Feast.

22:26 And the LORD spake unto Moses, saying, **22:27** When a bullock, or a sheep, or a goat, is brought forth [born], then it shall be seven days under the dam; and from the eighth day and thenceforth it shall be accepted for an offering made by fire unto the LORD.

The mother and the young may not be killed on the same day

22:28 And whether it be cow, or ewe, ye shall not kill it and her young both in one day.

The Thank Offering must be eaten on the same day it is offered

22:29 And when ye will offer a sacrifice of thanksgiving unto the LORD, offer it at your own will. **22:30** On the same day it shall be eaten up; ye shall leave none of it until the morrow: I am the LORD.

22:31 Therefore shall ye keep my commandments, and do them: I am the LORD.

Just as Mosaic Israel was to hallow God and exalt him above all else in the heavens and the earth; so we of the New Covenant called out are to do likewise; we are to exalt our most holy God above all things in heaven or on the earth to worship and obey him; learning and keeping every Word of God forever!

Because God called Israel and brought them out of bondage in Egypt they are to exalt him as most holy forever; and Because God called spiritual Israel and brought them out of bondage to Satan and sin [of which Egypt was a type] WE are to exalt him as most holy forever, and we are to be zealous to learn and to live by every Word of God without any hint of compromise, forever.

22:32 Neither shall ye profane my holy name; but I will be hallowed among the children of Israel: I am the LORD which hallow you [makes you holy], **22:33** That brought you out of the land of Egypt, to be your God: I am the LORD.

Leviticus 23

Leviticus 23:1 And the LORD spake unto Moses, saying, **23:2** Speak unto the children of Israel, and say unto them, Concerning the feasts of the LORD, which ye shall proclaim to be holy convocations, even these are my feasts.

The Weekly Sabbath is an unbroken repetitive cycle of seven days as a memorial of the physical creation and an acknowledgment of the Creator.

Those who claim that they must begin a count of seven days form the new moon break this commandment of God to maintain the seven day cycle from its beginning at creation because each month they break that cycle. If they count four seven day cycles to 28 days and then they ignore a day or two before restarting the cycle, they reject the Word of God for their own false reasoning.

23:3 Six days shall work be done: but the seventh day [Friday sunset to Saturday sunset] is the sabbath of rest, an holy convocation; ye shall do no work therein: it is the sabbath of the LORD in all your dwellings.

The Weekly Sabbath and the Annual Holy Days are Holy Time: No work of any kind is to be done on them. That means no food preparation and cooking and no buying of food or drink. All food and drink must be prepared on the previous day which is the Preparation Day for the Weekly and Annual Sabbaths.

Cooking, Buying and Work on the Weekly Sabbath

The Sabbath was instituted by our Creator on the seventh day after the completion of six days of creative activity. (Gen 2:2-3). The Sabbath was made for man (Mark 2:27) so that man could follow the example of his Creator and rest from his labors and spend time with God. It is not reasonable to think that God should need to rest, therefore he rested as an example for us.

It is lawful to do those things that God has commanded us to do on the Sabbath, since God is also the maker of the Sabbath and can therefore tell us what he wants done on HIS Sabbath. For this reason the Priests may fulfill their God commanded duties on the Sabbath.

Since the Sabbath was made for the good of man we may also do acts of compassion and mercy. We are NOT to use the "ox in the ditch" excuse to justify habitual Sabbath breaking. We are not to travel on the Sabbath to the extent that it becomes a tiring labor, nor are we to burden others by buying gas, food, drink and lodgings on God's Sabbaths. We are to use the Preparation Day to properly prepare for the Sabbath.

We are not to do any cooking on the Sabbath (Ex 16:22-24) nor are we to do our own things nor even think our own thoughts. We are to be totally dedicated to our God on his Holy Sabbath Day (Is 56 and Is 58).

We are to do no work at all on God's Holy Sabbath except for that which God himself commands and acts of mercy for the health of others; nor should we be responsible for any others doing any work on God's Sabbaths. To pay others to serve us in a restaurant is no different than to pay others to work at any other service. To pay anyone else to do what we would not do ourselves is HYPOCRISY! We are to avoid all appearance of sin.

> **Exodus 20:10** But the seventh day is the sabbath of the LORD thy God: in it thou shalt not do any work, thou, nor thy son, nor thy daughter, thy manservant, nor thy maidservant, nor thy cattle, nor thy stranger that is within thy gates:

Cooking, Buying and Work on Holy Days

> **Exodus 12:15** And in the first day there shall be an holy convocation, and in the seventh day there shall be an holy convocation to you; no manner of work shall be done in them, **save that which every man must eat, that only may be done of you.**

This statement that food may be prepared during the Feast of Unleavened Bread has at times been used to justify for preparation on all other Holy Day Annual Sabbaths. Is that a valid assumption?

This verse actually refers to the very First Feast of Unleavened Bread and its two High Holy Days, allowing food to be prepared and eaten. Some extrapolate from this verse that food may also be prepared and eaten on all subsequent Feasts of Unleavened Bread and all other High Holy Days.

It is necessary to understand that this particular scripture is a history of Israel coming out of Egypt.

After that FIRST Passover all leftovers had been burned, there was no prepared food available. As a singular act of mercy, God permitted food to be prepared and eaten on this one emergency occasion when Israel was engaged in marching out of Egypt at God's command. Nowhere else in all scripture is such a liberty [to prepare food on a Sabbath or High Day] mentioned. This is simply a record of a special allowance, an act of mercy; made for a special situation which was caused by the people obeying God and marching out of the land of Egypt.

This one time act of mercy is an exception to the rule and does NOT justify habitual breaking of the commandments for the weekly Sabbath or annual High Day Sabbaths!

Brethren, we have sinned against God and His weekly and annual Sabbaths! We must quickly repent and turn from this sin of using Holy Time for our own purposes and pleasures before we are corrected like physical Israel / Judah were historically corrected for the same sin!

Later in the first century A.D. it was well understood that the Passover was the preparation day for the first annual Sabbath of the Feast of Unleavened Bread, on which it was well understood that no work including cooking was to be done. This is made clear by the faithful who rushed to entomb Jesus BEFORE the High Day of Unleavened Bread began at sunset that evening.

> **John 19:31** The Jews therefore, **because it was the preparation,** that the bodies should not remain upon the cross on the sabbath day, (for **that sabbath day was an high day,**) besought Pilate that their legs might be broken, and that they might be taken away.

Servile Work

In Leviticus 23 the statements regarding the High Holy Days refer to commands not to do any work of any kind.

No work of any kind, including food preparation and purchasing is to be done on any weekly or annual Sabbath! Only acts of mercy for unexpected emergency health and safety issues, and anything specifically commanded by God to be done on the weekly and annual Sabbaths may be done. We are to properly prepare on the preparation day so that all might rest from physical duties and engage in spiritual pursuits, learning about God on His Holy Time

Those who follow the Rabbinic Calendar, just ask the Rabbins! They will tell you that I speak the truth on this subject. Claiming that the Rabbins must be followed in certain other matters is dishonestly cherry picking what Rabbinic teaching to follow.

Of course we know the answer to that; most folks will follow whatever is personally convenient and fits in with their preconceived beliefs, no matter how confused and inconsistent or how wrong they are! M ost would never think of living by every Word of God!

The Festivals, Holy Convocations and Appointed Times

God's commanded observances are covered intensively in our festival categories on the right hand sidebar. I will make a few comments here. To cover each High Day properly requires a post in itself and it would be wise to go to the three festivals categories at the sidebar for more.

The early harvest festivals of the called out from the Egypt; picture the spiritually called out from bondage to sin.

Leviticus 23:4 These are the feasts of the LORD, even holy convocations, which ye shall proclaim in their seasons.

Passover

Passover is on the 14th day and is NOT on the 15th day as some suppose. We observe Passover as the sun sets beginning the fourteenth day because that was the time of its observance in Egypt just BEFORE midnight when the Destroyer came through the land; and because we follow the example of Jesus Christ.

23:5 In the fourteenth day of the first month at even [beginning the 14th day, because the destroyer passed over the land at midnight n the 14th day] is the LORD's passover.

After sunset beginning the 15th day, Israel marched out of Egypt

The Feast of Unleavened Bread

This Feast pictures God calling out a few people as a kind of early spring harvest for seven thousand years as represented by the seven days of the Feast, with a resurrection at the end of the 6th day [at the end of 6,000 years]; followed by a High Day on the final seventh day, picturing the 7th, one thousand year period, during which the early spring harvest is expanded to include all people then living.

Eating the unleavened bread made with pure whole grain, pure olive oil, water and salt every day of this Feast, pictures the called out early harvest internalizing the very nature of God.

23:6 And on the fifteenth day of the same month is the feast of unleavened bread unto the LORD: seven days ye must eat unleavened bread.

23:7 In the first day ye shall have an holy convocation: ye shall do no servile work therein.

23:8 But ye shall offer an offering made by fire unto the LORD seven days: in the seventh day is an holy convocation: ye shall do no servile work therein.

The Wave Offering

23:9 And the LORD spake unto Moses, saying, **23:10** Speak unto the children of Israel, and say unto them, When ye be come into the land which I give unto you, and shall reap the harvest thereof, then ye shall bring a sheaf of the firstfruits of your harvest unto the priest: **23:11**

And he shall wave the sheaf before the LORD, to be accepted for you: on the morrow after the sabbath [a Sunday] the priest shall wave it.

This pictures the resurrection of Jesus Christ at the time the sheaf was cut, immediately after the sun set ending the Sabbath [Saturday]; and the ascension of the resurrected Christ to God the Father in heaven the next morning [the first of the harvest from the flesh] at the same time that the Wave Sheaf was lifted up after the Sunday Morning Daily Sacrifice.

23:12 And ye shall offer that day when ye wave the sheaf an he lamb without blemish of the first year for a burnt offering unto the LORD. **23:13** And the meat offering thereof shall be two tenth deals of fine flour mingled with oil, an offering made by fire unto the LORD for a sweet savour: and the drink offering thereof shall be of wine, the fourth part of an hin. **23:14** And ye shall eat neither bread, nor parched corn, nor green ears, until the selfsame day that ye have brought an offering unto your God: it shall be a statute for ever throughout your generations in all your dwellings.

The count to Pentecost, which is a count of seven weekly Sabbaths from the Sunday of the Wave Offering; and the day AFTER the seventh Sabbath [a Sunday] is the Feast of First Fruits often called Pentecost.

23:15 And ye shall count unto you from the morrow after the sabbath, from the day that ye brought the sheaf of the wave offering; seven sabbaths shall be complete: **23:16** Even unto the morrow after the seventh sabbath shall ye number fifty days; and ye shall offer a new meat offering unto the LORD.

The Feast of Pentecost

On Pentecost two loaves are offered picturing INCREASE; they are to be made with leaven picturing sin, which is in turn covered by a sin offering.

This offering does not picture the resurrection of the first fruits who have been called to God over the past 6,000 years.

This offering and the Feast of Pentecost pictures;

1. The formal establishment of the New Covenant, which happened on Pentecost in the first century as described in the book of Acts, and
2. It pictures the expansion of the first fruits to all of humanity then living with the pouring out of God's Spirit on all flesh (Joel 2:28) on a future Pentecost to begin and fulfill the remaining seventh day [the 7th one thousand year] of the Spring Harvest of First Fruits called out since Abel.

The Feast of Unleavened Bread is not just six days long, it is seven days long. Yes, there is a resurrection to spirit at the end of the sixth day [at the end of 6,000 years], but the remainder of the first fruits harvest continues through the remaining 7th one thousand year millennium.

1. Pentecost pictures the formal beginning of the New Covenant in the first century, and
2. The establishment of the kingdom of God over all the earth after Messiah the Christ comes and
3. The New Covenant being expanded to include all flesh after Christ comes.

23:17 Ye shall bring out of your habitations two wave loaves of two tenth deals; they shall be of fine flour; they shall be baken with leaven; they are the firstfruits unto the LORD.

23:18 And ye shall offer with the bread seven lambs without blemish of the first year, and one young bullock, and two rams: they shall be for a burnt offering unto the LORD, with their meat offering, and their drink offerings, even an offering made by fire, of sweet savour unto the LORD.

23:19 Then ye shall sacrifice **one kid of the goats for a sin offering** [to cover sin as represented by the leaven], and two lambs of the first year for a sacrifice of peace offerings.

23:20 And the priest shall wave them with the bread of the firstfruits for a wave offering before the LORD, with the two lambs: they shall be holy to the LORD for the priest.

On the Feast of First Fruits [Pentecost] no work of any kind may be done except that which is specifically commanded by God

23:21 And ye shall proclaim on the selfsame day, that it may be an holy convocation unto you: ye shall do no servile [no work of any kind] work therein: it shall be a statute for ever in all your dwellings throughout your generations.

The law of mercy called gleaning is given

It is placed here because besides being an act of mercy for the physically poor, this was an allegory that the first fruits are a small gleaning from the earth, and the main harvest of humanity is yet to come.

23:22 And when ye reap the harvest of your land, thou shalt not make clean riddance of the corners of thy field when thou reapest, neither shalt thou gather any gleaning of thy harvest: thou shalt leave them unto the poor, and to the stranger: I am the LORD your God.

The Fall Festivals

The physical fall harvest Festivals picture the main spiritual harvest of humanity

The Feast of Trumpets

On the first day of the seventh month the whole of humanity is called to rejoice before God concerning the final victory over Satan. See the Fall Festivals category on the right hand sidebar.

23:23 And the LORD spake unto Moses, saying, **23:24** Speak unto the children of Israel, saying, In the seventh month, in the first day of the month, shall ye have a sabbath, a memorial of blowing of trumpets, an holy convocation. **23:25** Ye shall do no servile work therein: but ye shall offer an offering made by fire unto the LORD.

The Day of Atonement

The fast of Atonement pictures the removal of Satan forever and sincere repentance with Christ's atoning sacrifice applied to all peoples.

23:26 And the LORD spake unto Moses, saying, **23:27** Also on the tenth day of this seventh month there shall be a day of atonement: it shall be an holy convocation unto you; and ye shall afflict your souls [a total fast of repentance] , and offer an offering made by fire unto the LORD. **23:28** And ye shall do no work in that same day: for it is a day of atonement, to make an atonement for you before the LORD your God.

23:29 For whatsoever soul it be that shall not be afflicted in that same day, he shall be cut off from among his people. **23:30** And whatsoever soul it be that doeth any work in that same day, the same soul will I destroy from among his people. **23:31** Ye shall do no manner of work: it shall be a statute for ever throughout your generations in all your dwellings. **23:32** It shall be unto you a sabbath of rest, and ye shall afflict your souls: in the ninth day of the month at even, from even unto even, shall ye celebrate your sabbath.

The final end of Satan and the call to the fasting of sincere repentance then leads to the bringing in of the main harvest of humanity during the Feast of Tabernacles.

The Feast of Tabernacles

23:33 And the LORD spake unto Moses, saying, **23:34** Speak unto the children of Israel, saying, The fifteenth day of this seventh month shall be the feast of tabernacles for seven days unto the LORD. **3:35** On the first day shall be an holy convocation: ye shall do no servile work therein.

23:36 Seven days ye shall offer an offering made by fire unto the LORD: on the eighth day shall be an holy convocation unto you; and ye shall offer an offering made by fire unto the LORD: it is a solemn assembly; and ye shall do no servile work therein.

23:37 These are the feasts of the LORD, which ye shall proclaim to be holy convocations, to offer an offering made by fire unto the LORD, a burnt offering, and a meat offering, a sacrifice, and drink offerings, every thing upon his day: **23:38** Beside the sabbaths of the LORD, and beside your gifts, and beside all your vows, and beside all your freewill offerings, which ye give unto the LORD.

Some commands regarding how we are to celebrate the Feast of Tabernacles.

The Feast of the Eighth Day

23:39 Also in the fifteenth day of the seventh month, when ye have gathered in the fruit of the land, ye shall keep a feast unto the LORD seven days: on the first day shall be a sabbath, and on the eighth day shall be a sabbath.

Instructions for the Feast of Tabernacles

We must cut small branches of good trees and rejoice with them for seven days. This is covered in detail in the Fall Festivals category. Nothing is said about making booths from the branches which is an assumption of men.

23:40 And ye shall take you on the first day the boughs of goodly trees, branches of palm trees, and the boughs of thick trees, and willows of the brook; and ye shall rejoice before the LORD your God seven days. **23:41** And ye shall keep it a feast unto the LORD seven days in the year.

The cutting of branches on the first day and rejoicing with them for seven days is to be done forever, yet this commandment is NOT obeyed by most today: Therefore most of today's Spiritual Ekklesia have never kept the Feast of Tabernacles in the manner which God has commanded!

Each year they go out to keep God's Feasts by their own ways on their own wrong [apostate Rabbinic Calendar] dates, contrary to the Word of God; and then they think that they are pleasing God! How very strange! To please God we must do what God commands!

. . . It shall be a statute for ever in your generations: ye shall celebrate it in the seventh month.

Now comes a separate command to dwell in booths, which are actually tabernacles or tents or any temporary structure, so that we may learn that being called out of this world we have become foreigners and strangers seeking a better world of righteousness.

23:42 Ye shall dwell in booths [tents and temporary structures like Israel had in the wilderness of Sinai] seven days; all that are Israelites born [including spiritual Israelites] shall dwell in booths: **23:43** That your generations may know that I made **the children of Israel to dwell in booths, when I brought them out of the land of Egypt**: I am the LORD your God.

23:44 And Moses declared unto the children of Israel the feasts of the LORD.

Leviticus 24

The command to make the seven branched lamp stand of the Menorah [think of the seven churches of Revelation 2-3] which would burn pure olive oil to light the court of the tabernacle/temple.

The pure olive oil represents the Holy Spirit, the presence and use of which makes the faithful; the light of the world. Today, by vexing God's Spirit in turning away from any zeal to learn and live by every Word of God, the Ekklesia are no longer the example of godliness and light to the world that we should be.

Instead we lean to our own ways, quenching the light of God's Spirit by rejecting any zeal to learn and grow and keep the whole Word of God. Our light of zeal for God is flickering and going out, and we know it not; because we are intent on zeal for our leaders and organizations instead of on zeal to live by every Word of God.

Leviticus 24:1 And the LORD spake unto Moses, saying, **24:2** Command the children of Israel, that they bring unto **thee pure oil olive beaten for the light, to cause the lamps to burn continually**.

24:3 Without the vail [outside the most holy place; in the priests courtyard of the tabernacle/temple] of the testimony, in the tabernacle of the congregation, shall Aaron order it from the evening unto the morning before the LORD continually: it shall be a statute for ever in your generations.

This is a symbolic promise that after the resurrection to godly eternal life the light of God will never go out in his true people

> **Matthew 16:18** And I say also unto thee, That thou art Peter, and upon this rock [Jesus Christ] I will build my church; and the **gates of hell** shall not prevail against it.

Leviticus 24:4 He shall order the lamps upon the pure candlestick [oil burning lamp stand] before the LORD continually.

The Bread of Presence pictures the presence of Jesus Christ as the Bread of Life for the Called Out of physical Israel; as an instructional allegory of the faithful internalizing the presence and nature of God in spiritual New Covenant Israel.

24:5 And thou shalt take fine flour, and bake twelve cakes thereof: two tenth deals shall be in one cake. **24:6** And thou shalt set them in two rows, six on a row, upon the pure table before the LORD.

Frankincense is to be placed on each piece, picturing the pleasant perfume of the Word of God

24:7 And thou shalt put pure frankincense upon each row, that it may be on the bread for a memorial [of the pleasant perfume of godliness], even an offering made by fire unto the LORD.

The Bread of Presence symbolizing the presence of the Husband and Creator of Israel was to be placed on the holy table each weekly Sabbath day. Just as Jesus Christ the Creator spent the first Sabbath with Adam, so he desires to be among his people on every Sabbath day.

24:8 Every sabbath he shall set it in order before the LORD continually, being taken from the children of Israel by an everlasting covenant.

The Bread of Presence is to be eaten only by the priests as a thing most holy to God, because the physical priests are a type of the spiritual priesthood of Melchizedek [Jesus Christ]. See our articles on the Priesthood and Ministry.

24:9 And it shall be Aaron's and his sons'; and they shall eat it in the holy place: for it is most holy unto him of the offerings of the LORD made by fire [baked in the fire] by a perpetual statute.

The law concerning all those who blaspheme God

Compromising with any part of the Word of God and leading the brethren away from any zeal for the practical application of the Word of God is an act of blasphemy.

24:10 And the son of an Israelitish woman, whose father was an Egyptian, went out among the children of Israel: and this son of the Israelitish woman and a man of Israel strove together in the camp; **24:11** And the Israelitish woman's son blasphemed the name of the Lord, and cursed. And they brought him unto Moses: (and his mother's name was Shelomith, the daughter of Dibri, of the tribe of Dan:) **24:12** And they put him in ward, that the mind of the LORD might be shewed them.

24:13 And the LORD spake unto Moses, saying, **24:14** Bring forth him that hath cursed without the camp; and let all that heard him lay their hands upon his head, and let all the congregation stone him.

Because many have followed their leaders away from any zeal for the Word of God, equating zeal for a man or for corporate churches with zeal for God is the sin of idolatry; those who do this will not be held guiltless before God, they will most certainly be corrected by our Mighty One.

24:15 And thou shalt speak unto the children of Israel, saying, Whosoever curseth his God shall bear his sin. **24:16** And he that blasphemeth the name of the LORD, he shall surely be put to death, and all the congregation shall certainly stone him: as well the stranger, as he that is born in the land, when he blasphemeth the name of the Lord, shall be put to death.

The murderer of innocent blood must surely be put to death

This applies to the physical murderer and also to the spiritual murderer who seeks to steal the Father's flock to turn the brethren away from their zeal for the Word of God, to follow after themselves. Such men, in leading people to equate loyalty to themselves as loyalty to God; are spiritual murderers leading people away from the way of life into the broad highway to destruction. They will be sternly corrected and if they will not sincerely repent they will surely be destroyed.

24:17 And he that killeth any man shall surely be put to death.

To wilfully steal an animal or to kill an animal not belonging to us is theft, and even if the killing was accidental the killer must restore the value to the owner.

24:18 And he that killeth a beast shall make it good; beast for beast.

The phrase below refers to equity in correction. Some would call this very harsh, yet in today's libertarian world there is vastly more crime than in ancient times. The moderation of the penalty to a fine or imprisonment opens the way for a rich man to simply pay a fine for his outrages.

24:19 And if a man cause a blemish in his neighbour; as he hath done, so shall it be done to him; **24:20** Breach for breach, eye for eye, tooth for tooth: as he hath caused a blemish in a man, so shall it be done to him again.

This has its spiritual application. God is just and demands fairness, equity and justice, he is not a respecter of persons and neither should we be.

24:21 And he that killeth a beast, he shall restore it: and he that killeth a man, he shall be put to death.

There is to be ONE foundational law for every person in our assemblies; THE LAW OF GOD. Anyone who teaches us to diminish our zeal for the Word of God, is in rebellion against God and is to be rejected from our assemblies.

When wickedness comes to a climax as it has in our time; where the vast majority laugh at and condemn zeal to live by every Word of God and follow idols of men rather than zealously testing every word of man by the Word of God [rejecting men's words which are not consistent with the Word of God]: Then we are to leave off assembling with such people in order to remain faithfully steadfast in passionate zeal for learning and living by every Word of God.

24:22 Ye shall have one manner of law, as well for the stranger, as for one of your own country: for I am the LORD your God.

24:23 And Moses spake to the children of Israel, that they should bring forth him that had cursed out of the camp, and stone him with stones. And the children of Israel did as the LORD commanded Moses.

Leviticus 25

The Land Sabbath

Leviticus 25:1 And the LORD spake unto Moses in mount Sinai, saying, **25:2** Speak unto the children of Israel, and say unto them, When ye come into the land which I give you, then shall the land keep a sabbath unto the LORD.

The land is to have a complete rest from cultivation and from commercial reaping

25:3 Six years thou shalt sow thy field, and six years thou shalt prune thy vineyard, and gather in the fruit thereof; **25:4** But in the seventh year shall be a sabbath of rest unto the land, a sabbath for the LORD: thou shalt neither sow thy field, nor prune thy vineyard. **25:5** That which groweth of its own accord of thy harvest thou shalt not reap, neither gather the grapes of thy vine undressed: for it is a year of rest unto the land.

This rest of the land is to be a complete one year Sabbath of rest for those who till or use the land; therefore this seventh year land Sabbath is a sabbatical year for BOTH the land and the people.

25:6 And the sabbath of the land shall be meat [one may eat but not harvest to take away or sell] for you; for thee, and for thy servant, and for thy maid, and for thy hired servant, and for thy stranger that sojourneth with thee.

That which grows of itself may be eaten by people and animals, but is not to be harvested for commercial sale.

It has been discovered that most insect pests increase in cycles and that a land rest in the seventh year has the effect of denying food to and thereby destroying many agricultural pests by breaking their cycles of increase.

Like the seventh day Sabbath, the seventh year is to be dedicated to spiritual pursuits.

25:7 And for thy cattle, and for the beast that are in thy land, shall all the increase thereof be meat.

The Jubilee Year

25:8 And thou shalt number seven sabbaths of years unto thee, seven times seven years; and the space of the seven sabbaths of years shall be unto thee forty and nine years.

The forty ninth year is a land Sabbath and the fiftieth year is the Jubilee. The Jubilee Year begins on the Day of Atonement late in the 49th year, and ends on the Day of Atonement in the fiftieth year.

The Jubilee year uses an Atonement to Atonement year, as opposed to the Spring to Spring year of the early harvest called out. This fall to fall year tells us that this Jubilee of years is the main fall harvest counterpart of the Jubilee of days of the spring, called Pentecost.

25:9 Then shalt thou cause the trumpet of the jubile to sound on the tenth day of the seventh month, **in the day of atonement** shall ye make the trumpet sound throughout all your land.

The fiftieth year is Holy to God, and is to be kept as Holy by us. This Jubilee Year is the latter main harvest counterpart of Pentecost, the early harvest of the called out.

Just as Pentecost represents the restoration of Godliness and the establishment of the New Covenant over all the earth for the early spring harvest; the fast of Atonement pictures the repentance of the main harvest of humanity and the Jubilee represents the restoration of all the ways of God over all the earth for the main fall harvest.

Please see: Sabbatical Years and Jubilee Years

Atonement and the Jubilee of years picture the MAIN HARVEST; they represent LIBERTY from the bondage of sin and freedom for every person from all forms of bondage as they repent and are made free through sincere repentance and the application of the sacrifice of the Lamb of God!

25:10 And ye shall hallow the fiftieth year, and **proclaim liberty throughout all the land unto all the inhabitants thereof: it shall be a jubile unto you; and ye shall return every man unto his possession, and ye shall return every man unto his family.**

Like the Sabbath, the Jubilee Year is to be a time of full freedom from all types of physical bondage as an allegorical type of freedom from all bondage to sin and Satan the god-king of this world.

25:11 A jubile shall that fiftieth year be unto you: ye shall not sow, neither reap that which groweth of itself in it, nor gather the grapes in it of thy vine undressed. **25:12** For it is the jubile; it shall be holy unto you: ye shall eat the increase thereof out of the field. **25:13** In the year of this jubile ye shall return every man unto his possession.

25:14 And if thou sell ought unto thy neighbour, or buyest ought of thy neighbour's hand, ye shall not oppress one another: **25:15** According to the number of years after the jubile thou shalt buy of thy neighbour, and according unto the number of years of the fruits he shall sell unto thee: **25:16** According to the multitude of years thou shalt increase the price thereof, and according to the fewness of years thou shalt diminish the price of it: for according to the number of the years of the fruits doth he sell unto thee.

25:17 Ye shall not therefore oppress one another; but thou shalt fear thy God: for I am the LORD your God. **25:18** Wherefore ye shall do my statutes, and keep my judgments, and do them; and ye shall dwell in the land in safety.

It is for the oppressing of the brethren and for the lack of zeal to apply the Word of God in our lives, that we will soon be cast into the coming great correction.

Blessings on the land in the Mosaic Covenant were in direct proportion to the degree of zeal in obedience to God. In the same way, the blessings of spiritual growth and entry into the Promised Land of eternal life in the New Covenant are directly proportionate to our zealous learning and living by every Word of God.

25:19 And the land shall yield her fruit, and ye shall eat your fill, and dwell therein in safety.

God will provide only as we believe and obey him

25:20 And if ye shall say, What shall we eat the seventh year? behold, we shall not sow, nor gather in our increase:

God will give increase on the harvest of the sixth year to last over the seventh year Land Sabbath until the harvest of the eighth year.

25:21 Then I will command my blessing upon you in the sixth year, and it shall bring forth fruit for three years. **25:22** And ye shall sow the eighth year, and eat yet of old fruit [of the sixth year] until [up to] the ninth year; until her fruits come [in the harvest at the end of the eighth year] in ye shall eat of the old store.

God promises that the harvest of the 48th year will be sufficient for eating on the 49th year Land Sabbath and will also last through the 50th year Jubilee year.

The possessions of land in the physical promised land belonged to each family forever. They could only sell in the sense of renting out the land until the Jubilee Year. This pictured an eternal possession for the faithful overcomers in the spiritual Promised Land of eternal life.

25:23 The land shall not be sold for ever: for the land is mine, for ye are strangers and sojourners with me.

Any farmland "sold" could be bought back by the seller or his kin at any time they chose, or it would revert back to the original possessor automatically on the Jubilee.

25:24 And in all the land of your possession ye shall grant a redemption for the land. **25:25** If thy brother be waxen poor, and hath sold away some of his possession, and if any of his kin come to redeem it, then shall he redeem that which his brother sold.

Anyone can buy back or redeem his farmland at a fair price based on the number of years remaining until the Jubilee.

25:26 And if the man have none [A man may buy back his land based on a fair price and the number of years remaining until the Jubilee of year.] to redeem it, and himself be able to redeem it; **25:27** Then let him count the years of the sale thereof, and restore the overplus unto the man to whom he sold it; that he may return unto his possession.

25:28 But if he be not able to restore it to him, then that which is sold shall remain in the hand of him that hath bought it **until the year of jubile:** and in the jubile it shall go out, and he shall return unto his possession.

Houses in fortified [major cities, as opposed to agricultural villages] may be redeemed within one year of sale; and if not redeemed within one year they will become the permanent property of the buyer until he sells it.

25:29 And if a man sell a dwelling house in a walled city, then he may redeem it within a whole year after it is sold; within a full year may he redeem it. **25:30** And if it be not redeemed within the space of a full year, then the house that is in the walled city shall be established for ever to him that bought it throughout his generations: it shall not go out in the jubile.

Only agricultural land and property in agricultural villages as well as all Levitical property, will return to the original owners at the Jubilee.

25:31 But the houses of the villages which have no wall round about them shall be counted as the fields of the country: they may be redeemed, and they shall go out in the jubile.

25:32 Notwithstanding the cities of the Levites, and the houses of the cities of their possession, may the Levites redeem at any time. **25:33** And if a man purchase of the Levites, then the house that was sold, and the city of his possession, shall go out [return to its Levitical owner] in the year of jubile: for the houses of the cities of the Levites are their possession among the children of Israel.

The Levites may not sell their fields

25:34 But the field of the suburbs of their cities may not be sold; for it is their perpetual possession.

We are to always help out the poor among us; not the lazy but those that are in genuine need.

25:35 And if thy brother be waxen poor, and fallen in decay with thee; then thou shalt relieve him: yea, though he be a stranger, or a sojourner; that he may live with thee.

We are forbidden to change interest or charge a fee for helping out a person in need of physical necessities. This is for those in genuine physical need and is not in reference to business loans intended to create a personal profit. In that case the provider of the capital has a right to benefit from the business gain created by his loan.

25:36 Take thou no usury of him, or increase: but fear thy God; that thy brother may live with thee. **25:37** Thou shalt not give him thy money upon usury, nor lend him thy victuals for increase.

25:38 I am the LORD your God, which brought you forth out of the land of Egypt, to give you the land of Canaan, and to be your God.

If a person becomes your servant due to inability to pay his debts he is to be treated with respect and given an allowance for his daily needs. Regardless of what he owes he shall become free when the trumpet of the Jubilee sounds on the fast of Atonement; representing that all humanity will become free from bondage to Satan when Satan is judged and removed forever on the Fast of Atonement.

25:39 And if thy brother that dwelleth by thee be waxen poor, and be sold unto thee; thou shalt not compel him to serve as a bondservant: **25:40** But as an hired servant, and as a sojourner, he shall be with thee, and shall serve thee unto the year of jubile. **25:41** And then shall he depart from thee, both he and his children with him, and shall return unto his own family, and unto the possession of his fathers shall he return.

All Mosaic Israel were to be the true servants of God who were redeemed and called out of Egypt by their Deliverer: Typifying that all the faithful spiritually called out are called out of bondage to sin in the spiritual Egypt of this world and have been redeemed and our freedom purchased by the price of the life of our Creator, Jesus Christ.

The called out of spiritual Egypt are not to be ruled over with rigor as bondmen and slaves; as is often done by leaders in today's Ekklesia. The elders are to set a godly example and to lead and teach godliness, never taking advantage of, nor bullying, nor seeking personal advantage, and never making merchandise of the free people of Almighty God.

Elders and leaders are to focus all brethren on gaining as much zeal as they can to live by every Word of God and are never to lead anyone to blindly and unquestioningly follow any man or organization!

The flock of God is not our flock! It has been redeemed by God at a great price; leaders and elders are merely caretakers who must give an account for their treatment of the flock of God.

25:42 For they are my servants, which I brought forth out of the land of Egypt: they shall not be sold as bondmen. 25:43 Thou shalt not rule over him with rigour; but shalt fear thy God.

Under the Mosaic Covenant those in the Covenant may not buy and sell their own Covenant people like merchandise [although they can be made bond servants for debts, they cannot be sold to another party]; but they may sell the outsiders [unconverted]. This reflects that the Covenant people already belong to their Deliverer while the others are still in bondage to Satan and sin.

Elders and leaders in the Spiritual Ekklesia are never to rule with rigor like worldly leaders do. they must understand that we are ALL called out to become kings and priests of Jesus Christ and that we ALL belong to him, having been bought with a great price.

25:44 Both thy bondmen, and thy bondmaids, which thou shalt have, shall be of the heathen that are round about you; of them shall ye buy bondmen and bondmaids. **25:45** Moreover of the children of the strangers that do sojourn among you, of them shall ye buy, and of their families that are with you, which they begat in your land: and they shall be your possession. **25:46** And ye shall take them as an inheritance for your children after you, to inherit them for a possession; they shall be your bondmen for ever: but **over your brethren the children of Israel, ye shall not rule one over another with rigour.**

25:47 And if a sojourner or stranger wax rich by thee, and thy brother that dwelleth by him wax poor, and sell himself unto the stranger or sojourner by thee, or to the stock of the stranger's family: **25:48** After that he is sold he may be redeemed again; one of his brethren may redeem him: **25:49** Either his uncle, or his uncle's son, may redeem him, or any that is nigh of kin unto him of his family may redeem him; or if he be able, he may redeem himself.

The redemption price is to be based on the value of the length of service remaining until the Jubilee.

25:50 And he shall reckon with him that bought him from the year that he was sold to him unto the year of jubile: and the price of his sale shall be according unto the number of years, according to the time of an hired servant shall it be with him.

25:51 If there be yet many years behind, according unto them he shall give again the price of his redemption out of the money that he was bought for. **25:52** And if there remain but few years unto the year of jubile, then he shall count with him, and according unto his years shall he give him again the price of his redemption.

25:53 And as a yearly hired servant shall he be with him: and the other [his master] **shall not rule with rigour over him in thy sight. 25:54** And if he be not redeemed in these years, **then he shall go out in the year of jubile, both he, and his children with him.**

The children of physical Israel were called out of bondage in Egypt as an allegory of spiritual Israel being redeemed by Jesus Christ and called out of bondage to Satan and sin.

Brethren, the spiritually called out have been called to serve God the Father and Jesus Christ, and to learn and to live by every Word of God! We are NOT to blindly slavishly follow the words of men and corporate church entities without questioning them.

> **1 Thessalonians 5:21** Prove all things; hold fast that which is good [by the holy scriptures]. **5:22** Abstain from all appearance of evil.

Leviticus 25:55 For unto me the children of [both physical and spiritual] Israel are servants; they are my servants whom I brought forth out of the land of Egypt: I am the LORD your God.

Leviticus 26

Physical idols of stone are types of the idols that we have made of men and organizations. Anything that we obey instead of God's Word is our idol: Anyone that we exalt as equal to or above God is our idol.

It is a gross sin to exalt the messenger above the God who sent the message.

Leviticus 26:1 Ye shall make you no idols nor graven image, neither rear you up a standing image, neither shall ye set up any image of stone in your land, to bow down unto it: for I am the LORD your God.

Today one of our greatest sins is to declare the Sabbath holy and then by our actions pollute it and fail to keep it holy. We buy on God's Sabbaths paying others to serve us on the Sabbath and High Days, thereby holding the Word of God [represented by the altar, the table of the Lord] in contempt.

26:2 Ye shall keep my sabbaths, and reverence my sanctuary: I am the LORD.

If we were zealous to diligently learn and live by every Word of God, we would be blessed with spiritual growth and understanding.

26:3 If ye walk in my statutes, and keep my commandments, and do them; **26:4** Then I will give you rain in due season, and the land shall yield her increase, and the trees of the field shall yield their fruit. **26:5** And your threshing shall reach unto the vintage, and the vintage shall reach unto the sowing time: and ye shall eat your bread to the full, and dwell in your land safely.

Just as Mosaic Israel would be blessed for learning and keeping the whole Word of God, so spiritual Israel would be showered with spiritual blessings of increase in understanding and wisdom and by being made fit for the resurrection of the first fruits to spirit; if we would only live by every Word of God.

The spiritually faithful need never fear, because the promise of Christ of the resurrection to spirit for the zealously faithful is SURE.

26:6 And I will give peace in the land, and ye shall lie down, and none shall make you afraid: and I will rid evil beasts out of the land, neither shall the sword go through your land.

In the resurrection to spirit the faithful will be made rulers and teachers in all the earth and all enemies shall flee before them to sincere repentance or total destruction.

26:7 And ye shall chase your enemies, and they shall fall before you by the sword. **26:8** And five of you shall chase an hundred, and an hundred of you shall put ten thousand to flight: and your enemies shall fall before you by the sword.

The Mosaic Covenant is an instructional allegory of the New Covenant

The Mosaic Covenant would be maintained by the zeal of the people to obey and follow their Husband. The New Covenant is maintained by the faithful zeal of the called out to learn and passionately love their Husband to live by every Word of God.

26:9 For I will have respect unto you, and make you fruitful, and multiply you, and establish my covenant with you.

Just as a faithful Mosaic Israel would have to throw out the old grain to make room for the new harvest for very abundance of their physical harvest; faithful spiritual Israel will be resurrected to spirit to be laborers to bring in the vast abundance of the main harvest of humanity. What an honor to be called out to become the laborers of God to bring multitudes into his family!

26:10 And ye shall eat old store, and bring forth the old because of the new.

Just as the God who later gave up his godhood to become flesh as Jesus Christ would dwell in the physical nation of Mosaic Israel if they remained faithful to live by every Word of God: Jesus Christ will dwell in the faithful steadfast of the New Covenant who live by every Word of God.

Jesus Christ abhors the wicked deeds of evil doers. If we wash away our wickedness through sincere repentance and a dedicated zeal to internalize the whole Word and nature of God, and go forward to sin no more; the abhorrent sins that separate us from God our Father would be covered by the application of the sacrifice of Christ.

If we continue in sin and fail to be zealous to live by every Word of God after we are reconciled to God the Father; then our abhorrent sins remain in us and keep us separated from God.

26:11 And I set my tabernacle among you: and my soul shall not abhor you. **26:12** And I will walk among you, and will be your God, and ye shall be my people.

Jesus Christ is the Mighty One who has delivered us from bondage to Satan and sin; why would we choose to continue in that bondage? Let us put off the old man of sin and become a new person in Jesus Christ.

26:13 I am the LORD your God, which brought you forth out of the land of Egypt, that ye should not be their bondmen; and I have broken the bands of your yoke, and made you go upright.

If we turn away from any zeal to learn and zealously keep the whole Word of God, we will face the same curses [including on a spiritual level] of the rebellious of Mosaic Israel.

26:14 But if ye will not hearken unto me, and will not do all these commandments; **26:15** And if ye shall despise my statutes, or if your soul abhor my judgments, so that ye will not do all my commandments, but that ye break my covenant:

When the Ekklesia preach the "Gospel" today, it is not the true gospel but their own ways; and they are sowing that seed in vain because there will be no godly increase because those who respond are accepting the false ways being taught and not the truth of the whole Word of God.

By compromising with the Word of God and by doing what we want instead of doing what God commands, we have turned aside from any zeal for the Word of God to follow our own vain imaginations.

26:16 I also will do this unto you; I will even appoint over you terror, consumption, and the burning ague, that shall consume the eyes, and cause sorrow of heart: and ye shall sow your seed in vain, for your enemies shall eat it.

We will surely be cast into the strong correction of great tribulation if we exalt men, the false traditions of men and organizational entities above any zeal to live by every Word of God.

26:17 And I will set my face against you, and ye shall be slain before your enemies: they that hate you shall reign over you; and ye shall flee when none pursueth you. **26:18** And if ye will not yet for all this hearken unto me, then I will punish you seven times more for your sins.

We speak of the breaking of the pride of national power, not considering that the pride of the power of today's Spiritual Ekklesia is being broken because of our idolatry of men and our many sins.

We are blind to the meaning of the splitting and splitting of congregations and the many trials of today's Ekklesia; and we are blind to the correction that is coming upon us because of our rejection of the warnings and our refusal to turn to our Great God in sincere repentance.

26:19 And I will break the pride of your power; and I will make your heaven as iron, and your earth as brass: **26:20** And your strength shall be spent in vain: for your land shall not yield her increase, neither shall the trees of the land yield their fruits.

We are at the point where we have received a solid and comprehensive warning and most still refuse to sincerely repent, being full of pride in our own ways. Therefore we are about to be spewed out by Jesus Christ (Rev 3:16), into the severe correction of great tribulation.

26:21 And **if ye walk contrary unto me, and will not hearken unto me; I will bring seven times more plagues upon you according to your sins**.

The literal wild beasts would include smaller pests like rodents as well as insects like mosquitoes, biting flies and hornets; larger wild creatures could include things like packs of wild starving dogs roaming the streets. In spiritual terms the "wild beasts" are types of the unconverted attacking as they are motivated by the fury of Satan.

26:22 I will also send wild beasts among you, which shall rob you of your children, and destroy your cattle, and make you few in number; and your high ways shall be desolate.

If we do not sincerely repent, Jesus Christ will be against us because we have turned away from him; and he shall cast us into great tribulation for our merciful correction in the hope that he might save us spiritually by afflicting our flesh.

26:23 And if ye will not be reformed by me by these things, but will walk contrary unto me; **26:24** Then will I also walk contrary unto you, and will punish you yet seven times for your sins.

The sword of the enemy will fall on both physical and spiritual Israel because of our departure from our baptismal Marriage Covenant with Jesus Christ, to learn and live by every Word of God.

26:25 And I will bring a sword upon you, that shall avenge the quarrel of my covenant: and when ye are gathered together within your cities, I will send the pestilence among you; and ye shall be delivered into the hand of the enemy.

We will be afflicted by the thirst of drought, famine and lack of food.

26:26 And when I have broken the staff of your bread, ten women shall bake your bread in one oven, and they shall deliver you your bread again by weight [food will be rationed]: and ye shall eat, and not be satisfied. **26:27** And if ye will not for all this hearken unto me, but walk contrary unto me; **26:28** Then I will walk contrary unto you also in fury; and I, even I, will chastise you seven times for your sins.

Some will turn to eating human flesh and possibly even the flesh of their own beloved families out of the madness of intense hunger.

26:29 And ye shall eat the flesh of your sons, and the flesh of your daughters shall ye eat.

Jesus Christ is determined to destroy all our idols, and that includes our wealth, our idols of men and corporate churches and all those things that we pursue instead of being zealous for our God. The term idols includes all things that come between God and his people and all things that we have exalted above the Word of God.

Jesus Christ will assuredly destroy all of the corporate organizations of today's spiritual Ekklesia; and he will correct all of his wayward people until they have all learned that The Eternal is God and beside HIM there is NO OTHER, and it is the Eternal who is to be exalted and obeyed above all else.

> **Deuteronomy 4:39** Know therefore this day, and consider it in thine heart, that the Lord he is God in heaven above, and upon the earth beneath: there is none else.

We MUST learn to question the words of all men by the whole Word of God and to hold fast the good and to reject anything contrary to the Word of God.

Leviticus 26:30 And I will destroy your high places [places of worship], and cut down your images, and cast your carcases upon the carcases of your idols, and my soul shall abhor you. **26:31** And I will make your cities waste, and bring your sanctuaries unto desolation, and I will not smell the savour of your sweet odours. **26:32** And I will bring the land into desolation: and your enemies which dwell therein shall be astonished at it.

Many will be scattered in search of food and water and will flee the violence in the land, and others will be made captives and forced to work in dangerous jobs under extremely harsh conditions.

26:33 And I will scatter you among the heathen, and will draw out a sword after you: and your land shall be desolate, and your cities waste.

26:34 Then shall the land enjoy her sabbaths, as long as it lieth desolate, and ye be in your enemies' land; even then shall the land rest, and enjoy her sabbaths. **26:35** As long as it lieth desolate it shall rest; because it did not rest in your sabbaths, when ye dwelt upon it.

Our people of both physical and spiritual Israel will become full of apprehension, mental insecurity and fear; and people will trample all over one another to escape, often when no one is pursuing.

26:36 And upon them that are left alive of you I will send a faintness into their hearts in the lands of their enemies; and the sound of a shaken leaf shall chase them; and they shall flee, as fleeing from a sword; and they shall fall when none pursueth. **26:37** And they shall fall one upon another, as it were before [in a panic as when being chased by] a sword, when none pursueth: and ye shall have no power to stand before your enemies.

Very many will die in their own land, and also in the land of their enemies.

26:38 And ye shall perish among the heathen, and the land of your enemies shall eat you up.

When spiritual and physical Israel's great pride has been crushed to contrition, then the warnings will be remembered and many will sincerely repent; then God will remember us and deliver us. Messiah will come to resurrect the chosen of spiritual Israel and will then deliver physical Israel. Then the kingdom of God will be established on a Feast of Pentecost.

26:39 And they that are left of you shall pine away in their iniquity in your enemies' lands; and also in the iniquities of their fathers shall they pine away with them.

26:40 If they shall confess their iniquity, and the iniquity of their fathers, with their trespass which they trespassed against me, and that also they have walked contrary unto me; **26:41** And that I also have walked contrary unto them, and have brought them into the land of their enemies; if then their uncircumcised hearts be humbled, and they then accept of the punishment of their iniquity: **26:42** Then will I remember my covenant with Jacob, and also my covenant with Isaac, and also my covenant with Abraham will I remember; and I will remember the land.

During the tribulation the Spiritual Ekklesia will be humbled and will remember the Husband of their espousal and will turn to him with a whole heart. Physical Israel and the nations will also be humbled and will be made ready to accept the coming of Messiah the Christ and his kingdom over all the earth.

Today's apostate Spiritual Ekklesia, the church of pride and idolatry; will be humbled to contrition and we will be saved! We will remember how we had despised any zeal to live by every Word of God in order to live as we thought right and we will sincerely repent!

26:43 The land also shall be left of them, and shall enjoy her sabbaths, while she lieth desolate without them: and **they shall accept of the punishment of their iniquity**: because, even because they despised my judgments, and because their soul abhorred my statutes.

Our merciful Christ will come to save humanity; so that physical and spiritual Israel and the nations of men are not totally destroyed from off the earth.

26:44 And yet for all that, when they be in the land of their enemies, I will not cast them away, neither will I abhor them, to destroy them utterly, and to break my covenant with them: for I am the LORD their God.

How wonderful and faithful is our Husband, our God, our Deliverer who will not reject us totally in our sin, but who will correct us in the hope that he might save us and grant his eternal promises to us!

26:45 But I will for their sakes remember the covenant of their ancestors, whom I brought forth out of the land of Egypt in the sight of the heathen, that I might be their God: I am the LORD.

26:46 These are the statutes and judgments and laws, which the LORD made between him and the children of Israel in mount Sinai by the hand of Moses.

Leviticus 27

Here the word "vow" is taken from the words פָּלָא pala a Special נֶדֶר neder Votive Offering. This refers to a special votive offering which is generally a thank offering for a particular blessing which was received often due to a request made to God.

Here God gives instructions on the amounts of special offerings [which are called vows in the KJV] which are to be given to the Levites [ministry].

Leviticus 27:1 And the LORD spake unto Moses, saying, **27:2** Speak unto the children of Israel, and say unto them, When a man shall make a singular (Strong's 6381 a special 5088 offering) vow, the persons shall be for the LORD by thy estimation.

27:3 And thy estimation shall be of the male from twenty years old even unto sixty years old, even thy estimation shall be fifty shekels of silver, after the shekel of the sanctuary. **27:4** And if it be a female, then thy estimation shall be thirty shekels.

Children

27:5 And if it be from five years old even unto twenty years old, then thy estimation shall be of the male twenty shekels, and for the female ten shekels. **27:6** And if it be from a month old even unto five years old, then thy estimation shall be of the male five shekels of silver, and for the female thy estimation shall be three shekels of silver.

The Elderly

27:7 And if it be from sixty years old and above; if it be a male, then thy estimation shall be fifteen shekels, and for the female ten shekels.

Mercy for the Poor

27:8 But if he be poorer than thy estimation, then he shall present himself before the priest, and the priest shall value him; according to his ability that vowed shall the priest value him.

Gifts

Clean Animals

27:9 And if it be a beast, whereof men bring an offering unto the LORD, all that any man giveth of such unto the LORD shall be holy. **27:10** He shall not alter it, nor change it, a good for a bad, or a bad for a good: and if he shall at all change beast for beast, then it and the exchange thereof shall be holy.

Unclean Animals

27:11 And if it be any unclean beast, of which they do not offer a sacrifice unto the LORD, then he shall present the beast before the priest: **27:12** And the priest shall value it, whether it be good or bad: as thou valuest it, who art the priest, so shall it be.

The unclean animal may be redeemed by adding a fifth of its value to its true value as an offering.

27:13 But if he will at all redeem it, then he shall add a fifth part thereof unto thy estimation.

The gift of a house

27:14 And when a man shall sanctify his house to be holy unto the LORD, then the priest shall estimate it, whether it be good or bad: as the priest shall estimate it, so shall it stand. **27:15** And if he that sanctified it will redeem his house, then he shall add the fifth part of the money of thy estimation unto it, and it shall be his.

The gift of agricultural land shall have its value reckoned by the years to a Jubilee and an homer of barley seed shall be valued at fifty shekels of silver.

27:16 And if a man shall sanctify unto the LORD some part of a field of his possession, then thy estimation shall be according to the seed thereof: an homer of barley seed shall be valued at fifty shekels of silver. **27:17** If he sanctify his field from the year of jubile, according to thy estimation it shall stand. **27:18** But if he sanctify his field after the jubile, then the priest shall reckon unto him the money according to the years that remain, even unto the year of the jubile, and it shall be abated from thy estimation.

Agricultural land vowed as a gift may be redeemed by paying its value plus a fifth part [20%].

27:19 And if he that sanctified the field will in any wise redeem it, then he shall add the fifth part of the money of thy estimation unto it, and it shall be assured to him.

The giver may refuse to receive his own field back at the Jubilee, and in that case it shall become permanently for the Levites.

27:20 And if he will not redeem the field, or if he have sold the field to another man, it shall not be redeemed any more. **27:21** But the field, when it goeth out in the jubile, shall be holy unto the LORD, as a field devoted; the possession thereof shall be the priest's.

If a field is not the owners inheritance but has been bought from another's inheritance until the Jubilee; the present user of the field may give the produce of that field to the priest but the field itself shall return back to its original owner.

27:22 And if a man sanctify unto the LORD a field which he hath bought, which is not of the fields of his possession; **27:23** Then the priest shall reckon unto him the worth of thy estimation, even unto the year of the jubile: and **he shall give thine estimation** in that day, as a holy thing unto the LORD.

27:24 In the year of the jubile the field shall return unto him of whom it was bought, even to him to whom the possession of the land did belong.

Definition of a shekel **27:25** And all thy estimations shall be according to the shekel of the sanctuary: **twenty gerahs shall be the shekel.**

First Fruits

The first born may not be consecrated to God because they already belong to God, because the Passover Lamb has atoned for the firstborn, saving them from death in Egypt.

Spiritually God the Father in heaven gave his first born son as the New Covenant Passover Lamb and therefore all first born belong to him.

27:26 Only the firstling of the beasts, which should be the LORD's firstling, no man shall sanctify it; whether it be ox, or sheep: it is the LORD's.

The first born of an unclean animal shall have its value estimated and may then either be given to the priests and the Levites, or it may be redeemed by the owner; by paying the value plus 20%.

27:27 And if it be of an unclean beast, then he shall redeem it according to thine estimation, and shall add a fifth part of it thereto: or if it be not redeemed, then it shall be sold according to thy estimation.

Anything devoted by vow to God may not be redeemed or withheld; all vows must be paid in full.

27:28 Notwithstanding no devoted thing, that a man shall devote unto the LORD of all that he hath, both of man and beast, and of the field of his possession, shall be sold or redeemed: every devoted thing is most holy unto the LORD. **27:29** None devoted, which shall be devoted of men, shall be redeemed; but shall surely be put to death.

Redeeming agricultural products

A tithe of all our agricultural increase is required by God, and if we desire to keep a certain animal possibly for breeding etc; then we are to pay its value plus 20% in money. This law changes the actual tithe from the animal into money for donation.

27:30 And all the tithe of the land, whether of the seed of the land, or of the fruit of the tree, is the LORD's: it is holy unto the LORD. **27:31** And if a man will at all redeem ought of his tithes, he shall add thereto the fifth part thereof.

All firstborn animals were separated out as belonging to God then the other newborn animals were separated from their parents and made to pass in single file before a man who counted them by touching each animal with his rod and shouting out to the recorder; 1, 2 ,3 etc. the tenth animal was then separated out whether good or bad [lame etc] as belonging to God and given to the Levites.

If it was desired to keep the animal for breeding etc, then it could be valued be the priest and the sum paid with the addition of 20%.

27:32 And concerning the tithe of the herd, or of the flock, even of whatsoever passeth under the rod, the tenth shall be holy unto the LORD. **27:33** He shall not search whether it be good or bad, neither shall he change it: and if he change it at all, then both it and the change thereof shall be holy; it shall not be redeemed.

27:34 These are the commandments, which the LORD commanded Moses for the children of Israel in mount Sinai.

Numbers

Numbers Introduction

The Five Books of Moses

1. Genesis is a history from creation to the entering into Egypt of the family of Israel [Jacob].

2. Exodus is a history of the deliverance of physical Israel as an allegory and prophecy of deliverance from bondage to sin for the Spiritual Ekklesia of the New Covenant.

3. Leviticus is instructions for the physical and the spiritual priesthood.

The physical priesthood of Aaron was to teach godliness to the people and offer physical sacrifices. All of the physical sacrifices were lessons and pictures of the atoning work and sacrifice of Jesus Christ the Lamb of God. All of the called out of the New Covenant are called to become priests of the High Priesthood of Jesus Christ after their resurrection.

4. Numbers is about the wondering after Sinai and before entering the physical promised land. This is a lesson on the life of the New Covenant converted as wanderers in an evil world, from their baptism until their death or change to spirit and entry into that spiritual Promised Land of eternal life.

5. Deuteronomy is the last instructions and warnings to the people immediately before their entry to the promised land. This is also a reminder to us of who may and who may not enter the spiritual Promised Land of eternal life. Only those who are zealously faithful to live by every Word of God may enter and remain in the spiritual Promised Land of eternal life.

Numbers Overview

Numbers begins at Mount Sinai, where the Israelites have received the law and covenant from God; and God has taken up residence among them in the tabernacle sanctuary. The task before them is now to take possession of the physical promised land.

The people are numbered and preparations are made for resuming their journey. The Israelites begin the journey, but they "murmur" (complain against God) at the hardships along the way and complain against Moses and Aaron because of the hardships. For these acts, God destroys approximately 15,000 of them through various means.

They arrive at the borders of Canaan and send spies into the land, but upon hearing the spies report concerning the conditions in Canaan the Israelites refuse to enter the land, and God condemns them to die in the wilderness until a new generation can grow up and carry out the task. The book ends with the new generation of Israelites in the plain of Moab ready for the crossing of the Jordan River.

God orders Moses to number those able to bear arms—of all the men "from twenty years old and upward;" and God appoints captains over each tribe. 603,550 Israelite men are found to be fit for military service. In chapter 26, a generation later and after forty years of wandering the desert, the Lord orders a second census and 601,730 men are counted.

The tribe of Levi is exempted from military service and therefore not included in the census totals. Moses consecrates the Levites for the service of the tabernacle in place of the first-born sons in Israel.

The Levites are divided into three families, the Gershonites, the Kohathites, and the Merarites, each under a chief, and all headed by the new high priest Aaron, and then Eleazar the son of Aaron.

The first journey of the Israelites after the Tabernacle had been constructed

The people murmur against God and are punished; Moses complains of the stubbornness of the Israelites and is given seventy elders [the later

Sanhedrin is based on this model] to assist him in the government of the people.

Miriam and Aaron insult Moses at Hazeroth, which angers God; Miriam is punished with leprosy and is shut out of camp for seven days, at the end of which the Israelites proceed to the desert of Paran. Twelve spies are sent out into Canaan and come back to report to Moses.

Joshua and Caleb, two of the spies, report that the land is abundant and is "flowing with milk and honey;" the other spies report the land is inhabited by giants, and the Israelites refuse to enter the land.

Yahweh decrees that the Israelites will be punished for their loss of faith by having to wander in the wilderness for 40 years, thus revealing that only by faith and the works of faith can anyone enter the spiritual Promised land of eternal life.

Moses is ordered by God to make plates to cover the altar with the two hundred fifty censers left after God's destruction of Korah's band for trying to usurp the authority of Moses and Aaron. The children of Israel murmur against Moses and Aaron on account of the destruction of Korah's men and are stricken with a plague, with 14,700 perishing.

Aaron and his family are declared by God to be responsible for any iniquity committed in connection with the sanctuary. This means that today's elders will be held responsible by God for the sin and false doctrine that they permit in the assemblies (Ezekiel 33)!

The Levites are again appointed to help in the keeping of the tabernacle. The Levites are ordered to give to the priests a tenth of the tithes given to them.

Miriam dies at Kadesh Barnea and the Israelites set out for Moab, on Canaan's eastern border.

The Israelites blame Moses for the lack of water and Moses is ordered by God to speak to a rock but disobeys striking the rock, and is punished by the announcement that he will not be allowed to enter Canaan.

The king of Edom refuses permission to the Israelites to pass through his land and they go around it. Aaron dies on Mount Hor. The Israelites are bitten by fiery serpents for speaking against God and Moses.

The Israelites arrive on the plains of Moab. A new census gives the total number of males from twenty years and upward as 601,730, and the number of the Levites from a month old and upward as 23,000.

God commands that he land is to be divided by lot. The daughters of Zelophehad, their father having no sons, are to share in the allotment.

Moses is ordered to appoint Joshua as his successor. Prescriptions for the observance of the feasts, and the offerings for different occasions are enumerated.

Just as Egypt was a type of bondage, and physical Israel was a type of the called out; the Canaanites were types of unrepentant sinners and their total destruction was representative of the final judgment of all unrepentant sinners and all false teaching in the lake of fire.

The Reubenites and the Gadites request Moses to assign them the land east of the Jordan. Moses grants their request after they promise to help in the conquest of the land west of the Jordan. The land east of the Jordan is divided among the tribes of Reuben, Gad, and the half-tribe of Manasseh.

Moses recalls the stations at which the Israelites halted during their forty years' wanderings and instructs the Israelites to exterminate the Canaanites and destroy their idols. The boundaries of the land are spelled out; the land is to be divided under the supervision of Eleazar, Joshua, and twelve princes, one from each tribe.

Numbers 1

Two weeks after Passover in the second year after the exodus, God instructs Moses to prepare to enter the physical promised land.

Under the Mosaic Covenant the whole nation was to be God's nation and was to make war by God's command as the instrument of God's policies. When the Mosaic Covenant ended with the death of the Husband of Israel, the God Being who had given up his Godhood to be made flesh; a New Covenant officially began in part (Jer 31:31).

In this dispensation we are a scattered people and we are not to take part in the unjust wars of this world's nations. Right now our warfare is spiritual, warring against the sin within ourselves (2 Cor 10:4).

During the present dispensation those scattered individuals called to God are in training to enter the New Covenant in its fullness at the resurrection to spirit when we shall be fully born again, this time as a spirit being.

At present the called out spiritual Ekklesia is not the wife of Christ, we are espoused to and in training to become a part of the resurrected bride; and if we are chosen we will be resurrected to spirit and we will become the full wife of Christ at the Marriage of the Lamb before the throne of God the Father in heaven (Rev 15). For even more detail see this article on "The Marriage of the Lamb."

At this time the spiritual Ekklesia is not a nation but a very scattered people, yet we have been called out to become a spiritual holy nation (1 Pet 2:9) which we are working to become.

The chosen will become a royal priesthood [kings and priests (Rev 1:6, 5:10)] and a holy spiritual nation at the resurrection to spirit and the Marriage of the Lamb, when we will enter in to a New Marriage Covenant with Christ; no longer espoused to Christ but becoming fully married to HIM at the Heavenly Wedding Feast at the Marriage of the Lamb (Rev 15)!

In this dispensation we are a scattered people and we are not to take part in the unjust wars of this world's nations. Right now our warfare is spiritual, warring against the sin within ourselves (2 Cor 10:4).

Later after the resurrection when we become a holy nation fully married to and at one with Jesus Christ the Lamb of God; and in full unity with God the Father and the very One who had been the Husband and leader of Mosaic Israel, we will make war at his direction alone and not by our own reasoning's.

Numbers 1:1 And the LORD spake unto Moses in the wilderness of Sinai, in the tabernacle of the congregation, on the first day of the second month, in the second year after they were come out of the land of Egypt, saying, **1:2** Take ye the sum of all the congregation of the children of Israel, after their families, by the house of their fathers, with the number of their names, every male by their polls; **1:3 From twenty years old and upward, all that are able to go forth to war in Israel**: thou and Aaron shall number them by their armies.

God selects and reveals to Moses who God wanted as commander of the fighting men of each tribe of Israel.

1:4 And with you there shall be a man of every tribe; every one head of the house of his fathers.

1:5 And these are the names of the men that shall stand with you: of the tribe of Reuben; Elizur the son of Shedeur.

1:6 Of Simeon; Shelumiel the son of Zurishaddai.

1:7 Of Judah; Nahshon the son of Amminadab.

1:8 Of Issachar; Nethaneel the son of Zuar.

1:9 Of Zebulun; Eliab the son of Helon.

1:10 Of the children of Joseph: of Ephraim; Elishama the son of Ammihud: of Manasseh; Gamaliel the son of Pedahzur.

1:11 Of Benjamin; Abidan the son of Gideoni.

1:12 Of Dan; Ahiezer the son of Ammishaddai.

1:13 Of Asher; Pagiel the son of Ocran.

1:14 Of Gad; Eliasaph the son of Deuel.

1:15 Of Naphtali; Ahira the son of Enan.

1:16 These were the renowned of the congregation, princes of the tribes of their fathers, heads of thousands in Israel.

The commanders which God had chosen gathered together and were introduced to the fighting men placed under their charge.

1:17 And Moses and Aaron took **these men which are expressed by their names**: **1:18** And **they assembled all the congregation together** on the first day of the second month, and they declared their pedigrees after their families, by the house of their fathers, according to the number of the names, **from twenty years old and upward,** by their polls.

1:19 As the LORD commanded Moses, so he numbered them in the wilderness of Sinai.

A list of the numbers of each tribe

1:20 And the children of Reuben, Israel's eldest son, by their generations, after their families, by the house of their fathers, according to the number of the names, by their polls, every male from twenty years old and upward, all that were able to go forth to war; **1:21** Those that were numbered of them, even of the **tribe of Reuben, were forty and six thousand and five hundred**.

1:22 Of the children of Simeon, by their generations, after their families, by the house of their fathers, those that were numbered of them, according to the number of the names, by their polls, every male from twenty years old and upward, all that were able to go forth to war; **1:23** Those that were numbered of them, even of **the tribe of Simeon, were fifty and nine thousand and three hundred.**

1:24 Of the children of Gad, by their generations, after their families, by the house of their fathers, according to the number of the names, from twenty years old and upward, all that were able to go forth to war; **1:25** Those that were numbered of them, even of **the tribe of Gad, were forty and five thousand six hundred and fifty.**

1:26 Of the children of Judah, by their generations, after their families, by the house of their fathers, according to the number of the names, from twenty years old and upward, all that were able to go forth to war; **1:27**

Those that were numbered of them, even of **the tribe of Judah, were threescore and fourteen thousand and six hundred.**

1:28 Of the children of Issachar, by their generations, after their families, by the house of their fathers, according to the number of the names, from twenty years old and upward, all that were able to go forth to war; **1:29** Those that were numbered of them, even of **the tribe of Issachar, were fifty and four thousand and four hundred.**

1:30 Of the children of Zebulun, by their generations, after their families, by the house of their fathers, according to the number of the names, from twenty years old and upward, all that were able to go forth to war; **1:31** Those that were numbered of them, even of **the tribe of Zebulun, were fifty and seven thousand and four hundred.**

1:32 Of the children of Joseph, [Joseph was given the right of the first born and had a double portion through his two sons Ephraim and Manasseh] namely, of the children of Ephraim, by their generations, after their families, by the house of their fathers, according to the number of the names, from twenty years old and upward, all that were able to go forth to war; **1:33** Those that were numbered of them, even of **the tribe of Ephraim, were forty thousand and five hundred. 1:34** Of the children of Manasseh, by their generations, after their families, by the house of their fathers, according to the number of the names, from twenty years old and upward, all that were able to go forth to war; **1:35** Those that were numbered of them, even of **the tribe of Manasseh, were thirty and two thousand and two hundred.**

1:36 Of the children of Benjamin, by their generations, after their families, by the house of their fathers, according to the number of the names, from twenty years old and upward, all that were able to go forth to war; **1:37** Those that were numbered of them, even of **the tribe of Benjamin, were thirty and five thousand and four hundred.**

1:38 Of the children of Dan, by their generations, after their families, by the house of their fathers, according to the number of the names, from twenty years old and upward, all that were able to go forth to war; **1:39** Those that were numbered of them, even of **the tribe of Dan, were threescore and two thousand and seven hundred.**

1:40 Of the children of Asher, by their generations, after their families, by the house of their fathers, according to the number of the names, from twenty years old and upward, all that were able to go forth to war; **1:41** Those that were numbered of them, even of **the tribe of Asher, were forty and one thousand and five hundred.**

1:42 Of the children of Naphtali, throughout their generations, after their families, by the house of their fathers, according to the number of the names, from twenty years old and upward, all that were able to go forth to war; **1:43** Those that were numbered of them, even of **the tribe of Naphtali, were fifty and three thousand and four hundred.**

These are the twelve tribes of Israel, exclusive of Levi which was the priesthood tribe

1:44 These are those that were numbered, which Moses and Aaron numbered, and the princes of Israel, being twelve men: each one was for the house of his fathers. **1:45** So were all those that were numbered of the children of Israel, by the house of their fathers, from twenty years old and upward, all that were able to go forth to war in Israel; **1:46** Even **all they that were numbered were six hundred thousand and three thousand and five hundred and fifty.**

In the following case the term "Levites" refers to the entire tribe of Levi, including both the priests and the Levites. Aaron and his sons were to be the priests and the other sons of Levi were to be the Levites [helpers of the priests, like modern deacons]; but the whole tribe of Levi was to be the tribe of God, called to serve in the holy things of God.

1:47 But the Levites after the tribe of their fathers were not numbered among them.

1:48 For the LORD had spoken unto Moses, saying, **1:49 Only thou shalt not number the tribe of Levi, neither take the sum of them among the children of Israel:**

The priests were to offer the sacrifices; while the responsibilities of the Levites are ordained by God here. Just as Israel was called out of Egypt, the tribe of Levi was called out from Israel to minister before God for them.

1:50 But thou shalt appoint the Levites over the tabernacle of testimony, and over all the vessels thereof, and over all things that belong to it: they shall bear the tabernacle, and all the vessels thereof; and they shall minister unto it, and shall encamp round about the tabernacle. **1:51** And when the tabernacle setteth forward, the Levites shall take it down: and when the tabernacle is to be pitched, the Levites shall set it up: and **the stranger that cometh nigh shall be put to death.**

The armies of Israel were then organized into groups [within their tribes] and each man belonged to his own regiment under his own tribal leader.

1:52 And the children of Israel shall pitch their tents, every man by his own camp, and every man by his own standard, throughout their hosts.

The Levites camped around the tabernacle of God so that no person would be destroyed for approaching God improperly. In the same way, Jesus Christ is now our High Priest and the ONLY Intercessor between us and God the Father, atoning for us; so that we are not destroyed for our sins when we approach God the Father.

1:53 But the Levites shall pitch round about the tabernacle of testimony, that there be no wrath upon the congregation of the children of Israel: and the Levites shall keep the charge of the tabernacle of testimony.

1:54 And the children of Israel did according to all that the LORD commanded Moses, so did they.

Numbers 2

The war camp of Israel

The people were organized by their tribes and clans [extended families]. These numbers of men include only the fighting men from the age of 20 who were capable of fighting in battle.

Physical Israel was a type of the spiritually called out of bondage to Satan and sin, while ancient Egypt was a type of bondage and Canaan was a type of unrepentant sinners.

This war machine represented the faithful and zealous New Covenant called out; who are called out of bondage to conquer sin and defeat wickedness within themselves.

Brethren, we are not to take part in this world's wars, we have been called out of this world to be mighty men of war against Satan, and sin!

We are NOT called out to compromise with or tolerate sin and false teachings! But to conquer and destroy them through living by every Word of God! and by faithfully and zealously obeying and following God the Father and our espoused Husband Jesus Christ!

Numbers 2:1 And the LORD spake unto Moses and unto Aaron, saying, **2:2** Every man of the children of Israel shall pitch by his own standard, with the ensign of their father's house: far off about the tabernacle of the congregation shall they pitch.

Army Group East

Judah, Issachar and Zebulun

2:3 And on the east side toward the rising of the sun shall they of the standard of the camp of Judah pitch throughout their armies: and Nahshon the son of Amminadab shall be captain of the children of Judah. **2:4** And his host, and those that were numbered of them, were **threescore and fourteen thousand and six hundred [74,600]**.

2:5 And those that do pitch next unto him shall be the tribe of **Issachar**: and Nethaneel the son of Zuar shall be captain of the children of Issachar. **2:6** And his host, and those that were numbered thereof, were **fifty and four thousand and four hundred [54,400]**.

2:7 Then the tribe of **Zebulun**: and Eliab the son of Helon shall be captain of the children of Zebulun. **2:8** And his host, and those that were numbered thereof, were **fifty and seven thousand and four hundred [57,400]**.

2:9 All that were numbered in the camp of **Judah** [**Issachar** and **Zebulun**] were an hundred thousand and fourscore thousand and six thousand and four hundred, throughout their armies. These shall first set forth. [186,400]

Army Group South

Reuben, Simeon and Gad

2:10 On the south side shall be the standard of the camp of **Reuben** according to their armies: and **the captain of the children of Reuben shall be Elizur the son of Shedeur**. **2:11** And his host, and those that were numbered thereof, were forty and six thousand and five hundred. [46,500]

2:12 And those which pitch by him shall be the tribe of **Simeon**: and **the captain of the children of Simeon shall be Shelumiel the son of Zurishaddai**. **2:13** And his host, and those that were numbered of them, were fifty and nine thousand and three hundred. [59,300]

2:14 Then the tribe of **Gad**: and **the captain of the sons of Gad shall be Eliasaph the son of Reuel**. **2:15** And his host, and those that were numbered of them, were forty and five thousand and six hundred and fifty. [45,650]

2:16 All that were numbered in the camp of **Reuben** [Simeon and Gad] were an hundred thousand and fifty and one thousand and four hundred and fifty, throughout their armies. And they shall set forth in the second rank. [151,450]

The Descendants of Levi

The Levites including the priests surrounded the tabernacle in the center of the camp.

2:17 Then the tabernacle of the congregation shall set forward with the camp of the Levites in the midst of the camp: as they encamp, so shall they set forward, every man in his place by their standards.

Army Group West

Ephraim, Manasseh and Benjamin

2:18 On the west side shall be the standard of the camp of **Ephraim** according to their armies: and **the captain of the sons of Ephraim shall be Elishama the son of Ammihud. 2:19** And his host, and those that were numbered of them, were forty thousand and five hundred. [40,500]

2:20 And by him shall be the tribe of **Manasseh**: and **the captain of the children of Manasseh shall be Gamaliel the son of Pedahzur. 2:21** And his host, and those that were numbered of them, were thirty and two thousand and two hundred. [32,200]

2:22 Then the tribe of **Benjamin**: and **the captain of the sons of Benjamin shall be Abidan the son of Gideoni. 2:23** And his host, and those that were numbered of them, were thirty and five thousand and four hundred. [35,400]

2:24 All that were numbered of the camp of Ephraim [Manasseh and Benjamin] were an hundred thousand and eight thousand and an hundred, throughout their armies. And they shall go forward in the third rank. [108,100]

Army Group North

Dan, Asher and Naphtali

2:25 The standard of the camp of **Dan** shall be on the north side by their armies: and **the captain of the children of Dan shall be Ahiezer the son of Ammishaddai. 2:26** And his host, and those that were numbered of them, were threescore and two thousand and seven hundred. [62,700]

2:27 And those that encamp by him shall be the tribe of **Asher**: and **the captain of the children of Asher shall be Pagiel the son of Ocran. 2:28** And his host, and those that were numbered of them, were forty and one thousand and five hundred. [41,500]

2:29 Then the tribe of **Naphtali: and the captain of the children of Naphtali shall be Ahira the son of Enan. 2:30** And his host, and those that were numbered of them, were fifty and three thousand and four hundred. [53,400]

2:31 All they that were numbered in the camp of Dan [Asher and Naphtali] were an hundred thousand and fifty and seven thousand and six hundred. They shall go hindmost with their standards. [157,600]

The Total Number of Fighting Men

2:32 These are those which were numbered of the children of Israel by the house of their fathers: all those that were numbered of the camps throughout their hosts were six hundred thousand and three thousand and five hundred and fifty. [603,550]

2:33 But the Levites were not numbered among the children of Israel; as the LORD commanded Moses.

2:34 And the children of Israel did according to all that the LORD commanded Moses: so they pitched by their standards, and so they set forward, every one after their families, according to the house of their fathers.

Numbers 3

Brethren, these things are instructional examples for us.

Jesus Christ has replaced the high priesthood of Aaron and has restored the High Priesthood of Melchizedek becoming our eternal High Priest! Those who attain the first general resurrection to spirit will become the priests of Jesus Christ, if we remain steadfast in overcoming sin and remaining full of zeal for the whole Word of God!

Moses as the Mosaic Covenant mediator, was a type of Christ the Mediator of the New Covenant; and Aaron as the high priest of the Mosaic Covenant, was a type of the High Priest of a New Covenant, Jesus Christ.

Separately the Levites were called to assist the priests in the physical things and as such were equivalent to today's deacons.

When Christ comes a new physical temple will be built and the latter day descendant of Levi will be converted to the New Covenant and through the descendants of Zadok they will serve in the physical Ezekiel Temple!

Just as before, their job will be to serve God in the things of the physical temple: With the physical priests offering sacrifices and the physical Levites assisting them; while being overseen by the spirit High Priest of the New Covenant Jesus Christ, and all of his spirit priesthood!

This will be further explained in the Ezekiel study.

One of the purposes of these studies is to prepare for Passover, and studies in Hebrews and the Epistles alongside these studies in the Books of Moses would be of great help in that preparation.

Numbers 3:1 These also are the generations of Aaron and Moses in the day that the LORD spake with Moses in mount Sinai.

The Descendants of Aaron; the Priesthood

Aaron had four sons.

3:2 And these are the names of the sons of Aaron; Nadab the firstborn, and Abihu, Eleazar, and Ithamar. **3:3** These are the names of the sons of Aaron, the priests which were anointed, whom he consecrated to minister in the priest's office.

Only Eleazar and Ithamar had descendants, so the priesthood was divided between these two lines of Aaron.

3:4 And **Nadab and Abihu died before the LORD**, when they offered strange fire before the LORD, in the wilderness of Sinai, and **they had no children**: and Eleazar and Ithamar ministered in the priest's office in the sight of Aaron their father.

The tribe of Levi includes all of the descendants of Levi; while the priesthood is Aaron's and his descendants. The sons of Aaron were to be the priests and offer the sacrifices and minister in the tabernacle, later the temple; while their brothers of Levi who not descended from Aaron were called to serve and assist the priests descended from Aaron.

3:5 And the LORD spake unto Moses, saying, **3:6** Bring the tribe of Levi near, and present them before Aaron the priest, that they may minister unto him. **3:7** And they shall keep his charge, and the charge of the whole congregation before the tabernacle of the congregation, to do the service of the tabernacle. **3:8** And they shall keep all the instruments of the tabernacle of the congregation, and the charge of the children of Israel, to do the service of the tabernacle.

The other descendants of Levi were given to the priests descended from Aaron, to assist them in serving God.

3:9 And thou shalt give the Levites unto Aaron and to his sons: they are wholly given unto him out of the children of Israel.

The priests were to serve God, helped by the Levites; and no stranger [unconverted person] was allowed in the tabernacle, or temple area. This commandment forbids knowingly baptizing and taking into the assemblies of today's spiritual Ekklesia, any unconverted person; (Exodus 12:48) not committed to live by every Word of God.

3:10 And thou shalt appoint Aaron and his sons, and they shall wait on their priest's office: and **the stranger that cometh nigh shall be put to death.**

The Levites are to serve the priesthood in place of the first born which were redeemed by the blood of the lamb in Egypt.

3:11 And the LORD spake unto Moses, saying, **3:12** And I, behold, I **have taken the Levites from among the children of Israel instead of all the firstborn** that openeth the matrix among the children of Israel: therefore the Levites shall be mine;

The first born of the called out are hallowed unto God, because God the Father gave his first born son for them. The Passover lambs in Egypt were sacrificed for the first born of Israel in Egypt, being a type of the Lamb of God who would be sacrificed for us.

In the place of the first born of Israel, God has provided the Levites to serve him by assisting the priesthood.

3:13 Because all the firstborn are mine; for on the day that I smote all the firstborn in the land of Egypt I hallowed unto me all the firstborn in Israel, both man and beast: mine shall they be: I am the LORD.

The Levites Are Counted

3:14 And the LORD spake unto Moses in the wilderness of Sinai, saying, **3:15** Number the children of Levi after the house of their fathers, by their families: every male from a month old and upward shalt thou number them. **3:16** And Moses numbered them according to the word of the LORD, as he was commanded.

The family of Levi according to the three sons of Levi.

3:17 And these were the sons of Levi by their names; **Gershon, and Kohath, and Merari.**

The sons of Gershon, Kohath and Merari listed

3:18 And these are the names of the **sons of Gershon** by their families; **Libni, and Shimei.**

3:19 And the **sons of Kohath** by their families; **Amram, and Izehar, Hebron, and Uzziel.**

3:20 And the **sons of Merari** by their families; **Mahli, and Mushi.** These are the families of the Levites according to the house of their fathers.

3:21 Of Gershon was the family of the Libnites, and the family of the Shimites: these are the families of the Gershonites.

The total of these men of Levi in the second year at Sinai was:

3:22 Those that were numbered of them, according to the number of all the males, from a month old and upward, even those that were numbered of them were seven thousand and five hundred. [7,500]

The Levites are now organized

The Gershonites led by Eliasaph the son of Lael would camp to the west of the tabernacle.

3:23 The families of the Gershonites shall pitch behind the tabernacle westward. **3:24** And the chief of the house of the father of the Gershonites shall be Eliasaph the son of Lael.

The responsibilities of the sons of Gershon.

They are to be in charge of the tent [the covering of the tabernacle] and curtains with their cords.

3:25 And the charge of the sons of Gershon in the tabernacle of the congregation shall be **the tabernacle, and the tent, the covering thereof, and the hanging for the door of the tabernacle of the congregation, 3:26 And the hangings of the court, and the curtain for the door of the court, which is by the tabernacle, and by the altar round about, and the cords of it for all the service thereof.**

The family of Kohath

3:27 And of Kohath was the family of the **Amramites**, and the family of the **Izeharites,** and the family of the **Hebronites**, and the family of the **Uzzielites**: these are the families of the Kohathites. **3:28** In the number of all the males, from a month old and upward, were eight thousand and six hundred, keeping the charge of the sanctuary. [8,600]

The family of Kohath camped south of the tabernacle.

3:29 The families of the sons of Kohath shall pitch on the side of the tabernacle southward.

3:30 And **the chief of the house of the father of the families of the Kohathites shall be Elizaphan the son of Uzziel.**

The responsibilities of the sons of Kohath

3:31 And their **charge shall be the ark, and the table, and the candlestick** [lamp stand, menorah]**, and the altars, and the vessels of the sanctuary wherewith they minister, and the hanging, and all the service thereof.**

The high priest was to be the ruler of all the families of the Levites.

3:32 And Eleazar the son of Aaron the priest shall be chief over the chief of the Levites, and have the oversight of them that keep the charge of the sanctuary.

The families of Merari

3:33 Of Merari was the family of the **Mahlites**, and the family of the **Mushites**: these are the families of Merari. **3:34** And those that were numbered of them, according to the number of all the males, from a month old and upward, were six thousand and two hundred. [6,200]

Merari would camp to the north of the tabernacle.

3:35 And **the chief of the house of the father of the families of Merari was Zuriel** the son of Abihail: these shall pitch on the side of the **tabernacle northward.**

The sons of Merari shall have responsibility for the wood, metal and pillars of the tabernacle

3:36 And under the custody and charge of the sons of Merari shall be **the boards of the tabernacle, and the bars thereof, and the pillars thereof, and the sockets thereof, and all the vessels thereof, and all that serveth thereto, 3:37 And the pillars of the court round about, and their sockets, and their pins, and their cords.**

Moses and Aaron were to camp to the east of the tabernacle so that they must go to the west to seek God. That is, they will have their back to the east and its rising sun; most pagans and the wicked always look to the east.

3:38 But those that encamp before the tabernacle toward the east, even before the tabernacle of the congregation eastward, shall be Moses, and Aaron and his sons, keeping the charge of the sanctuary for the charge of the children of Israel; and **the stranger** [unconverted] **that cometh nigh shall be put to death**.

We are never to baptize a person who is repentant in name only, and lacks basic understanding, NEVER

3:39 All that were numbered of the Levites, which Moses and Aaron numbered at the commandment of the LORD, throughout their families, all the males from a month old and upward, were twenty and two thousand. [22,000 total Levites]

The male firstborn of Israel are then counted

3:40 And the LORD said unto Moses, Number all the firstborn of the males of the children of Israel from a month old and upward, and take the number of their names.

3:41 And thou shalt take the Levites for me (I am the LORD) instead of all the firstborn among the children of Israel; and the cattle of the Levites instead of all the firstlings among the cattle of the children of Israel.

3:42 And Moses numbered, as the LORD commanded him, all the firstborn among the children of Israel. **3:43** And all the firstborn males by the number of names, from a month old and upward, of those that were numbered of them, were twenty and two thousand two hundred and threescore and thirteen. [22,272]

God then commands an exchange of Levites for the first born of Israel who were bought [redeemed] with the blood of the lamb [representing the later sacrifice of the Lamb of God] in Egypt. The first born of cattle [large and small, bovine and sheep/goats] were also redeemed or passed over in Egypt and therefore they also belong to God; which is why the firstborn of beasts is to be given to the Eternal.

3:44 And the LORD spake unto Moses, saying, **3:45** Take the Levites instead of all the firstborn among the children of Israel, and the cattle of the Levites instead of their cattle; and the Levites shall be mine: I am the LORD.

Those first born of Israel outnumbering the Levites were to be redeemed with five shekels of silver each, to be given to the priests.

3:46 And for those that are to be redeemed of the two hundred and threescore and thirteen of the firstborn of the children of Israel, which are more than the Levites; **3:47** Thou shalt even **take five shekels apiece by the poll, after the shekel of the sanctuary shalt thou take them: (the shekel is twenty gerahs:) 3:48 And thou shalt give the money, wherewith the odd number of them is to be redeemed, unto Aaron and to his sons.**

3:49 And Moses took the redemption money of them that were over and above them that were redeemed by the Levites: **3:50** Of the firstborn of the children of Israel took he the money; a thousand three hundred and threescore and five shekels [1,365], after the shekel of the sanctuary: **3:51** And Moses gave the money of them that were redeemed unto Aaron and to his sons, according to the word of the LORD, as the LORD commanded Moses.

Numbers 4

At this point the counting of **the Levites from one month old and upward as an exchange for the firstborn of Israel has been completed;** and Moses is now commanded to count the number of Levites qualified to serve the priesthood in the heavy work of the tabernacle, being those between 30 and 50 years old.

This means that today's spiritual Ekklesia should follow the command of God and the example of Jesus who began his ministry at age 30, and no elder under the age of 30 should be ordained. See also the articles on the ministry here.

This is in preparation for moving the tabernacle and beginning the journey into the promised land.

Remember that all of the descendants of Levi were Levites, while the priesthood belonged only to the descendants of Aaron the descendant of Levi.

The duties of the non-Aaronic Levites were about moving the tabernacle and about assisting the priests the descendants of Aaron in the physical aspects of the temple functions. It is from this office of Levites, that the office of deacons to help the physical New Covenant called out elders came.

Today the elders are to remain focused on spiritual service and intense study of the whole Word of God; to study continually, to learn, to set a godly example and to rebuke all sin, and teach the righteousness of the Word of God. They are to leave physical activities like organizing sports or camps or other functions to others [that is what deacons were ordained for]; and the ministry is to focus on the spiritual!

Numbers 4:1 And the LORD spake unto Moses and unto Aaron, saying, **4:2** Take the sum of **the sons of Kohath** from among the sons of Levi, after their families, by the house of their fathers, **4:3** From **thirty years old and upward even until fifty years old**, all that enter into the host, to do the work in the tabernacle of the congregation.

This is speaking of serving Levites as helps for the priests.

4:4 This shall be the service of the sons of Kohath in the tabernacle of the congregation, about the most holy things:

When the tabernacle was to be moved, the high priest and all the priests were to wrap all of the things of the tabernacle in coverings: so that the Levitical Kohath family which will carry them, will not come into direct contact with the holy things which only the priests are allowed to touch.

4:5 And when **the camp setteth forward** [is to be moved], **Aaron shall come, and his sons, and they shall take down the covering vail, and cover the ark of testimony with it:**

4:6 And shall put thereon the covering of badgers' skins, and shall spread over it a cloth wholly of blue, and shall put in the staves thereof.

> **Badgers skins:** The word **"tachash,"** mistakenly rendered "badger" in the Authorized Version, refers to ram's skins dyed royal blue. The ancient versions seem nearly all agreed that it denotes not an animal but the color, royal-blue. Badgers did not live in that region and are unclean; we should know by now what God thinks of any unclean thing associated with him, his tabernacle or his temple.

The royal blue covering of ram's skins dyed blue, represents Jesus Christ as BOTH King and Atoning Sacrifice, while the blue cloth pictures the kingship and sovereignty of Christ as Husband of Israel.

The twelve pieces of unleavened bread were covered with scarlet picturing the twelve tribes of physical Israel, representing spiritual Israel being covered by the blood of the Lamb, Jesus Christ.

The table of the Lord [in this case the table of the bread of presence] was to be covered with a royal blue tablecloth; then the twelve pieces of the Unleavened Bread of Life were to be covered by a cloth of scarlet on the bread including the dishes, picturing the atoning sacrifice of Christ; which scarlet cloth is in its turn to be covered by the ram's skins dyed royal blue as a sign of God's Royal Sovereignty over the twelve tribes.

This is the meaning of the table of the Lord in Malachi 1, which is called contemptible by the church of God today.

How So? They reject the sovereignty of God the Father and Jesus Christ and therefore reject the Bread of God's Presence by choosing to follow their own false traditions above living by every Word of God!

The Table of the Bread of Presence

4:7 And upon the table of shewbread they shall spread **a cloth of blue**, and put thereon the dishes, and the spoons, and the bowls, and covers to cover withal: and the continual bread shall be thereon: **4:8** And they shall spread upon them **a cloth of scarlet**, and cover the same with a covering of badgers' skins [ram's skin dyed royal blue], and shall put in the staves thereof.

The Menorah

4:9 And they shall take **a cloth of blue**, and cover the candlestick [lamp stand of oil burning lamps; menorah] of the light, and his lamps, and his tongs, and his snuffdishes, and all the oil vessels thereof, wherewith they minister unto it: **4:10** And they shall put it and all the vessels thereof within a covering of badgers' skins [Ram's skins dyed royal blue], and shall put it upon a bar [as a hanging curtain].

How to Move The Golden Altar and It's Implements

4:11 And upon the golden altar they shall spread a **cloth of blue,** and cover it with a covering of badgers' skins [ram's skins dyed royal blue], and shall put to the staves thereof:

4:12 And they shall take all the instruments of ministry, wherewith they minister in the sanctuary, and put them **in a cloth of blue,** and cover them with a covering of badgers' skins [ram's skins dyed blue], and shall put them on a bar: **4:13** And they shall take away the ashes from the altar, and spread a purple cloth thereon: **4:14** And they shall put upon it all the vessels thereof, wherewith they minister about it, even the censers, the fleshhooks, and the shovels, and the basons, all the vessels of the altar; and they shall spread upon it a covering of badgers' skins [rams skins dyed blue], and put to the staves of it.

After the holy things have been prepared by Aaron and his descendants the priests; then the sons of Kohath the Levites may come to move them.

4:15 And when Aaron and his sons have made an end of covering the sanctuary, and all the vessels of the sanctuary, as the camp is to set forward; after that, **the sons of Kohath shall come to bear it: but they shall not touch any holy thing, lest they die**. These things are the burden of the sons of Kohath in the tabernacle of the congregation.

The high priest is to supply the pure olive oil for the lamps, the anointing oil and the Unleavened Bread offering; which is symbolic of Jesus Christ our High Priest supplying the sinless unleavened Bread of Life, and the anointing oil of the Holy Spirit of salvation so that the light of the Word of God may shine within us.

4:16 And to the office of Eleazar the son of Aaron the priest pertaineth the oil for the light, and the sweet incense, and the daily meat [unleavened bread] offering, and the anointing oil, and the oversight of all the tabernacle, and of all that therein is, in the sanctuary, and in the vessels thereof.

The Levitical family of Kohath may not even see the holy things uncovered by the priests.

4:17 And the LORD spake unto Moses and unto Aaron saying,

The priests were not to allow the Kothathites to be destroyed by touching or seeing the holy things uncovered.

4:18 Cut ye not off the tribe of the families of the Kohathites from among the Levites: **4:19** But thus do unto them, that they may live, and not die, when they approach unto the most holy things: Aaron and his sons shall go in, and appoint them every one to his service and to his burden: **4:20** But they shall not go in [be curious to see what these things look like and open their coverings] to see when the holy things are covered, lest they die.

The Levitical duties of the sons of Gershon

4:21 And the LORD spake unto Moses, saying, **4:22** Take also the sum of the sons of Gershon, throughout the houses of their fathers, by their families; **4:23 From thirty years old and upward until fifty years old** shalt thou number them; all that enter in to perform the service, to do the work in the tabernacle of the congregation.

4:24 This is the service of the families of the Gershonites, to serve, and for burdens: **4:25** And they shall bear the curtains of the tabernacle, and the tabernacle of the congregation, his covering, and the covering of the badgers' skins [ram's skins dyed blue] that is above upon it, and the hanging for the door of the tabernacle of the congregation, **4:26** And the hangings of the court, and the hanging for the door of the gate of the court, which is by the tabernacle and by the altar round about, and their cords, and all the instruments of their service, and all that is made for them: so shall they serve.

The Levitical sons of Gershon were under the hand [authority of] of Ithamar [and his descendants], the son of Aaron the priest.

4:27 At the appointment of Aaron and his sons shall be all the service of the sons of the Gershonites, in all their burdens, and in all their service: and ye shall appoint unto them in charge all their burdens. **4:28** This is the service of the families of the sons of Gershon in the tabernacle of the congregation: and their charge shall be under the hand of Ithamar the son of Aaron the priest.

The Levitical service of the sons of Merari

4:29 As for the sons of Merari, thou shalt number them after their families, by the house of their fathers; **4:30** From thirty years old and upward even unto fifty years old shalt thou number them, every one that entereth into the service, to do the work of the tabernacle of the congregation.

4:31 And this is the charge of their burden, according to all their service in the tabernacle of the congregation; the boards of the tabernacle, and the bars thereof, and the pillars thereof, and sockets thereof, **4:32** And the pillars of the court round about, and their sockets, and their pins, and their cords, with all their instruments, and with all their service: and by name ye shall reckon the instruments of the charge of their burden.

4:33 This is the service of the families of the sons of Merari, according to all their service, in the tabernacle of the congregation, under the hand of Ithamar the son of Aaron the priest.

Moses obeyed God and numbered the Levites from 30 to 50 years old for their service in the tabernacle.

4:34 And Moses and Aaron and the chief of the congregation **numbered the sons of the Kohathites** after their families, and after the house of their fathers, **4:35** From thirty years old and upward even unto fifty years old, every one that entereth into the service, for the work in the tabernacle of the congregation: **4:36** And those that were numbered of them by their families were two thousand seven hundred and fifty. [2,750] **4:37** These were they that were numbered of the families of the Kohathites, all that might do service in the tabernacle of the congregation, which Moses and

Aaron did number according to the commandment of the LORD by the hand of Moses.

4:38 And those that were **numbered of the sons of Gershon,** throughout their families, and by the house of their fathers, **4:39** From thirty years old and upward even unto fifty years old, every one that entereth into the service, for the work in the tabernacle of the congregation, **4:40** Even those that were numbered of them, throughout their families, by the house of their fathers, were two thousand and six hundred and thirty. [2,630] **4:41** These are they that were numbered of the families of the sons of Gershon, of all that might do service in the tabernacle of the congregation, whom Moses and Aaron did number according to the commandment of the LORD.

4:42 And those that were **numbered of the families of the sons of Merari,** throughout their families, by the house of their fathers, **4:43** From thirty years old and upward even unto fifty years old, every one that entereth into the service, for the work in the tabernacle of the congregation, **4:44** Even those that were numbered of them after their families, were three thousand and two hundred. [3,200] **4:45** These be those that were numbered of the families of the sons of Merari, whom Moses and Aaron numbered according to the word of the LORD by the hand of Moses.

4:46 All those that were numbered of the Levites, whom Moses and Aaron and the chief of Israel numbered, after their families, and after the house of their fathers, **4:47** From thirty years old and upward even unto fifty years old, every one that came to do the service of the ministry, and the service of the burden in the tabernacle of the congregation. **4:48** Even those that were numbered of them, were eight thousand and five hundred and fourscore, [The serving Levites at Sinai totaled 8,560]

4:49 According to the commandment of the LORD they were numbered by the hand of Moses, every one according to his service, and according to his burden: thus were they numbered of him, as the LORD commanded Moses

RECAP

The whole tribe, all the children of Levi, were separated out as belonging to God. Later the male descendants of Aaron were called out of Levi to be the priests of God.

The Levites who were not descendants of Aaron, were to be helps and to assist the priests, the sons of Aaron.

The Levites were not priests but assisted the priests. The priests carried out the tasks involving the sacrifices and directly serving God, while the

Levites served and assisted in the physical necessities of the tabernacle and later the temple.

Later the Levites were given additional duties including singing at the tabernacle/temple and teaching the people in the Synagogue schools across the land, especially at the Levitical cities. For details see the Priests and Levites article.

The physical Mosaic high priest as the intermediary between men and God is typical of the New Covenant High Priest Jesus Christ, being the ONLY intercessor between God the Father and humanity.

The New Covenant High Priest Jesus Christ is the ONLY Mediator of the New Covenant and stands between the people and God the Father; and all those Called Out to become priests of Jesus Christ are to perform the works of a Holy Priesthood and teach the way to reconciliation with God the Father and salvation through Jesus Christ. See the Hebrews study.

> **1 Peter 2:4** To whom coming, as unto a living stone [Jesus Christ], disallowed indeed of men, but chosen of God, and precious,

We are being called to the priesthood of Jesus Christ, and we are to offer spiritual sacrifices which is our intense zeal to learn and live by every Word of God. A thing that we, for the most part have left off doing, in order to exalt our idols of men and corporate entities.

> **2:5 Ye also, as lively stones, are built up a spiritual house, an holy priesthood, to offer up spiritual sacrifices, acceptable to God by Jesus Christ.**

To believe is not enough, for belief without the works of sincere repentance and faith is dead.

> **James 2:19** Thou believest that there is one God; thou doest well: the devils also believe, and tremble. **2:20** But wilt thou know, O vain man, that faith without works is dead?

> **1 Peter 2:6** Wherefore also it is contained in the scripture, **Behold, I lay in Sion a chief corner stone, elect, precious: and he that believeth on him shall not be confounded.**

Jesus Christ is a stumbling block to the disobedient, because the wicked believe that Christ winks at and tolerates disobedience.

> **2:7** Unto you therefore which believe he is precious: but **unto them which be disobedient, the stone which the builders disallowed, the same is made the head of the corner, 2:8 And a stone of stumbling, and a rock of offence, even to them which stumble at**

the [obedience to the whole Word of God] **word, being disobedient: whereunto also they were appointed.**

The Called Out are called into the priesthood of Jesus Christ; who has REPLACED the high priesthood of Aaron, restoring the priesthood of Melchizedek which office Jesus Christ had held before he was made flesh and BEFORE Aaron ever existed. The New Covenant Spiritual Ekklesia are called to follow Jesus Christ [Melchizedek] as our High Priest and to qualify to replace the priests of Aaron in the resurrection.

> **2:9** But **ye are a chosen generation, a royal priesthood, an holy nation, a peculiar** [special] **people;** that ye should shew forth the praises of him [By setting an example of living by every Word of God] who hath called you out of darkness [of ignorance and sin (commandment breaking)] into his marvellous light [the light of learning and keeping the whole Word of God]; **2:10** Which in time past were not a people [being individuals], but are now the people of God: which had not obtained mercy, but now have obtained mercy.

We see then that the high priest of Aaron was only a physical type of the spiritual High Priest, Jesus Christ; and that the priests of Aaron were only physical types of those called to become spiritual priests of our spiritual High Priest, Jesus Christ.

Brethren, in the spiritual sense; not only the ministry but every single one of the Called Out, has been called to become Priests of the New Covenant! (Rev 1:6, 5:10 and 20:6)! Yet in the New Covenant several different RESPONSIBILITIES have been given to aid the brethren as helps to focus us on every Word of God!

Numbers 5

Remember that this is a Battle Group and not the everyday camp, and that Jesus Christ is to be in their midst leading them into the physical battle against Canaan which was a type of sin!

Therefore purity and godliness is paramount in order that Jesus Christ who will not tolerate any sin, might remain in their midst!

Brethren, just as they were going into physical battle, we are in a spiritual fight with sin, led by Jesus Christ dwelling in us through his Spirit! Just as Jesus Christ required purity and cleanness in the physical army; even so he requires both physical and spiritual cleanness and purity from any tolerance of or compromise with wilful sin among his New Covenant called out.

Tolerance for diversity of doctrine [false teachings] and for sin is an abomination to Jesus Christ! As priests of Jesus Christ in training we are to rebuke with power all wilful sin and we are to destroy every false doctrine while accepting every good thing; by proving it according to the scriptures.

Let us obey this Word of God and put every wilful sin and all spiritual uncleanness of tolerating sin out of our lives, so that our Mighty One may dwell among us and lead us to victory over the sin that we are now falling prey to! Let the bride make herself ready by removing every spot of sin on her garments and be clothed with the righteous of every Word of God!

Numbers 5:1 And the LORD spake unto Moses, saying, **5:2** Command the children of Israel, that they put out of the camp every leper, and every one that hath an issue, and whosoever is defiled by the dead: **5:3** Both male and female shall ye put out, without the camp shall ye put them; that they defile not their camps, in the midst whereof I dwell. **5:4** And the children of Israel did so, and put them out without the camp: as the LORD spake unto Moses, so did the children of Israel.

The Law of Trespass

When we do damage to another we are to repay him and add an additional 20% for his trouble. For example, if we accidentally kill one of his animals we are to repay its value plus an added 20%.

5:5 And the LORD spake unto Moses, saying, **5:6** Speak unto the children of Israel, When a man or woman shall commit any sin that men commit, to do a trespass against the LORD, and that person be guilty; **5:7** Then they shall confess their sin which they have done: and he shall recompense his trespass with the principal thereof, and add unto it the fifth part thereof, and give it unto him against whom he hath trespassed.

If the offended person is not found, the repayment is to be made to his family; and if he has no family the money is to be given to the priesthood, in addition to the sacrifice of the trespass offering.

5:8 But if the man have no kinsman to recompense the trespass unto, let the trespass be recompensed unto the LORD, even to the priest; beside the ram of the atonement, whereby an atonement shall be made for him.

5:9 And every offering of all the holy things of the children of Israel, which they bring unto the priest, shall be his [the officiating priest's]. **5:10** And every man's hallowed things shall be his: whatsoever any man giveth the priest, it shall be his [the officiating priest's, the ministry are to be paid according to the extent of their service].

The Law of Jealousy

5:11 And the LORD spake unto Moses, saying, **5:12** Speak unto the children of Israel, and say unto them, If any man's wife go aside, and commit a trespass against him, **5:13** And a man lie with her carnally, and it be hid from the eyes of her husband, and be kept close, and she be defiled, and there be no witness against her, neither she be taken with the manner;

5:14 And the spirit of jealousy come upon him, and he be jealous of his wife, and she be defiled: or if the spirit of jealousy come upon him, and he be jealous of his wife, and she be not defiled:

This particular unleavened bread offering can have no symbol of the Holy Spirit [oil], nor the symbol of the sweetness of prayer and praise [frankincense] because its purpose is to expose sin.

5:15 Then shall the man bring his wife unto the priest, and he shall bring her offering for her, the tenth part of an ephah of barley meal; he shall pour no oil upon it, nor put frankincense thereon; for it is an offering of jealousy, an offering of memorial, bringing iniquity to remembrance.

5:16 And the priest shall bring her near, and set her before the LORD: **5:17** And the priest shall take holy water [pure blessed water, symbolic of the living water of faithfulness to the Word of God] in an earthen vessel; and of the dust [symbolic of the evil being trodden under foot] that is in the floor of the tabernacle the priest shall take, and put it into the water:

5:18 And the priest shall set the woman before the LORD, and uncover [remove the symbol of loyalty to her husband] the woman's head [in Israel married women covered their heads [hair] while prostitutes covered their faces to avoid recognition], and put the offering of memorial [the barley meal] in her hands, which is the jealousy offering: and the priest shall have in his hand the bitter water that causeth the curse:

The priest shall pronounce the terms of the trial

5:19 And the priest shall charge her by an oath, and say unto the woman, If no man have lain with thee, and if thou hast not gone aside to uncleanness with another instead of thy husband, be thou free from this bitter water that causeth the curse:

5:20 But if thou hast gone aside to another instead of thy husband, and if thou be defiled, and some man have lain with thee beside thine husband: **5:21** Then the priest shall charge the woman with an oath of cursing, and the priest shall say unto the woman, The LORD make thee a curse and an oath among thy people, when the LORD doth make thy thigh to rot, and thy belly to swell; **5:22** And this water that causeth the curse shall go into thy bowels, to make thy belly to swell, and thy thigh to rot: And the woman shall say, Amen, amen.

5:23 And the priest shall write these curses in a book, and he shall blot them out with the bitter water: **5:24** And he shall cause the woman to drink the bitter water that causeth the curse: and the water that causeth the curse shall enter into her, and become bitter.

5:25 Then the priest shall take the jealousy offering [the grain [barley meal) offering] out of the woman's hand, and shall wave the offering before the LORD, and offer it upon the altar: **5:26** And the priest shall take an handful of the offering [the barley meal], even the memorial thereof, and burn it upon the altar, and afterward shall cause the woman to drink the water.

5:27 And when he hath made her to drink the water, then it shall come to pass, that, if she be defiled, and have done trespass against her husband, that the water that causeth the curse shall enter into her, and become bitter, and her belly shall swell, and her thigh shall rot: and the woman shall be a curse among her people.

This is a physical lesson that God knows when we follow other gods and we are unfaithful to him, even if such a thing is not openly and publicly evident to the assembly.

Jesus Christ knows who the false wolves in sheep's clothing are in our assemblies, and he is allowing them to remain for a short time to test the faithfulness of his people as to whether they will remain faithful to live by every Word of God, or whether they will turn to follow after these false teachers.

Those who are falsely accused and persecuted by their brethren, will ultimately be revealed and exonerated and they will bring forth much spiritual fruit.

5:28 And if the woman be not defiled, but be clean; then she shall be free, and shall conceive seed.

5:29 This is the law of jealousies, when a wife goeth aside to another instead of her husband, and is defiled; **5:30** Or when the spirit of jealousy cometh upon him, and he be jealous over his wife, and shall set the woman before the LORD, and the priest shall execute upon her all this law.

If we are guilty of spiritual adultery we shall bear our sin and the correction for our sin, unless we quickly and sincerely repent.

5:31 Then shall the man be guiltless from iniquity, and this woman shall bear her iniquity

Numbers 6

In the Mosaic Covenant any Israelite of any tribe or sex [not just a priest or Levite] can volunteer to serve God.

In the New Covenant: Everyone called in the early harvest to the first general resurrection has been called to become the priests of God.

The Law of the Nazarite

Numbers 6:1 And the LORD spake unto Moses, saying, **6:2** Speak unto the children of Israel, and say unto them, When **either man or woman** shall separate themselves to vow a vow of a Nazarite, **to separate themselves unto the LORD:**

They must avoid eating any grapes of the vine or anything made from those grapes. Drinking a little alcohol is not sin; however in the Set Apart condition of the Nazarite, it is representative of false human pride which is like the leaven of sin.

In scripture; Sanctified Wine which is poured out with the sacrifice or drunk with a sacrificial meal is symbolic of death; since the life is in the blood. The sanctified wine offering is symbolic of the death of Jesus Christ the Lamb of God, for the sincerely repented sins of the world.

For the Nazarite alcohol is symbolic of the pride which is a root cause of sin and death; and pride comes forth from the sin of living our own ways and not being zealous to live by every Word of God.

Most of today's Spiritual Ekklesia is intoxicated with pride as this prophecy of Isaiah proclaims. We are full of our own ways and have no zeal to keep the ways of God.

> **Isaiah 29:9** Stay yourselves, and wonder; cry ye out, and cry: **they are drunken, but not with wine; they stagger, but not with strong drink. 29:10** For the Lord hath poured out upon you **the spirit of deep sleep**, and hath closed your eyes: the prophets and your rulers, the seers hath he covered. **29:11** And the vision of all is become unto you as the words of a book that is sealed, which men deliver to one that is learned, saying, Read this, I pray thee: and he saith, I cannot; for it is sealed: **29:12** And the book is delivered to him that is not learned, saying, Read this, I pray thee: and he saith, I am not learned.

Here is the sin of today's corporate Ekklesia

> **29:13** Wherefore the Lord said, **Forasmuch as this people draw near me with their mouth, and with their lips do honour me, but have removed their heart far from me, and their fear toward me is taught by the precept of men:**

Wine is also equated with the loss of a sound mind, and good judgment; which is analogous with the deception of false teachings and false religion.

Today we are filled with an unsound mind by being intoxicated with pride and our own false traditions. Today's spiritual Ekklesia is drunk with pride and in rebellion against any zeal to learn and live by the whole Word of God in any meaningful practical manner.

This has come upon us because so many accept the false Babylonian concept of Nicolaitane governance [obeying the ministry as if they were God, and not living by every Word of God] in the assemblies.

> **Jeremiah 51:6** Flee out of the midst of Babylon [reject blindly following men as if they were God], and deliver every man his soul: be not cut off in her iniquity; for this is the time of the Lord's vengeance; he will render unto her a recompence.
>
> **51:7 Babylon hath been a golden cup in the Lord's hand, that made all the earth drunken: the nations have drunken of her wine; therefore the nations are mad.**
>
> **51:8** Babylon is suddenly fallen and destroyed: howl for her; take balm for her pain, if so be she may be healed.

Numbers 6:3 He [a Nazarite] shall **separate himself from wine and strong drink**, and shall drink no vinegar of wine, or vinegar of strong drink, neither shall he drink any liquor [juice] of grapes, nor eat moist grapes, or dried. **6:4** All the days of his separation shall he eat nothing that is made of the vine tree, from the kernels even to the husk.

NOTHING that pertains to wine [including all alcoholic drinks or other intoxicants] or grapes may be consumed by a Nazarite. God's Word is to be our desire and not the intoxicating false imaginations and pride of our own ways of men.

No hair of the head is to be cut, symbolizing the Nazarite as a part of the bride of Christ and submissive to the authority of the spirit Husband Jesus Christ and the whole Word of God.

The Nazarite's hair is a symbol of voluntary consecration to God and is therefore holy to God. It is to be cut at the end of the period of consecration and burned as holy upon the altar, the smoke ascending up to God as a pleasant perfume representing heart felt voluntary service, to be accepted by Him.

6:5 All the days of the vow of his separation there shall no razor come upon his head: until the days be fulfilled, in the which he separateth himself unto the LORD, he shall be holy, and shall let the locks of the hair of his head grow.

The Nazarite must not touch any dead body because he must be HOLY and pure from all defilement of death, which is the wages of sin; because the Nazarite is consecrated [Set Apart] to holiness.

6:6 All the days that he separateth himself unto the LORD he shall come at no dead body. **6:7** He shall not make himself unclean for his father, or for his mother, for his brother, or for his sister, when they die: **because the consecration of his God is upon his head**. **6:8** All the days of his separation he is holy unto the LORD.

If the Nazarite is accidentally defiled by a dead person

6:9 And if any man die very suddenly by him, and he hath defiled the head of his consecration; then he shall shave his head in the day of his cleansing, on the seventh day shall he shave it.

6:10 And on the eighth day [an eighth day always represents a new beginning] he shall bring two turtles [turtle doves], or two young pigeons, to the priest, to the door of the tabernacle of the congregation: **6:11** And the priest shall offer the one for a sin offering, and the other for a burnt offering, and make an atonement for him, for that he sinned by the dead, and shall hallow his head that same day.

The Nazarite who was accidentally defiled must begin the days of his Set Apartness vow anew, after being cleansed of the defilement

6:12 And he shall consecrate unto the LORD the days of his separation, and shall bring a lamb of the first year for a trespass offering: but **the days that were before shall be lost,** because his separation was defiled.

The offering to conclude the period of service

6:13 And this is the law of the Nazarite, when the days of his separation are fulfilled: he shall be brought unto the door of the tabernacle of the congregation: **6:14** And he shall offer his offering unto the LORD, **one he lamb** of the first year without blemish for **a burnt offering** [symbolic of meek voluntary wholehearted zealous service], and **one ewe lamb of the first year** [from one month to a full year old; that is, the sacrifice must be within the first year of life] without blemish for a sin offering, and **one ram** without blemish for **peace offerings**, **6:15** And a basket of **unleavened bread**, cakes of fine flour **mingled with oil** [the unleavened bread mingled with oil pertains to having the Holy Spirit and internalizing the unleavened (sinless) Bread of Life which is Jesus Christ and every Word of God], and wafers of **unleavened bread anointed with oil,** [the unleavened bread anointed with oil is to show the anointing (Set Apartness) with the Holy Spirit for service to God] and their meat offering, and their drink offerings.

This was a very expensive offering and it was usual for sponsors and contributors to assist the Nazarite in his dedicated service to God and in these offerings.

6:16 And the priest shall bring them before the LORD, and shall offer his sin offering, and his burnt offering: **6:17** And he shall offer the ram for a sacrifice of peace offerings unto the LORD, with the basket of unleavened bread: the priest shall offer also his meat offering, and his drink offering.

At this point the hair of separation is to be shaved and burned in the fire of the Peace Offering.

The Peace Offering representing the faithful zealous wholehearted voluntary service bringing the Nazarite into a state of peace with and in complete unity with God. The smoke of the burning hair rising up represented the voluntary service as a wonderful and acceptably pleasant thing to God.

6:18 And the Nazarite shall shave the head of his separation at the door of the tabernacle of the congregation, and shall take the hair of the head of his separation, and put it in the fire which is under the sacrifice of the peace offerings.

6:19 And the priest shall take the sodden shoulder of the ram, and one unleavened cake out of the basket, and one unleavened wafer, and shall put them upon the hands of the Nazarite, after the hair of his separation is shaven:

After placing these pieces in the hands of the Nazarite and then lifting them up to be accepted by God as a representation of the Nazarite's service; the Holy Set Apartness of the Nazarite as accepted and the vow is completed.

6:20 And the priest shall wave them for a wave offering before the LORD: this is holy for the priest, with the wave breast and heave shoulder: and after that the Nazarite may drink wine.

No specific time span is commanded for a Nazarite vow, the period of commitment being left to the volunteer, but in Israel the vow was often taken for 30 to 90 days.

Besides the sacrifices completing the vow, the Nazarite must also pay any other commitments that he had made as a part of his vow.

In certain rare cases [Samson and John Baptist] God has commanded that a certain person be a special Nazarite from birth.

6:21 This is the law of the Nazarite who hath vowed, and of his offering unto the LORD for his separation, beside that that his hand shall get: according to the vow which he vowed, so he must do after the law of his separation.

6:22 And the LORD spake unto Moses, saying, **6:23** Speak unto Aaron and unto his sons, saying, On this wise ye shall bless the children of Israel, saying unto them,

Christ teaches the priests how to bless the brethren, [and this blessing comes ONLY through diligent zeal to learn and to keep the whole Word of God!]

6:24 The LORD bless thee, and keep thee: **6:25** The LORD make his face shine upon thee, and be gracious unto thee: **6:26** The LORD lift up his countenance upon thee, and give thee peace.

In the spiritual sense, placing the name of God on the people, does not refer to the verbal name by which people are called. It refers to teaching the people to become like God, to become holy as God is holy; and then the people will become at one with God in his holiness, and shall be brought into the family of God, and given the family name of God!

6:27 And they shall put my name upon the children of Israel, and I will bless them

EVERYTHING in the scriptures was written for the instruction of those who are called into the New Covenant.

> **2 Timothy 3:16** All scripture is given by inspiration of God, and is profitable for doctrine, for reproof, for correction, for instruction in righteousness: **3:17** That the man of God may be perfect, thoroughly furnished unto all good works.

> **1 Corinthians 10:11** Now all these things happened unto them for examples: and they are written for our admonition, upon whom the ends of the world are come.

> **Romans 15:4** For whatsoever things were written aforetime were written for our learning, that we through patience and comfort of the scriptures might have hope.

Brethren, the whole of scripture was written for us today and ultimately for all mankind. The whole of scripture was for our instruction or for our example, not just the New Testament. That includes the example of the Nazarite vow!

The Nazarite was set apart from all sin; set apart to godly holiness!

Brethren, the spiritually called out to the New Covenant of Jeremiah 31:31 are to be separated from sin through the power of the Holy Spirit of God.

They are called out to be set apart from sin and death; called out to be set apart unto holiness and godliness through sincere repentance, a baptismal commitment to "go and sin no more," and the removal of sin and spiritual death by the application of the sacrifice of the Lamb of God Jesus Christ, followed by the empowerment of Christ living in them by the agency of the Holy Spirit.

> **1 Thessalonians 5:21** Prove all things; hold fast that which is good. **5:22 Abstain from all appearance of evil.**

The Mosaic Covenant was a marriage covenant between God and the physical nation of Israel.

That covenant contained a priesthood to fulfill ecclesiastical duties and act as intercessors between God and physical Israel. The priesthood together with the Levites were of only one tribe by God's direction, which means that everyone else was left out of any deep personal relationship with God.

The Law of the Nazarite allowed people in the nation to voluntarily dedicate themselves to godly service.

The Babylonian church government system condemned by God

Today many have fallen into the error of leading the people to follow themselves instead of following the whole Word of God, just as much of the priesthood of Mosaic Israel did at various times, when they led people astray after themselves and their idols instead of focusing the people on obedience to God's Word.

Today many elders have become infatuated with their supposed authority and instead of leading people to obey God they lead people astray to obey themselves. They reason that God has placed them in authority over God's people and that they should be obeyed as if they are God; and reason that they have the right to make decisions and to bind and loose the Word of God at their own pleasure. See the Binding and Loosing article.

This abominable heresy is generally known as the "Primacy of Peter" and is widely accepted by the ministry and brethren today [even if not by that term] and large groups of brethren idolize men even today.

Brethren, we are to prove all things by the Word of God and to follow men ONLY as they follow God. If we follow any man contrary to the whole Word of God; we have turned away from the Eternal to make gods of men and to follow them!

> **Deuteronomy 28:14** And thou shalt not go aside from any of the words which I command thee this day, to the right hand, or to the left, to go after other gods to serve them.

Many men make themselves into the idols [false gods] of many and use the name of Christ to focus the brethren on themselves or their false traditions or church organization, as it is written to the disciples. See the Priesthood and Ministry and See also The Nicolaitanes.

> **Matthew 24:4** And Jesus answered and said unto them, Take heed that no man deceive you. **24:5** For many shall come in my name, saying, I [that Jesus is Christ] am Christ; and shall deceive many.

Also see our article on Nazarites.

Numbers 7

Numbers 7 is about preparing for anointing the altar and the consecration of the Levites to their service.

See the Priesthood and Ministry series for more on the Priests, Levites, the Mosaic Administration and the New Testament Ministry.

When the tabernacle was completed the elders of the tribes brought wagons and oxen as a gift to God.

Numbers 7:1 And it came to pass on the day that Moses had fully set up the tabernacle, and had anointed it, and sanctified it, and all the instruments thereof, both the altar and all the vessels thereof, and had anointed them, and sanctified them; **7:2** That the princes of Israel, heads of the house of their fathers, who were the princes of the tribes, and were over them that were numbered, offered: **7:3** And they brought their offering before the LORD, **six covered wagons, and twelve oxen; a wagon for two of the princes, and for each one an ox:** and they brought them before the tabernacle.

These gifts of conveyances were is preparation for the moving of the items of the tabernacle. These wagons were to be used to carry the utensils and coverings of the tabernacle. This history may have later led David to mistakenly try to move the Ark of the Covenant on an ox pulled cart.

7:4 And the LORD spake unto Moses, saying, **7:5** Take it of them, that they may be to do the service of the tabernacle of the congregation; and thou shalt give them unto the Levites, to every man according to his service. **7:6** And Moses took the wagons and the oxen, and gave them unto the Levites.

The wagons were given to the two families of Levi, Gershon and Merari, to carry their part of the tabernacle as in Numbers 4.

The holy things were to be wrapped by the priests and then carried by hand by the sons of Kohath.

7:7 Two wagons and four oxen he gave unto the sons of Gershon, according to their service: **7:8** And **four wagons and eight oxen he gave unto the sons of Merari**, according unto their service, under the hand of Ithamar the son of Aaron the priest. **7:9** But **unto the sons of Kohath he gave none: because the service of the sanctuary belonging unto them was that they should bear upon their shoulders.**

7:10 And the princes offered for dedicating of the altar in the day that it was anointed, even the princes offered their offering before the altar.

Then on each day for twelve days, each new ruler of the various tribes offered an offering for the new tabernacle out of their particular tribe: In this way providing for the anointing and consecration of the Altar. These offerings included silver and gold implements and grain for the unleavened bread offerings, and animals for sacrifices.

7:11 And the LORD said unto Moses, They shall offer their offering, each prince on his day, for the dedicating of the altar.

7:12 And he that offered his **offering the first day was Nahshon the son of Amminadab, of the tribe of Judah: 7:13** And his offering was **one silver charger, the weight thereof was an hundred and thirty shekels, one silver bowl of seventy shekels,** after the shekel of the sanctuary; **both of them were full of fine flour mingled with oil for a** [an unleavened bread offering] **meat offering: 7:14 One spoon of ten shekels of gold, full of incense: 7:15 One young bullock, one ram, one lamb of the first year, for a burnt offering: 7:16 One kid of the goats for a sin offering: 7:17** And **for a sacrifice of peace offerings, two oxen, five rams, five he goats, five lambs of the first year** [in their first year]: this was the offering of Nahshon the son of Amminadab.

7:18 On the **second day Nethaneel the son of Zuar, prince of Issachar**, did offer: **7:19** He offered for his offering **one silver charger, the weight whereof was an hundred and thirty shekels, one silver bowl of seventy shekels**, after the shekel of the sanctuary; **both of them full of fine flour mingled with oil for a meat offering**: **7:20 One spoon of gold of ten shekels, full of incense: 7:21 One young bullock, one ram, one lamb of the first year, for a burnt offering: 7:22 One kid of the goats for a sin offering: 7:23 And for a sacrifice of peace offerings, two oxen, five rams, five he goats, five lambs of the first year**: this was the offering of Nethaneel the son of Zuar.

7:24 On the **third day Eliab the son of Helon, prince of the children of Zebulun**, did offer: **7:25** His offering **was one silver charger, the weight whereof was an hundred and thirty shekels, one silver bowl of seventy shekels**, after the shekel of the sanctuary; both of them full of fine flour mingled with oil for a meat offering: **7:26 One golden spoon of ten shekels, full of incense: 7:27 One young bullock, one ram, one lamb of the first year, for a burnt offering: 7:28 One kid of the goats for a sin offering: 7:29 And for a sacrifice of peace offerings, two oxen, five rams, five he goats, five lambs of the first year**: this was the offering of Eliab the son of Helon.

7:30 On the **fourth day Elizur the son of Shedeur, prince of the children of Reuben**, did offer: **7:31** His offering was **one silver charger of the weight of an hundred and thirty shekels, one silver bowl of seventy shekels, after the shekel of the sanctuary; both of them full of fine flour mingled with oil for a meat offering: 7:32 One golden spoon of ten shekels, full of incense: 7:33 One young bullock, one ram, one lamb of the first year, for a burnt offering: 7:34 One kid of the goats for a sin offering: 7:35 And for a sacrifice of peace offerings, two oxen, five rams, five he goats, five lambs of the first year:** this was the offering of Elizur the son of Shedeur.

7:36 On the **fifth day Shelumiel the son of Zurishaddai, prince of the children of Simeon**, did offer: **7:37** His offering was **one silver charger, the weight whereof was an hundred and thirty shekels, one silver bowl of seventy shekels, after the shekel of the sanctuary; both of them full of fine flour mingled with oil for a meat offering: 7:38 One golden spoon of ten shekels, full of incense: 7:39 One young bullock, one ram, one lamb of the first year, for a burnt offering: 7:40 One kid of the goats for a sin offering: 7:41 And for a sacrifice of peace offerings, two oxen, five rams, five he goats, five lambs of the first year:** this was the offering of Shelumiel the son of Zurishaddai.

7:42 On the **sixth day Eliasaph the son of Deuel, prince of the children of Gad,** offered: **7:43** His offering was **one silver charger of the weight of an hundred and thirty shekels, a silver bowl of seventy shekels, after the shekel of the sanctuary; both of them full of fine flour mingled with oil for a meat offering: 7:44 One golden spoon of ten shekels, full of incense: 7:45 One young bullock, one ram, one lamb of the first year, for a burnt offering: 7:46 One kid of the goats for a sin offering: 7:47 And for a sacrifice of peace offerings, two oxen, five rams, five he goats, five lambs of the first year:** this was the offering of Eliasaph the son of Deuel.

7:48 On the **seventh day Elishama the son of Ammihud, prince of the children of Ephraim**, offered: **7:49** His offering was **one silver charger, the weight whereof was an hundred and thirty shekels, one silver bowl of seventy shekels, after the shekel of the sanctuary; both of them full of fine flour mingled with oil for a meat offering: 7:50 One golden spoon of ten shekels, full of incense: 7:51 One young bullock, one ram, one lamb of the first year, for a burnt offering: 7:52 One kid of the goats for a sin offering: 7:53 And for a sacrifice of peace offerings, two oxen, five rams, five he goats, five lambs of the first year:** this was the offering of Elishama the son of Ammihud.

7:54 On the **eighth day offered Gamaliel the son of Pedahzur, prince of the children of Manasseh: 7:55** His offering was **one silver charger of the weight of an hundred and thirty shekels, one silver bowl of seventy shekels, after the shekel of the sanctuary; both of them full of fine flour mingled with oil for a meat offering: 7:56 One golden spoon of ten shekels, full of incense: 7:57 One young bullock, one ram, one lamb of the first year, for a burnt offering: 7:58 One kid of the goats for a sin offering: 7:59 And for a sacrifice of peace offerings, two oxen, five rams, five he goats, five lambs of the first year:** this was the offering of Gamaliel the son of Pedahzur.

7:60 On the **ninth day Abidan the son of Gideoni, prince of the children of Benjamin**, offered: **7:61** His offering was **one silver charger, the weight whereof was an hundred and thirty shekels, one silver bowl of seventy shekels, after the shekel of the sanctuary; both of them full of fine flour mingled with oil for a meat offering: 7:62 One golden spoon of ten shekels, full of incense: 7:63 One young bullock, one ram, one lamb of the first year, for a burnt offering: 7:64 One kid of the goats for a sin offering: 7:65 And for a sacrifice of peace offerings, two oxen, five rams, five he goats, five lambs of the first year:** this was the offering of Abidan the son of Gideoni.

7:66 On the **tenth day Ahiezer the son of Ammishaddai, prince of the children of Dan**, offered: **7:67** His offering was **one silver charger, the weight whereof was an hundred and thirty shekels, one silver bowl of seventy shekels, after the shekel of the sanctuary; both of them full of fine flour mingled with oil for a meat offering: 7:68 One golden spoon of ten shekels, full of incense: 7:69 One young bullock, one ram, one lamb of the first year, for a burnt offering: 7:70 One kid of the goats for a sin offering: 7:71 And for a sacrifice of peace offerings, two oxen, five rams, five he goats, five lambs of the first year:** this was the offering of Ahiezer the son of Ammishaddai.

7:72 On the **eleventh day Pagiel the son of Ocran, prince of the children of Asher**, offered: **7:73** His offering was **one silver charger, the weight whereof was an hundred and thirty shekels, one silver bowl of seventy shekels, after the shekel of the sanctuary; both of them full of fine flour mingled with oil for a meat offering: 7:74 One golden spoon of ten shekels, full of incense: 7:75 One young bullock, one ram, one lamb of the first year, for a burnt offering: 7:76 One kid of the goats for a sin offering: 7:77 And for a sacrifice of peace offerings, two oxen, five rams, five he goats, five lambs of the first year:** this was the offering of Pagiel the son of Ocran.

7:78 On the **twelfth day Ahira the son of Enan, prince of the children of Naphtali**, offered: **7:79** His offering was **one silver charger, the weight whereof was an hundred and thirty shekels, one silver bowl of seventy shekels, after the shekel of the sanctuary; both of them full of fine flour mingled with oil for a meat offering: 7:80 One golden spoon of ten shekels, full of incense: 7:81 One young bullock, one ram, one lamb of the first year, for a burnt offering: 7:82 One kid of the goats for a sin offering: 7:83 And for a sacrifice of peace offerings, two oxen, five rams, five he goats, five lambs of the first year:** this was the offering of Ahira the son of Enan.

We should notice that while the gifts of each tribe were identical; each tribe, its leader and its gift is carefully listed. This because this is for the dedication and consecration of the tabernacle, which is to be the residence of God through the dwelling of the Holy Spirit, the Shekinah of God; within the whole assembly of Israel. This being a picture of God dwelling within His people through the Shekinah or Holy Spirit in the New Covenant of Jeremiah 31.

After the end of the bringing of these gifts, the altar was dedicated and consecrated [Set Apart] as Holy.

7:84 This was the dedication of the altar, in the day when it was anointed, by the princes of Israel: twelve chargers of silver, twelve silver bowls, twelve spoons of gold: **7:85** Each charger of silver weighing an hundred and thirty shekels, each bowl seventy: all the silver vessels weighed two thousand and four hundred shekels, after the shekel of the sanctuary: **7:86** The golden spoons were twelve, full of incense, weighing ten shekels apiece, after the shekel of the sanctuary: all the gold of the spoons was an hundred and twenty shekels.

The physical sin offering pictures the sacrifice of the Lamb of God to atone for all sin in the spiritual sense; and then after our repentance and the application of the Sin Offering of the Lamb of God, we are to go and sin no more!

Sinning no more and instead going on to wholeheartedly live by every Word of God is pictured by the Burnt Offering.

The whole animal of the Burnt Offering is to be consumed in the fire, picturing a continual zeal and wholehearted service to God the Father in heaven; with the smoke rising up, symbolic of the faithful dedicated service of the offerors as rising up before God as a very sweet and acceptable thing to God the Father in heaven.

The opposite of this wholehearted service to God is the lukewarm, spiritually lax and compromising service to God of today's Spiritual Ekklesia, who love following idols of men, corporate entities and false traditions more than loving living by every Word of God. The Laodicean attitude which has overwhelmed today's corporate Ekklesia groups is an ABOMINATION to God the Father and to Jesus Christ.

7:87 All the oxen for the burnt offering were twelve bullocks, the rams twelve, the lambs of the first year twelve, with their meat offering: and the kids of the goats for sin offering twelve.

Once sin has been sincerely repented of we are to go on to never again sin wilfully; instead serving God and living by every Word of God with a wholehearted dedication of will and deeds; then we will come into a unity of spirit with God the Father in heaven and with the Son.

True Spiritual Unity of the people comes through unity with God through a deep dedication to learn and to keep his Word. Those who seek a corporate unity based on tolerating the false teachings of men; separate themselves from God!

It is through enthusiastically living by every Word of God that we become totally at one with God the Father; and reach a state of reconciliation and full peace with God as represented by the peace offering.

7:88 And all the oxen for the sacrifice of the peace offerings were twenty and four bullocks, the rams sixty, the he goats sixty, the lambs of the first year sixty. This was the dedication of the altar, after that it was anointed.

7:89 And when Moses was gone into the tabernacle of the congregation to speak with him [God], then he heard the voice of one speaking unto him from off the mercy seat that was upon the ark of testimony, from between the two cherubims: and he spake unto him.

Then God commanded Moses to sanctify the Levites to their service, which is recorded in Chapter 8.

Numbers 8

In King James England olive oil was not common and wax candles were used for light which confused the translation to candles instead of the correct oil lamp.

God's commandments concerning the seven branched lamp stand and its seven lights which are wicks each one set in a bowl at the top of each branch, the bowls filled with pure olive oil and the wicks lighted.

Numbers 8:1 And the LORD spake unto Moses, saying, **8:2** Speak unto Aaron and say unto him, When thou lightest the lamps, the seven lamps [one lamp or Menorah with seven branches] shall give light over against the candlestick [lamp stand]. **8:3** And Aaron did so; he lighted the lamps thereof over against the candlestick, as the LORD commanded Moses.

The seven branched lamp stands or menorah to be placed in the tabernacle were to be made of beaten gold. The light produced by burning pure olive oil, pictured the light of Godliness produced by using the indwelling of the Holy Spirit and following that Holy Spirit into Christ-like zeal to live by every Word of God.

> **Matthew 5:14 Ye are the light of the world.** A city that is set on an hill cannot be hid. **5:15** Neither do men light a candle [lamp], and put it under a bushel, but on a candlestick [lamp stand]; and it giveth light unto all that are in the house.

Let the light of your zeal for the whole Word of God shine brightly in your example of passion to learn and live by every Word of God, which is the product and proof of the indwelling of the Spirit of God within you. It is the indwelling of God's Spirit and our zeal to follow it, which leads us into unity with God and makes the light of our example to shine before all who see us.

> **5:16 Let your light so shine before men, that they may see your good works**, and glorify your Father which is in heaven.

Numbers 8:4 And this work of the candlestick was of beaten gold, unto the shaft thereof, unto the flowers thereof, was beaten work: according unto the pattern which the LORD had shewed Moses, so he made the candlestick.

> **Exodus 25:31** And thou shalt make a candlestick of pure gold: of beaten work shall the candlestick be made: his shaft, and his branches, his bowls, his knops [buds], and his flowers, shall be of the same.
>
> **25:32** And six branches shall come out of the sides of it; three branches of the candlestick out of the one side, and three branches of the candlestick out of the other side:
>
> **25:33** Three bowls made like unto almonds, with a knop [bud] and a flower in one branch; and three bowls made like almonds in the other branch, with a knop and a flower: so in the six branches that come out of the candlestick.
>
> **25:34** And in the candlesticks shall be four bowls made like unto almonds, with their knops [buds] and their flowers.
>
> **25:35** And there shall be a knop [bud] under two branches of the same, and a knop under two branches of the same, and a knop under two branches of the same, according to the six branches that proceed out of the candlestick.
>
> **25:36** Their knops [buds] and their branches shall be of the same: all it shall be one beaten work of pure gold.

The consecration of the Levites

Numbers 8:5 And the LORD spake unto Moses, saying, **8:6** Take the Levites from among the children of Israel, and cleanse them.

The Levites were to shave off all the hair on their bodies and then to wash themselves and their clothes, so as to be completely clean.

8:7 And thus shalt thou do unto them, to cleanse them: Sprinkle water of purifying upon them, and let them shave all their flesh, and let them wash their clothes, and so make themselves clean.

8:8 Then let them take a young bullock with his meat offering, even fine flour mingled with oil, and another young bullock shalt thou take for a sin offering.

Then the people were to lay hands on and ordain the Levites to the service of God; from this and other examples comes the modern ordination to ministerial offices and even the laying on of hands after baptism.

Just like God called the Levites to his service we are to lay hands on [ordain] ONLY those who God has clearly chosen as revealed by their fruits of faithful diligence in the righteousness of the whole Word of God. The ordaining of people for graduating from a college or for their loyalties to men as is commonly done is a false ordination and is not respected by God.

8:9 And thou shalt bring the Levites before the tabernacle of the congregation: and thou shalt gather the whole assembly of the children of Israel together: **8:10** And thou shalt bring the Levites before the LORD: and **the children of Israel shall put their hands upon the Levites: 8:11** And Aaron shall offer the Levites before the LORD for an offering of the children of Israel, that they may execute the service of the LORD.

The Levites then offered a bull for a Sin Offering to cover their sins; and then offered another bull as a Burnt Offering representing the patient, powerful, single minded, wholehearted service to which they were called.

8:12 And the Levites shall lay their hands upon the heads of the bullocks: and thou shalt offer the one for a sin offering, and the other for a burnt offering, unto the LORD, to make an atonement for the Levites.

Then the Levites were presented to the priests as an offering of service to God, and a help to the priests.

8:13 And thou shalt set the Levites before Aaron, and before his sons, and offer them for an offering unto the LORD.

This whole process in how the priests and Levites are to be consecrated to their service is analogous of the consecration of baptism of the New Covenant called out to become priests of today's New Covenant High Priest Jesus Christ. The Mosaic priests and Levites had to wash and remove all uncleanness and sin, and baptism is the washing away of all past uncleanness of service to false gods and sin.

8:14 Thus shalt thou separate the Levites from among the children of Israel: and the Levites shall be mine.

The Levites were given to serve God by assisting the priests in place of the first born of Israel; and after their consecration they were sanctified to serve in the physical things of the tabernacle: The actual sacrifices and holy things, being reserved for the priesthood.

8:15 And after that shall the Levites go in to do the service of the tabernacle of the congregation: and thou shalt cleanse them, and offer them for an offering.

The first born of Israel were saved in Egypt by the blood of the lamb on their doorposts and they all belong to God because he spared them.

This is a symbol that all of the sincerely repentant of the New Covenant, have also had the blood of the Lamb applied to the doorposts of their hearts and have been spared from their bondage to sin as a kind of first fruits of a much larger harvest of lives; the Lamb himself being the first born of many brethren.

Therefore they [and we] belong to God the Father and Jesus Christ and are NOT their [or our] own; we are to fully and wholeheartedly become like God the Father and Jesus Christ for we belong to them! We are to learn and to keep the whole Word of God, which is the nature of God the Father and Jesus Christ in print; which is our reasonable service to God.

8:16 For they are wholly given unto me from among the children of Israel; instead of such as open every womb, even instead of the firstborn of all the children of Israel, have I taken them unto me.

8:17 For **all the firstborn of the children of Israel are mine, both man and beast: on the day that I smote every firstborn in the land of Egypt I sanctified them for myself.**

8:18 And I have taken the Levites for all the firstborn of the children of Israel.

8:19 And **I have given the Levites as a gift to Aaron and to his sons** from among the children of Israel, to do the service of the children of Israel in the tabernacle of the congregation, and to make an atonement for the children of Israel: that there be no plague among the children of Israel, when the children of Israel come nigh unto the sanctuary.

8:20 And Moses, and Aaron, and all the congregation of the children of Israel, did to the Levites according unto all that the LORD commanded Moses concerning the Levites, so did the children of Israel unto them. **8:21** And the Levites were purified, and they washed their clothes; and Aaron offered them as an offering before the LORD; and Aaron made an atonement for them to cleanse them. **8:22** And after that went the Levites in to do their service in the tabernacle of the congregation before Aaron, and before his sons: as the LORD had commanded Moses concerning the Levites, so did they unto them.

The physical work of the Levites was from the age of 25 to the age of 50; after which they were to retire from physical labor to teach and supervise others.

8:23 And the LORD spake unto Moses, saying, **8:24** This is it that belongeth unto the Levites: from twenty and five years old and upward they shall go in to wait upon the service of the tabernacle of the congregation: **8:25** And from the age of fifty years they shall cease waiting upon the service thereof, and shall serve no more: **8:26 But shall minister** [supervise and teach] **with their brethren in the tabernacle of the congregation, to keep the charge, and shall do no service** [no physical work]. Thus shalt thou do unto the Levites touching their charge.

Numbers 9

Here we have an inset back to the Passover of the first month of the second year of the Exodus; the previous events in Numbers came in the second month of the second year.

Numbers 9:1 And the LORD spake unto Moses in the wilderness of Sinai, in the first month of the second year after they were come out of the land of Egypt, saying, **9:2** Let the children of Israel also keep the passover at his appointed season. **9:3 In the fourteenth day of this month, at even** [the beginning of the evening starting the 14th day, since the destroyer went through Egypt at midnight on the fourteenth day] , ye shall keep it in his appointed season: according to all the rites of it, and according to all the ceremonies thereof, shall ye keep it.

The Passover is to be kept on the fourteenth day, and therefore is not to be kept after the sunset which ended the 14th day; which would actually be on the 15th day. Since the Passover is to be kept on the evening and also ON the 14th day it is to be kept just after sunset BEGINNING the 14th day.

9:4 And Moses spake unto the children of Israel, that they should keep the passover. **9:5** And they kept the passover **on the fourteenth day**; of the first month at even in the wilderness of Sinai: according to all that the LORD commanded Moses, so did the children of Israel.

A solution for those unable to keep the Passover in the 14th day of the first month.

9:6 And there were certain men, who were defiled by the dead body of a man, that they could not keep the passover on that day: and they came before Moses and before Aaron on that day: **9:7** And those men said unto him, We are defiled by the dead body of a man: wherefore are we kept back, that we may not offer an offering of the LORD in his appointed season among the children of Israel? **9:8** And Moses said unto them, Stand still, and I will hear what the LORD will command concerning you.

Being physically unclean or far off is a symbol of being separated from God and far off from HIM through spiritual uncleanness by reason of unrepented sin. Spiritually, Passover cannot be taken while in a state of unrepented sin.

Genuine repentance is a sincere and wholehearted commitment to go and sin no more. It is because the vast majority of today's spiritual Ekklesia take the Passover unworthily by repenting in name only and insisting on their own ways, that so much correction is falling upon them.

Here we also have a command to eat the Passover lamb with unleavened bread and bitter herbs. Eating the lamb and the unleavened bread represents internalizing the life and sinless nature of Jesus Christ to live as he lived. The bitter herbs represented the acceptance of our trials as he accepted his trials. See the Passover Symbols article.

9:9 And the LORD spake unto Moses, saying, **9:10** Speak unto the children of Israel, saying, If any man of you or of your posterity shall be unclean by reason of a dead body, or be in a journey afar off, **yet he shall keep the passover unto the LORD. 9:11 The fourteenth day of the second month at even they shall keep it,** andeat it **with unleavened bread and bitter herbs.**

During the time that this command was given all Israel was in one camp at Sinai with the tabernacle at its center.

The Second Passover and the Feast of Unleavened Bread

Later when Israel entered and spread across Palestine the people were to travel to the place where the tabernacle [later the temple] was located, to kill and eat the Passover before God. They were then to remain before God at the tabernacle/temple for the seven days of the Feast of Unleavened Bread.

Since they were to present themselves before God at the tabernacle/temple for Passover AND the seven day feast of Unleavened Bread, the full eight days was a pilgrim feast to God, just like the seven days of Tabernacles together with the Feast of the Eighth Day.

The Passover and the Feast of Unleavened are inseparable from one another: Passover picturing the application of the sacrifice of the Lamb of God and the seven day Feast picturing coming out of sin and internalizing the Nature of God.

Passover Details

No bone shall be broken, just as no bone of Messiah was broken in his life or in his death. No part of the Passover could be left over until the morning [all leftovers must be burned]; symbolizing that Jesus would be buried before the sunset ending the 14th day of the first month.

9:12 They shall leave none of it unto the morning, nor break any bone of it: according to all the ordinances of the passover they shall keep it.

Taking the Passover was essential to remain in the Mosaic Covenant, it is also essential to take the Passover at the appointed time to remain reconciled to God the Father in the New Covenant.

Eating the Passover with unleavened bread and eating unleavened bread for each of the seven days of the Feast of Unleavened Bread after Passover, pictures internalizing the very nature of Jesus Christ and God the Father.

Failing to eat the Passover or to eat unleavened bread for each of the seven subsequent days is a rejection of the commandment of God and pictures a refusal to internalize the Word and Nature of God.

Those who do take the Passover without sincerely repenting of all sin and compromising with the Word of God; are making a mockery of the sacrifice of Jesus Christ the Lamb of God.

Brethren, today we are in grave danger of reaching the state where we will not repent and would rather follow men and not God, having been deceived into thinking that blindly following men is the same as following God; It is NOT!

We think of ourselves as righteous while we justify our sin of idolizing men and the false traditions of men, refusing to repent of our idolatry; which refusal to repent is unpardonable.

Our only hope is that we have been deceived into this evil and that our Lord will cast us into great tribulation so that we might see the errors of standing on the false traditions of men contrary to any part of the whole

Word of God, and sincerely repent turning to a wholehearted zeal to live by every Word of God.

> **Hebrews 6:4** For it is impossible for those who were once enlightened, and have tasted of the heavenly gift, and were made partakers of the Holy Ghost, **6:5** And have tasted the good word of God, and the powers of the world to come,

If we take the Passover without repenting of our lack of faithful zeal to live by every Word of God and our not exalting the Ruler of Eternity above all else; we make a mockery of the sacrifice of the Lamb of God!

> **6:7** If they shall fall away, to renew them again unto repentance; seeing **they crucify to themselves the Son of God afresh, and put him to an open shame.**

Numbers 9:13 But the man that is clean, and is not in a journey, and forbeareth to keep the passover, even the same soul shall be cut off from among his people: because he brought not the offering of the LORD in his appointed season, that man shall bear his sin.

The stranger [unconverted person] may keep the Passover only if he sincerely repents, symbolized at that time by being circumcised, and commits to live by every Word of God in future.

> **Genesis 12:48** And when a stranger shall sojourn with thee, and will keep the passover to the Lord, let all his males be circumcised, and then let him come near and keep it; and he shall be as one that is born in the land: for no uncircumcised person shall eat thereof.

Numbers 9:14 And if a stranger shall sojourn among you, and will keep the passover unto the LORD; according to the ordinance of the passover, and according to the manner thereof, so shall he do: ye shall have one ordinance, both for the stranger, and for him that was born in the land.

The explanation of how the people knew when to stay put or to move in their journey. They followed Christ by following the movement of the cloud, for the God Being who later gave up his God-hood to be made flesh as Jesus Christ was in the cloud from the time that they began to leave Egypt.

This too is an allegory for us; the cloud of water and the pillar of fire representing the lead of God's Word and the Holy Spirit. We are to follow ONLY the Word of God through the power of the Holy Spirit from the time that we are called out of bondage in spiritual Egypt: The Word of God is the nature of God the Father and Jesus Christ in print.

9:15 And on the day that the tabernacle was reared up the cloud covered the tabernacle, namely, the tent of the testimony: and at even there was upon the tabernacle as it were the appearance of fire, until the morning.

9:16 So it was alway: the cloud covered it by day, and the appearance of fire by night. 9:17 And when the cloud was taken up from the tabernacle, then after that the children of Israel journeyed: and in the place where the cloud abode, there the children of Israel pitched their tents. **9:18** At the commandment of the LORD the children of Israel journeyed, and at the commandment of the LORD they pitched: as long as the cloud abode upon the tabernacle they rested in their tents. **9:19** And when the cloud tarried long upon the tabernacle many days, then the children of Israel kept the charge of the LORD, and journeyed not.

Brethren, we are to ONLY follow the lead of God the Father and Jesus Christ who is the chief cornerstone of the whole Word of Almighty God. God and God alone, leads us out of the bondage to Satan and sin of spiritual Egypt, and out of the sin of breaking or compromising with any part of God's Word.

The Lamb of God is our ONLY Effectual Sacrifice and Deliverer; not the traditions of men!

9:20 And so it was, when the cloud was a few days upon the tabernacle; according to the commandment of the LORD they abode in their tents, and according to the commandment of the LORD they journeyed.

9:21 And so it was, when the cloud abode from even unto the morning, and that **the cloud was taken up in the morning, then they journeyed: whether it was by day or by night that the cloud was taken up, they journeyed.**

9:22 Or whether it were two days, or a month, or a year, that the cloud tarried upon the tabernacle, remaining thereon, the children of Israel abode in their tents, and journeyed not: but when it was taken up, they journeyed.

The Passover is a commitment to learn, follow and to live by every Word God, which is the Holy Scriptures; without compromise or any hint of turning to the left or to the right: FOREVER!

9:23 At the commandment of the LORD they rested in the tents, and at the commandment of the LORD they journeyed: they kept the charge of the LORD, at the commandment of the LORD by the hand of Moses.

Numbers 10

The two silver trumpets

Numbers 10:1 And the LORD spake unto Moses, saying, **10:2** Make thee two trumpets of silver; of a whole piece shalt thou make them: that thou mayest use them for the calling of the assembly, and for the journeying of the camps.

The two silver trumpets are to be made of one piece of silver; this is speaking of each trumpet coming from a very large piece of pure silver. They both to be sounded together, and their purpose is to call all the people to assemble.

The two silver trumpets are to sound to call all the people to assemble before the mediator of the covenant Moses, at the door of the tabernacle before God.

The silver trumpets are also to be sounded over the New Moon and High Day sacrifices, v 10.

10:3 And when they shall blow with them [both], all the assembly shall assemble themselves **to thee at the door of the tabernacle of the congregation.**

If only one is sounded the captains and elders of the people were to assemble.

10:4 And if they blow but **with one trumpet, then the princes, which are heads of the thousands of Israel,** shall gather themselves unto thee.

If the alarm of the trumpet blast sounds when the people are gathered and ready to move, it is the signal for the camp move forward. The meaning of the word blast, here translated as "alarm," is not clear and it could mean a special kind of call.

10:5 When ye blow an alarm, then the camps that lie on the east parts shall go forward. **10:6** When ye blow an alarm the second time, then the camps that lie on the south side shall take their journey: they shall blow an alarm for their journeys.

10:7 But when the congregation is to be gathered together, ye shall blow [to call an assembly], but ye shall not sound an alarm.

Only the priests may sound the silver trumpets, while any person could sound the shofar.

10:8 And **the sons of Aaron, the priests, shall blow with the trumpets**; and they shall be to you for an **ordinance for ever throughout your generations**.

The priests must sound these special silver trumpets calling the people to assemble before God during times of war. If the people rally to God they will be remembered by God and saved from their enemies.

The meaning of this is that victory in war comes through rallying to and following God; this is an allegory that spiritual victory over Satan and sin comes only through the power of God and that victory over sin only comes through diligently obeying and following our God.

10:9 And if ye go to war in your land against the enemy that oppresseth you, then **ye shall blow an alarm with the trumpets; and ye shall be remembered before the LORD your God, and ye shall be saved from your enemies.**

The two silver trumpets [along with shofars] are to be sounded on the new moons, and on the High Days as a memorial for the people to remember and come to God, so that God may remember the people who are called to assemble before him,

We are to gather before God to learn of him and to learn to live by every Word of God our Mighty One!

These two silver trumpets are to be sounded over all the burnt and peace offerings on ALL of the High Days and new moons, which are indicative of the faithful wholehearted service of Jesus Christ to God the Father as an example that we should do likewise.

10:10 Also in the day of your gladness, and in your solemn days, and in the beginnings of your months, ye shall blow with the trumpets over your burnt offerings, and over the sacrifices of your peace offerings; that they may be to you for a memorial before your God: I am the LORD your God.

Physical Israel having been called out of the bondage of Egypt and married to Christ at Sinai; the commandments, law, statutes, and judgments received by Israel and the Priests and Levites now sanctified to their service and the army organized; the journey to the physical promised land begins.

10:11 And it came to pass on the **twentieth day of the second month, in the second year,** that the cloud was taken up from off the tabernacle of the testimony.

10:12 And the children of Israel took their journeys out of the wilderness of Sinai; and the cloud rested in the wilderness of Paran. **10:13** And they first took their journey according to the commandment of the LORD by the hand of Moses.

10:14 In the first place went the standard of the camp of the children of Judah according to their armies: and over his host was Nahshon the son of Amminadab. **10:15** And over the host of the tribe of the children of Issachar was Nethaneel the son of Zuar. **10:16** And over the host of the tribe of the children of Zebulun was Eliab the son of Helon.

10:17 And the tabernacle was taken down; and the sons of Gershon and the sons of Merari set forward, bearing the tabernacle.

10:18 And the standard of the camp of Reuben set forward according to their armies: and over his host was Elizur the son of Shedeur. **10:19** And over the host of the tribe of the children of Simeon was Shelumiel the son of Zurishaddai. **10:20** And over the host of the tribe of the children of Gad was Eliasaph the son of Deuel.

10:21 And the Kohathites set forward, bearing the sanctuary: and the other did set up the tabernacle against they came.

10:22 And the standard of the camp of the children of Ephraim set forward according to their armies: and over his host was Elishama the son of Ammihud. **10:23** And over the host of the tribe of the children of Manasseh was Gamaliel the son of Pedahzur. **10:24** And over the host of the tribe of the children of Benjamin was Abidan the son of Gideoni. **10:25** And the standard of the camp of the children of Dan set forward, which was the rereward of all the camps throughout their hosts: and over his host was Ahiezer the son of Ammishaddai.

10:26 And over the host of the tribe of the children of Asher was Pagiel the son of Ocran. **10:27** And over the host of the tribe of the children of Naphtali was Ahira the son of Enan.

10:28 Thus were the journeyings of the children of Israel according to their armies, when they set forward.

Moses and his father in law separate close to the border of the physical promised land.

10:29 And Moses said unto Hobab, the son of Raguel the Midianite, Moses' father in law, We are journeying unto the place of which the LORD said, I will give it you: come thou with us, and we will do thee good: for the LORD hath spoken good concerning Israel.

10:30 And he said unto him, I will not go; but I will depart to mine own land, and to my kindred.

Moses asks this Bedouin chief to be his guide to inform him of the land and promises to share all things with him, but he returns to his own people.

10:31 And he said, Leave us not, I pray thee; forasmuch as thou knowest how we are to encamp in the wilderness, and **thou mayest be to us instead of eyes**. **10:32** And it shall be, if thou go with us, yea, it shall be, **that what goodness the LORD shall do unto us, the same will we do unto thee.**

They took a three day journey from Mt Sinai

10:33 And they departed from the mount of the LORD three days' journey: and the ark of the covenant of the LORD went before them in the three days' journey, to search out a resting place for them.

10:34 And the cloud of the LORD was upon them by day, when they went out of the camp.

Moses called upon Christ to scatter and destroy the enemies of God whenever the cloud obscuring the presence of God went forward.

Should we not do the same thing and call out to God for our deliverance, faithfully following the lead of the Spirit of God to live by every Word of God instead of trusting in the false traditions of men?

Let us keep the whole Word of God with consummate zeal; let us keep the sanctity of the Sabbath, not buying or selling or working or paying others to serve us on God's Holy Sabbath Day! Let us keep the sanctity of all the things of God: Let us rejoice to do the will of our Greatly Beloved regardless of what men can do!

10:35 And it came to pass, when the ark set forward, that Moses said, **Rise up, LORD, and let thine enemies be scattered; and let them that hate thee flee before thee.**

10:36 And when it rested, he said, **Return, O LORD, unto the many thousands of Israel.**

Numbers 11

The camp moved to Taberah where the people began to complain and were corrected by the God who later gave up his God-hood to be made flesh as Jesus Christ.

These complaints were not about going to God and asking for his help to bring them relief, these folks in Sinai were complaining AGAINST God.

This is a repeated theme in Numbers and was recorded as an example for us, to teach us that we should not blame God and his Word for our trials, but that we should understand that such trials come to test their loyalty and steadfastness to God and his Word, and to build strength and character. See The Job studies.

Just as they received the fire of correction for falling away from the Word of God and failing the test, so today's spiritual Ekklesia will also be corrected in the furnace of affliction.

Numbers 11:1 And when the people complained, it displeased the LORD: and the LORD heard it; and his anger was kindled; and the fire of the LORD burnt among them, and consumed them that were in the uttermost parts of the camp.

The people repented, but they repented in name only to try and avoid correction.

They did not sincerely and wholeheartedly turn from their own ways to embrace their Husband and every Word of God!

How like them we are! We trust in our own ways and when things go wrong we repent in word only, and then we continue to compromise further and further away from any zeal to live by every Word of God!

11:2 And the people cried unto Moses; and when Moses prayed unto the LORD, the fire was quenched. **11:3** And he called the name of the place Taberah: because the fire of the LORD burnt among them.

A mixed people [typical of tares amongst the wheat] took the opportunity to leave Egypt with Israel, and within the assembly they stirred up dissent against the sound doctrine of the Word of God and affected Israel by their example.

This is an instructional example of what has happened today's church of God which has overall adopted the Business Model Outreach and knowingly allowed very many unconverted into the assembly; baptizing sincere people who may support the corporate entity, but who did not understand that they were making a commitment to live by every Word of God.

To this day the corporate Ekklesia commits the same error of baptizing those who are repentant in name only and without any depth of understanding, just to gain finances and to inflate numbers.

The mixed people longed to go back into Egypt because of the hardships involved and they infected Israel with the same longing: Even as some today long to go back into the spiritual Egypt of bondage to sin, and seek to do so by compromising with the Word of God and doing as they think good instead of doing as God commands.

11:4 And the mixt multitude that was among them fell a lusting: and the children of Israel also wept again, and said, Who shall give us flesh to eat? **11:5** We remember the fish, which we did eat in Egypt freely; the cucumbers, and the melons, and the leeks, and the onions, and the garlick:

These things are covered in Exodus 16

Manna

11:6 But now our soul is dried away: there is nothing at all, beside this manna, before our eyes.

The manna was a kind of granule out of which bread could be made

11:7 And the manna was as coriander seed, and the colour thereof as the colour of bdellium. **11:8** And the people went about, and gathered it, and **ground it in mills, or beat it in a mortar**, and baked it in pans, and **made cakes of it**: and the taste of it was as the taste of fresh oil.

Manna came down in the night with the dew

11:9 And when the dew fell upon the camp in the night, the manna fell upon it.

Christ was greatly angered by the complaints of the people, which began in the associated mixed people and increased until this unclean attitude had leavened the whole lump of Israel.

Brethren, this is why we are not to tolerate unclean doctrine or sin, or the willfully self-justifying sinful in our assemblies! Lest they corrupt us and leaven our whole assembly with spiritual uncleanness and false doctrine!

> **Galatians 5:9** A little leaven leaveneth the whole lump.
>
> **Titus 3:10** A man that is an heretick after the first and second admonition reject; 11 Knowing that he that is such is subverted, and sinneth, being condemned of himself.

Brethren, how long will it be before we learn the lesson of the clean and the unclean; and put a difference between the holy and the profane; to burn with zeal for the holy and to reject the profane? See our article on Clean and Unclean.

How long will it be before we STOP sinning and compromising with the Word of God, making it easy for Satan to sow his tares among us and pollute our assemblies with false teachings and sin?

How long will we lust after mammon or worldly pleasures, and fail to be totally faithful to the Word of God?

Numbers 11:10 Then Moses heard the people weep throughout their families, every man in the door of his tent: and the anger of the LORD was kindled greatly; Moses also was displeased.

Moses was highly displeased, just as every true servant of God would be highly displeased by such a rebellious attitude.

11:11 And Moses said unto the LORD, Wherefore hast thou afflicted thy servant? and wherefore have I not found favour in thy sight, that thou layest the burden of all this people upon me? **11:12** Have I conceived all this people? have I begotten them, that thou shouldest say unto me, Carry them in thy bosom, as a nursing father beareth the sucking child, unto the land which thou swarest unto their fathers? **11:13** Whence should I have flesh to give unto all this people? for they weep unto me, saying, Give us flesh, that we may eat.

Moses was so disgusted that the people wanted to go back into Egypt and preferred the pleasures of bondage to sin above the perfection of the Word of God; that he wanted to die, for he saw no hope for Israel.

It is the same today, as the corporate Ekklesia compromises with the Word of God and idolizes men and corporations above their Deliverer, committing spiritual idolatry and adultery against the Husband of their baptismal covenant.

11:14 I am not able to bear all this people alone, because it is too heavy for me. **11:15** And if thou deal thus with me, kill me, I pray thee, out of hand, if I have found favour in thy sight; and let me not see my wretchedness.

Jesus Christ commands that the 70 elders be brought before him; and promised that he will place his Spirit on the 70 so that they could assist Moses in judging and leading the people. This is the scripture used to establish the later Sanhedrin of 70 men plus one president. See The Mosaic Administration study.

11:16 And the LORD said unto Moses, Gather unto me seventy men of the elders of Israel, whom thou knowest to be the elders of the people, and officers over them; and bring them unto the tabernacle of the congregation, that they may stand there with thee. **11:17** And I will come down and talk with thee there: and I will take of the spirit which is upon thee, and will put it upon them; and they shall bear the burden of the people with thee, that thou bear it not thyself alone.

The people had desired to eat flesh, yet they had many flocks and herds; the real issue was that they were intimidated by the hardships and difficulties of coming out from the bondage of Egypt and were looking for an excuse to go back to the pleasures of bondage to sin typified by Egypt.

This is a lesson for us that Satan comes after us when we are delivered from his bondage; and pressures us and tempts us into thinking that his way, the worldly way is better, and that God's way is a very heavy burden; which is of course a big lie!

God's way is easy and his burden light; it is Satan's attacks on the godly that are a heavy burden and are intended to get us to compromise with God's ways and to cause us to give up and turn back into the bondage to worldliness that we were delivered from.

The mixed people and physical Israel had their great herds and flocks and yet lusted after flesh and the things of Egypt; therefore Jesus Christ gave them flesh and killed thousands with that flesh, because of their lust.

Many of us also compromise with the Word of God, lusting after the pleasures of this world; and Jesus Christ is just as angry with us today as he was with physical Israel at that time. He is preparing to correct us and to destroy our idols of men, false traditions and corporate groups.

11:18 And say thou unto the people, Sanctify yourselves against to morrow, and ye shall eat flesh: for ye have wept in the ears of the LORD, saying, Who shall give us flesh to eat? for it was well with us in Egypt: therefore the LORD will give you flesh, and ye shall eat.

11:19 Ye shall not eat one day, nor two days, nor five days, neither ten days, nor twenty days; **11:20** But even a whole month, until it come out at your nostrils, and it be loathsome unto you: because that ye have despised the LORD which is among you, and have wept before him, saying, Why came we forth out of Egypt?

Moses is amazed that God promised to bring flesh to feed the multitudes and God tells him that his power will perform it.

11:21 And Moses said, The people, among whom I am, are six hundred thousand footmen; and thou hast said, I will give them flesh, that they may eat a whole month. **11:22** Shall the flocks and the herds be slain for them, to suffice them? or shall all the fish of the sea be gathered together for them, to suffice them? **11:23** And the LORD said unto Moses, Is the LORD's hand waxed short? thou shalt see now whether my word shall come to pass unto thee or not.

The 70 elders receive God's Spirit and prophesy. Here is another of those places where people had God's Holy Spirit given to them before Pentecost 31 A.D. God has been calling out people since Abel for six thousand years; at the end of which will be the resurrection of the chosen, followed by the millennial Sabbath of rest. That is the prophetic lesson of the Feast of Unleavened Bread.

11:24 And Moses went out, and told the people the words of the LORD, and gathered the seventy men of the elders of the people, and set them round about the tabernacle. **11:25** And the LORD came down in a cloud, and spake unto him, and **took of the spirit that was upon him, and gave it unto the seventy elders:** and it came to pass, that, when the spirit rested upon them, they prophesied, and did not cease.

NOTICE the attitude of Moses and how godly it was, being the absolute opposite of the lusting for the chief seats of many ungodly elders and leaders in today's Spiritual Ekklesia.

11:26 But there remained two of the men in the camp, the name of the one was Eldad, and the name of the other Medad: and the spirit rested upon them; and they were of them that were written, but went not out unto the tabernacle: and they prophesied in the camp. **11:27** And there ran a young man, and told Moses, and said, Eldad and Medad do prophesy in the camp.

Here Joshua the "apprentice" of Moses; learns a lesson that will stay with him all of his life

11:28 And Joshua the son of Nun, the servant of Moses, one of his [Moses' helpers] young men, answered and said, My lord Moses, forbid them.

11:29 And Moses said unto him, Enviest thou for my sake? would God that all the LORD's people were prophets, and that the LORD would put his spirit upon them!

11:30 And Moses gat him into the camp, he and the elders of Israel.

After this God sent a strong wind which carried to the camp a dense concentration of quails about three feet deep over all the camp to a distance of about 15 miles or more, on either side.

11:31 And there went forth a wind from the LORD, and brought quails from the sea, and let them fall by the camp, **as it were a day's journey on this side, and as it were a day's journey on the other side,** round about the camp, and as it were **two cubits high** upon the face of the earth.

11:32 And the people stood up all that day, and all that night, and all the next day, and they gathered the quails: he that gathered least gathered ten homers: and they spread them all abroad for themselves round about the camp.

These quails were brought to demonstrate the power of God, after which God corrected them for the sin of complaining against him and lusting to return to the pleasures of Egypt

11:33 And while the flesh was yet between their teeth, ere it was chewed, the wrath of the LORD was kindled against the people, and the LORD smote the people with a very great plague. **11:34** And he called the name of that place Kibrothhattaavah: because there they buried the people that lusted.

11:35 And the people journeyed from Kibrothhattaavah unto Hazeroth; and abode at Hazeroth.

Numbers 12

Moses marries an Ethiopian [black] woman. This is an allegory that people will be called out from all nations to be a part of the bride of the Mediator of the New Covenant, Jesus Christ.

Numbers 12:1 And Miriam [English: Mary] and Aaron spake against Moses because of the Ethiopian woman whom he had married: for he had married an Ethiopian woman.

Moses was the mediator of the Mosaic Covenant, and as such was a representation of Jesus Christ the Mediator of the New Covenant, who's bride will include people from all nations.

12:2 And they said, Hath the LORD indeed spoken only by Moses? hath he not spoken also by us? And the LORD heard it.

In this, Miriam and Aaron exalted themselves over the mediator of the Mosaic Covenant; just like many leaders and groups in today's Ekklesia exalt themselves over the Mediator of the New Covenant, to turn the brethren away from zeal to live by every Word of God towards exalting men, corporate churches and the false traditions of men.

God heard Miriam and Aaron and God judged Miriam

12:3 (Now the man Moses was very meek, above all the men which were upon the face of the earth.) **12:4** And the LORD spake suddenly unto

Moses, and unto Aaron, and unto Miriam, Come out ye three unto the tabernacle of the congregation. And they three came out.

The God who later gave up his God-hood to be made flesh as Jesus Christ called Miriam and Aaron and spoke to them out of a cloud

12:5 And the LORD came down in the pillar of the cloud, and stood in the door of the tabernacle, and called Aaron and Miriam: and they both came forth.

12:6 And he said, Hear now my words: If there be a prophet among you, I the LORD will make myself known unto him in a vision, and will speak unto him in a dream. **12:7** My servant Moses is not so, who is faithful in all mine house.

12:8 With him will I speak mouth to mouth, even apparently, and not in dark speeches; and the similitude of the LORD shall he behold: wherefore then were ye not afraid to speak against my servant Moses? **12:9** And the anger of the LORD was kindled against them; and he departed.

At the correction of Christ, Miriam and Aaron repented of their rebellion against the mediator of the Mosaic Covenant

12:10 And the cloud departed from off the tabernacle; and, behold, Miriam became leprous, white as snow: and Aaron looked upon Miriam, and, behold, she was leprous. **12:11** And Aaron said unto Moses, Alas, my lord, I beseech thee, lay not the sin upon us, wherein we have done foolishly, and wherein we have sinned. **12:12** Let her not be as one dead, of whom the flesh is half consumed when he cometh out of his mother's womb.

Moses, the aggrieved person, cried out in complete forgiveness for the afflicted and repentant Miriam

12:13 And Moses cried unto the LORD, saying, Heal her now, O God, I beseech thee.

Christ forgives but maintains the correction for seven days. Even so the repentant often have to continue to suffer for their sins for a time so as to learn not to sin any more.

12:14 And the LORD said unto Moses, If her father had but spit in her face, should she not be ashamed seven days? let her be shut out from the camp seven days, and after that let her be received in again. **12:15** And Miriam was shut out from the camp seven days: and the people journeyed not till Miriam was brought in again.

12:16 And afterward the people removed from Hazeroth, and pitched in the wilderness of Paran.

Numbers 13

At the border of the physical promised land God commanded Moses to send a man from each tribe to spy out the land. Consider: there was no need for such a mission, for God could direct their path. This mission was a test of faith for the people.

Numbers 13:1 And the LORD spake unto Moses, saying, **13:2** Send thou men, that they may search the land of Canaan, which I give unto the children of Israel: of every tribe of their fathers shall ye send a man, every one a ruler among them.

13:3 And Moses by the commandment of the LORD sent them from the wilderness of Paran: **all those men were heads of the children of Israel**.

The names of these leading men were:

13:4 And these were their names: of the tribe of Reuben, Shammua the son of Zaccur.

13:5 Of the tribe of Simeon, Shaphat the son of Hori.

13:6 Of the tribe of **Judah, Caleb the son of Jephunneh.**

13:7 Of the tribe of Issachar, Igal the son of Joseph.

13:8 Of the tribe of **Ephraim, Oshea [Joshua] the son of Nun.**

13:9 Of the tribe of Benjamin, Palti the son of Raphu.

13:10 Of the tribe of Zebulun, Gaddiel the son of Sodi.

13:11 Of the tribe of Joseph, namely, of the tribe of Manasseh, Gaddi the son of Susi.

13:12 Of the tribe of Dan, Ammiel the son of Gemalli.

13:13 Of the tribe of Asher, Sethur the son of Michael.

13:14 Of the tribe of Naphtali, Nahbi the son of Vophsi.

13:15 Of the tribe of Gad, Geuel the son of Machi.

13:16 These are the names of the men which Moses sent to spy out the land.

And **Moses called Oshea the son of Nun Jehoshua**. [Joshua; this is KJV spelling, the name is the same as the name Yeshua, or Jesus: meaning Salvation]

Moses gives them their mission

13:17 And Moses sent them to spy out the land of Canaan, and said unto them, Get you up this way southward, and go up into the mountain: **13:18** And see the land, what it is, and the people that dwelleth therein, whether they be strong or weak, few or many; **13:19** And what the land is that they dwell in, whether it be good or bad; and what cities they be that they dwell in, whether in tents, or in strong holds; **13:20** And what the land is, whether it be fat or lean, whether there be wood therein, or not. And be ye of good courage, and bring of the fruit of the land. Now the time was the time of the firstripe grapes.

13:21 So they went up, and searched the land from the wilderness of Zin unto Rehob, as men come to Hamath. **13:22** And they ascended by the south, and came unto Hebron; where Ahiman, Sheshai, and Talmai, the children of Anak, were. (Now Hebron was built seven years before Zoan in Egypt.)

13:23 And they came unto the brook of Eshcol, and cut down from thence a branch with one cluster of grapes, and they bare it between two upon a staff; and they brought of the pomegranates, and of the figs. **13:24** The place was called the brook Eshcol, because of the cluster of grapes which the children of Israel cut down from thence.

They covered a vast area for being on foot, and returned only after 40 days

13:25 And they returned from searching of the land after forty days.

13:26 And they went and came to Moses, and to Aaron, and to all the congregation of the children of Israel, unto the wilderness of Paran, to Kadesh; and brought back word unto them, and unto all the congregation, and shewed them the fruit of the land.

The report of the twelve

13:27 And they told him, and said, We came unto the land whither thou sentest us, and surely it floweth with milk and honey; and this is the fruit of it. **13:28** Nevertheless the people be strong that dwell in the land, and the cities are walled, and very great: and moreover we saw the children of Anak there. **13:29** The Amalekites dwell in the land of the south: and the Hittites, and the Jebusites, and the Amorites, dwell in the mountains: and the Canaanites dwell by the sea, and by the coast of Jordan.

How like physical Israel we are today! We see the wonders of the spiritual Promised Land of eternity, yet we lack the faith and the moral courage to stand steadfast to trust and live by every Word of God!

While they were too afraid of men to enter the land; we are also afraid of what men can do and therefore we are afraid to zealously live by every Word of God; which is the KEY to entering eternity!

Satan uses our fears and deceives us into believing in a false "no pain" entry into eternal life; perverting grace as a license to compromise and to remain in sin through repenting in name only (see the book of Jude)!

Then Caleb [of Judah] stood strong and full of faith in the promises and power of God.

Where are the Joshua's and Caleb's today? Where are the men of faith and courage, who dare to stand up and be counted; who dare to openly rebuke sin and to teach passionate zeal to follow Jesus Christ and to live by every Word of God?

Where are those who have the faith and courage to take a stand for God's Word and to stand fast and unmovable on the foundation of the Prophets, Apostles and Jesus Christ the Cornerstone of Salvation?

13:30 And Caleb stilled the people before Moses, and said, **Let us go up at once, and possess it; for we are well able to overcome it.**

Of course Israel was not able to overcome these things on their own if they forgot to faithfully follow their Mighty God, who is well able to deliver the victory over all opposition and to give them the land of the birthright of the promise to their forefathers.

Even so, today's Spiritual Ekklesia lacks faith in our Mighty One and his power to lead us and deliver us from our trials, and we therefore lack courage and faith to go forward, trusting on our God to deliver us. Just like those ancient people, we compromise with God's Word, and reject living by every Word of God.

We fear men, and because we fear men and lust after the pleasures of sin [spiritual Egypt]; we back off on our commitment to our espoused Husband! Just as they lost their chance to enter the physical promised land; we are losing our opportunity to enter that spiritual Promised Land of eternity by making idols of men and polluting God's Sabbaths!

13:31 But the men that went up with him said, We be not able to go up against the people; for they are stronger than we.

13:32 And they brought up an evil report of the land which they had searched unto the children of Israel, saying, The land, through which we have gone to search it, is a land that eateth up the inhabitants thereof; and all the people that we saw in it are men of a great stature.

13:33 And there we saw the giants, the sons of Anak, which come of the giants: and we were in our own sight as grasshoppers [tiny men like insects in comparison to them], and so we were in their sight.

> **Hebrews 3:7** Wherefore (as the Holy Ghost saith, To day if ye will hear his voice,
>
> **3:8** Harden not your hearts, as in the provocation, in the day of temptation in the wilderness: **3:9** When your fathers tempted me, proved me, and saw my works forty years. **3:10** Wherefore I was grieved with that generation, and said, They do alway err in their heart; and they have not known my ways. **3:11** So I sware in my wrath, They shall not enter into my rest.)
>
> **3:12** Take heed, brethren, lest there be in any of you **an evil heart of unbelief, in departing from** [following the whole Word of] **the living God.**

Did Paul say that we are to hide away our light of sound doctrine and zeal for God's Word and tolerate evil to have some kind of false organizational unity? Is that the lesson God teaches concerning Israel and the spies?

NO, we are to encourage one another daily lest anyone be deceived by false doctrine and led into the deceitfulness of tolerating and committing sin.

> **3:13** But **exhort one another daily,** while it is called To day; lest any of you be hardened through the deceitfulness of sin.

We are to remain in Christ and to live as Christ lived, without sin: and if we do so, we will surely face opposition and the temptation to sin. Nevertheless we must remain steadfast in growing and living by every Word of God.

3:14 For we are made partakers of Christ, if we hold the beginning of our confidence stedfast unto the end;

We are NOT to lust after worldliness nor are we to turn away from our calling to return to the bondage of spiritual Egypt [bondage to Satan and sin]. We are to live as Christ lived and to remain steadfast in learning and living by every Word of God with passionate zeal, turning neither to the left nor to the right.

3:15 While it is said, To day if ye will hear his voice, harden not your hearts, as in the provocation. **3:16** For some, when they had heard, did provoke: howbeit not all that came out of Egypt by Moses.

Just as Christ was grieved with the faithless in physical Israel who lusted after the pleasures of Egypt, and grumbled over difficulties; So he is grieved with all those of the New Covenant who are faithless and grumble over difficulties, desiring the pleasures of worldliness and the easy way more than we are zealous for our God.

3:17 But with whom was he grieved forty years? was it not with them that had sinned, whose carcases fell in the wilderness? **3:18** And to whom sware he that they should not enter into his rest, but to them that believed not? **3:19** So we see that they could not enter in because of unbelief.

Just as those ancient folks could not enter into the physical promised land because of fear and unbelief; we also will NOT enter into the Promised Land of eternal life if we fear men and do not believe that God is able to deliver us from all our trials.

If we depart from a zeal to live by every Word of God to try and alleviate our trials by compromising with our zeal and obedience to God our Father and our espoused Husband; we CANNOT enter into the spiritual Promised Land of eternal life!

Numbers 13

At the border of the promised land God commands Moses to send a man from each tribe to spy out the land. Consider: there was no need for such a mission, for God could direct their path. This mission was a test of faith for the people.

Numbers 13:1 And the LORD spake unto Moses, saying, **13:2** Send thou men, that they may search the land of Canaan, which I give unto the children of Israel: of every tribe of their fathers shall ye send a man, every one a ruler among them.

13:3 And Moses by the commandment of the LORD sent them from the wilderness of Paran: **all those men were heads of the children of Israel**.

The names of these leading men were:

13:4 And these were their names: of the tribe of Reuben, Shammua the son of Zaccur.

13:5 Of the tribe of Simeon, Shaphat the son of Hori.

13:6 Of the tribe of Judah, Caleb the son of Jephunneh.

13:7 Of the tribe of Issachar, Igal the son of Joseph.

13:8 Of the tribe of Ephraim, Oshea [Joshua] the son of Nun.

13:9 Of the tribe of Benjamin, Palti the son of Raphu.

13:10 Of the tribe of Zebulun, Gaddiel the son of Sodi.

13:11 Of the tribe of Joseph, namely, of the tribe of Manasseh, Gaddi the son of Susi.

13:12 Of the tribe of Dan, Ammiel the son of Gemalli.

13:13 Of the tribe of Asher, Sethur the son of Michael.

13:14 Of the tribe of Naphtali, Nahbi the son of Vophsi.

13:15 Of the tribe of Gad, Geuel the son of Machi.

13:16 These are the names of the men which Moses sent to spy out the land.

And **Moses called Oshea the son of Nun Jehoshua**. [Joshua; this is KJV spelling, the name is the same as the name Yeshua, or Jesus: meaning Salvation]

Moses gives them their mission

13:17 And Moses sent them to spy out the land of Canaan, and said unto them, Get you up this way southward, and go up into the mountain: **13:18** And see the land, what it is, and the people that dwelleth therein, whether they be strong or weak, few or many; **13:19** And what the land is that they dwell in, whether it be good or bad; and what cities they be that they dwell in, whether in tents, or in strong holds; **13:20** And what the land is, whether it be fat or lean, whether there be wood therein, or not. And be ye of good courage, and bring of the fruit of the land. Now the time was the time of the firstripe grapes.

13:21 So they went up, and searched the land from the wilderness of Zin unto Rehob, as men come to Hamath. **13:22** And they ascended by the south, and came unto Hebron; where Ahiman, Sheshai, and Talmai, the children of Anak, were. (Now Hebron was built seven years before Zoan in Egypt.)

13:23 And they came unto the brook of Eshcol, and cut down from thence a branch with one cluster of grapes, and they bare it between two upon a staff; and they brought of the pomegranates, and of the figs. **13:24** The place was called the brook Eshcol, because of the cluster of grapes which the children of Israel cut down from thence.

They covered a vast area for being on foot and returned only after 40 days

13:25 And they returned from searching of the land after forty days.

13:26 And they went and came to Moses, and to Aaron, and to all the congregation of the children of Israel, unto the wilderness of Paran, to Kadesh; and brought back word unto them, and unto all the congregation, and shewed them the fruit of the land.

The report of the twelve

13:27 And they told him, and said, We came unto the land whither thou sentest us, and surely it floweth with milk and honey; and this is the fruit of it. **13:28** Nevertheless the people be strong that dwell in the land, and the cities are walled, and very great: and moreover we saw the children of Anak there. **13:29** The Amalekites dwell in the land of the south: and the Hittites, and the Jebusites, and the Amorites, dwell in the mountains: and the Canaanites dwell by the sea, and by the coast of Jordan.

How like physical Israel we are today! We see the wonders of the spiritual Promised Land of eternity, yet we lack the faith and the moral courage to stand steadfast to trust and live by every Word of God!

While they were too afraid of men to enter the land; we are also afraid of what men can do, and therefore we are afraid to zealously live by every Word of God; which is the KEY to entering eternity!

Satan uses our fears and deceives us into believing in a false "no pain" entry into eternal life; perverting grace as a license to compromise and to remain in sin through repenting in name only (the book of Jude)!

Then Caleb [of Judah] stood strong and full of faith in the promises and power of God.

Where are the Caleb's today? Where are the men of faith and courage, who dare to stand up and be counted; who dare to openly rebuke sin and to teach passionate zeal to follow Jesus Christ and to keep his whole word?

Where are those who have the faith and courage to take a stand for God's Word and to stand fast and unmovable on the foundation of the Prophets, Apostles and Jesus Christ the Cornerstone of Salvation?

13:30 And Caleb stilled the people before Moses, and said, **Let us go up at once, and possess it; for we are well able to overcome it.**

Of course Israel was not able to overcome these things on their own if they forgot to faithfully follow their Mighty God, who is well able to deliver the victory over all opposition and to give them the land of the birthright of their calling.

Even so, today's spiritual Ekklesia lacks faith in our Mighty One and his power to lead us and deliver us from our trials, and we therefore lack courage and faith to go forward, trusting on our God to deliver us. Just like those ancient people, we compromise with God's Word, and reject living by every Word of God.

We fear men, and because we fear men and lust after the pleasures of sin [spiritual Egypt]; we back off on our commitment to our espoused

Husband! Just as they lost their chance to enter the physical promised land; we are losing our opportunity to enter that spiritual Promised Land of eternity by making idols of men and polluting God's Sabbaths!

13:31 But the men that went up with him said, We be not able to go up against the people; for they are stronger than we.

13:32 And they brought up an evil report of the land which they had searched unto the children of Israel, saying, The land, through which we have gone to search it, is a land that eateth up the inhabitants thereof; and all the people that we saw in it are men of a great stature.

13:33 And there we saw the giants, the sons of Anak, which come of the giants: and we were in our own sight as grasshoppers, and so we were in their sight.

> **Hebrews 3:7** Wherefore (as the Holy Ghost saith, To day if ye will hear his voice,
>
> **3:8** Harden not your hearts, as in the provocation, in the day of temptation in the wilderness: **3:9** When your fathers tempted me, proved me, and saw my works forty years. **3:10** Wherefore I was grieved with that generation, and said, They do alway err in their heart; and they have not known my ways. **3:11** So I sware in my wrath, They shall not enter into my rest.)
>
> **3:12** Take heed, brethren, lest there be in any of you **an evil heart of unbelief, in departing from** [following the whole Word of] **the living God.**

Did Paul say that we are to hide away our light of sound doctrine and zeal for God's Word and tolerate evil to have some kind of false organizational unity? Is that the lesson God teaches concerning Israel and the spies?

NO, we are to encourage one another daily lest anyone be deceived by false doctrine and led into the deceitfulness of tolerating and committing sin.

> **3:13** But **exhort one another daily,** while it is called To day; lest any of you be hardened through the deceitfulness of sin.

We are to remain in Christ and to live as Christ lived, without sin; and if we do so, we shall surely face opposition and the temptation to sin. Nevertheless we must remain steadfast in growing and living by every Word of God.

> **3:14** For we are made partakers of Christ, if we hold the beginning of our confidence stedfast unto the end;

We are NOT to lust after worldliness, nor are we to turn away from our calling to return to the bondage of spiritual Egypt[bondage to Satan and sin]. We are to live as Christ lived and to remain steadfast in learning and living by every Word of God, with passionate zeal, turning neither to the left nor to the right.

> **3:15** While it is said, To day if ye will hear his voice, harden not your hearts, as in the provocation. **3:16** For some, when they had heard, did provoke: howbeit not all that came out of Egypt by Moses.

Just as Christ was grieved with the faithless who lusted after the pleasures of Egypt, and grumbled over difficulties; so He is grieved with those of US, who are faithless and grumble over difficulties, desiring the pleasures of worldliness and the easy way more than we are zealous for our God.

> **3:17** But with whom was he grieved forty years? was it not with them that had sinned, whose carcases fell in the wilderness? **3:18** And to whom sware he that they should not enter into his rest, but to them that believed not? **3:19** So we see that they could not enter in because of unbelief.

Just as those folks could not enter into the physical promised land because of fear and unbelief; we also will NOT enter into the Promised Land of eternal life if we fear men and do not believe that God is able to deliver us from all our trials.

If we depart from a zeal to live by every Word of God to try and alleviate our trials by compromising with our zeal and obedience to God our Father and our espoused Husband; we CANNOT enter into the spiritual Promised Land of eternal life!

Numbers 14

The people wept over the sufferings which had been brought on by their lust to return to Egypt, and repented not. Instead they continued to blame God for their troubles and to lust for the pleasures of worldliness.

How very like them we are today. We fast and beg God to bless us, while we continue to exalt our corporate entities, false traditions and leaders above the Word of God and trample all over any possible zeal to live by every Word of God! We call out to God as we trample all over his Word and follow our own ways!

Numbers 14:1 And all the congregation lifted up their voice, and cried; and the people wept that night.

14:2 And all the **children of Israel murmured against Moses and against Aaron**: and the whole congregation said unto them, **Would God that we had died in the land of Egypt!** [they regretted being called out to obey God] or would God we had died in this wilderness! **14:3** And wherefore hath the LORD brought us unto this land, to fall by the sword, that our wives and our children should be a prey? were it not better **for us to return into Egypt? 14:4** And they said one to another, **Let us make a captain, and let us return into Egypt.**

Today's Spiritual Ekklesia has made themselves many captains; who are leading them AWAY from any zeal for the practical application of the Word of God to follow men and organizations in idolatry and spiritual adultery! Like the ancient rebels they lead today's brethren back into the worldliness of spiritual Egypt.

Moses and Aaron fell on their faces before God and the people; knowing that the fierce anger of Jesus Christ had been aroused. Moses as mediator of the Mosaic Covenant and Aaron as the high priest and also a mediator between the people and God.

14:5 Then Moses and Aaron fell on their faces before all the assembly of the congregation of the children of Israel.

Joshua and Caleb rose up and took a stand against the other spies before the people, to tell the truth that our Mighty God is above all others and can deliver us from all adversaries.

Just as Egypt was a type of bondage; Canaan was a type of wickedness and sin. The fight to possess Canaan was a type of the fight of the called out to OVERCOME all sin and to wash away all sin, by internalizing the very nature of God through a diligent study and living by every Word of God.

The physical battle of Israel to possess Canaan, was a type of the spiritual battle to OVERCOME all sin by the faithful called out to the New Covenant and to enter the spiritual Promised Land of eternal life!

Canaan was a type of unrepentant sin and that is why they were to be utterly destroyed. They will be raised up and given their opportunity during the Feast of Tabernacles main harvest of humanity.

Physical Israel was commanded to destroy all of Canaan as a type of wickedness and unrepentant sin, so that we will learn that all unrepentant sinners will be destroyed.

We have been called out to DESTROY all sin and compromise with any part of the Word of God from within ourselves and ultimately in the whole world as leaders after the resurrection.

Let us stand strong against all sin, compromise and toleration of false doctrine [teachings]; with the FAITH and the ZEAL of Jesus, Caleb and Joshua!

14:6 And Joshua the son of Nun, and Caleb the son of Jephunneh, which were of them that searched the land, rent their clothes: **14:7** And they spake unto all the company of the children of Israel, saying, The land, which we passed through to search it, is an exceeding good land.

If we make God and the things and Word of God our delight, to follow and obey every Word of God; then God will delight in us!

14:8 If the LORD delight in us, then he will bring us into this land, and give it us; a land which floweth with milk and honey.

Fear not men and never exalt the word of men above the Word of God the Almighty!

Have courage and faith to live by every Word of God, which is for our good! Run to our God to find his deliverance, and NEVER tolerate false ways, or fall away into compromise with sin for the sake of any fear of men and never fall to any enticement to sin!

14:9 Only rebel not ye against the LORD, neither fear ye the people of the land; for they are bread for us: their defence is departed from them, and the LORD is with us: fear them not.

Those who take a stand for the Word of God may face intense persecution from even those who are in the congregation; yet God will love the zealous for him and God will deliver his faithful on that day and they shall shine like the stars forever and ever (Dan 12).

14:10 But all the congregation bade stone them with stones. And the glory of the LORD appeared in the tabernacle of the congregation before all the children of Israel.

The fury of Christ against the rebellions of the brethren is the same today as it was thousands of years ago. Today, we stand at the very point of complete rejection by Jesus Christ into the correction of great tribulation, because of the overspreading of our rebellions, idolatries and spiritual adulteries (Rev 3:14-22).

Jesus said; I will destroy this people and make of Moses a great nation; and Moses mediated for the people to save them.

14:11 And the LORD said unto Moses, How long will this people provoke me? and how long will it be ere they believe me, for all the signs which I have shewed among them? **14:12** I will smite them with the pestilence, and disinherit them, and will make of thee a greater nation and mightier than they.

14:13 And Moses said unto the LORD, Then the Egyptians shall hear it, (for thou broughtest up this people in thy might from among them;) **14:14** And they will tell it to the inhabitants of this land: for they have heard that thou LORD art among this people, that thou LORD art seen face to face, and that thy cloud standeth over them, and that thou goest before them, by day time in a pillar of a cloud, and in a pillar of fire by night.

14:15 Now if thou shalt kill all this people as one man, then the nations which have heard the fame of thee will speak, saying, **14:16** Because the LORD was not able to bring this people into the land which he sware unto them, therefore he hath slain them in the wilderness.

When most of us are given over to great affliction of the flesh, it is so that the spirit can be saved.

Today's spiritual Ekklesia justifies itself and has fallen into the depths of a complete unwillingness to repent, because of this we now face eternal death for our willingness to obey men [commit idolatry] above the Word of God.

Today's Spiritual Ekklesia call the imaginations of their leaders good while they reject any zeal to live by every Word of God! We do indeed make a mockery of Jesus Christ by rejecting faithfulness and Christ-like zeal to live by God's Word, and we put Jesus Christ to an open shame by claiming to be his while having no zeal for his Word.

Indeed we are in greater danger of the judgment than the Pharisees were, for we claim to have the Spirit of God and yet we reject any zeal for God's Word for our own ways; while they did not have God's Spirit.

They had their excuse, but where is the cloak for our sin ?

By bringing the Ekklesia to repentance God will save us; and God will be glorified in his wisdom that he is able to do his will; for nothing is beyond his might!

14:17 And now, I beseech thee, let the power of my LORD be great, according as thou hast spoken, saying, **14:18** The LORD is longsuffering, and of great mercy, forgiving iniquity and transgression, and by no means clearing the guilty, visiting the iniquity of the fathers upon the children unto the third and fourth generation. **14:19** Pardon, I beseech thee, the iniquity of this people according unto the greatness of thy mercy, and as thou hast forgiven this people, from Egypt even until now.

14:20 And the LORD said, I have pardoned according to thy word: 14:21 But as truly as I live, all the earth shall be filled with the glory of the LORD.

The God who later gave up is God-hood to be made flesh as Jesus Christ then proclaimed that only those who have been zealously faithful to him may enter the promised land. The same is true of that spiritual Promised Land of eternal life!

14:22 Because all those men which have seen my glory, and my miracles, which I did in Egypt and in the wilderness, and have tempted me now these ten times, and have not hearkened to my voice; **14:23** Surely they shall not see the land which I sware unto their fathers, neither shall any of them that provoked me see it: **14:24** But my servant Caleb, because he had another spirit with him, and hath followed me fully, him will I bring into the land whereinto he went; and his seed shall possess it.

The people are commanded to leave the area, because the enemy is gathering to resist them.

14:25 (Now the Amalekites and the Canaanites dwelt in the valley.) Tomorrow turn you, and get you into the wilderness by the way of the Red sea.

14:26 And the LORD spake unto Moses and unto Aaron, saying, **14:27** How long shall I bear with this evil congregation, which murmur against me? I have heard the murmurings of the children of Israel, which they murmur against me.

Except for the two faithful, all physical Israel was prevented from entering the physical promised land for their rebellion and false words. Again, this is a lesson for us; that only the faithful to follow and live by every Word of God, can inherit the spiritual Promised Land of eternal life.

Today our Lord is also losing patience with our idolatry and sin (Rev 3:15). Just as physical Israel died in the wilderness, all Spiritual Israel who turns back from their task of overcoming, and turns away from any zeal to live by every Word of God, shall die in a wilderness of affliction; in the hope that by afflicting the flesh we might repent and our spirits might be saved

14:28 Say unto them, As truly as I live, saith the LORD, as ye have spoken in mine ears, so will I do to you: **14:29** Your carcases shall fall in this wilderness; and all that were numbered of you, according to your whole number, from twenty years old and upward which have murmured against me. **14:30** Doubtless ye shall not come into the land, concerning which I sware to make you dwell therein, save Caleb the son of Jephunneh, and Joshua the son of Nun.

Only the children of those people could enter the physical promised land. Spiritually only these who are humble and teachable and run to follow and live by the Word of God their Father in heaven, may enter the spiritual Promised Land of eternal life.

> **Matthew 18:2** And Jesus called a little child unto him, and set him in the midst of them, **18:3** And said, Verily I say unto you, Except ye be converted, and become as little children, ye shall not enter into the kingdom of heaven. **18:4** Whosoever therefore shall humble himself as this little child, the same is greatest in the kingdom of heaven.

Numbers 14:31 But your little ones, which ye said should be a prey, them will I bring in, and they shall know the land which ye have despised.

14:32 But as for you, your carcases, they shall fall in this wilderness. **14:33** And your children shall wander in the wilderness forty years, and bear your whoredoms, until your carcases be wasted in the wilderness. **14:34** After the number of the days in which ye searched the land, even forty days, each day for a year, shall ye bear your iniquities, even forty years, and ye shall know my breach of promise. **14:35** I the LORD have said, I will surely do it unto all this evil congregation, that are gathered together against me: in this wilderness they shall be consumed, and there they shall die.

Many then died immediately by a plague from God

14:36 And the men, which Moses sent to search the land, who returned, and made all the congregation to murmur against him, by bringing up a slander upon the land, **14:37** Even those men that did bring up the evil report upon the land, died by the plague before the LORD.

14:38 But Joshua the son of Nun, and Caleb the son of Jephunneh, which were of the men that went to search the land, lived still.

14:39 And Moses told these sayings unto all the children of Israel: and the people mourned greatly.

The people still did not understand about obedience to God in faith to keep his Word; and repenting for not entering the land they then committed the same sin of rebellion and refusal to accept and obey the Word of God, by trying to enter the land contrary to God's Word.

14:40 And they rose up early in the morning, and gat them up into the top of the mountain, saying, Lo, we be here, and will go up unto the place which the LORD hath promised: for we have sinned.

Moses warns them

14:41 And Moses said, Wherefore now do ye transgress the commandment of the LORD? but it shall not prosper. **14:42** Go not up, for the LORD is not among you; that ye be not smitten before your enemies. **14:43** For the Amalekites and the Canaanites are there before you, and ye shall fall by the sword: because ye are turned away from the LORD, therefore the LORD will not be with you.

Moses refused to let the Ark be moved to go with those rebellious people, and God allowed the people to be defeated for their rebellion against him: Just as God would not be with those who rebelled against his Word in ancient times, today God will not be with anyone who will not live by every Word of God.

14:44 But they presumed to go up unto the hill top: nevertheless the ark of the covenant of the LORD, and Moses, departed not out of the camp. **14:45** Then the Amalekites came down, and the Canaanites which dwelt in that hill, and smote them, and discomfited them, even unto Hormah.

Numbers 15

Commandments concerning offerings

Unleavened bread made with salt, pure water and olive oil is to be offered; the salt picturing the everlasting nature of our Covenant to live by every Word of God, and the oil representing the enabling Holy Spirit of God while the water pictures the washing and cleansing of the Word of God and the ground whole grain itself pictures the body and nature of Jesus Christ.

> **Leviticus 2:13** And every oblation of thy meat offering shalt thou season with salt; neither shalt thou suffer the salt of the covenant of thy God to be lacking from thy meat offering: with all thine offerings thou shalt offer salt.

Wine is poured out picturing the pouring out of the life of Jesus Christ the Lamb of God, for the wine is a type of the blood and the life is in the blood.

Numbers 15:1 And the LORD spake unto Moses, saying, **15:2** Speak unto the children of Israel, and say unto them, When ye be come into the land of your habitations, which I give unto you, **15:3** And will make an offering by fire unto the LORD, a burnt offering, or a sacrifice in performing a vow, or in a freewill offering, or in your solemn feasts, to make a sweet savour unto the LORD, of the herd or of the flock:

15:4 Then shall he that offereth his offering unto the LORD **bring a meat offering** of a tenth deal of flour mingled with the fourth part of an hin of oil. **15:5** And the fourth part of an hin **of wine** for a drink offering shalt thou prepare with the burnt offering or sacrifice, for one lamb.

15:6 Or for a ram, thou shalt prepare for **a meat offering** two tenth deals of flour mingled with the third part of an hin of oil. **15:7** And for **a drink offering** thou shalt offer the third part of an hin of wine, for a sweet savour unto the LORD.

15:8 And when thou preparest a bullock for a burnt offering, or for a sacrifice in performing a vow, or peace offerings unto the LORD: **15:9** Then shall he bring with a bullock **a meat offering** of three tenth deals of flour mingled with half an hin of oil. **15:10** And thou shalt bring for a drink offering half an hin of wine, **for an offering made by fire, of a sweet savour unto the LORD.**

15:11 Thus shall it be done for one bullock, or for one ram, or for a lamb, or a kid.

The unleavened bread of ground whole grain and water with oil and salt and the pouring out of wine; must be done as proscribed by God for each sacrificial animal.

This represents Jesus Christ the Lamb of God as the Bread of Life filled with the Holy Spirit, pouring out his life for the people. This tics the unleavened bread and wine commanded for Passover with all the various sacrifices.

15:12 According to the number that ye shall prepare, so shall ye do to every one according to their number.

The commandment here is not in regards to any Sin or Trespass Offering; but concerns the Burnt Offering. The unleavened bread and wine offering commanded here is to be offered with all things that are burnt on the altar, as representing a sweet service and peaceful relationship with God the Father in heaven. The smoke rising up represents faithful zealous service and unity with God the Father in heaven, rising up as a pleasing thing to be accepted by God the Father.

15:13 All that are born of the country shall do these things after this manner, in offering an offering made by fire, of a sweet savour unto the LORD. **15:14** And if a stranger sojourn with you, or whosoever be among you in your generations, and will offer an offering made by fire, of a sweet savour unto the LORD; as ye do, so he shall do. **15:15** One ordinance shall be both for you of the congregation, and also for the stranger that sojourneth with you, an ordinance for ever in your generations: as ye are, so shall the stranger be before the LORD.

15:16 One law and one manner shall be for you, and for the stranger that sojourneth with you.

Below is an allusion to the Wave Offering of Leviticus 23:9. Since the Wave Offering is commanded in Leviticus 23, why does today's Spiritual Ekklesia not obey it and at least have a service on the Wave Offering Sunday to discuss and expound on this commandment?

15:17 And the LORD spake unto Moses, saying, **15:18** Speak unto the children of Israel, and say unto them, When ye come into the land whither I bring you, **15:19** Then it shall be, that, when ye eat of the bread of the land, ye shall offer up an heave offering unto the LORD. **15:20** Ye shall offer up a cake of the first of your dough for an heave offering: as ye do the heave offering of the threshingfloor, so shall ye heave it. **15:21** Of the first of your dough ye shall give unto the LORD an heave offering in your generations.

When the whole assembly has erred without realizing it and later the leaders and people realize their error; the whole people are to offer a Burnt Offering along with a Sin Offering. This offering is for a organizational sin committed in ignorance. This offering like the Daily and all other offerings on behalf of the congregation was the responsibility of the High Priest.

15:22 And if ye have erred, and not observed all these commandments, which the LORD hath spoken unto Moses, **15:23** Even all that the LORD hath commanded you by the hand of Moses, from the day that the LORD commanded Moses, and henceforward among your generations; **15:24** Then it shall be, if ought be committed by ignorance without the knowledge of the congregation, that all the congregation shall offer one young bullock for a burnt offering, for a sweet savour unto the LORD, with his meat offering, and his drink offering, according to the manner, and one kid of the goats for a sin offering.

15:25 And the priest shall make an atonement for all the congregation of the children of Israel, and it shall be forgiven them; for it is ignorance: and they shall bring their offering, **a sacrifice made by fire** [a Burnt Offering] unto the LORD, and [accompanied by a Sin Offering] their sin offering before the LORD, for their ignorance: **15:26** And it shall be forgiven all the congregation of the children of Israel, and the stranger that sojourneth among them; seeing all the people were in ignorance.

If any individual sins in ignorance

15:27 And if any soul sin through ignorance, then he shall bring **a she goat of the first year for a sin offering**. **15:28** And the priest shall make an atonement for the soul that sinneth ignorantly, when he sinneth by ignorance before the LORD, to make an atonement for him; and it shall be forgiven him.

15:29 Ye shall have one law for him that sinneth through ignorance, both for him that is born among the children of Israel, and for the stranger that sojourneth among them.

There is no sacrifice for unrepented willful sin. When we justify our departure from living by every Word of God instead of sincerely repenting [which is the state of today's corporate Spiritual Ekklesia] we have rejected God, and God (Rev 3:15) will reject us and cut us off from being His people.

15:30 But the soul that doeth ought presumptuously [willfully, justifying the sin], whether he be born in the land, or a stranger, the same reproacheth the LORD; and that soul shall be cut off from among his people. **15:31** Because he hath despised the word of the LORD, and hath [willfully, justifying himself] broken his commandment, that soul shall utterly be cut off; his iniquity shall be upon him.

Upholding the sanctity of the Sabbath

This event is not just picking up a stick and playing with it, people gathered sticks and carried then on their backs back to the camp for firewood, and such burdens often weighed 40 or more pounds. This was hard work.

15:32 And while the children of Israel were in the wilderness, they found a man that gathered sticks upon the sabbath day. **15:33** And they that found him gathering sticks brought him unto Moses and Aaron, and unto all the congregation.

They held the person until they could inquire of God what to do

15:34 And they put him in ward, because it was not declared what should be done to him.

This is a judgment of God concerning working on the Sabbath. God's judgment is that anyone working on HIS Sabbaths, and that includes paying others to serve us in restaurants [or to serve us in other ways and places] on God's Sabbaths; must die. This includes the annual as well as the weekly Sabbaths.

> Consider: If it is proper to postpone Annual Sabbaths for our own convenience, then why not also postpone the weekly Sabbath as we want? Of course it is wrong and a grievous sin to postpone EITHER the Weekly or Annual Sabbaths!

This judgment is in effect today; and all those who do not repent of polluting the Weekly and Annual Sabbaths by postponing them to days other than the date that God has proscribed, or by profaning them by buying, selling, or by doing any work on them including cooking, will be cast into the severe correction of great tribulation.

That is the judgment of Almighty God, it is NOT my judgment.

15:35 And the LORD said unto Moses, The man shall be surely put to death: all the congregation shall stone him with stones without the camp. **15:36** And all the congregation brought him without the camp, and stoned him with stones, and he died; as the LORD commanded Moses.

The people were then commanded to place fringes on their garments as a sign to help them to remember to keep the commandments of God. See this article.

In the New Covenant, the Holy Spirit has been given to bring to remembrance the commandments and doctrines of God: Yet we call the Sabbath holy, showing that we know the commandments, while refusing to keep the Sabbath holy!

In view of our unconverted attitude and lack of zeal for the sanctity of God's Sabbaths; perhaps we should go back to wearing such fringes; lest we all suffer the same judgment of DEATH for our wickedness.

> **John 14:26** But the Comforter, which is the Holy Ghost, whom the Father will send in my name, he shall teach you all things, **and bring all things to your remembrance, whatsoever I have said unto you.**

Numbers 15:37 And the LORD spake unto Moses, saying, **15:38** Speak unto the children of Israel, and bid them that they make them fringes in the borders of their garments throughout their generations, and that **they put upon the fringe of the borders a ribband of blue:**

15:39 And it shall be unto you for a fringe, that ye may look upon it, and remember all the commandments of the LORD, and do them; and that ye seek not after your own heart and your own eyes, after which ye use to go a whoring: **15:40** That ye may remember, and do all my commandments, and be holy unto your God.

It is about time that we remember who our God should be! NOT any idol of men or corporate entities, but the Eternal Almighty One!

Remember the One who brought us out of the spiritual Egypt of bondage to Satan and sin; and is our HELP to overcome and destroy all sin so that we may enter the spiritual Promised Land of eternity!

It is God the Father and the whole Word of God that we must obey to attain eternal life, and it is the Lamb of God that is to be followed and to be adored as our espoused spiritual Husband!

15:41 I am the LORD your God, which brought you out of the land of Egypt, to be your God: I am the LORD your God.

Numbers 16

Korah a Levite, and Dathan and Abiram of Reuben lead 250 other leaders to rise up against Moses. For decades this has been misapplied as a lesson that we are to accept and to follow any man who takes to himself a title and that we are not to question his leadership.

The true lesson is the exact opposite of that false teaching.

Moses had been personally chosen by God and had proved his loyalty and zeal for God over many trials and many years; this faithful Moses was the mediator of the Mosaic Covenant, and as such; Moses was a type of the Mediator of the New Covenant, who is "that prophet" Jesus Christ (Deu 18:18).

These three men were leading a rebellion against the faithful mediator of the Mosaic Covenant; which was a type of rebellion against the faithful Mediator of the New Covenant, Jesus Christ!

The lesson here is that the Spiritual Ekklesia are to be absolutely faithful to every Word of God, which was inspired by the ONLY Mediator of the New Covenant, Jesus Christ, the Logos.

If someone says: "do not question me, remember Korah" he is misapplying this lesson, because it is Jesus Christ and no human being who the mediator of the spiritual New Covenant.

We have a command not to blindly follow any man, but to prove and test every word of men by every Word of God, and to reject anything that is different from the Word of God. Remember the Berean's

> **Acts 17:10** And the brethren immediately sent away Paul and Silas by night unto Berea: who coming thither went into the synagogue of the Jews. **17:11** These were more noble than those in Thessalonica, in that they received the word with all readiness of mind, and **searched the scriptures daily, whether those things were so**.

and the words of Paul:

> **1 Thessalonians 5:21 Prove all things**; hold fast that which is good [by the scriptures].

Moses was a type of Jesus Christ and these men were rebelling against Moses the mediator of the Mosaic Covenant.

To blindly support men without question is rebelling against Jesus Christ who is the HEAD of the faithful and the High Priest and Mediator of the New Covenant, under God the Father.

Blindly following any man without question is the same as rebelling like Korah; while questioning men and remaining faithful to God is to follow the example of those loyal to Moses!

> **1 Timothy 2:5** For there is one God, and one mediator between God and men, the man Christ Jesus;

To follow any man contrary to any part of the Word of God, is doing the same thing as these folks who followed Korah against Moses, it is rebellion against the Word of God and against the spiritual Mediator of the New Covenant.

Those who claim that questioning them is like the rebellion of Korah are exalting themselves to the same level as the Mediator of the New Covenant, Jesus Christ; they have forgotten who their HEAD is, and they are usurping the authority of the Mediator of the New Covenant, Jesus Christ!

Numbers 16:1 Now Korah, the son of Izhar, the son of Kohath, the son of Levi, and Dathan and Abiram, the sons of Eliab, and On, the son of Peleth, sons of Reuben, took men: **16:2** And they rose up before Moses, with certain of the children of Israel, two hundred and fifty princes of the assembly, famous in the congregation, men of renown:

16:3 And they gathered themselves together against Moses and against Aaron, and said unto them, Ye take too much upon you, seeing all the congregation are holy, every one of them, and the LORD is among them: wherefore then lift ye up yourselves above the congregation of the LORD?

Moses as a mortal man did not defend himself at all; instead he called on God to reveal God's will!

Why will so many elders not call on the Eternal to reveal his will for us today? Today there are many Korah's in the Spiritual Ekklesia, each one rejecting any zeal for the Mediator of the New Covenant and seeking the preeminence for himself, doing what he wants instead of doing as God commands.

16:4 And when Moses heard it, he fell upon his face: **16:5** And he spake unto Korah and unto all his company, saying, Even to morrow the LORD will shew who are his, and who is holy; and will cause him to come near unto him: even him whom he hath chosen will he cause to come near unto him.

Moses said take censors of incense [symbolic of rising prayers and appealing to God for God's judgment]; and the Eternal will judge and reveal who he wants to lead his people.

16:6 This do; Take you censers, Korah, and all his company; **16:7** And put fire therein, and put incense in them before the LORD to morrow: and **it shall be that the man whom the LORD doth choose**, he shall be holy: ye take too much upon you, ye sons of Levi.

Moses warns the Levites of their called out place and heritage, and asks them why they want to rise out of their place. Why are they not content with the honor of a Levite, seeking to take the preeminence of the priesthood also?

16:8 And Moses said unto Korah, Hear, I pray you, ye sons of Levi: **16:9** Seemeth it but a small thing unto you, that the God of Israel hath separated you from the congregation of Israel, to bring you near to himself to do the service of the tabernacle of the LORD, and to stand before the congregation to minister unto them? **16:10** And he hath brought thee near to him, and all thy brethren the sons of Levi with thee: and **seek ye the priesthood also?**

These men would not submit to the mediator of the Mosaic Covenant, Moses; nor would they submit to and serve the priesthood of Aaron: And although it was they themselves who had refused to go into the land, they claimed that Moses had not brought them into the promised land.

Today many elders in the Ekklesia engage in this same rebellion against God; insisting that the brethren must follow and obey them and their organization instead of living by every Word of God to enter the Promised Land of eternal life

16:11 For which cause both thou and all thy company are gathered together against the LORD: and what is Aaron, that ye murmur against him? **16:12** And Moses sent to call Dathan and Abiram, the sons of Eliab: which said, **We will not come up: 16:13** Is it a small thing that thou hast brought us up out of a land that floweth with milk and honey, to kill us in the wilderness, except thou make thyself altogether a prince over us? **16:14** Moreover thou hast not brought us into a land that floweth with milk and honey, or given us inheritance of fields and vineyards: wilt thou put out the eyes of these men? **we will not come up.**

Moses was furious that they would not submit to the will of God: Just so, Jesus Christ is furious with us today for our rebellion against him, to decide right and wrong for ourselves instead of living by every Word of God.

16:15 And Moses was very wroth, and said unto the LORD, Respect not thou their offering: I have not taken one ass from them, neither have I hurt one of them.

Moses demanded that these rebels appear before God with Moses and Aaron, to see who God had chosen for the office of mediator of the Mosaic Covenant.

16:16 And Moses said unto Korah, Be thou and all thy company before the LORD, thou, and they, and Aaron, to morrow: **16:17** And take every man his censer, and put incense in them, and bring ye before the LORD every man his censer, two hundred and fifty censers; thou also, and Aaron, each of you his censer.

16:18 And they took every man his censer, and put fire in them, and laid incense thereon, and stood in the door of the tabernacle of the congregation with Moses and Aaron.

Korah then came and brought very many supporters with him.

16:19 And Korah gathered all the congregation against them unto the door of the tabernacle of the congregation: and the glory of the LORD appeared unto all the congregation.

Jesus Christ then appeared in the cloud of glory and commanded the faithful to separate themselves from the wicked rebels so that the rebels might be destroyed.

Even so, the time is almost at hand in our day, where those who rebel against zealously living by every Word of God and who rebel against Jesus

Christ the Mediator of the New Covenant and their espoused Husband: will be separated from the zealous so that the faithful can be saved alive while those who refuse to live by every Word of God can be cast into the furnace of affliction.

16:20 And the LORD spake unto Moses and unto Aaron, saying, **16:21** Separate yourselves from among this congregation, that I may consume them in a moment.

God commands that the faithful to his Word separate themselves out from among those rebels, so that the faithful are not destroyed with the sinful.

The time of the separation of the zealous to live by every Word of God from those who rebel against any zeal for the whole Word of God is almost at hand. Yes, God IS the author of division; dividing the holy from the profane, the good from the evil and the faithful from the faithless! Did not Jesus cast the sinners out of the temple?

16:22 And they fell upon their faces, and said, O God, the God of the spirits of all flesh, shall one man sin, and wilt thou be wroth with all the congregation? **16:23** And the LORD spake unto Moses, saying, **16:24** Speak unto the congregation, saying, Get you up from about the tabernacle of Korah, Dathan, and Abiram.

My Dear and Much Beloved Brethren; it is those people who are not zealous for the sanctity of the Sabbath or for the practical keeping of the Word of God who are in rebellion against Jesus Christ the Mediator of the New Covenant!

The time is very near at hand to separate out the zealous from the idolaters of men, the false traditions of men and corporate entities; so that the idolaters who blindly follow men and those who compromise with the Word of God; can be cast into the furnace of affliction for their good, to humble them and bring them to sincere repentance.

16:25 And Moses rose up and went unto Dathan and Abiram; and the elders of Israel followed him. **16:26** And he spake unto the congregation, saying, Depart, I pray you, from the tents of these wicked men, and touch nothing of their's, lest ye be consumed in all their sins.

Then the faithful removed themselves because they believed the warnings and trusted in their God. The time for such a separation in today's Spiritual Ekklesia is at hand!

16:27 So they gat up from the tabernacle of Korah, Dathan, and Abiram, on every side: and Dathan and Abiram came out, and stood in the door of their tents, and their wives, and their sons, and their little children.

Moses then asked God to reveal who his true servants were

16:28 And Moses said, Hereby ye shall know that the LORD hath sent me to do all these works; for I have not done them of mine own mind. **16:29** If these men die the common death of all men, or if they be visited after the visitation of all men; then the LORD hath not sent me. **16:30 But if the LORD make a new thing, and the earth open her mouth, and swallow them up, with all that appertain unto them, and they go down quick into the pit; then ye shall understand that these men have provoked the LORD.**

At the words of Moses; Jesus Christ: yes, the same Christ which many falsely claim will wink at sin and overlook transgressions and tolerate false teachings [doctrines]; opened up the very earth and swallowed up these rebels against the Word of God.

16:31 And it came to pass, as he had made an end of speaking all these words, that the ground clave asunder that was under them: **16:32** And the earth opened her mouth, and swallowed them up, and their houses, and all the men that appertained unto Korah, and all their goods. **16:33** They, and all that appertained to them, went down alive into the pit, and the earth closed upon them: and they perished from among the congregation.

When these rebels began to scream as they felt the earth open under them, those nearby fled away

16:34 And all Israel that were round about them fled at the cry of them: for they said, Lest the earth swallow us up also.

Then the men who offered incense on behalf of Korah were killed by fire from God: this a direct answer from God revealing unmistakably that their rebellion against the mediator of the Mosaic Covenant was rejected.

God the Father and Jesus Christ WILL NOT TOLERATE any departure from the Word of God to idolize men and exalt men above the authority of the Word of God!!! NO! NO! NO! Ten thousand thousand times NO!

16:35 And there came out a fire from the LORD, and consumed the two hundred and fifty men that offered incense.

Then the God who later gave up his Godhood to become flesh as Jesus Christ [Hebrew: Yeshua Mashiach] commanded Eleazar to beat the censors of the rebels into plates to cover the altar, so that the people may see and remember to never again rebel against the Mediator of the Covenant or against any part of the Word of God.

16:36 And the LORD spake unto Moses, saying, **16:37** Speak unto Eleazar the son of Aaron the priest, that he take up the censers out of the burning, and scatter thou the fire yonder; for they are hallowed.

Those who compromise with or fail to zealously live by every Word of God, sin against their own lives.

16:38 The censers of **these sinners against their own souls,** let them make them broad plates for a covering of the altar: for they offered them before the LORD, therefore they are hallowed: and they shall be a sign unto the children of Israel. **16:39** And Eleazar the priest took the brasen censers, wherewith they that were burnt had offered; and they were made broad plates for a covering of the altar:

These Levites wanted to be the deciders and leaders and were in rebellion against God's chosen mediator and the Word of God, and they wanted to usurp this position by self-will and open rebellion.

Today in the Ekklesia, men rule by their own ways and are not diligent to live by every Word of God; thereby rebelling against the Spirit Mediator of the spiritual New Covenant and against many parts of the Word of God.

The time for separating the faithful to God from such people is close at hand.

16:40 To be **a memorial unto the children of Israel, that no stranger, which is not of the seed of Aaron, come near to offer incense before the LORD**; that he be not as Korah, and as his company: as the LORD said to him by the hand of Moses.

Astounding! The next day the people accused Moses of killing God's people!

16:41 But on the morrow all the congregation of the children of Israel murmured against Moses and against Aaron, saying, Ye have killed the people of the LORD.

The people gathered against Moses and Aaron; and Jesus Christ came down in the cloud of glory to meet them.

16:42 And it came to pass, when the congregation was gathered against Moses and against Aaron, that they looked toward the tabernacle of the congregation: and, behold, the cloud covered it, and the glory of the LORD appeared. **16:43** And Moses and Aaron came before the tabernacle of the congregation.

Then the Eternal then told Moses and Aaron and the faithful to immediately separate themselves from the sinning people so that he might destroy them.

This same event is to soon be repeated as God's two servants will call by the Word of the Eternal, for the faithful to separate themselves and leave so that the faithless may be corrected in great tribulation.

16:44 And the LORD spake unto Moses, saying, **16:45** Get you up from among this congregation, that I may consume them as in a moment. And they fell upon their faces.

Moses commanded Aaron to quickly offer an atonement for the people because the plague was upon them for their rejection of the Word and Will of God. This is the God Being who later became flesh as Jesus Christ doing this, and destroying the unrepentant who reject living by every Word of God to embrace the false ways of human imagination!

Because God has been a long time patient with us, it does not mean that our correction is not at hand.

16:46 And Moses said unto Aaron, Take a censer, and put fire therein from off the altar, and put on incense, and go quickly unto the congregation, and make an atonement for them: for there is wrath gone out from the LORD; the plague is begun.

16:47 And Aaron took as Moses commanded, and ran into the midst of the congregation; and, behold, the plague was begun among the people: and he put on incense, and made an atonement for the people. **16:48** And he stood between the dead and the living; and the plague was stayed. **16:49** Now **they that died in the plague were fourteen thousand and seven hundred**, beside them that died about the matter of Korah.

16:50 And Aaron returned unto Moses unto the door of the tabernacle of the congregation: and the plague was stayed.

Simply stated: The New Covenant is an espousal of marriage, a personal agreement between an individual and Jesus Christ formalized by a baptismal commitment to be absolutely faithful to and to live by every Word of God the Father and Jesus Christ.

Therefore any person, organization, tradition or thing which comes between us and our commitment to live by every Word of God is a Korah trying to usurp the position of our espoused Husband Jesus Christ.

Numbers 17

Jesus then moves to clearly identify who he has chosen as the high priest of Mosaic Israel.

Numbers 17:1 And the LORD spake unto Moses, saying, **17:2** Speak unto the children of Israel, and take of every one of them a rod according to the house of their fathers, of all their princes according to the house of their fathers twelve rods: write thou every man's name upon his rod.

The name of the head of each tribe is to be written on rods, with Aaron's name written on the rod of Levi. God was going to clearly identify which tribe and which person he had called to be the first high priest and father of the priesthood of physical Mosaic Israel.

The Aaronic Mosaic high priest being an instructional allegory of the spiritual High Priest of the order of Melchizedek [Jesus Christ] the High Priest of the New Covenant; and Aaron's rod being a symbol of the Branch Jesus Christ.

> **Isaiah 11:1** And there shall come forth a rod out of the stem of Jesse, and a Branch shall grow out of his roots:

Numbers 17:3 And thou shalt write **Aaron's name upon the rod of Levi**: for one rod shall be for the head of the house of their fathers. **17:4** And thou shalt lay them up in the tabernacle of the congregation before the testimony, where I will meet with you.

17:5 And it shall come to pass, **that the man's rod, whom I shall choose, shall blossom:** and I will make to cease from me the murmurings of the children of Israel, whereby they murmur against you.

Moses then obeyed and took a rod from each tribe. This is very similar to the choosing of Matthias by lot, as an apostle in Acts 1:26.

17:6 And Moses spake unto the children of Israel, and every one of their princes gave him a rod apiece, for each prince one, according to their fathers' houses, even twelve rods: and the rod of Aaron was among their rods. **17:7** And Moses laid up the rods before the LORD in the tabernacle of witness.

In the morning the rod of Aaron had budded and bloomed and brought forth the fruit of almonds.

Here I want to point out that the Menorah lamp stands in the tabernacle were to be decorated as almond branches with almond buds, flowers and fruit.

For those who can understand; the Menorah is a symbol of Jesus Christ the Branch (See the John 15 article) and Mediator of the New Covenant through whom flows the oil of the Holy Spirit into the seven churches (See the Revelation 1 article) who through that Holy Spirit are to be a shining light to the nations.

We are nothing on our own and our own ways are nothing. It is the internalizing of the whole Word of God and living by every Word of God through God's Holy Spirit dwelling in us [the Spirit of God the Father and Jesus Christ living in us], and our being totally zealous for the whole Word and Will of God the Father in heaven; which makes us shining lights in this dark world.

Tolerating false doctrine and sin while idolizing men above the Word of God; quenches God's Spirit and dims our light to extinction!

ONLY if we are filled with wholehearted Christ-like zeal to live by every Word of God; will we be given the Spirit of God. ONLY if we follow God's Spirit in passionate zeal to keep God's Word, can our light truly shine! And ONLY then will we spiritually grow, bud and blossom and bear much fruit!

17:8 And it came to pass, that on the morrow Moses went into the tabernacle of witness; and, behold, the rod of Aaron for the house of Levi was budded, and brought forth buds, and bloomed blossoms, and yielded almonds. **17:9** And Moses brought out all the rods from before the LORD unto all the children of Israel: and they looked, and took every man his rod.

Aaron's rod was then placed in the tabernacle as proof of the Mosaic priesthood of Aaron.

We who are called into the spiritual priesthood of Jesus Christ; if we remain steadfast and faint not, will grow, bud, blossom and bear fruit; as a shining light in the spiritual darkness of this world. Not by our own strength or ways, but through the Holy Spirit of God and a passionate zeal for the Word of God the Almighty.

17:10 And the LORD said unto Moses, Bring Aaron's rod again before the testimony, to be kept for a token against the rebels; and thou shalt quite take away their murmurings from me, that they die not. **17:11** And Moses did so: as the LORD commanded him, so did he.

The people now realized that God really meant it when he said that they would die in their sins.

Today's spiritual Ekklesia needs to learn the same lesson, that if we do as we think is right and we fail to live by every Word of God rebelling against God and Jesus Christ the Mediator of the New Covenant, we will also die in our sins.

17:12 And the children of Israel spake unto Moses, saying, Behold, we die, we perish, we all perish. **17:13** Whosoever cometh any thing near unto the tabernacle of the LORD shall die: shall we be consumed with dying?

Numbers 18

The Mosaic priesthood of Aaron interceded between Israel and God and covered the people's repented sins against the Mosaic Covenant by sacrificing for them. This is an instructional allegory that spiritually, Jesus Christ would bear the sins of sincerely repentant humanity against the spiritual New Covenant; offering himself as the Lamb of God.

Numbers 18:1 And the LORD said unto Aaron, Thou and thy sons and thy father's house with thee shall bear the iniquity of the sanctuary: and thou and thy sons with thee shall bear the iniquity of your priesthood.

The priests ministered in the holy things, and the Levites assisted hem with the physical needs of the tabernacle [later the temple].

18:2 And thy brethren also of the tribe of Levi, the tribe of thy father, bring thou with thee, that they may be joined unto thee, and minister unto thee: but thou and thy sons with thee shall minister before the tabernacle of witness. **18:3** And they shall keep thy charge, and the charge of all the tabernacle: only they [the non-priest Levites] shall not come nigh the vessels of the sanctuary and the altar, that neither they, nor ye also, die.

NO stranger [no unconverted person] was allowed to approach any holy thing.

This is representative of the fact that in the New Covenant, no person can approach God the Father except through the High Priest of the New Covenant, Jesus Christ.

18:4 And they shall be joined unto thee, and keep the charge of the tabernacle of the congregation, for all the service of the tabernacle: and a stranger shall not come nigh unto you.

The priests were to maintain the holiness of the holy things, by keeping them pure and clean from all pollution; just like the called out Spiritual Ekklesia is to keep our assemblies holy by keeping out those repentant in name only, and by rejecting all self- justifying and wilful sin and compromise with any part of the holiness of the Word of God.

Seeking numbers by watering down teachings is an abomination to God the Father and Jesus Christ! God wants Quality, Holiness and Spiritual Purity; he wants the brethren to be in full unity with God the Father: Which unity only comes through a passionate zeal to live by every Word of God so as to internalize the nature of God and become like HIM!

18:5 And ye shall keep the charge of the sanctuary, and the charge of the altar: that there be no wrath any more upon the children of Israel.

The Levites were to assist in the physical work and the priests were to be Set Apart to minister in the HOLY THINGS.

18:6 And I, behold, I have taken your brethren the Levites from among the children of Israel: to you they are given as a gift for the LORD, to do the service of the tabernacle of the congregation.

Those spiritually called to become priests of Jesus Christ, if we endure and overcome, will receive their reward in the first general resurrection to spirit: But no stranger who was not called out to the New Covenant of zeal to live by every Word of God, will be raised to eternal life to become a part of the holy priesthood of Jesus Christ.

> **Revelation 5:10** And hast made us unto our God **kings and priests**: **and** we shall reign on the earth.

Numbers 18:7 Therefore thou and thy sons with thee shall keep your priest's office for everything of the altar, and within the vail; and ye shall serve: I have given your priest's office unto you as a service of gift: and the stranger that cometh nigh shall be put to death.

The heave offerings are to be given to the priests for their service to God in the holy things.

18:8 And the LORD spake unto Aaron, Behold, I also have given thee the charge of mine heave offerings of all the hallowed things of the children of

Israel; unto thee have I given them by reason of the anointing, and to thy sons, by an ordinance for ever.

Those parts not burned in the fire are to be given to the priests as explained in Leviticus.

18:9 This shall be thine of the most holy things, reserved from the fire: every oblation of theirs, every **meat offering** of theirs, and every **sin offering** of theirs, and every **trespass offering** of theirs which they shall render unto me, shall be [reserved as] most holy for thee and for thy sons [the officiating priests].

18:10 In the most holy place shalt thou eat it; every male shall eat it: it shall be holy unto thee.

All offerings not burned but lifted up before the Lord, like the Wave Offering and the Pentecost first fruits offering etc. belong to the priests. These offerings are not only for the male priests but also belong to the female family members of the descendants of Aaron. The only restriction is that a person must be "clean" to eat these offerings.

In the spiritual sense of the New Covenant, being clean means being free from the pollution of any sin as well as from any physical uncleanness.

Today's Spiritual Ekklesia is full of spiritual uncleanness and sin, and most are not fit to have a part in the resurrection to the eternal priesthood of Jesus Christ until they sincerely repent.

18:11 And this is thine; **the heave offering of their gift, with all the wave offerings** of the children of Israel: I have given them unto thee, and to thy sons **and to thy daughters** with thee, by a statute for ever: **every one that is clean in thy house shall eat of it**.

18:12 All the best of the oil, and all the best of the wine, and of the wheat, the firstfruits of them which they shall offer unto the LORD, them have I given thee.

The first fruits belong to the priests; spiritually all of the New Covenant called out are called to become priests in the resurrection of the chosen first fruits and the nations will bring their first fruits to them in the kingdom of God.

18:13 And whatsoever is first ripe in the land, which they shall bring unto the LORD, shall be thine; every one that is clean in thine house shall eat of it.

All the things devoted to God belonged to the high priesthood of Aaron and his descendants, as an allegory that all holy things belong to the High

Priest of the New Covenant, Jesus Christ; and to his resurrected spiritual priesthood.

18:14 Every thing devoted in Israel shall be thine.

Every first born of man and beast along with the first fruits of the field belonged to God and were given to the physical high priesthood of Aaron, as an allegory that the resurrected chosen first fruits priesthood belong to the New Covenant High Priest of Jesus Christ who has redeemed us with his life.

18:15 Every thing that openeth the matrix in all flesh, which they bring unto the LORD, whether it be of men or beasts, shall be thine: nevertheless the **firstborn of man shalt thou surely redeem, and the firstling of unclean beasts shalt thou redeem.**

To redeem the firstborn of men, five shekels were to be paid to the sanctuary.

18:16 And those that are to be redeemed from a month old shalt thou redeem, according to thine estimation, for the money of five shekels, after the shekel of the sanctuary, which is twenty gerahs.

The first born of all sacrificial animals must be sacrificed and may NOT be redeemed.

18:17 But the firstling of a cow, or the firstling of a sheep, or the firstling of a goat, **thou shalt not redeem**; they are holy: **thou shalt sprinkle their blood upon the altar, and shalt burn their fat** for an offering made by fire, for a sweet savour unto the LORD.

18:18 And the flesh of them shall be thine [belong to the officiating priests], as the wave breast and as the right shoulder are thine. **18:19** All the heave offerings of the holy things, which the children of Israel offer unto the LORD, have **I given thee, and thy sons and thy daughters with thee,** by a statute for ever: it is a covenant of salt for ever before the LORD unto thee and to thy seed with thee.

The priests had no land except the Levitical cities and their suburbs to live in, for God is their inheritance; the priests are to fully trust in God to provide for them.

18:20 And the LORD spake unto Aaron, **Thou shalt have no inheritance in their land, neither shalt thou have any part among them: I am thy part and thine inheritance** among the children of Israel.

The people were to tithe exclusively to the Levites who assist the priests.

The Levites are then to give the priests a tithe of all that they have received (Nu 18:26); which pays for the sacrifices offered on behalf of the whole nation and the priestly expenses, and the priests are also to be supported by the sacrifices

18:21 And, behold, **I have given the children of Levi all the tenth in Israel for an inheritance**, for their service which they serve, even the service of the tabernacle of the congregation.

Israel is warned to keep away from the tabernacles and let the priests and Levites do their jobs.

18:22 Neither must the children of Israel henceforth come nigh the tabernacle of the congregation [the Inner Court of the Priests and The Most Holy Place], lest they bear sin, and die.

The inheritance of the Levites is the tithe of the people; they shall have no other inheritance in Israel [except the Levitical cities and their suburbs to dwell in] .

18:23 But the Levites shall do the service of the tabernacle of the congregation, and they shall bear their iniquity: it shall be a statute for ever throughout your generations, that among the children of Israel they have no inheritance. **18:24** But **the tithes of the children of Israel, which they offer as an heave offering unto the LORD, I have given to the Levites to inherit**: therefore I have said unto them, Among the children of Israel they shall have no inheritance.

The Levites are to take a tenth from the people and they are then to give a tenth of what they receive to the priests.

18:25 And the LORD spake unto Moses, saying, **18:26** Thus speak unto the Levites, and say unto them, When ye take of the children of Israel the tithes which I have given you from them for your inheritance, then ye shall offer up an heave offering of it for the LORD, **even a tenth part of the tithe**. **18:27** And this your heave offering shall be reckoned unto you, as though it were the corn of the threshingfloor, and as the fulness of the winepress. **18:28** Thus ye also shall offer an heave offering unto the LORD of all your tithes, which ye receive of the children of Israel; and **ye shall give thereof the LORD's heave offering to Aaron the priest.**

The Levites are also to share with the priests whatever gifts that they receive above the tithes of the people.

18:29 Out of all your gifts ye shall offer every heave offering of the LORD, of all the best thereof, even the hallowed part thereof out of it. **18:30** Therefore thou shalt say unto them, When ye have heaved the best thereof from it, then it shall be counted unto the Levites as the increase of the threshingfloor, and as the increase of the winepress.

The Levites may eat the tithe and gifts anywhere and need not eat them in the tabernacle. It is the sacrifices which must be eaten by the priests in the tabernacle or later the temple.

18:31 And ye shall eat it in every place, ye and your households: for it is your reward for your service in the tabernacle of the congregation.

The priests must not sin in desiring more than their share from the Levites, for they have been given the meat of the various offerings in addition to a tenth of the Levitical tithes. Neither shall the priests take for themselves any holy thing which is commanded to be burned on the altar.

18:32 And ye shall bear no sin by reason of it, when ye have heaved from it the best of it: neither shall ye pollute the holy things of the children of Israel, lest ye die.

Numbers 19

The Red Heifer

For non cattle people a heifer is a virgin cow, usually under two years old.

The Red Heifer must be killed before the high priest outside the camp, just as Jesus Christ was killed outside the city; and must be wholly burned with cedar wood, and hyssop, and with scarlet cast into the fire.

The redness of this heifer being typical of the red of the blood of Christ shed for us and the red heifer being of the cattle kind, was typical of strength and patient service, while its virginity was representative of total loyalty to God and absolute purity. These things are an allegory of Jesus Christ.

The burning of the whole heifer represented serving the God the Father wholeheartedly, the cedar was to be burned and to rise up as a sweet smelling smoke, typical of the service of Christ as a very sweet and acceptable thing to God the Father. The scarlet was typical of the shed blood of Christ, and the hyssop typical of the cleansing quality of the sacrifice of Christ.

Numbers 19:1 And the LORD spake unto Moses and unto Aaron, saying, **19:2** This is the ordinance of the law which the LORD hath commanded, saying, Speak unto the children of Israel, that they bring thee a red heifer without spot, wherein is no blemish, and **upon which never came yoke**:

The yoke being typical of the yoke of the bondage to Satan and sin; therefore, never having been yoked was representative of Jesus Christ who was never in bondage to any sin.

19:3 And ye shall give her unto Eleazar the priest, that he may bring her forth without the camp, and one shall slay her before his face: **19:4** And Eleazar the priest shall take of her blood with his finger, and sprinkle of her blood directly before the tabernacle of the congregation seven times: **19:5** And **one shall burn the heifer in his sight; her skin, and her flesh, and her blood, with her dung, shall he burn: 19:6 And the priest shall take cedar wood, and hyssop, and scarlet, and cast it into the midst of the burning of the heifer.**

The red heifer took on itself all uncleanness, just as Jesus Christ took upon himself the sincerely repented sin and uncleanness of the world. Therefore the high priest and everyone involved in the killing and the burning of this heifer was unclean [representing bearing sin] and must be washed and remain unclean until the sun set and a new day began.

19:7 Then the priest shall wash his clothes, and he shall bathe his flesh in water, and afterward he shall come into the camp, and the priest shall be unclean until the even. **19:8** And he that burneth her shall **wash his clothes in water, and bathe his flesh in water, and shall be unclean until the even.**

The ashes were then to be gathered up by a clean person and used to cleanse people from the uncleanness of exposure to death.

19:9 And a man that is clean shall gather up the ashes of the heifer, and lay them up without the camp in a clean place, and it shall be kept for the congregation of the children of Israel for a water of separation: it is a purification for sin.

The clean ash gatherers become unclean by their contact with the ashes.

19:10 And he that gathereth the ashes of the heifer shall wash his clothes, and be unclean until the even: and it shall be unto the children of Israel, and unto the stranger that sojourneth among them, for a statute for ever.

The Uses of the Red Heifer Ashes

Uncleanness by contact with a dead person

Death being the wages of sin, and all have sinned except Jesus Christ; contact with the dead is a type of contact and being made unclean by sin. The operative word here is DEATH.

Those who have become unclean by touching the dead are to cleanse themselves with the ashes of the red heifer mixed with water on the third and seventh days.

This cleansing was done on the third and seventh day's, and the unclean person was made clean at sunset ending the seventh day.

The beginning of the eighth day represents a new beginning for the person, cleansed from the uncleanness of association with death.

After the END of the seventh day of the Feast of Tabernacles; the Eighth Day Feast represents humanity cleansed from all sin and changed to spirit, going forward into eternity in peace with God: All the uncleanness of sin and death destroyed.

19:11 He that **toucheth the dead body of any man shall be unclean seven days. 19:12** He shall **purify himself with it** [the ashes of the red heifer mixed with water] **on the third day**, and on the seventh day he shall be clean: but if he purify not himself the third day, then the seventh day he shall not be clean.

The red heifer was an allegory of the need to apply the sacrifice of Jesus Christ [typified by the ashes mixed with water] to the sincerely repentant in the New Covenant.

The ashes represented Jesus Christ the ultimate sacrifice for all sincerely repented sin and uncleanness, and the water was typical of the Spirit and Word of God; both together washing away the uncleanness of the wages of sin which is death.

> **Ephesians 5:25** . . . even as Christ also loved the church, and gave himself for it; **5:26** That he might sanctify and cleanse it with **the washing of water by the word, 5:27 That he might present it to himself a glorious church, not having spot, or wrinkle, or any such thing; but that it should be holy and without blemish.**

Spiritually only those having their uncleanness of sin which brings death, atoned for by sincere repentance and the application of the sacrifice of Jesus Christ; and who then go onward to sin no more, zealously living by every Word of God: will be accepted as pure spiritual virgins and resurrected as a part of the congregation of the bride.

Numbers 19:13 Whosoever toucheth the dead body of any man that is dead, and purifieth not himself, defileth **the tabernacle of the LORD**; and that soul shall be cut off from Israel: because **the water of separation was not sprinkled upon him**, he shall be unclean; his uncleanness is yet upon him.

Here we see that Jesus Christ calls the converted human person; "the tabernacle of the LORD," indicating that he will live in God's faithful through the agency of God's holy Spirit.

ANY and ALL association with sin and the wages of sin [death] MUST be atoned for; because NO uncleanness of sin or pollution by any association with evil, will be permitted in the resurrection to eternal life. Those who claim that it is godly Christ-like love to tolerate sin: are LIARS!

We are to be zealous to prove every word of men, and we are to reject anything that is not consistent with every Word of God.

No one who tolerates a diversity of doctrine from God's Word, which departure from the holiness of the Word of God is the uncleanness of sin; will be in the resurrection to spirit!

Jesus Christ here condemns any association with death [which is the wages of sin and compromise with the Word of God], and requires cleansing atonement for this uncleanness, which is typical of all uncleanness of sin in the spiritual sense.

19:14 This is the law, when a man dieth in a tent: all that come into the tent, and all that is in the tent, shall be unclean seven days. **19:15** And every open vessel, which hath no covering bound upon it, is unclean. **19:16** And whosoever toucheth one that is slain with a sword in the open fields, or a dead body, or a bone of a man, or a grave, shall be unclean seven days.

Mosaic cleansing with the red heifer from defilement by any dead body

A clean person is to mix the ashes with running water [living as opposed to stagnant (dead) water], and sprinkled with a branch of hyssop [a plant with cleaning properties]; sprinkling the unclean person and things on the third and seventh days.

The clean person doing the sprinkling then also becomes unclean, and must himself wash and remain unclean until the evening [sunset].

Then the person and things remain unclean for seven days, and shall become clean at sunset ending the seventh day and then have a new beginning on the eighth day.

19:17 And for an unclean person they shall take of the ashes of the burnt heifer of purification for sin, and running water shall be put thereto in a vessel: **19:18** And a clean person shall take hyssop, and dip it in the water, and sprinkle it upon the tent, and upon all the vessels, and upon the persons that were there, and upon him that touched a bone, or one slain, or one dead, or a grave: **19:19 And the clean person shall sprinkle upon the unclean on the third day, and on the seventh day: and on the seventh day he shall purify himself, and wash his clothes, and bathe himself in water, and shall be clean at even.**

If a person does not sincerely repent and seek the cleansing of the sacrifice of Jesus Christ to be applied to him; he is cut off from God. Anyone who idolizes and follows any man contrary to the Word of God and is not zealous to live by every Word of God, will reap the wages of his sin and will be cut off from Jesus Christ and God the Father.

19:20 But the man that shall be unclean, and shall not purify [spiritually: sincerely repent] **himself, that soul shall be cut off from among the congregation, because he hath defiled the sanctuary of the LORD: the water of separation hath not been sprinkled upon him; he is unclean.**

19:21 And it shall be a perpetual statute unto them, that he that sprinkleth the water of separation shall wash his clothes; and he that toucheth the water of separation shall be unclean until even.

This teaching absolutely prohibits any tolerance for the spiritual uncleanness of doctrines diverse from the scriptures, including any tolerance for the willfully sinful among the assemblies of the called out.

19:22 And whatsoever the unclean person toucheth shall be unclean; and the soul that toucheth it shall be unclean until even.

See also The Law of God and the Unclean Thing.

Numbers 20

Instead of seeking deliverance from God the people complained and rebelled; today's Spiritual Ekklesia does the very same thing! Oh, we would deny that, but in fact we attempt to water down the commandments of God rather than run to Christ for deliverance and the strength to obey the Word of God!

Yes, we are NO different from those complainers when we call the Sabbath holy and then refuse to keep it holy!

We make the Word of God of no effect by our watering down of God's Word and our rejection of any zeal to live by every Word of God. We would rather judge the Word of God by the words of men than the other way around, because we exalt and idolize men above the Word of God.

Just like physical Israel in the wilderness, we complain about God's Word and seek to turn back into the bondage of the spiritual Egypt of our idols of men.

Numbers 20:1 Then came the children of Israel, even the whole congregation, into the desert of Zin in the first month: and the people abode in Kadesh; and Miriam died there, and was buried there. **20:2** And there was no water for the congregation: and they gathered themselves together against Moses and against Aaron. **20:3** And the people chode with Moses, and spake, saying, Would God that we had died when our brethren died before the LORD! **20:4** And why have ye brought up the congregation of the LORD into this wilderness, that we and our cattle should die there? **20:5** And wherefore have ye made us to come up out of Egypt, to bring us in unto this evil place? it is no place of seed, or of figs, or of vines, or of pomegranates; neither is there any water to drink.

While the people complained against God for their problems, faithful Moses and Aaron went to God and asked for help. Moses and Aaron did not water down teachings to bring in more numbers or money! NO absolutely not, they ran to their God for deliverance, instead of trying to deliver themselves by turning away from and compromising with the Word of God!

Brethren, this was recorded for OUR example!

20:6 And Moses and Aaron went from the presence of the assembly unto the door of the tabernacle of the congregation, and they fell upon their faces: and the glory of the LORD appeared unto them.

This is the second time in their journeys where this matter of water became a problem. Do you not think that God knew where the water was and could have led them to water. These things happened and were recorded for OUR instruction.

Spiritually this water represented the Holy Spirit and these events were instructional examples for us, teaching us that it is through the sacrifice of Jesus Christ the Rock of Our Salvation, that the water of the Holy Spirit and an understanding of and willingness to live by the Word of God comes.

The analogy being that first the Rock must be struck, meaning that Christ would die to cover our sins as the sacrificial Lamb of God; and that after that the water of the Holy Spirit would be given to those who seek to live by every Word of God and ask for God's Spirit. See the article on "The Living Waters of Salvation".

> **1 Corinthians 10** Moreover, brethren, I would not that ye should be ignorant, how that all our fathers were under the cloud, and all passed through the sea; **10:2** And were all baptized unto Moses in the cloud and in the sea; **10:3 And did all eat the same spiritual meat** [the Word of God]; **10:4 And did all drink the same spiritual drink: for they drank of that spiritual Rock that followed them: and that Rock was Christ. 10:5** But with many of them God was not well pleased: for they were overthrown in the wilderness. **10:6** Now **these things were our examples, to the intent we should not lust after evil things, as they also lusted.**

These two times were an allegory for us: The first time Moses was commanded to strike the rock and the water would come out. That was an allegory that the death of Christ would bring forth the living waters of salvation.

> **Exodus 17:5** And the Lord said unto Moses, Go on before the people, and take with thee of the elders of Israel; and thy rod, wherewith thou smotest the river, take in thine hand, and go. **17:6** Behold, I will stand before thee there upon the rock in Horeb; and **thou shalt smite the rock, and there shall come water out of it,** that the people may drink. And Moses did so in the sight of the elders of Israel.

The second time Moses was commanded to SPEAK to the rock and the living waters of salvation would flow out. This is in reference to the fact that Jesus Christ would only die [be struck] ONCE and that at the appointed time all who call on the name of the Lord would be saved.

> **Joel 2:32** And it shall come to pass, **that whosoever shall call on the name of the Lord shall be delivered:** for in mount Zion and in Jerusalem shall be deliverance, as the Lord hath said, and in the remnant whom the Lord shall call.

Numbers 20:7 And the LORD spake unto Moses, saying, **20:8** Take the rod, and gather thou the assembly together, thou, and Aaron thy brother, and **speak ye unto the rock** before their eyes; and it shall give forth his water, and thou shalt bring forth to them water out of the rock: so thou shalt give the congregation and their beasts drink.

Moses lost his temper and did not obey God by speaking to the rock, instead striking it twice and breaking the intended allegory. For this sin Moses was corrected because God is NOT a respecter of persons; therefore you elders and leaders take heed that Jesus Christ will indeed correct you for departing from him to lead the people astray to idolize men.

20:9 And Moses took the rod from before the LORD, as he commanded him. **20:10** And Moses and Aaron gathered the congregation together before the rock, and he said unto them, Hear now, ye rebels; must we fetch you water out of this rock? **20:11 And Moses lifted up his hand, and with his rod he smote the rock twice:** and the water came out abundantly, and the congregation drank, and their beasts also.

The water came out of the rock, to continue the allegory and to give drink to the people, but God corrected Moses. Indeed Jesus used this sin of Moses to teach us that no sinner who is not totally faithful to EVERY WORD of God may enter the spiritual Promised Land of eternal life.

Jesus Christ forbade Moses to enter the physical promised land as an instruction to us that he will NOT wink at any self-justified sin; and he will NOT let any sinner into his Promised Land of eternal life.

It's time that WE WOKE UP and understood that Jesus Christ will not tolerate any sin or false teachings and that he will NOT wink at any sin.

20:12 And the LORD spake unto Moses and Aaron, Because ye believed me not, to sanctify me in the eyes of the children of Israel, therefore **ye shall not bring this congregation into the land which I have given them.**

20:13 This is the water of Meribah; because the children of Israel strove with the LORD, and he was sanctified in them.

Israel made preparations to travel up the east side of Jordan and Moses sent a letter to the ruler of Edom.

20:14 And Moses sent messengers from Kadesh unto the **king of Edom,** Thus saith thy brother Israel, Thou knowest all the travail that hath befallen us: **20:15** How our fathers went down into Egypt, and we have dwelt in Egypt a long time; and the Egyptians vexed us, and our fathers: **20:16** And when we cried unto the LORD, he heard our voice, and sent an angel, and hath brought us forth out of Egypt: and, behold, we are in Kadesh, a city in the uttermost of thy border: **20:17 Let us pass, I pray thee, through thy country: we will not pass through the fields, or through the vineyards, neither will we drink of the water of the wells: we will go by the king's high way, we will not turn to the right hand nor to the left, until we have passed thy borders.**

Edom refuses passage and threatens to fight Israel if they enter his land

20:18 And Edom [Esau] said unto him, Thou shalt not pass by me, lest I come out against thee with the sword.

The dialogue continues with Moses offering to pay for anything that Israel might use

20:19 And the children of Israel said unto him, We will go by the high way: and if I and my cattle drink of thy water, then I will pay for it: I will only, without doing anything else, go through on my feet.

The king of Edom rejected Israel and mobilized his armies to defend his borders

20:20 And he said, Thou shalt not go through. And Edom came out against him with much people, and with a strong hand.

Israel turned back and stayed in the area, but outside the border of Canaan and Edom

20:21 Thus Edom refused to give Israel passage through his border: wherefore Israel turned away from him. **20:22** And the children of Israel, even the whole congregation, journeyed from Kadesh, and came unto mount Hor.

Aaron was also forbidden to enter the promised land.

20:23 And the LORD spake unto Moses and Aaron in mount Hor, by the coast of the land of Edom, saying, **20:24** Aaron shall be gathered unto his people: **for he shall not enter into the land which I have given unto the children of Israel, because ye rebelled against my word at the water of Meribah.**

Aaron is stripped of the garments of the high priest, and that sign of office was given to his son Eleazar as the indication that God had chosen him as the new high priest.

20:25 Take Aaron and Eleazar his son, and bring them up unto mount Hor: **20:26 And strip Aaron of his garments, and put them upon Eleazar his son**: and Aaron shall be gathered unto his people, and shall die there.

The congregation was gathered to witness the change of men in the office of high priest.

20:27 And Moses did as the LORD commanded: and they went up into mount Hor in the sight of all the congregation. **20:28** And Moses stripped Aaron of his garments, and put them upon Eleazar his son; and Aaron died there in the top of the mount: and Moses and Eleazar came down from the mount.

20:29 And when all the congregation saw that Aaron was dead, they mourned for Aaron thirty days, even all the house of Israel.

Numbers 21

A Canaanite king comes forth to battle, attacking in the area south west of Edom. The people then turned to God for deliverance.

They were slowly learning their lesson, the wanderings in Sinai for 40 years is an allegory of a spiritually called out person's journey to learn zeal for the Word and promises of God.

Numbers 21:1 And when king Arad the Canaanite, which dwelt in the south, heard tell that Israel came by the way of the spies; then he fought against Israel, and took some of them prisoners.

21:2 And Israel vowed a vow unto the LORD, and said, If thou wilt indeed deliver this people into my hand, then I will utterly destroy their cities.
21:3 And the LORD hearkened to the voice of Israel, and delivered up the Canaanites; and they utterly destroyed them and their cities: and he called the name of the place **Hormah**.

21:4 And they journeyed from mount Hor by the way of the Red sea, to compass [go around] the land of Edom: and the soul of the people was much discouraged because of the way.

How quickly we forget, the people were again complaining over the hardships of the journey; just as many in today's spiritual Israel of the called out, complain about the hardship of keeping the commandments of God.

21:5 And the people spake against God, and against Moses, Wherefore have ye brought us up out of Egypt to die in the wilderness? for there is no bread, neither is there any water; and our soul loatheth this light bread.

Jesus Christ then sent fiery serpents to torment and kill them. This was a lesson that "the way of the serpent" [Satan, and rebellion against zeal to keep the Word of God] is pain and death; the word "fiery" referring to an intense burning pain upon being bitten.

21:6 And the LORD sent fiery serpents among the people, and they bit the people; and much people of Israel died.

The people repent again and beg for relief

21:7 Therefore the people came to Moses, and said, We have sinned, for we have spoken against the LORD, and against thee; pray unto the LORD, that he take away the serpents from us. And Moses prayed for the people.

A likeness of the serpent is hanged on a pole. This being an instruction that Jesus Christ would be hanged on a pole and would bear the sins of the world: And that his sacrificial death was a complete and total victory over sin and the serpent [dragon, cherub] in the garden which brought sin into the world.

21:8 And the LORD said unto Moses, Make thee a fiery serpent, and set it upon a pole: and it shall come to pass, that every one that is bitten, when he looketh upon it, shall live. **21:9** And Moses made a serpent of brass, and put it upon a pole, and it came to pass, that if a serpent had bitten any man, when he beheld the serpent of brass, he lived.

The journeys of Israel to go around Edom and reach the Jordan River

21:10 And the children of Israel set forward, and pitched in Oboth.

21:11 And they journeyed from Oboth, and pitched at Ijeabarim, in the wilderness which is before Moab, toward the sunrising.

21:12 From thence they removed, and pitched in the valley of Zared.

21:13 From thence they removed, and pitched on the other side of Arnon, which is in the wilderness that cometh out of the coasts of the Amorites: for Arnon is the border of Moab, between Moab and the Amorites.

21:14 Wherefore it is said in the book of the wars of the LORD, What he did in the Red sea, and in the brooks of Arnon, **21:15** And at the stream of the brooks that goeth down to the dwelling of Ar, and lieth upon the border of Moab.

21:16 And from thence they went to **Beer: that is the well whereof the LORD spake unto Moses, Gather the people together, and I will give them water.**

21:17 Then Israel sang this song, Spring up, O well; sing ye unto it: **21:18** The princes digged the well, the nobles of the people digged it, by the direction of the lawgiver [Jesus Christ], with their staves. And from the wilderness they went to Mattanah: **21:19** And from Mattanah to Nahaliel: and from Nahaliel to Bamoth: **21:20** And from Bamoth in the valley, that is in the country of Moab, to the top of Pisgah, which looketh toward Jeshimon.

Israel appeals for passage through the land of the Amorites

21:21 And Israel sent messengers unto Sihon king of the Amorites, saying, **21:22** Let me pass through thy land: we will not turn into the fields, or into the vineyards; we will not drink of the waters of the well: but we will go along by the king's high way, until we be past thy borders.

Sihon would fight and not allow safe passage

21:23 And Sihon would not suffer Israel to pass through his border: but Sihon gathered all his people together, and went out against Israel into the wilderness: and he came to Jahaz, and fought against Israel.

The Amorites were defeated by the God who later gave up his Godhood to be made flesh as Jesus Christ, and Israel came to the border of Ammon

21:24 And Israel smote him with the edge of the sword, and possessed his land from Arnon unto Jabbok, even unto the children of Ammon: for the border of the children of Ammon was strong.

The Amorites also included the land of Moab which Sihon had subjugated. So Israel defeated the Amorites and took the land of the Amorites and the land of Moab which was occupied by the Amorites.

21:25 And Israel took all these cities: and **Israel dwelt in all the cities of the Amorites, in Heshbon, and in all the villages thereof. 21:26** For Heshbon was the city of Sihon the king of the Amorites, who had fought against the **former king of Moab, and taken all his land out of his hand, even unto Arnon.**

21:27 Wherefore they that speak in proverbs say, Come into Heshbon, let the city of Sihon be built and prepared: **21:28** For there is a fire gone out of Heshbon, a flame from the city of Sihon: it hath consumed Ar of Moab, and the lords of the high places of Arnon. **21:29** Woe to thee, Moab! thou art undone, O people of Chemosh: he hath given his sons that escaped, and his daughters, into captivity unto Sihon king of the Amorites. **21:30** We have shot at them; Heshbon is perished even unto Dibon, and we have laid them waste even unto Nophah, which reacheth unto Medeba.

Sihon ruled from the border of Edom south of the Dead Sea including Moab at the east side of the Dead Sea, right up to the border of Ammon. After conquering Sihon Israel went around Ammon and moved up into Bashan [modern Syria's side of the Golan]. Nevertheless the Amorites were a large nation of the Canaanites and certain other kings of the Amorites lived west of Jordan which were later destroyed by Joshua.

21:31 Thus Israel dwelt [occupied] in the land of the Amorites. **21:32** And Moses sent to spy out Jaazer, and they took the villages thereof, and drove out the Amorites that were there.

After destroying the Amorites they continued north to fight against Og king of the Golan region.

21:33 And they turned and went up by the way of Bashan: and **Og the king of Bashan** [the Golan region] went out against them, he, and all his people, to the battle at Edrei.

The God who later gave up his God-hood to be made flesh as Jesus Christ then told Moses to go forward fearlessly into the Golan region. Is this the wimpy, tolerate anything in the name of a false emotional love, false Christ of today's spiritual Ekklesia?

Those Canaanites were to be destroyed as an instructional allegory for us, teaching us that all unrepentant sinners will ultimately be destroyed!

Jesus Christ will deliver a great victory over all sin; if we will only follow him to live by every Word of God and seek God's deliverance against the sin and temptation that besets us.

21:34 And the LORD said unto Moses, **Fear him [Og] not: for I have delivered him into thy hand, and all his people, and his land; and thou shalt do to him as thou didst unto Sihon king of the Amorites, which dwelt at Heshbon.**

21:35 So they smote him [Og of Bashan, aka Golan], and his sons, and all his people, until there was none left him alive: and they possessed his land.

Numbers 22

Israel then turned back south to Moab and instead of welcoming their liberators from the Amorites Moab was sore afraid of Israel

22:1 And the children of Israel set forward, and pitched in the plains of Moab on this side Jordan by Jericho.

Balak was ruler of Moab and was greatly afraid because of Israel's destruction of the Amorites.

22:2 And Balak the son of Zippor saw all that Israel had done to the Amorites. **22:3** And Moab was sore afraid of the people, because they were many: and Moab was distressed because of the children of Israel. **22:4** And Moab said unto the elders of Midian, Now shall this company lick up all that are round about us, as the ox licketh up the grass of the field. And Balak the son of Zippor was king of the Moabites at that time.

Balak sends messengers to Balaam because Balaam had a great reputation to bless and to curse effectively. Balak asks Balaam to curse Israel, who were the called out of Egypt and the bride of the God who later became flesh as Jesus Christ.

22:5 He sent messengers therefore unto Balaam the son of Beor to Pethor, which is by the river of the land of the children of his people, to call him, saying, Behold, there is a people come out from Egypt: behold, they cover the face of the earth, and they abide over against me: **22:6** Come now therefore, I pray thee, curse me this people; for they are too mighty for me: peradventure I shall prevail, that we may smite them, and that I may drive them out of the land: for I wot that he whom thou blessest is blessed, and he whom thou cursest is cursed.

The messengers brought with them payment for Balaam; this being the rewards of divination. I have heard some imply that Balaam was a man of God, how they could get this idea about this wicked satanic man is beyond understanding. Balaam was a diviner and magician who's workings were by the power of Satan.

He had great power by Satan, yet Satan and his instruments are limited by God in what they are allowed to do.

22:7 And the elders of Moab and the elders of Midian departed with the rewards of divination in their hand; and they came unto Balaam, and spake unto him the words of Balak.

Balaam then inquires of God as to what he may do. This is not strange considering that Satan appears before God to give an account of his doings (Job 1:6-8).

22:8 And he said unto them, Lodge here this night, and I will bring you word again, as the LORD shall speak unto me: and the princes of Moab abode with Balaam.

God speaks to Balaam and Balaam makes his request

22:9 And God came unto Balaam, and said, What men are these with thee? **22:10** And Balaam said unto God, Balak the son of Zippor, king of Moab, hath sent unto me, saying, **22:11** Behold, there is a people come out of Egypt, which covereth the face of the earth: come now, curse me them; peradventure I shall be able to overcome them, and drive them out.

God forbids cursing Israel; and calls them blessed

22:12 And God said unto Balaam, Thou shalt not go with them; thou shalt not curse the people: for they are blessed.

Balaam informs the messengers that he has been refused permission to go with them to curse Israel. We should begin to get the picture that even though Satan is the God of this world, he is limited by the Eternal in what he may do. The God family is always in charge and in full control.

22:13 And Balaam rose up in the morning, and said unto the princes of Balak, Get you into your land: for the LORD refuseth to give me leave to go with you.

The messengers returned to the king and the king sent them back to Balaam with offers of greater rewards.

22:14 And the princes of Moab rose up, and they went unto Balak, and said, Balaam refuseth to come with us.

22:15 And Balak sent yet again princes, more, and more honourable than they. **22:16** And they came to Balaam, and said to him, Thus saith Balak the son of Zippor, Let nothing, I pray thee, hinder thee from coming unto me: **22:17** For I will promote thee unto very great honour, and I will do whatsoever thou sayest unto me: come therefore, I pray thee, curse me this people.

Balaam then admits that he is completely limited by the Word of God: So it is in this end time, when we have trials we are to run to our Mighty Deliverer who has power over every work of Satan.

22:18 And Balaam answered and said unto the servants of Balak, If Balak would give me his house full of silver and gold, **I cannot go beyond the word of the LORD my God, to do less or more.**

Balaam was enticed by the offers and decided to ask God once more

22:19 Now therefore, I pray you, tarry ye also here this night, that I may know what the LORD will say unto me more.

God allowed Balaam to go with the men, but admonishes him to speak only the words which God tells him.

22:20 And God came unto Balaam at night, and said unto him, If the men come to call thee, rise up, and go with them; but yet the word which I shall say unto thee, that shalt thou do. **22:21** And Balaam rose up in the morning, and saddled his ass, and went with the princes of Moab.

God was angry because Balaam wanted to take a reward from the king to curse those whom God had blessed: And he sent his angel to threaten to kill Balaam in order to impress upon him that he must say only what God would tell him to say.

22:22 And God's anger was kindled because he went: and the angel of the LORD stood in the way for an adversary against him. Now he was riding upon his ass, and his two servants were with him. **22:23** And the ass saw the angel of the LORD standing in the way, and his sword drawn in his hand: and the ass turned aside out of the way, and went into the field: and Balaam smote the ass, to turn her into the way.

The ass seeing the angel tried to turn aside in a narrow lane and crushed the foot of Balaam against a wall

22:24 But the angel of the LORD stood in a path of the vineyards, a wall being on this side, and a wall on that side. **22:25** And when the ass saw the angel of the LORD, she thrust herself unto the wall, and crushed Balaam's foot against the wall: and he smote her again.

The angel went a little distance further, where the ass on seeing him refused to go further and laid down.

22:26 And the angel of the LORD went further, and stood in a narrow place, where was no way to turn either to the right hand or to the left. **22:27** And when the ass saw the angel of the LORD, she fell down under Balaam: and Balaam's anger was kindled, and he smote the ass with a staff.

Then the ass was made to speak the words of God

22:28 And the LORD opened the mouth of the ass, and she said unto Balaam, What have I done unto thee, that thou hast smitten me these three times? **22:29** And Balaam said unto the ass, Because thou hast mocked me: I would there were a sword in mine hand, for now would I kill thee. **22:30** And the ass said unto Balaam, Am not I thine ass, upon which thou hast ridden ever since I was thine unto this day? was I ever wont to do so unto thee? And he said, Nay.

Then Balaam's eyes were opened so that he could see why the ass had tried to stop

22:31 Then the LORD opened the eyes of Balaam, and he saw the angel of the LORD standing in the way, and his sword drawn in his hand: and he bowed down his head, and fell flat on his face.

The angel tells Balaam that his life had been saved by his ass

22:32 And the angel of the LORD said unto him, Wherefore hast thou smitten thine ass these three times? behold, I went out to withstand thee, because thy way is perverse before me: **22:33** And the ass saw me, and turned from me these three times: unless she had turned from me, **surely now also I had slain thee, and saved her alive.**

Obviously, normally asses cannot speak, and this ass was allowed to speak by God's power so that Balaam would be thoroughly warned to say ONLY those things that God wanted said.

22:34 And Balaam said unto the angel of the LORD, I have sinned; for I knew not that thou stoodest in the way against me: now therefore, if it displease thee, I will get me back again. **22:35** And the angel of the LORD said unto Balaam, **Go with the men: but only the word that I shall speak unto thee, that thou shalt speak.** So Balaam went with the princes of Balak.

22:36 And when Balak heard that Balaam was come, he went out to meet him unto a city of Moab, which is in the border of Arnon, which is in the utmost coast.

Balaam now warns Balak that he may speak only the word that God gives him; regardless of any reward

22:37 And Balak said unto Balaam, Did I not earnestly send unto thee to call thee? wherefore camest thou not unto me? am I not able indeed to promote thee to honour? **22:38** And Balaam said unto Balak, Lo, I am come unto thee: **have I now any power at all to say any thing? the word that God putteth in my mouth, that shall I speak.**

22:39 And Balaam went with Balak, and they came unto Kirjathhuzoth. **22:40** And Balak offered [sacrificed to his gods] oxen and sheep, and sent to Balaam, and to the princes that were with him. **22:41** And it came to pass on the morrow, that Balak took Balaam, and brought him up into the high places of Baal, that thence he might see the utmost part of the people [of Israel].

Numbers 23

Balaam sought to entice God with offerings; making offerings with evil in his heart.

How many today make big offerings in an attempt to ease their consciences while having malice or some evil like Sabbath pollution in their hearts? How many people give a large High Day offering and then rush out to pollute the High Day by buying in a restaurant?

Numbers 23:1 And Balaam said unto Balak, Build me here seven altars, and prepare me here seven oxen and seven rams. **23:2** And Balak did as Balaam had spoken; and Balak and Balaam offered on every altar a bullock and a ram. **23:3** And Balaam said unto Balak, Stand by thy burnt offering, and I will go: peradventure the LORD will come to meet me: and whatsoever he sheweth me I will tell thee. And he went to an high place.

God commands Balaam concerning what he should speak

23:4 And God met Balaam: and he said unto him, I have prepared seven altars, and I have offered upon every altar a bullock and a ram. **23:5** And the LORD put a word in Balaam's mouth, and said, Return unto Balak, and thus thou shalt speak.

23:6 And he [Balaam] returned unto him [king Balak], and, lo, he stood by his burnt sacrifice, he, and all the princes of Moab.

Then Balaam declared the Word of God to the king

23:7 And he took up his parable, and said, Balak the king of Moab hath brought me from Aram, out of the mountains of the east, saying, Come, curse me Jacob, and come, defy Israel.

Jacob [Israel] is blessed by God through the words of Balaam

23:8 How shall I curse, whom God hath not cursed? or how shall I defy, whom the LORD hath not defied? **23:9** For from the top of the rocks I see him, and from the hills I behold him: lo, the people shall dwell alone, and shall not be reckoned among the nations.

23:10 Who can count the dust of Jacob, and the number of the fourth part of Israel? Let me die the death of the righteous, and let my last end be like his!

Balak who paid for a curse is enraged that a blessing is accounted to Israel

23:11 And Balak said unto Balaam, What hast thou done unto me? I took thee to curse mine enemies, and, behold, thou hast blessed them altogether. **23:12** And he answered and said, Must I not take heed to speak that which the LORD hath put in my mouth?

Balak tried to get a curse on Israel from Balaam again.

23:13 And Balak said unto him, Come, I pray thee, with me unto another place, from whence thou mayest see them: thou shalt see but the utmost part of them, and shalt not see them all: and curse me them from thence. **23:14** And he brought him into the field of Zophim, to the top of Pisgah, and built seven altars, and offered a bullock and a ram on every altar.

Balaam then again consults with the God who later gave up his Godhood to become flesh as Jesus Christ, perhaps unaware of the fact that this God was the Husband of Israel and that he was asking a Husband to curse his beloved wife.

23:15 And he said unto Balak, Stand here by thy burnt offering, while I meet the LORD yonder.

God tells Balaam what to say

23:16 And the LORD met Balaam, and put a word in his mouth, and said, Go again unto Balak, and say thus. **23:17** And when he came to him, behold, he stood by his burnt offering, and the princes of Moab with him. And Balak said unto him, What hath the LORD spoken?

Balaam admits that he cannot reverse the Word of God, just as today Satan cannot resist the will of God.

23:18 And he took up his parable, and said, Rise up, Balak, and hear; hearken unto me, thou son of Zippor: **23:19** God is not a man, that he should lie; neither the son of man, that he should repent: hath he said, and shall he not do it? or hath he spoken, and shall he not make it good? **23:20** Behold, I have received commandment to bless: and he hath blessed; and I cannot reverse it.

This statement is now about both physical Israel and the resurrected spiritual Israel.

23:21 He hath not beheld iniquity in Jacob, neither hath he seen perverseness in Israel: the LORD his God is with him, and the shout of a king is among them. **23:22** God brought them out of Egypt; he hath as it were the strength of an unicorn [more correctly translated as: a strong ox].

Just as physical Israel overcame many enemies by the power of the God who later became flesh as Christ to take possession of the physical promised land; so the faithful of spiritual Israel shall also overcome all adversity to steadfastly conquer sin, by the power of our Mighty One.

23:23 Surely there is no enchantment against Jacob, neither is there any divination against Israel: according to this time it shall be said of Jacob and of Israel, What hath God wrought! **23:24** Behold, the people shall rise up as a great lion, and lift up himself as a young lion: he shall not lie down until he eat of the prey, and drink the blood of the slain.

Balak commanded Balaam not to speak of Israel again, because he does not want Israel blessed

23:25 And Balak said unto Balaam, Neither curse them at all, nor bless them at all. **23:26** But Balaam answered and said unto Balak, Told not I thee, saying, All that the LORD speaketh, that I must do?

Balak later asks Balaam to try one more time

23:27 And Balak said unto Balaam, Come, I pray thee, I will bring thee unto another place; peradventure it will please God that thou mayest curse me them from thence. **23:28** And Balak brought Balaam unto the top of Peor, that looketh toward Jeshimon. **23:29** And Balaam said unto Balak, Build me here seven altars, and prepare me here seven bullocks and seven rams. **23:30** And Balak did as Balaam had said, and offered a bullock and a ram on every altar.

Numbers 24

Numbers 24:1 And when Balaam saw that it pleased the LORD to bless Israel, he went not, as at other times, **to seek for enchantments, but he set his face toward the wilderness.**

God then inspired Balaam by God's Spirit to prophesy again concerning Israel

24:2 And Balaam lifted up his eyes, and he saw Israel abiding in his tents according to their tribes; and the spirit of God came upon him.

Balaam in a trance from God, delivers a blessing and a prophecy of Israel

24:3 And he took up his parable, and said, Balaam the son of Beor hath said, and the man whose eyes are open hath said: **24:4** He hath said, which heard the words of God, which saw the vision of the Almighty, falling into a trance, but having his eyes open:

This is a prophecy of physical Israel at that time, about entering Canaan and possessing the land; and it is a prophecy of millennial physical Israel being the head of all nations. It is also a prophecy of spiritual Israel overcoming all sin through zeal to live by every Word of God and entering the Promised Land of eternal life.

24:5 How goodly are thy tents, O Jacob, and thy tabernacles, O Israel! **24:6** As the valleys are they spread forth, as gardens by the river's side, as the trees of lign aloes which the LORD hath planted, and as cedar trees beside the waters.

24:7 He shall pour the water out of his buckets, and his seed shall be in many waters, and his king shall be higher than Agag, and his kingdom shall be exalted.

24:8 God brought him forth out of Egypt; he hath as it were the strength of an unicorn: he shall eat up the nations his enemies, and shall break their bones, and pierce them through with his arrows.

24:9 He couched, he lay down as a lion, and as a great lion: who shall stir him up? Blessed is he that blesseth thee, and cursed is he that curseth thee.

King Balak is furious at Balaam

24:10 And Balak's anger was kindled against Balaam, and he smote his hands together: and Balak said unto Balaam, I called thee to curse mine enemies, and, behold, thou hast altogether blessed them these three times. **24:11** Therefore now flee thou to thy place: I thought to promote thee unto great honour; but, lo, the LORD hath kept thee back from honour.

24:12 And Balaam said unto Balak, Spake I not also to thy messengers which thou sentest unto me, saying, **24:13** If Balak would give me his house full of silver and gold, **I cannot go beyond the commandment of the LORD, to do either good or bad of mine own mind; but what the LORD saith, that will I speak?**

Another prophecy of the latter days

24:14 And now, behold, I go unto my people: come therefore, and **I will advertise thee what this people shall do to thy people in the latter days.**

24:15 And he took up his parable, and said, Balaam the son of Beor hath said, and the man whose eyes are open hath said: **24:16** He hath said, which heard the words of God, and knew the knowledge of the most High, which saw the vision of the Almighty, falling into a trance, but having his eyes open:

Balaam prophesies of the coming of Jesus Christ and the destruction of the nations which had destroyed end time physical Israel.

Psalm 83 shows us that the nations of the Middle East will ally themselves with the king of the North [the New Federal Europe] to defeat and to occupy Jerusalem and Judea until the armies of the East come to gather at Jerusalem. Then Messiah will come with all his resurrected chosen to take rulership over the whole earth.

24:17 I shall see him, **but not now:** I shall behold him, **but not nigh** [in Balaam's day the coming of Messiah was far off] : there shall come a Star out of Jacob, and a Sceptre shall rise out of Israel, and shall smite the corners of Moab, and destroy all the children of Sheth.

24:18 And Edom [Turkey] shall be a possession, Seir [Turkey] also shall be a possession for his enemies; and Israel shall do valiantly.

24:19 Out of Jacob shall come he that shall have dominion [Jesus Christ], and shall destroy him [the wicked] that remaineth of the city.

24:20 And when he looked on Amalek, he took up his parable, and said, Amalek was the first of the nations; but his latter end shall be that he perish for ever.

24:21 And he looked on the Kenites, and took up his parable, and said, Strong is thy dwellingplace, and thou puttest thy nest in a rock. **24:22** Nevertheless the Kenite shall be wasted, until Asshur shall carry thee away captive.

> The Kenites appear to be associated with Midian the ancestors of the Bedouin. Moses' father-in-law, Jethro, also known as Reuel, was "the priest of Midian" and a Kenite (Judges 1:16). Ashur (אַשּׁוּר) was the second son of Shem, the son of Noah. Ashur was the father of the Assyrians, his brothers were Elam, Arphaxad, Lud, and Aram.

24:23 And he took up his parable, and said, Alas, who shall live when God doeth this! **24:24** And ships shall come from the coast of Chittim, and shall afflict Asshur, and shall afflict Eber, and he also shall perish for ever.

24:25 And Balaam rose up, and went and returned to his place: and Balak also went his way.

Numbers 25

Here we find that Balaam unable to curse Israel for king Balak, advised Moab that they could cause Israel to bring a curse upon themselves by enticing them into sinning against the commandments of God (Rev 2:14).

This is exactly how Satan works. He uses a combination of pressure and persecution, together with enticements and temptations to sin.

We must remember Satan's methods in our own personal lives, and the leaders and brethren should remember these things and be ever alert to remain steadfastly grounded on the whole Word of God.

Numbers 25:1 And Israel abode in Shittim [the acacia woods], and **the people began to commit whoredom with the daughters of Moab.**

Israel had defeated the Amorites and liberated both Moab and Midian, and Israel was actually camped in Midian (Num 26:1) by Moab on the east side of Jordan near Jericho. Both Moab and Midian listened to Balaam and both were enticing Israel to sin with their gods through sexual enticement.

The people of Moab [and Midian] sent out the willing among their women to entice Israel to sin; offering themselves to fornicate and then inviting those Israelites they consorted with, to come to the sacrifices and feasts of their gods. Later Solomon was enticed into the same sins by his unconverted wives. This is why we must never knowingly marry an unconverted mate.

Very many in today's Spiritual Ekklesia are enticed into many sins by loving others more than they love God; who commands us NOT to participate in the sins of others.

> **1 Timothy 5:22** . . . neither be partaker of other men's sins: keep thyself pure.

Numbers 25:2 And **they called the people unto the sacrifices of their gods: and the people did eat, and bowed down to their gods.**

> **Baalpeor:** Lord of the opening, a god of the Moabites (Num. 25:3; 31:16; Josh. 22:17), worshiped by indiscriminate sexual orgies. So called from the mountain pass of Mount Peor, where this worship was celebrated, the Baal [the lord or god] of Mount Peor. The Israelites fell into the worship of this idol (Num. 25:3, 5, 18; Deut. 4:3; Ps. 106:28; Hos. 9:10).

Peor the "opening" was not some sexual thing as some suggest, instead it referred to a mountain pass on the border.

Numbers 25:3 And **Israel joined himself unto Baalpeor**: and the anger of the LORD was kindled against Israel.

Satan cannot bring a curse on today's Spiritual Ekklesia, therefore Satan has secretly brought in false leaders [see Jude] to lead us into idolizing men and the false traditions of men and thereby bring a curse on ourselves by departing from living by every Word of God.

This is Satan's trap; to entice us into sin and today's Ekklesia has fallen into the trap.

Today, some in the Ekklesia dare to claim that Jesus will overlook sin so they can go ahead and compromise with God's commandments and tolerate diversity of doctrine [false teachings that turn us away from the truth and of the Word of God] with impunity!

No, Jesus Christ is not the pathetic man who would permit his espoused wife to commit spiritual adultery and reject zeal for HIM, in favor of zeal for others.

> **Exodus 34:13** But ye shall destroy their altars, break their images, and cut down their groves: **34:14 For thou shalt worship no other god: for the Lord, whose name is Jealous, is a jealous God:**

Brethren, we are to destroy every idol of organizations and men; every false doctrine, every false teaching and every false way from among us; and we are to live by every Word of God!

We are NEVER to tolerate and overlook sin, nor are we to fail to strongly rebuke the sin that brings sorrow and death!

Deuteronomy 6:13 Thou shalt fear the Lord thy God, and serve him, and shalt swear by his name. **6:14 Ye shall not go after other gods,** of the gods of the people which are round about you;

6:15 (For the Lord thy God is a jealous God among you) lest the anger of the Lord thy God be kindled against thee, and destroy thee from off the face of the earth. 6:16 Ye shall not tempt the Lord your God, as ye tempted him in Massah.

6:17 Ye shall diligently keep the commandments of the Lord your God, and his testimonies, and his statutes, which he hath commanded thee.

6:18 And thou shalt do that which is right and good in the sight of the Lord: that it may be well with thee, and that thou mayest go in and possess the good land which the Lord sware unto thy fathers.

We are commanded by God the Father and Jesus Christ to be strong, intense and zealous to destroy every false way and to be passionately committed to live by every Word of God.

God knows and will afflict those who commit spiritual adultery by tolerating and following false teachings; and by exalting the word of men above the Word of God.

Jesus Christ knows those who have a false feigned love for him and will not keep God's Word in passionate Christ-like zeal; and he will NOT close his eyes to our sins.

Jesus Christ knows those who are zealous and absolutely faithful to HIM and GOD'S WORD, and he will care for them and defend them like the jealous protecting God he is. He calls us to sincerely repent of following any false teacher who tolerates and overlooks idolatry and the spiritual adultery of sin against the Husband of our baptismal commitment!

Nahum 1:1 The burden of Nineveh. The book of the vision of Nahum the Elkoshite.

1:2 God is jealous, and the Lord revengeth; the Lord revengeth, and is furious; the Lord will take vengeance on his adversaries [those who break God's commandments and go contrary to God's Word], **and he reserveth wrath for his enemies** [who teach false doctrine and a false Christ who tolerates sin].

The men who teach a false tolerant of sin, evangelical emotional love love Christ, are the enemies of the true Jesus Christ. Jesus Christ will NOT tolerate sin and he will judge every person by their works according to the Word of God!

He will not at all acquit the wicked nor will he apply his sacrifice to the unrepentant, or those repentant in name only.

> **1:3** The Lord is slow to anger, and great in power, and **will not at all acquit the wicked:** the Lord hath his way in the whirlwind and in the storm, and the clouds are the dust of his feet.

Jesus Christ is Mighty to Save his faithful beloved who follow the Lamb whithersoever he goeth; and he is Mighty to Destroy the unrepentant sinful.

> **1:4** He rebuketh the sea, and maketh it dry, and drieth up all the rivers: Bashan languisheth, and Carmel, and the flower of Lebanon languisheth. **1:5** The mountains quake at him, and the hills melt, and the earth is burned at his presence, yea, the world, and all that dwell therein. **1:6 Who can stand before his indignation? and who can abide in the fierceness of his anger?** his fury is poured out like fire, and the rocks are thrown down by him.

Jesus Christ is Strong to Save those who are faithful and diligent to learn and keep the whole Word of God, who love Christ and God the Father enough to DO what they say and to internalize the very nature of God by learning and living by every Word of God without any compromise or turning to the left or to the right.

Let us flee temptation, and stand fast in trials; let us always take refuge in the arms of our Mighty One!

> **1:7** The Lord is good, a strong hold in the day of trouble; and he knoweth them that trust in him.

God commands Moses to tell the leaders of the people to slay the wicked who fell into idolatry. The Ekklesia today is full of idolatry and spiritual adultery and is now facing their own powerful affliction and correction. They will soon be spewed out of the body of Christ the spiritual Ekklesia [which was typified by physical Israel] into great tribulation (Rev 3:16).

The God who later became flesh as Jesus Christ was and is a jealous Husband, here he commanded Moses to slay all the leaders of the people who allowed this apostasy from the commandments of God.

Numbers 25:4 And the LORD said unto Moses, Take all the heads [leaders] of the people, and hang them up before the LORD against the sun, that the fierce anger of the LORD may be turned away from Israel. **25:5 And Moses said unto the judges of Israel, Slay ye every one his men that were joined unto Baalpeor.**

Israel had defeated the Amorites and liberated both Moab and Midian, and Israel was actually camped in Midian (Num 26:1) by Moab on the east side of Jordan near Jericho. Both Moab and Midian listened to Balaam and both were enticing Israel to sin with their gods through sexual enticement.

Later, after the leaders of Israel had been killed for their sins, the people continued the same sins with the women of Moab and Midian, and a man brought in a woman of Midian and openly consorted with her.

This is done in type today, as many leaders in the Spiritual Ekklesia openly commit spiritual adultery by turning away from any zeal for the Word of God.

25:6 And, behold, one of the children of Israel came and brought unto his brethren a Midianitish woman in the sight of Moses, and in the sight of all the congregation of the children of Israel, who were weeping before the door of the tabernacle of the congregation.

Remember that they had been commanded by God to destroy the idolaters who had gone to the feasts of Baalpeor of Moab in rebellion against the Word of God.

Now here was a sinner of Israel who was openly fornicating with a woman of Midian, AFTER God had already passed judgment on those who had fallen into this evil; and Phinehas the priest, full of zeal for God, acted.

25:7 And when Phinehas, the son of Eleazar, the son of Aaron the priest, saw it, he rose up from among the congregation, and took a javelin in his hand; **25:8** And he went after the man of Israel into the tent, **and thrust both of them through, the man of Israel, and the woman through her belly. So the plague was stayed from the children of Israel.**

25:9 And those that died in the plague were twenty and four thousand.

Phinehas, the zealous for God the Father, Jesus Christ and the Word of God, is granted an exceptional blessing; while those who justified attending pagan feasts and following pagan ways to commit spiritual adultery against their Husband were destroyed.

Those in the spiritual Ekklesia who do the same sin today by following the idols of men and organizations, will also be afflicted in this latter time.

Today, those who take a stand against the general overwhelming idolatry and spiritual adultery in the spiritual Ekklesia; are like a latter day Phinehas and will receive an everlasting spiritual priesthood.

25:10 And the LORD spake unto Moses, saying, **25:11** Phinehas, the son of Eleazar, the son of Aaron the priest, hath turned my wrath away from the children of Israel, while **he was zealous for my sake among them**, that I consumed not the children of Israel in my jealousy.

This matter of Phinehas was recorded for our instruction. If we are zealous for the Word of God to learn it and to keep it; we shall also receive an everlasting priesthood of eternal life as priests and kings of our God (Rev 5:10), in the resurrection to spirit.

25:12 Wherefore say, Behold, **I give unto him my covenant of peace: 25:13 And he shall have it, and his seed after him, even the covenant of an everlasting priesthood; because he was zealous for his God, and made an atonement for the children of Israel.**

The names of the wicked were also recorded. Today those who compromise with the Word of God and follow men and organizations in spiritual idolatry will be corrected in great tribulation, and if they will still not repent after exhausting all opportunity, they will be destroyed in the lake of fire and held in eternal contempt.

> **Daniel 12:2** And many of them that sleep in the dust of the earth shall awake, some to everlasting life, and **some to shame and everlasting contempt**.

Numbers 25:14 Now the name of the Israelite that was slain, even that was slain with the Midianitish woman, was **Zimri, the son of Salu, a prince of a chief house among the Simeonites. 25:15** And the name of the Midianitish woman that was slain was **Cozbi, the daughter of Zur; he was head over a people, and of a chief house in Midian.**

Jesus Christ then commanded Israel to attack and destroy Midian. It seems apparent that Moab had been confederate with Midian in these things, but that God had other things in mind for Moab.

25:16 And the LORD spake unto Moses, saying, **25:17 Vex the Midianites, and smite them**: **25:18** For they vex you with their wiles, wherewith they have beguiled you in the matter of Peor, and in the matter of Cozbi, the daughter of a prince of Midian, their sister, which was slain in the day of the plague for Peor's sake.

At this point Moses covers other subjects and returns to the war against Midian in Chapter 31.

Numbers 26

God commands Moses to count the army of Israel

Numbers 26:1 And it came to pass after the plague, that the LORD spake unto Moses and unto Eleazar the son of Aaron the priest, saying, **26:2** Take the sum of all the congregation of the children of Israel, from twenty years old and upward, throughout their fathers' house, all that are able to go to war in Israel.

They were camped in Midian by Moab on the east side of Jordan near Jericho. The army is being numbered and prepared to attack Midian [by God's command in Chapter 25] for following the advice of Balaam and leading Israel into sin.

26:3 And Moses and Eleazar the priest spake with them in the plains of Moab by Jordan near Jericho, saying, **26:4** Take the sum of the people, **from twenty years old and upward;** as the LORD commanded Moses and the children of Israel, which went forth out of the land of Egypt.

The families of Reuben

26:5 Reuben, the eldest son of Israel: the children of Reuben; Hanoch, of whom cometh the family of the Hanochites: of Pallu, the family of the Palluites: **26:6** Of Hezron, the family of the Hezronites: of Carmi, the family of the Carmites. **26:7** These are the families of the Reubenites: and they that were numbered of them were forty and three thousand and seven hundred and thirty. [43,730]

An explanation of the family of Reuben in reference to Dathan and Abiram

26:8 And the sons of Pallu; Eliab. **26:9** And the sons of Eliab; Nemuel, and Dathan, and Abiram. This is that **Dathan and Abiram**, which were famous in the congregation, who strove against Moses and against Aaron in the company of Korah, when they strove against the LORD: **26:10** And the earth opened her mouth, and swallowed them up together with Korah, when that company died, what time the fire devoured two hundred and fifty men: and they became a sign. **26:11 Notwithstanding the children of Korah died not.**

The family of Simeon

26:12 The sons of Simeon after their families: of Nemuel, the family of the Nemuelites: of Jamin, the family of the Jaminites: of Jachin, the family of the Jachinites: **26:13** Of Zerah, the family of the Zarhites: of Shaul, the family of the Shaulites. **26:14** These are the families of the Simeonites, twenty and two thousand and two hundred. [22,200]

The family of Gad

26:15 The children of Gad after their families: of Zephon, the family of the Zephonites: of Haggi, the family of the Haggites: of Shuni, the family of the Shunites: **26:16** Of Ozni, the family of the Oznites: of Eri, the family of the Erites: **26:17** Of Arod, the family of the Arodites: of Areli, the family of the Arelites. **26:18** These are the families of the children of Gad according to those that were numbered of them, forty thousand and five hundred. [40,500]

The family of Judah

26:19 The sons of Judah were Er and Onan: and Er and Onan died in the land of Canaan. **26:20** And the sons of Judah after their families were; of Shelah [the son that Judah was afraid to give Tamar], the family of the Shelanites [the twins of Tamar by Judah were accounted as the children of Shelah]: of Pharez, the family of the Pharzites: of Zerah, the family of the Zarhites.

26:21 And the sons of Pharez were; of Hezron, the family of the Hezronites: of Hamul, the family of the Hamulites.

26:22 These are the families of Judah according to those that were numbered of them, threescore and sixteen thousand and five hundred. [76,500]

The family of Issachar

26:23 Of the sons of Issachar after their families: of Tola, the family of the Tolaites: of Pua, the family of the Punites: **26:24** Of Jashub, the family of the Jashubites: of Shimron, the family of the Shimronites. **26:25** These are the families of Issachar according to those that were numbered of them, threescore and four thousand and three hundred. [64,300]

The family of Zebulun

26:26 Of the sons of Zebulun after their families: of Sered, the family of the Sardites: of Elon, the family of the Elonites: of Jahleel, the family of the Jahleelites. **26:27** These are the families of the Zebulunites according to those that were numbered of them, threescore thousand and five hundred. [60,500]

The family of Joseph; Joseph was given the place of the first born and exalted over his brothers to receive a double portion.

26:28 The sons of Joseph after their families were **Manasseh and Ephraim**.

26:29 Of **the sons of Manasseh**: of Machir, the family of the Machirites: and Machir begat Gilead: of Gilead come the family of the Gileadites. **26:30** These are the sons of Gilead: of Jeezer, the family of the Jeezerites: of Helek, the family of the Helekites: **26:31** And of Asriel, the family of the Asrielites: and of Shechem, the family of the Shechemites: **26:32** And of Shemida, the family of the Shemidaites: and of Hepher, the family of the Hepherites.

Verse 33 will become relevant later

26:33 And **Zelophehad the son of Hepher had no sons, but daughters: and the names of the daughters of Zelophehad were Mahlah, and Noah, Hoglah, Milcah, and Tirzah.**

26:34 These are the families of Manasseh, and those that were numbered of them, fifty and two thousand and seven hundred. [52,500]

26:35 These are **the sons of Ephraim** after their families: of Shuthelah, the family of the Shuthalhites: of Becher, the family of the Bachrites: of Tahan, the family of the Tahanites. **26:36** And these are the sons of Shuthelah: of Eran, the family of the Eranites. **26:37** These are the families of the sons of Ephraim according to those that were numbered of them, thirty and two thousand and five hundred. These are the sons of Joseph after their families. [32.500]

The family of Benjamin

26:38 The sons of Benjamin after their families: of Bela, the family of the Belaites: of Ashbel, the family of the Ashbelites: of Ahiram, the family of the Ahiramites: **26:39** Of Shupham, the family of the Shuphamites: of Hupham, the family of the Huphamites. **26:40** And the sons of Bela were Ard and Naaman: of Ard, the family of the Ardites: and of Naaman, the family of the Naamites. **26:41** These are the sons of Benjamin after their families: and they that were numbered of them were forty and five thousand and six hundred. [45,600]

The family of Dan

26:42 These are the sons of Dan after their families: of Shuham, the family of the Shuhamites. These are the families of Dan after their families. **26:43** All the families of the Shuhamites, according to those that were numbered of them, were threescore and four thousand and four hundred. [64,400]

The family of Asher

26:44 Of the children of Asher after their families: of Jimna, the family of the Jimnites: of Jesui, the family of the Jesuites: of Beriah, the family of the Beriites. **26:45** Of the sons of Beriah: of Heber, the family of the Heberites: of Malchiel, the family of the Malchielites. **26:46** And the name of the daughter of Asher was Sarah. **26:47** These are the families of the sons of Asher according to those that were numbered of them; who were fifty and three thousand and four hundred. [53,400]

The family of Naphtali

26:48 Of the sons of Naphtali after their families: of Jahzeel, the family of the Jahzeelites: of Guni, the family of the Gunites: **26:49** Of Jezer, the family of the Jezerites: of Shillem, the family of the Shillemites. **26:50** These are the families of Naphtali according to their families: and they that were numbered of them were forty and five thousand and four hundred. [45,400]

The total fighting men of all Israel

26:51 These were the numbered of the children of Israel, six hundred thousand and a thousand seven hundred and thirty. [601,730]

They were numbered by their families for the war and also so that lots can be cast in the names of the various families for the dividing of the land.

26:52 And the LORD spake unto Moses, saying, **26:53** Unto **these the land shall be divided for an inheritance according to the number of names.** **26:54** To many thou shalt give the more inheritance, and to few thou shalt give the less inheritance: to every one shall his inheritance be given according to those that were numbered of him.

God was to decide who would possess each part of the physical promised land; and God will decide who occupies various offices in the Promised Land of eternity

> **Proverbs 16:33** The lot is cast into the lap; but the whole disposing thereof is of the Lord.

Numbers 26:55 Notwithstanding the land shall be divided by lot: according to the names of the tribes of their fathers they shall inherit. **26:56** According to the lot shall the possession thereof be divided between many and few.

Now comes the counting of the Levites.

26:57 And these are they that were numbered of the Levites after their families: **of Gershon**, the family of the Gershonites: **of Kohath**, the family of the Kohathites: **of Merari**, the family of the Merarites.

26:58 These are the families of the Levites: the family of the Libnites, the family of the Hebronites, the family of the Mahlites, the family of the Mushites, the family of the Korathites. And **Kohath begat Amram.**

Amram and Jochebed were born in Egypt of the family of Kohath the son of Levi, as descendants of Levi. The mother of Moses, Aaron and Miriam; is identified as Jochebed, and their father was Amram.

Moses, Aaron and Miriam were Kohathites of Levi.

26:59 And the name of Amram's wife was Jochebed, the daughter [descendent of] of Levi, whom her mother bare to Levi in Egypt: and she bare unto Amram Aaron and Moses, and Miriam their sister.

Aaron had four sons of which two died for placing strange fire on the altar of God

26:60 And unto Aaron was born Nadab, and Abihu, Eleazar, and Ithamar. **26:61** And **Nadab and Abihu died, when they offered strange fire before the LORD.**

26:62 And those that were numbered of them were twenty and three thousand, [23,000] all males **from a month old and upward**: for they were not numbered among the children of Israel, because there was no inheritance given them among the children of Israel.

26:63 These are they that were numbered by Moses and Eleazar the priest, who numbered the children of Israel in the plains of Moab by Jordan near Jericho.

ONLY Caleb, Joshua and Moses remained of Israel from forty years previous; and not one person remained of those who had refused to follow Christ into the physical promised land.

Moses was to also die, not being allowed to enter the land.

26:64 But among these there was not a man of them whom Moses and Aaron the priest numbered, when they numbered the children of Israel in the wilderness of Sinai. **26:65** For the LORD had said of them, They shall surely die in the wilderness. And there was not left a man of them, save Caleb the son of Jephunneh, and Joshua the son of Nun.

Numbers 27

A judgment is sought regarding inheritance of land

A judgment in the context of the scriptural law is a request for God to decide a matter, which is then recorded in the scriptures.

Numbers 27:1 Then came the **daughters of Zelophehad**, the son of Hepher, the son of Gilead, the son of Machir, the son of Manasseh, of the families **of Manasseh the son of Joseph**: and these are the names of his daughters; **Mahlah, Noah, and Hoglah, and Milcah, and Tirzah**.

27:2 And they stood before Moses, and before Eleazar the priest, and before the princes and all the congregation, by the door of the tabernacle of the congregation, saying, **27:3** Our father died in the wilderness, and **he was not in the company** of them that gathered themselves together against the LORD **in the company of Korah**; but died in his own sin, and had no sons. **27:4 Why should the name of our father be done away from among his family, because he hath no son? Give unto us therefore a possession among the brethren of our father.**

27:5 And Moses brought their cause before the LORD.

27:6 And the LORD spake unto Moses, saying, **27:7** The **daughters of Zelophehad speak right: thou shalt surely give them a possession of an inheritance among their father's brethren; and thou shalt cause the inheritance of their father to pass unto them.**

The judgment of God

This is in regards to the inheritance of the perpetual possession of farmland, to keep every tribe on its own land. If a man dies without a son, the inheritance should be given to his daughters, and if he also has no daughters, then his inheritance should go to his brothers; and if he has no brothers then the inheritance shall go to his father's brothers.

27:8 And thou shalt speak unto the children of Israel, saying, **If a man die, and have no son, then ye shall cause his inheritance to pass unto his daughter. 27:9** And **if he have no daughter, then ye shall give his inheritance unto his brethren. 27:10 And if he have no brethren, then ye shall give his inheritance unto his father's brethren.**

27:11 And if his father have no brethren, then ye shall give his inheritance unto his kinsman that is next to him of his family, and he shall possess it: and **it shall be unto the children of Israel a statute of judgment, as the LORD commanded Moses.**

Moses could not enter the land, but he is allowed to see the physical promised land before he dies

27:12 And the LORD said unto Moses, Get thee up into this mount Abarim, and see the land which I have given unto the children of Israel. **27:13** And when thou hast seen it, thou also shalt be gathered unto thy people, as Aaron thy brother was gathered.

Moses could not enter the physical promised land because he struck the rock instead of speaking to it, which was an act of disobedience. Will not Jesus Christ also hold us fully accountable for our lack of zeal to fully and correctly perform every Word of God? Our entry into the Promised Land of eternity is directly contingent upon our zeal to learn and to live by every Word of God.

27:14 For ye rebelled against my commandment in the desert of Zin, in the strife of the congregation, to sanctify me at the water before their eyes: that is the water of Meribah in Kadesh in the wilderness of Zin.

Moses then asks God to appoint a leader to replace him

27:15 And Moses spake unto the LORD, saying, **27:16** Let the LORD, the God of the spirits of all flesh, set a man over the congregation, **27:17** Which may go out before them, and which may go in before them, and which may lead them out, and which may bring them in; that the congregation of the LORD be not as sheep which have no shepherd.

Then the God Being who later became flesh as Jesus Christ commanded Moses to lay hands on Joshua before all the people. From this comes the concept of the laying on of hands. However notice that Moses laid hands on the person who was selected by GOD!

He did not lay hands or anyone because they finished a course of study or had proved organizationally loyal or loyal to himself. Hands are to be laid on those who have proved themselves to be absolutely loyal to God and full of the Holy Spirit which leads us into the zealous keeping of every Word of God.

Today, very many of those who have had the hands of men laid on them [been ordained by men], are not qualified to lead the assemblies because they are loyal to men and organizations and they are not faithful to live by every Word of God.

27:18 And the LORD said unto Moses, Take thee Joshua the son of Nun, **a man in whom is the spirit, and lay thine hand upon him**; **27:19** And set him before Eleazar the priest, and before all the congregation; and give him a charge in their sight. **27:20** And **thou shalt put some of thine honour upon him**, that all the congregation of the children of Israel may be obedient.

27:21 And he shall stand before Eleazar the priest, who shall ask counsel for him after the judgment of Urim before the LORD: at his word shall they go out, and at his word they shall come in, both he, and all the children of Israel with him, even all the congregation.

27:22 And Moses did as the LORD commanded him: and he took Joshua, and set him before Eleazar the priest, and before all the congregation: **27:23** And he laid his hands upon him, and gave him a charge, as the LORD commanded by the hand of Moses.

Numbers 28

The Daily Sacrifice

God commands daily offerings to be made by the high priest on behalf of the whole congregation, as differentiated from individual personal offerings. This includes the Daily evening and morning Burnt Offering.

The Daily consists of a lamb in its first year for a Burnt Offering, accompanied by unleavened bread made with ground whole grain, pure water, olive oil and salt.

> 1. The Daily pictures the Lamb of God giving himself wholly and completely in service to God the Father, as the only Mediator between God the Father and the whole congregation.

> 2. The evening and morning sacrifices refers to a whole 24 a day of service, just as the evening and the morning are one whole day.

> 3. The unleavened bread grain offering pictures Jesus Christ as the Bread of Life for the whole collective called out, of physical and spiritual Egypt. The water is the water of salvation the Word and Spirit of God, the olive oil represents the Holy Spirit, and the salt pictures the perpetual nature of the New Covenant.

> 4. These things were to be wholly burned in the fire with the smoke ascending upward as symbolic of the very pleasant and acceptable service of Christ on behalf of the nation rising up to God the Father.

5. This is to be done continually each morning at sunrise and each evening at sunset day by day, demonstrating that it is the Lamb of God which reconciles the assembly of the called out to God the Father in Heaven.

6. The physical Daily is symbolic of the spiritual daily service of Christ as the Intercessor for the spiritually called out of bondage to sin.

7. With the change in the priesthood from the physical priesthood of Aaron to the spirit priesthood of Jesus Christ [Melchizedek]; there was a change in the Daily Sacrifice from a daily physical evening and morning offering to a continual spiritual intercession in heaven by Jesus Christ, between God the Father and the New Covenant Ekklesia.

8. In this latter day the spiritual daily intercession of Jesus Christ for the collective body of the called out with God the Father will be halted because of the overspreading of our idolatry, spiritual adultery and our many sins; like Sabbath pollution and rejecting any zeal to live by every Word of God in favor of a zeal to follow the words of men.

The stopping of the spiritual daily, means the stopping of the intercession of Jesus Christ for the called out as a collective body of people because of all our sins; so that we may be cast out from any relationship with God the Father and Jesus Christ (Rev 3:14-22), into great tribulation for the affliction of our flesh, in the hope of humbling us to sincere repentance and the saving of the spirit.

While the collective body is cast out by Christ; individuals can still have a good relationship with God the Father and Jesus Christ by their individual zeal for the whole Word of God.

The reestablishment of a physical Daily before the tribulation is NOT necessary.

Numbers 28:1 And the LORD spake unto Moses, saying, **28:2** Command the children of Israel, and say unto them, My offering, and my bread for my sacrifices made by fire, for a sweet savour unto me, shall ye observe to offer unto me in their due season.

28:3 And thou shalt say unto them, This is the offering made by fire which ye shall offer unto the LORD; **two lambs of the first year without spot day by day, for a continual burnt offering. 28:4 The one lamb shalt thou offer in the morning, and the other lamb shalt thou offer at even;**

28:5 And a tenth part of an ephah of flour for a meat offering, mingled with the fourth part of an hin of beaten oil.

28:6 It is a continual burnt offering, which was ordained in mount Sinai for a sweet savour, a sacrifice made by fire unto the LORD.

The wine or Drink Offering represents the blood, the poured out life of the Lamb of God, Jesus Christ.

28:7 And the drink offering thereof shall be the fourth part of an hin for the one lamb: **in the holy place shalt thou cause the strong wine to be poured unto the LORD for a drink offering.**

28:8 And the other lamb shalt thou offer at even: as the meat offering of the morning, and as the drink offering thereof, thou shalt offer it, a sacrifice made by fire, of a sweet savour unto the LORD.

The special Sabbath offering which is in addition to the daily sacrifice

28:9 And on **the sabbath day two lambs of the first year without spot, and two tenth deals of flour for a meat offering, mingled with oil, and the drink offering thereof: 28:10 This is the burnt offering of every sabbath, beside the continual burnt offering, and his drink offering.**

The new moons beginning the months are to be sanctified by special offerings. Since there is now no physical temple no physical sacrifices may be offered in this dispensation.

> **The New Moon is to be observed** with congregational bible studies, or personal bible studies if it is not possible to meet with a like-minded congregation. I recommend that visitors go to the "Sabbath and Calendar" category and review these things this New Moon Day.
>
> God's Word tells us to begin the new month with the first visible light of the new moon as seen from Jerusalem. The new moon day is an Appointed Time like Passover and is not a High Day, it is to be observed with Bible Studies and the Shofar.
>
> When Christ comes and the Ezekiel Temple is built, special new moon sacrifices will be offered and in addition to the Shofar being sounded in every town, the two silver trumpets will be sounded over the sacrifices in the Temple at Jerusalem.
>
> Remember that when Christ comes he will require all humanity to observe the New Moons. **Isaiah 66:23** And it shall come to pass, that **from one new moon to another,** and from one sabbath to another, **shall all flesh come to worship before me, saith the Lord.**

Numbers 28:11 And **in the beginnings of your months ye shall offer a burnt offering** unto the LORD; two young bullocks, and one ram, seven lambs of the first year without spot; **28:12** And three tenth deals of flour for a meat offering, mingled with oil, for one bullock; and two tenth deals of flour for a meat offering, mingled with oil, for one ram; **28:13** And a several tenth deal of flour mingled with oil for a meat offering unto one lamb; for a burnt offering of a sweet savour, a sacrifice made by fire unto the LORD. **28:14** And their drink offerings shall be half an hin of wine unto a bullock, and the third part of an hin unto a ram, and a fourth part of an hin unto a lamb: this is the burnt offering of every month throughout the months of the year.

A Sin Offering must also be made on every new moon, besides the continual Daily Burnt Offering and the special New Moon Burnt Offerings and if applicable the Sabbath offering.

28:15 And one kid of the goats for a sin offering unto the LORD shall be offered, beside the continual burnt offering, and his drink offering.

The Passover in on the 14th day of the first month, and the Feast of Unleavened Bread begins at sunset starting the 15th day of the first month.

28:16 And in the fourteenth day of the first month is the passover of the LORD. **28:17** And in the fifteenth day of this month is the feast: seven days shall unleavened bread be eaten.

The first day of the Feast of Unleavened Bread which is the 15th day of the first month, is a holy convocation. On a personal level this day represents the beginning of an individual's journey out of sin: On the prophetic level this day represents God beginning to call out a kind of first fruits with righteous Able which then continues over seven thousand years.

28:18 In the first day shall be an holy convocation; ye shall do no manner of servile work [work of any kind] therein:

The special offerings of the Feast of Unleavened Bread.

These are heavy with meaning and help to give us an understanding of this Festival.

28:19 But ye shall offer a **sacrifice made by fire for a burnt offering** unto the LORD; two young bullocks, and one ram, and seven lambs of the first year: they shall be unto you without blemish: **28:20** And their meat offering shall be of flour mingled with oil: three tenth deals shall ye offer for a bullock, and two tenth deals for a ram; **28:21** A several tenth deal shalt thou offer for every lamb, throughout the seven lambs:

28:22 And one goat for a sin offering, to make an atonement for you. **28:23** Ye shall offer these beside the burnt offering in the morning, which is for a continual burnt offering.

The Feast of Unleavened Bread daily Sin and Burnt Offerings are to be made immediately after the regular Daily Burnt Offering. These special Festival Sin and Burnt Offerings with the Meat Offering [unleavened bread] must be offered daily for the entire seven days of this Feast.

28:24 After this manner **ye shall offer daily, throughout the seven days,** the meat [the unleavened bread accompanying the Burnt Offering] of the sacrifice made by fire, of a sweet savour unto the LORD: **it shall be offered beside the continual burnt offering, and his drink offering.**

28:25 And on the seventh day ye shall have an holy convocation; ye shall do no servile work.

The First and Seventh days of the Feast are High Holy Days:

The first day representing the beginning of God calling out an early harvest from bondage to sin, which calling to God began with righteous Abel and has continued for almost 6,000 years.

At the end of the 6,000 years there will be a resurrection to spirit of God's faithful.

The seventh day High Holy Day represents a millennial Sabbath of rest with Satan removed; capping the resurrection to spirit of the chosen late on the sixth day of the Feast of Unleavened Bread when Israel rose up out of the Red Sea in a type of the resurrection of those called out of bondage to Satan and sin.

The seventh day of this Feast celebrates deliverance from bondage in physical Egypt; and deliverance from bondage to Satan, sin and the grave for the spiritually called out of the early harvest.

The sacrifices of the Feast of First Fruits, sometimes called Pentecost

28:26 Also in the day of the firstfruits, when ye bring a new meat [unleavened bread] offering unto the LORD, **after** your weeks be out [after the seventh week is completed, that is, on the fiftieth day] , ye shall have an holy convocation; ye shall do no servile work [work of any kind]: See the Pentecost articles.

28:27 But ye shall offer the burnt offering for a sweet savour unto the LORD; two young bullocks, one ram, seven lambs of the first year; **28:28** And their meat offering of flour mingled with oil, three tenth deals unto one bullock, two tenth deals unto one ram, **28:29** A several tenth deal unto one lamb, throughout the seven lambs; **28:30** And one kid of the goats, to make an atonement for you.

28:31 Ye shall offer them beside the continual burnt offering, and his meat [unleavened bread] offering, (they shall be unto you without blemish) and their drink [wine] offerings.

Numbers 29

Special sacrifices for the Feast of Trumpets

Numbers 29:1 And **in the seventh month, on the first day of the month,** ye shall have an holy convocation; ye shall do no servile work [work of any kind]: it is a day of blowing [blasting] the trumpets unto you.

29:2 And ye shall offer a burnt offering for a sweet savour unto the LORD; one young bullock, one ram, and seven lambs of the first year without blemish: **29:3** And their meat offering shall be of flour mingled with oil, three tenth deals for a bullock, and two tenth deals for a ram, **29:4** And one tenth deal for one lamb, throughout the seven lambs: **29:5** And one kid of the goats for a sin offering, to make an atonement for you:

The above offerings are in addition to the regular Daily and the New Moon offerings, and where this Feast falls on a weekly Sabbath, the Sabbath offerings.

29:6 Beside the burnt offering of the month, and his meat offering, and the daily burnt offering, and his meat offering, and their drink offerings, according unto their manner, for a sweet savour, a sacrifice made by fire unto the LORD.

The Fast of Atonement special offerings

29:7 And ye shall have on the tenth day of this seventh month an holy convocation; and ye shall afflict your souls: ye shall not do any work therein: **29:8** But ye shall offer a burnt offering unto the LORD for a sweet savour; one young bullock, one ram, and seven lambs of the first year; they shall be unto you without blemish: **29:9** And their meat offering shall be of flour mingled with oil, three tenth deals to a bullock, and two tenth deals to one ram, **29:10** A several tenth deal for one lamb, throughout the seven lambs: **29:11** One kid of the goats for a sin offering; beside the sin offering of atonement, and the continual burnt offering, and the meat offering of it, and their drink offerings.

The Offerings of the Feast of Tabernacles

The first day is a High Holy Day, followed by six more days for a complete seven day fall Feast

29:12 And on **the fifteenth day of the seventh month ye shall have an holy convocation; ye shall do no servile work** [no work of any kind], and ye shall keep a feast unto the LORD seven days:

The acknowledged expert on the Temple and its services is Albert Edersheim. Here is an extraction of his comments on the Feast of Tabernacles. Notice that the Last Great Day is clearly identified as the seventh day of Tabernacles and it is NOT the Eighth Day Feast.

The Feast of Tabernacles, Burnt Offerings and the Seventy Nations of Mankind

> "The Tabernacles Offerings were altogether unique. The sin-offering for each of the seven days was 'one kid of the goats.' A parallel of the Fast of Atonement, with a goat [typical of the of the main harvest, as the lamb was the sin offering for the early harvest called out.
>
> The burnt-offerings consisted of bullocks, rams, and lambs, with their appropriate meat [Unleavened Bread]- and drink-offerings. But, whereas the number of the rams and lambs remained the same on each day of the festival, that of the bullocks decreased every day by one— thirteen on the first to seven bullocks on the seventh and last day of Tabernacles, 'that great day of the feast.'
>
> As no special injunctions are given about the drink-offering, we infer that it was, as usually (Num 15:1-10), 1/4 of a hin of wine for each lamb, 1/3 for each ram, and 1/2 for each bullock (the hin = 1

gallon 2 pints). The 'meat-offering' is expressly fixed (Num 19:12, etc.) at 1/10 of an ephah of flour, mixed with 1/4 of a hin of oil, for each lamb; 2/10 of an ephah with 1/3 hin of oil, for each ram; and 3/10 of an ephah, with 1/2 hin of oil, for each bullock.

The offerings for Tabernacles are greatly increased for those of the Feast of Unleavened bread, this signifying the main fall harvest as opposed to the small early harvest in the spring.

Three things are remarkable about these burnt-offerings.

First, they are evidently the characteristic sacrifice of the Feast of Tabernacles. As compared with the Feast of Unleavened Bread, the number of the rams and lambs is double, while that of the bullocks is fivefold (14 during the Passover week, 5 x 14 during that of Tabernacles).

Second, the number of the burnt-sacrifices, whether taking each kind by itself or all of them together, is always divisible by the sacred number seven. We have for the week 70 bullocks, 14 rams, and 98 lambs, or altogether 182 sacrifices (26 x 7), to which must be added 336 (48 x 7) tenths of ephahs of flour for the meat-offering; whereas the sacred number 7 appeared at the Feast of Unleavened Bread only in the number of its days, and at Pentecost in the period up to its observance (7 x 7 days after Passover), **the Feast of Tabernacles lasted seven days, took place when the seventh month was at its full height, and had the number 7 impressed on its characteristic sacrifices.**

Third, is the daily diminution in the number of bullocks offered. and that **these sacrifices were offered, not for Israel, but for the nations of the world**: 'There were seventy bullocks, to correspond to the number of the seventy nations in the world."

See also the Fall Festivals articles or see the Fall Festivals book.

At Babel mankind was divided by language and race into seventy families or basic nations

The burnt offering of a bullock pictures the strength and patient labour of the ox; as an example of the powerful and patient service of Jesus Christ, in this case to reconcile all of humanity to God the Father.

The burning of the whole bullock and its smoke rising up, is indicative of the sweetness to God the Father of the strong patient labour and dedication of Christ, in labouring to reconcile humanity to God the Father. The work of Christ is much more than an atonement for past sin; his work is also to spiritually heal the people so that they will sin no more.

This is a fall Festival and the sacrifice of the seventy bullocks, pictures the labor and strength of Christ to bring the seventy families - the entirety of mankind - into the Family of God.

The lambs in Burnt Offerings picture the meek child-like trust and dedication of Christ to serve God the Father; and the rams in Burnt Offerings picture Jesus Christ as the head of the flock [the Ekklesia] under God the Father [the owner of the flock] leading the flock to keep the whole Word of God, and into internalizing the nature of God the Father, and into eternal Salvation.

The goat Sin Offering at this Fall Festival like the goat of Atonement is a sin offering for the main fall harvest of humanity; while the Passover Lamb Sin Offering was for the called out of the early harvest.

29:13 And ye shall offer a burnt offering, a sacrifice made by fire, of a sweet savour unto the LORD; thirteen young bullocks, two rams, and fourteen lambs of the first year; they shall be without blemish: **29:14** And their meat offering shall be of flour mingled with oil, three tenth deals unto every bullock of the thirteen bullocks, two tenth deals to each ram of the two rams, **29:15** And a several tenth deal to each lamb of the fourteen lambs: **29:16** And one kid of the goats for a sin offering; beside the continual burnt offering, his meat offering, and his drink offering.

29:17 And on the second day ye shall offer twelve young bullocks, two rams, fourteen lambs of the first year without spot: **29:18** And their meat offering and their drink offerings for the bullocks, for the rams, and for the lambs, shall be according to their number, after the manner: **29:19** And one kid of the goats for a sin offering; beside the continual burnt offering, and the meat offering thereof, and their drink offerings.

29:20 And on the third day eleven bullocks, two rams, fourteen lambs of the first year without blemish; **29:21** And their meat offering and their drink offerings for the bullocks, for the rams, and for the lambs, shall be according to their number, after the manner: **29:22** And one goat for a sin offering; beside the continual burnt offering, and his meat offering, and his drink offering.

29:23 And on the fourth day ten bullocks, two rams, and fourteen lambs of the first year without blemish: **29:24** Their meat offering and their drink offerings for the bullocks, for the rams, and for the lambs, shall be according to their number, after the manner: **29:25** And one kid of the goats for a sin offering; beside the continual burnt offering, his meat offering, and his drink offering.

29:26 And on the fifth day nine bullocks, two rams, and fourteen lambs of the first year without spot: **29:27** And their meat offering and their drink offerings for the bullocks, for the rams, and for the lambs, shall be according to their number, after the manner: **29:28** And one goat for a sin offering; beside the continual burnt offering, and his meat offering, and his drink offering.

29:29 And on the sixth day eight bullocks, two rams, and fourteen lambs of the first year without blemish: **29:30** And their meat offering and their drink offerings for the bullocks, for the rams, and for the lambs, shall be according to their number, after the manner: **29:31** And one goat for a sin offering; beside the continual burnt offering, his meat offering, and his drink offering.

29:32 And on the seventh day seven bullocks, two rams, and fourteen lambs of the first year without blemish: **29:33** And their meat offering and their drink offerings for the bullocks, for the rams, and for the lambs, shall be according to their number, after the manner: **29:34** And one goat for a sin offering; beside the continual burnt offering, his meat offering, and his drink offering.

See the Seventy Sacrifices article or see the Fall Festivals book.

The Feast of the Eighth Day Sacrifices

29:35 On the eighth day ye shall have a solemn assembly: ye shall do no servile work [no work of any kind] therein: **29:36** But ye shall offer a burnt offering, a sacrifice made by fire, of a sweet savour unto the LORD: one bullock, one ram, seven lambs of the first year without blemish: **29:37** Their meat offering [unleavened bread] and their drink [wine] offerings for the bullock, for the ram, and for the lambs, shall be according to their number, after the manner: **29:38** And one goat for a sin offering; beside the continual burnt offering, and his meat [unleavened bread] offering, and his drink [wine] offering.

29:39 These things ye shall do unto the LORD in your set feasts, beside your vows, and your freewill offerings, for your burnt offerings, and for your meat [unleavened bread] offerings, and for your drink [wine] offerings, and for your peace offerings.

29:40 And Moses told the children of Israel according to all that the LORD commanded Moses.

See the Feast of the Eighth Day article or see the Fall Festivals book.

Numbers 30

The law of vows, in its spiritual sense, is a law of deliverance from all sin

Remember that God the Father is the Head of Jesus Christ and that Christ is the Head and Husband of the chosen called out (1 Cor 11:3); therefore this law of vows permits Jesus Christ to annul all of his wife's [our] previous vows made to others; including past vows to false religions, and such wickedness as the Masonic vows and this law also permits God as our Father to annul our vows.

This law also means that we must be absolutely faithful to our baptismal commitment [vow] of espousal to marriage with Jesus Christ; and it means that God the Father and Jesus Christ WILL KEEP their solemn promises as well.

If we compromise with the Word of God to follow any person other than God the Father and our espoused Husband, we are breaking our vow of espousal to be absolutely faithful to, and to follow our espoused spirit Husband Jesus Christ above all others.

In the physical sense; if we divorce the physical spouse that we vowed to be faithful to for life; we are breaking our vow made before and in the presence of God!

Any person who divorces their spouse in the faith, and marries another, is not worthy of their calling and should be immediately ejected from the assembly; yet the Ekklesia of today allows divorce almost at will and even has elders living in this commandment breaking condition of adultery, committing the divorce and remarriage sin. See the article on Divorce and Remarriage at theshininglight.info web site.

By equating any loyalty to men, or organizations, or friends, or physical family; with loyalty to our espoused Husband Jesus Christ; we are breaking our baptismal commitment [marriage vow] and we are committing spiritual adultery.

Numbers 30:1 And Moses spake unto the heads of the tribes concerning the children of Israel, saying, This is the thing which the LORD hath commanded. **30:2 If a man vow a vow unto the LORD, or swear an oath to bind his soul with a bond; he shall not break his word, he shall do according to all that proceedeth out of his mouth.**

30:3 If a woman also vow a vow unto the LORD, and bind herself by a bond, being in her father's house in her youth; **30:4 And her father hear her vow, and her bond wherewith she hath bound her soul, and her father shall hold his peace at her; then all her vows shall stand, and every bond wherewith she hath bound her soul shall stand.**

When we sincerely repent and commit to follow the Lamb of God whithersoever he goeth and to sin no more; all our vows and promises to follow others contrary to any part of the Word of God will be annulled by Jesus Christ the Husband of our baptismal espousal and by God our Father in heaven.

Then the sacrifice of Jesus Christ the Lamb of God will be applied to us and wash us clean from all such uncleanness and evil and we shall be accounted spiritual virgins and fit to be a part of the collective bride; as long as we remain completely faithful to Jesus Christ and God the Father, and remain zealous to learn and keep every Word of God!

There are those who believe that they are bound by the blood curdling vows of masonry to Lucifer, and there are others who believe they are bound by vows to other religions and groups. Don't you believe it! Jesus Christ is conqueror of the Pharaoh of this world, and liberates us from all bondage; if we will turn to him in sincere repentance! Satan has NO power over anyone when Christ lifts his strong right arm to deliver us!

30:5 But **if her father disallow** her in the day that he heareth; **not any of her vows, or of her bonds wherewith she hath bound her soul, shall stand**: and the LORD shall forgive her, because her father disallowed her.

If God the Father or our Husband Jesus Christ approves of any vow and does not annul it then the vow stands; but if they hear it and annul it the vow will not stand. All evil vows made before conversion are annulled by God the Father upon our repentance and conversion; but all vows made to God from conversion onward must be kept.

30:6 And if she had at all an husband, when she vowed, or uttered ought out of her lips, wherewith she bound her soul; **30:7** And her husband heard it, and held his peace at her in the day that he heard it: then her vows shall stand, and her bonds wherewith she bound her soul shall stand.

30:8 But if her husband disallowed her on the day that he heard it; then he shall make her vow which she vowed, and that which she uttered with her lips, wherewith she bound her soul, of none effect: and the LORD shall forgive her.

Spiritually when we are espoused to Jesus Christ, he becomes an authority over us and annuls all our past foolish vows

30:9 But every vow of a widow, and of her that is divorced, wherewith they have bound their souls, shall stand against her.

30:10 And if she vowed in her husband's house, or bound her soul by a bond with an oath; **30:11** And her husband heard it, and held his peace at her, and disallowed her not: then all her vows shall stand, and every bond wherewith she bound her soul shall stand.

30:12 But if her husband hath utterly made them void on the day he heard them; then whatsoever proceeded out of her lips concerning her vows, or concerning the bond of her soul, shall not stand: her husband hath made them void; and the LORD shall forgive her.

30:13 Every vow, and every binding oath to afflict the soul, **her husband may establish it, or her husband may make it void.**

30:14 But if her husband altogether hold his peace at her from day to day; then he establisheth all her vows, or all her bonds, which are upon her: **he confirmeth them, because he held his peace at her in the day that he heard them.**

If the husband frees his wife or daughter from her vows, he bears the responsibility for doing so. Jesus Christ has borne the iniquity of our evil vows through his atoning sacrifice, so that we may come to God the Father through him.

If we remain totally faithful to our vow [baptismal commitment] of espousal to Jesus Christ at baptism to live by every Word of God and to do all that he requires: All our sincerely repented past sins including foolish vows are wiped clean.

30:15 But if he shall any ways make them void after that he hath heard them; then **he shall bear her iniquity.**

30:16 These are the statutes, which the LORD commanded Moses, between a man and his wife, between the father and his daughter, being yet in her youth in her father's house.

Numbers 31

Midian had spread over a large area and when Moses had fled Egypt he went to a nomadic southern branch of Midian by Sinai (Gen 25, Num 10:29).

Moses had found refuge and married into the nomadic family of Midian called Kenites (Judges 1:16): this later war was with the Midianites on the border of Moab.

In Numbers 25:16 Jesus Christ commanded Moses to attack the Midianites; the narrative then turns to other issues in Numbers 26-30 and is now returning to the war between Israel and the Midianites.

Israel had defeated the Amorites and liberated both Moab and Midian, and Israel was actually camped in Midian (Num 26:1) by Moab on the east side of Jordan near Jericho.

Both Moab and Midian listened to Balaam and both had been enticing Israel to sin with their gods through sexual enticement.

> **Numbers 22:4** And **Moab** said unto **the elders of Midian**, Now shall this company lick up all that are round about us, as the ox licketh up the grass of the field. And Balak the son of Zippor was king of the Moabites at that time. **22:5** He sent messengers therefore unto Balaam the son of Beor to Pethor, which is by the river of the land of the children of his people, to call him, saying, Behold, there is a people come out from Egypt: behold, they cover the face of the

earth, and they abide over against me: **22:6** Come now therefore, I pray thee, curse me this people; for they are too mighty for me: peradventure I shall prevail, that we may smite them, and that I may drive them out of the land: for I wot that he whom thou blessest is blessed, and he whom thou cursest is cursed. **22:7** And **the elders of Moab and the elders of Midian** departed with the rewards of divination in their hand [to pay Balaam]; and they came unto Balaam, and spake unto him the words of Balak.

God had forbidden Israel to war against Moab and commands Israel to now deal with Midian alone.

Numbers 31:1 And the LORD spake unto Moses, saying, **31:2** Avenge the children of Israel of the Midianites: afterward shalt thou be gathered unto thy people. **31:3** And Moses spake unto the people, saying, Arm some of yourselves unto the war, and let them go against the Midianites, and avenge the LORD of Midian.

Moses calls for a thousand from each tribe except Levi, to go up to fight Midian for enticing Israel into idolatry and fornication on the advice of Balaam.

Spiritually we must also fight all temptation and enticement to sin with the powerful irresistible strength of Jesus Christ the Deliverer going before us to give us victory.

31:4 Of every tribe a thousand, throughout all the tribes of Israel, shall ye send to the war. **31:5** So there were delivered out of the thousands of Israel, a thousand of every tribe, twelve thousand armed for war.

The twelve thousand, with Phinehas the priest [who had stayed the plague in Israel by his zeal against the idolatry of Baalpeor and fornication with Midian] and the silver trumpets, with the God who later gave up his Godhood to become flesh as Jesus Christ in the midst of the army they went forward to make war.

Even so, we are to go forward to make war against all sin and compromise with the Word of God, and against the committing of spiritual idolatry by exalting any man or organizations above the Word of God!

31:6 And Moses sent them to the war, a thousand of every tribe, them and Phinehas the son of Eleazar the priest, to the war, with the holy instruments, and the trumpets to blow in his hand.

Physical Israel defeated Midian by the power of God with them; demonstrating that spiritually we can have victory over all sin through Jesus Christ dwelling in us by his Spirit; doing in us what he has always done; zealously living by every Word of God the Father in heaven.

Dear brethren, how sad it is that we choose to follow our idols of men and we choose to compromise or to even reject much of the Word of God for our own false traditions.

How very sad that there is virtually no zeal in today's Ekklesia to follow the Lamb of God, our own espoused Husband whithersoever he goeth. For HE alone can give victory over the bondage of Satan the present god king of this world and the forces of sin.

Jesus Christ [A member of the YHVH family.] is Strong, he is Mighty, he is Worthy to be Followed and Praised; and he will NEVER compromise with or overlook any sin, or fail to rebuke and destroy unrepentant sinners.

It is to their SHAME, that so many have forgotten the Might of our Lord and turned away; welcoming him in name only while denying his authority and power and his instructions to live by every Word of God.

>   **2 Timothy 3:5** Having a form of godliness, but denying the power [authority] thereof: from such turn away.

Christ gave them victory over Midian as an example that he also gives victory over all sin to those who follow him.

When we are tempted by sin to turn away from zeal for the Word of God: We must reject these temptations and run to the Strong Refuge of our Husband, to seek his Powerful Deliverance, and to rededicate ourselves to a passionate zeal for God's Word and Will!

Numbers 31:7 And they warred against the Midianites, as the LORD commanded Moses; and they slew all the males. **31:8** And they slew the kings of Midian, beside the rest of them that were slain; namely, Evi, and Rekem, and Zur, and Hur, and Reba, five kings of Midian: **Balaam also the son of Beor they slew with the sword.**

The men of Israel still desired the women of Midian who had led them into sin and idolatry; which sins had brought the plagues upon Israel.

31:9 And the children of Israel took all the women of Midian captives, and their little ones, and took the spoil of all their cattle, and all their flocks, and all their goods. **31:10** And they burnt all their cities wherein they dwelt, and all their goodly castles, with fire. **31:11** And they took all the spoil, and all the prey, both of men and of beasts. **31:12** And they brought the captives, and the prey, and the spoil, unto Moses, and Eleazar the priest, and unto the congregation of the children of Israel, unto the camp at the plains of Moab, which are by Jordan near Jericho.

Moses rebuked the army for the sin of sparing the wicked women of Midian; For Jesus Christ had commanded them to destroy Midian lest they be again led astray by the women of Midian. Does this sound like a wimpy Jesus Christ who paid for our sins in advance so that we need not depart from sin, only mouth the words "I repent" and repent in name only? This is an instruction for us, that we should not involve ourselves in false religions and false doctrines nor take unconverted mates nor indulge in any sin.

Why do you think that the Unitarian One God Movement is so prevalent in the Ekklesia today? Its purpose is to deny that Jesus Christ inspired the whole Word of God and destroyed the wicked, in order to introduce a false Christ who will tolerate sin. Read the words of Jude; these wicked men were prophesied of long ago.

31:13 And Moses, and Eleazar the priest, and all the princes of the congregation, went forth to meet them without the camp. **31:14** And Moses was wroth with the officers of the host, with the captains over thousands, and captains over hundreds, which came from the battle.

Moses rebuked the army for saving the women who had been the guilty party in leading them into fornication/adultery and idolatry! It was their lust for these very women which had been their downfall!

Our desire for the pleasures of worldliness, like buying in restaurants on God's Holy Sabbath and Holy Days is also leading us to our destruction.

31:15 And Moses said unto them, **Have ye saved all the women alive? 31:16 Behold, these caused the children of Israel, through the counsel of Balaam, to commit trespass against the LORD in the matter of Peor**, and there was a plague among the congregation of the LORD.

Moses commands to kill every mature woman [who would have been involved in leading them into idolatry] and to leave only the very young females alive.

31:17 Now therefore kill every male among the little ones, and kill every woman that hath known man by lying with him. **31:18** But all the women children, that have not known a man by lying with him [at that time and in that society those under about 12 years old], keep alive for yourselves.

Moses then commands the soldiers to purify themselves from the uncleanness of the dead on the third and seventh days and then to return into the camp on the Eighth Day as the law of the Red Heifer required.

31:19 And do ye abide without the camp seven days: whosoever hath killed any person, and whosoever hath touched any slain, purify both yourselves and your captives on the third day, and on the seventh day. **31:20** And purify all your raiment, and all that is made of skins, and all work of goats' hair, and all things made of wood.

As for the metal only, it was passed through the fire and then sprinkled with the water of the Red Heifer to be purified, and all the other spoil that cannot survive the fire was washed in water and sprinkled with the water of the Red Heifer.

31:21 And Eleazar the priest said unto the men of war which went to the battle, This is the ordinance of the law which the LORD commanded Moses; **31:22** Only the gold, and the silver, the brass, the iron, the tin, and the lead, **31:23** Every thing that may abide the fire, ye shall make it go through the fire, and it shall be clean: nevertheless it shall be purified with the water of separation: and all that abideth not the fire ye shall make go through the water. **31:24** And ye shall wash your clothes on the seventh day, and ye shall be clean, and afterward ye shall come into the camp.

The dividing of the spoils as commanded by God; Moses, Eleazar and the leaders were to assess the spoil and to divide it exactly as God commanded.

31:25 And the LORD spake unto Moses, saying, **31:26** Take the sum of the prey that was taken, both of man and of beast, thou, and Eleazar the priest, and the chief fathers of the congregation:

Those who had defeated the enemy and taken the spoil were to have one half. The congregation are to have the other half.

31:27 And divide the prey into two parts; between them that took the war upon them, who went out to battle, and between all the congregation:

An offering is to be given by the men who fought the battle, because of the great victory and spoil given to them. The tribute was to be one part out of each five hundred parts of the spoil.

31:28 And levy a tribute unto the Lord of the men of war which went out to battle: **one soul of five hundred**, both of the persons, and of the beeves, and of the asses, and of the sheep: **31:29 Take it of their half, and give it unto Eleazar the priest, for an heave offering of the LORD.**

The whole congregation that did not go to the battle must then give one part out of each fifty parts of the spoil that they received. The men going to battle being required to give less because they followed Christ in faith and hazarded their lives; while the congregation remained in the camp.

31:30 And of the children of Israel's half, thou shalt take **one portion of fifty**, of the persons, of the beeves, of the asses, and of the flocks, of all manner of beasts, and give them unto the Levites, which keep the charge of the tabernacle of the LORD. **31:31 And Moses and Eleazar the priest did as the LORD commanded Moses. 31:32** And the [total spoil] booty, being the rest of the prey which the men of war had caught, was six hundred thousand and seventy thousand and five thousand sheep [675,000], **31:33** And threescore and twelve thousand beeves [72,000], **31:34** And threescore and one thousand asses [61,000], **31:35** And thirty and two thousand persons in all [32,000 female children], of women that had not known man by lying with him.

31:36 And the half, which was the portion of them that went out to war, was in number three hundred thousand and seven and thirty thousand and five hundred sheep [337,500]: **31:37** And **the LORD's tribute of the sheep** was six hundred and threescore and fifteen [675]. **31:38** And the beeves were thirty and six thousand [36,000 cattle]; of which **the LORD's tribute** was threescore and twelve [72]. **31:39** And the asses were thirty thousand and five hundred [30,500]; of which the LORD's tribute was threescore and one [61]. **31:40** And the persons were sixteen thousand [16,000 female children]; of which the LORD's tribute was thirty and two persons [32] .

31:41 And Moses gave the tribute, which was the LORD's heave offering, unto Eleazar the priest, as the LORD commanded Moses.

31:42 And of the children of Israel's half, which Moses divided from the men that warred, **31:43** (Now the half that pertained unto the congregation was three hundred thousand and thirty thousand and seven thousand and five hundred sheep [337,500], **31:44** And thirty and six thousand beeves [36,000], **31:45** And thirty thousand asses and five hundred [30,500], **31:46** And sixteen thousand persons; [16,000]) **31:47** Even of the children of Israel's half, Moses took one portion of fifty, both of man and of beast, and **gave them unto the Levites**, which kept the charge of the tabernacle of the LORD; as the LORD commanded Moses.

Not one Israelite man of war was killed in the battle because the LORD went before them. This is a lesson for us that we are to live by every Word of God and run to our Deliverer trusting in him to deliver us from Satan, sin and death.

31:48 And the officers which were over thousands of the host, the captains of thousands, and captains of hundreds, came near unto Moses: **31:49** And they said unto Moses, Thy servants have taken the sum of the men of war which are under our charge, and **there lacketh not one man of us.**

Because not a life was lost, the army voluntarily chose to give some of the jewels, and precious metals as an additional special Thank Offering for their deliverance.

31:50 We have therefore brought an oblation for the LORD, what every man hath gotten, of jewels of gold, chains, and bracelets, rings, earrings, and tablets, to make an atonement for our souls before the LORD. **31:51** And Moses and Eleazar the priest took the gold of them, even all wrought jewels. **31:52** And all the gold of the offering that they offered up to the LORD, of the captains of thousands, and of the captains of hundreds, was sixteen thousand seven hundred and fifty shekels [16,750 shekels weight] .

31:53 (For the men of war had taken spoil, every man for himself.) **31:54** And Moses and Eleazar the priest took the gold of the captains of thousands and of hundreds, and brought it into the tabernacle of the congregation, for a memorial for the children of Israel before the LORD.

Numbers 32

Reuben and Gad ask for land in modern Golan

Numbers 32:1 Now the children of Reuben and the children of Gad had a very great multitude of cattle: and when they saw the land of Jazer, and the land of Gilead, that, behold, the place was a place for cattle; **32:2** The children of Gad and the children of Reuben came and spake unto Moses, and to Eleazar the priest, and unto the princes of the congregation, saying, **32:3** Ataroth, and Dibon, and Jazer, and Nimrah, and Heshbon, and Elealeh, and Shebam, and Nebo, and Beon, **32:4** Even the country which the LORD smote before the congregation of Israel, is a land for cattle, and thy servants have cattle: **32:5** Wherefore, said they, if we have found grace in thy sight, let this land be given unto thy servants for a possession, and bring us not over Jordan.

Moses initially rejects this, thinking the idea came from a fear of the wars to come. They were accused of not wanting to enter the land to fight with their brethren.

32:6 And Moses said unto the children of Gad and to the children of Reuben, Shall your brethren go to war, and shall ye sit here? **32:7** And wherefore discourage ye the heart of the children of Israel from going over into the land which the LORD hath given them? **32:8** Thus did your fathers, when I sent them from Kadeshbarnea to see the land. **32:9** For when they went up unto the valley of Eshcol, and saw the land, they discouraged the heart of the children of Israel, that they should not go into the land which the LORD had given them.

32:10 And the LORD's anger was kindled the same time, and he sware, saying, **32:11** Surely none of the men that came up out of Egypt, from twenty years old and upward, shall see the land which I sware unto Abraham, unto Isaac, and unto Jacob; because they have not wholly followed me: **32:12 Save Caleb the son of Jephunneh the Kenezite, and Joshua the son of Nun: for they have wholly followed the LORD.**

32:13 And the LORD's anger was kindled against Israel, and he made them wander in the wilderness forty years, until all the generation, that had done evil in the sight of the LORD, was consumed. **32:14** And, behold, ye are risen up in your fathers' stead, an increase of sinful men, to augment yet the fierce anger of the LORD toward Israel. **32:15** For if ye turn away from after him, he will yet again leave them in the wilderness; and ye shall destroy all this people.

Reuben and Gad then offered to go up to war against the Canaanites until all the tribes had inherited their land, before returning to Bashan [Golan]

32:16 And they came near unto him, and said, **We will build sheepfolds here for our cattle, and cities for our little ones: 32:17 But we ourselves will go ready armed before the children of Israel, until we have brought them unto their place: and our little ones shall dwell in the fenced cities** because of the inhabitants of the land.

32:18 We will not return unto our houses, until the children of Israel have inherited every man his inheritance. 32:19 For we will not inherit with them on yonder side Jordan, or forward; because our inheritance is fallen to us on this side Jordan eastward.

Then Moses agreed that they should have the land north of Ammon and into Syria as pasturage for their many cattle and for their land. Moses agreed because he had the promise from God that Israel would inherit all the land from El Arish in Sinai to the Euphrates if they would only follow and keep the whole Word of God.

> **Genesis 15:18** In the same day the Lord made a covenant with Abram, saying, Unto thy seed have I given this land, from the **river of Egypt** unto the great **river**, the **river** Euphrates:

It is worthy of note that the tribes of Judah and Benjamin were given only the land from Jerusalem south to Egypt.

Entering and remaining in the land is completely conditional on zeal to keep the whole Word of God; therefore there will be one more and final correction for Judah/Benjamin for the overspreading of sin in today's Jewish State.

Numbers 32:20 And Moses said unto them, If ye will do this thing, if ye will go armed before the LORD to war, **32:21** And will go all of you armed over Jordan before the LORD, until he hath driven out his enemies from before him, **32:22** And the land be subdued before the LORD: then afterward ye shall return, and be guiltless before the LORD, and before Israel; and this land shall be your possession before the LORD.

Moses warns them against any failure to keep their vow to God to help their brethren

32:23 But if ye will not do so, behold, ye have sinned against the LORD: and be sure your sin will find you out.

Moses then permits them to build defensed cities to secure their women and children [doubtless also secured by garrisons of men].

32:24 Build you cities for your little ones, and folds for your sheep; and do that which hath proceeded out of your mouth.

32:25 And the children of Gad and the children of Reuben spake unto Moses, saying, Thy servants will do as my lord commandeth. **32:26** Our little ones, our wives, our flocks, and all our cattle, shall

be there in the cities of Gilead: **32:27** But thy servants will pass over, every man armed for war, before the LORD to battle, as my lord saith.

Moses then charges his successor Joshua and also the high priest with enforcing the agreement with Reuben and Gad and allowing them an inheritance east of the Jordan

32:28 So concerning them Moses commanded Eleazar the priest, and Joshua the son of Nun, and the chief fathers of the tribes of the children of Israel: **32:29** And Moses said unto them, If the children of Gad and the children of Reuben will pass with you over Jordan, every man armed to battle, before the LORD, and the land shall be subdued before you; then ye shall give them the land of Gilead for a possession: **32:30** But if they will not pass over with you armed, they shall have possessions among you in the land of Canaan.

32:31 And the children of Gad and the children of Reuben answered, saying, As the LORD hath said unto thy servants, so will we do. 32:32 We will pass over armed before the LORD into the land of Canaan, that the possession of our inheritance on this side Jordan may be ours.

Here Manasseh also enters the agreement. Manasseh was then split with one half west and one half east of the Jordan river.

32:33 And Moses gave unto them, even to the children of **Gad,** and to the children of **Reuben**, and unto half the tribe of **Manasseh** the son of Joseph, the kingdom of Sihon king of the Amorites, and the kingdom of Og king of Bashan, the land, with the cities thereof in the coasts, even the cities of the country round about.

A list of the cities which each tribe took east of Jordan, before Israel moved into Canaan across the Jordan river.

32:34 And the **children of Gad** built Dibon, and Ataroth, and Aroer, **32:35** And Atroth, Shophan, and Jaazer, and Jogbehah, **32:36** And Bethnimrah, and Bethharan, fenced cities: and folds for sheep.

32:37 And the **children of Reuben** built Heshbon, and Elealeh, and Kirjathaim, **32:38** And Nebo, and Baalmeon, (their names being changed,) and Shibmah: and gave other names unto the cities which they builded.

32:39 And the **children of Machir the son of Manasseh** went to Gilead, and took it, and dispossessed the Amorite which was in it. **32:40** And Moses gave Gilead unto Machir the son of Manasseh; and he dwelt therein.

32:41 And **Jair the son of Manasseh** went and took the small towns thereof, and called them Havothjair.

32:42 And **Nobah** went and took Kenath, and the villages thereof, and called it Nobah, after his own name.

Numbers 33

A list of the camps of Israel from the time that they left Egypt until the crossing of the Jordan river

This physical journey to the Mosaic physical promised land is an instructional allegory that the journey to the spiritual Promised Land of eternal life, is also not an easy one, being filled with trials and temptations to turn aside from diligently following our Might One!

Numbers 33:1 These are the journeys of the children of Israel, which went forth out of the land of Egypt with their armies under the hand of Moses and Aaron. **33:2** And Moses wrote their goings out according to their journeys by the commandment of the LORD: and these are their journeys according to their goings out.

They left Egypt as the sun set ending the 14th and beginning the 15th day of the first month, while the Egyptians were burying their dead after the Passover of the destroyer at midnight on the 14th day of the first month.

The City of Ramses

> The city which Israel had greatly enlarged and to which they gathered was called Avaris. Much later Ramses renamed Avaris after himself calling it Ramses, and the scribes translating the scriptures modernized the name Avaris with Ramses so that people

would understand which city was meant. This has led to enormous chronological confusion because people later misunderstood and misdated the exodus during the reign of Ramses instead of properly in the reign of Thutmose.

Numbers 33:3 And they departed from **Rameses in the first month, on the fifteenth day of the first month**; on the morrow after the passover the children of Israel went out with an high hand in the sight of all the Egyptians. **33:4** For the Egyptians buried all their firstborn, which the LORD had smitten among them: upon their gods also the LORD executed judgments.

33:5 And the children of Israel removed from Rameses, and pitched in Succoth.

There were only three camps between leaving Egypt and the crossing of the Red Sea

33:6 And they departed from **Succoth**, and pitched in **Etham**, which is in the edge of the wilderness. **33:7** And they removed from Etham, and turned again unto **Pihahiroth**, which is before Baalzephon: and they pitched before Migdol. **33:8** And **they departed from before Pihahiroth, and passed through the midst of the sea into the wilderness**, and went three days' journey in the wilderness of Etham, and pitched in Marah.

Please do visit **the Spring Festivals category on the sidebar** for articles on the true meaning of the biblical harvest Festivals and High Days.

After crossing the sea they journeyed to Sinai

33:9 And they removed from Marah, and came unto **Elim**: and in Elim were twelve fountains of water, and threescore and ten palm trees; and they pitched there.

33:10 And they removed from Elim, and encamped by the Red sea. **33:11** And they removed from the Red sea, and encamped in **the wilderness of Sin**.

33:12 And they took their journey out of the wilderness of Sin, and encamped in **Dophkah**.

33:13 And they departed from Dophkah, and encamped in **Alush**.

33:14 And they removed from Alush, and encamped at **Rephidim**, where was no water for the people to drink.

33:15 And they departed from Rephidim, and pitched in **the wilderness of Sinai**.

33:16 And they removed from the desert of Sinai, and pitched at **Kibrothhattaavah.**

33:17 And they departed from Kibrothhattaavah, and encamped at **Hazeroth.**

33:18 And they departed from Hazeroth, and pitched in **Rithmah.**

33:19 And they departed from Rithmah, and pitched at **Rimmonparez.**

33:20 And they departed from Rimmonparez, and pitched in **Libnah.**

33:21 And they removed from Libnah, and pitched at **Rissah.**

33:22 And they journeyed from Rissah, and pitched in **Kehelathah.**

33:23 And they went from Kehelathah, and pitched in **mount Shapher.**

33:24 And they removed from mount Shapher, and encamped in **Haradah.**

33:25 And they removed from Haradah, and pitched in **Makheloth.**

33:26 And they removed from Makheloth, and encamped at **Tahath.**

33:27 And they departed from Tahath, and pitched at **Tarah.**

33:28 And they removed from Tarah, and pitched in **Mithcah.**

33:29 And they went from Mithcah, and pitched in **Hashmonah.**

33:30 And they departed from Hashmonah, and encamped at **Moseroth.**

33:31 And they departed from Moseroth, and pitched in **Benejaakan.**

33:32 And they removed from Benejaakan, and encamped at **Horhagidgad.**

33:33 And they went from Horhagidgad, and pitched in **Jotbathah.**

33:34 And they removed from Jotbathah, and encamped at **Ebronah.**

33:35 And they departed from Ebronah, and encamped at **Eziongaber.**

33:36 And they removed from Eziongaber, and pitched in the wilderness of Zin, which is **Kadesh.**

33:37 And they removed from Kadesh, and pitched in **mount Hor, in the edge of the land of Edom.**

33:38 And **Aaron the priest went up into mount Hor at the commandment of the LORD, and died there, in the fortieth year after the children of Israel were come out of the land of Egypt, in the first day of the fifth month. 33:39 And Aaron was an hundred and twenty and three years old when he died in mount Hor.**

33:40 And **king Arad the Canaanite, which dwelt in the south in the land of Canaan, heard of the coming of the children of Israel.**

33:41 And they departed from mount Hor, and pitched in **Zalmonah.**

33:42 And they departed from Zalmonah, and pitched in **Punon.**

33:43 And they departed from Punon, and pitched in **Oboth.**

33:44 And they departed from Oboth, and pitched in **Ijeabarim, in the border of Moab**.

33:45 And they departed from Iim, and pitched in **Dibongad.**

33:46 And they removed from Dibongad, and encamped in **Almondiblathaim.**

33:47 And they removed from Almondiblathaim, and pitched **in the mountains of Abarim, before Nebo.**

33:48 And they departed from the mountains of Abarim, and **pitched in the plains of Moab by Jordan near Jericho.**

33:49 And they pitched by Jordan, from Bethjesimoth even unto Abelshittim in the plains of Moab.

Here, as they were ready to cross Jordan, God gave Moses instructions to warn Israel to be faithful, and to follow his instructions and to destroy the Canaanites [as typical of unrepentant sinners, which they were], and to divide the land by lot.

These instructions are also instructions for us, so that we must be faithful to follow the Lamb of God and not sin; and an instruction that inheritance in the spiritual Promised Land by the resurrected chosen will be distributed by God.

> **John 5:22** For the Father **judge**th no man, but hath committed all judgment unto the Son:

We shall all be judged and rewarded by our zeal to live by every Word of God

> **John 12:48** He that rejecteth me, and receiveth not my words, hath one that judgeth him: **the word that I have spoken, the same shall judge him in the last day.**

Numbers 33:50 And the LORD spake unto Moses in the plains of Moab by Jordan near Jericho, saying, **33:51** Speak unto the children of Israel, and say unto them, When ye are passed over Jordan into the land of Canaan; **33:52** Then ye shall drive out all the inhabitants of the land from before you, and destroy all their pictures, and destroy all their molten images, and quite pluck down all their high places: **33:53** And ye shall dispossess the inhabitants of the land, and dwell therein: for I have given you the land to possess it.

33:54 And ye shall divide the land by lot for an inheritance among your families: and to the more ye shall give the more inheritance, and to the fewer ye shall give the less inheritance: every man's inheritance shall be in the place where his lot falleth; according to the tribes of your fathers ye shall inherit.

Israel was not to allow the Canaanites, who were types of unrepented sinners, to remain among them.

Brethren, this was a example for us, that we are not to permit false doctrine and open unrebuked sin in our assemblies

33:55 But **if ye will not drive out the inhabitants of the land from before you; then it shall come to pass, that those which ye let remain of them shall be pricks in your eyes, and thorns in your sides, and shall vex you in the land wherein ye dwell.**

By the business model outreach of catering to the perceived desires of what people want to hear, as opposed to the God commanded gospel message of warning, sincere repentance, condemnation of unrepentant sin and the good news of salvation; we have brought very many sincere but still unconverted into our assemblies. People with no understanding and with no zeal to live by every Word of God are overwhelming the zeal of the truly converted and leading them astray into tolerance for sin.

Therefore, by tolerating sin and rejecting sound doctrine and rejecting any zeal to live by every Word of God; today's Spiritual Ekklesia are facing the serious correction of the great tribulation unless we sincerely repent.

33:56 Moreover it shall come to pass, that I shall do unto you, as I thought to do unto them.

Numbers 34

The borders of millennial Israel have been defined by the God Personage who later gave up his Godhood to become flesh as Jesus Christ and who will come as King of kings over all the earth. The border on the West will be the Mediterranean Sea; southeast is the east side of the Dead Sea, south is the Red Sea and the Sinai Wadi of El Arish and the northern border will be around Lebanon and then north to the Euphrates river.

Numbers 34:1 And the LORD spake unto Moses, saying, **34:2** Command the children of Israel, and say unto them, When ye come into the land of Canaan; (this is the land that shall fall unto you for an inheritance, even the land of Canaan with the coasts thereof:)

34:3 Then your south quarter shall be from the wilderness of Zin along by the coast of Edom, and your south border shall be the outmost coast of the salt sea eastward: **34:4** And your border shall turn from the south to the ascent of Akrabbim, and pass on to Zin: and the going forth thereof shall be from the south to Kadeshbarnea, and shall go on to Hazaraddar, and pass on to Azmon: **34:5** And the border shall fetch a compass from Azmon unto the river of Egypt, and the goings out of it shall be at the sea. **34:6** And as for the western border, ye shall even have the great sea for a border: this shall be your west border.

The northern border is to be a straight line from the Mediterranean Sea east to mount Hor and then northwards to Hamath and the Euphrates

34:7 And this shall be your north border: from the great sea ye shall point out for you mount Hor: **34:8** From mount Hor ye shall point out your border unto the entrance of Hamath; and the goings forth of the border shall be to Zedad: **34:9** And the border shall go on to Ziphron, and the goings out of it shall be at Hazarenan: this shall be your north border.

The border then come down from the Euphrates in the north and ends at the border of Moab at the brook Arnon as it flows into the Dead Sea

34:10 And ye shall point out your east border from Hazarenan to Shepham: **34:11** And the coast shall go down from Shepham to Riblah, on the east side of Ain; and the border shall descend, and shall reach unto the side of the sea of Chinnereth eastward: **34:12** And the border shall go down to Jordan, and the goings out of it shall be at the salt sea: this shall be your land with the coasts thereof round about.

34:13 And Moses commanded the children of Israel, saying, This is the land which ye shall inherit by lot, which the LORD commanded to give unto the nine tribes, and to the half tribe: **34:14** For the tribe of the children of Reuben according to the house of their fathers, and the tribe of the children of Gad according to the house of their fathers, have received their inheritance; and half the tribe of Manasseh have received their inheritance: **34:15** The two tribes and the half tribe have received their inheritance on this side Jordan near Jericho eastward, toward the sunrising.

The physical promised land's eastern border runs from the Euphrates at Hamath south to the land of Moab and then south along the Dead Sea directly down to the Red Sea.

34:16 And the LORD spake unto Moses, saying, **34:17** These are the names of the men which shall divide the land unto you: Eleazar the priest, and Joshua the son of Nun.

The leaders chosen by God to divide the land to the tribes

34:18 And ye shall take one prince of every tribe, to divide the land by inheritance. **34:19** And the names of the men are these: Of the tribe of Judah, Caleb the son of Jephunneh. **34:20** And of the tribe of the children of Simeon, Shemuel the son of Ammihud. **34:21** Of the tribe of Benjamin, Elidad the son of Chislon. **34:22** And the prince of the tribe of the children of Dan, Bukki the son of Jogli.

34:23 The prince of the children of Joseph, for the tribe of the children of Manasseh, Hanniel the son of Ephod. **34:24** And the prince of the tribe of the children of Ephraim, Kemuel the son of Shiphtan. **34:25** And the prince of the tribe of the children of Zebulun, Elizaphan the son of Parnach. **34:26** And the prince of the tribe of the children of Issachar,

Paltiel the son of Azzan. **34:27** And the prince of the tribe of the children of Asher, Ahihud the son of Shelomi. **34:28** And the prince of the tribe of the children of Naphtali, Pedahel the son of Ammihud.

34:29 These are they whom the LORD commanded to divide the inheritance unto the children of Israel in the land of Canaan.

Numbers 35

The Levitical cities commanded by God, the Levites were given 48 cities scattered throughout all Israel for them to dwell in.

It was intended that these cities would be centers of religious education spread throughout all Israel so that the Levites could teach the Word of God to the twelve tribes, and that courses of Levites would go up to serve for a time at the tabernacle and later the temple.

35:1 And the LORD spake unto Moses in the plains of Moab by Jordan near Jericho, saying, **35:2** Command the children of Israel, that they give unto the Levites of the inheritance of their possession cities to dwell in; and ye shall give also unto the Levites suburbs for the cities round about them. **35:3 And the cities shall they have to dwell in; and the suburbs of them shall be for their cattle, and for their goods, and for all their beasts.**

35:4 And the suburbs of the cities, which ye shall give unto the Levites, **shall reach from the wall of the city and outward a thousand cubits round about.**

35:5 And ye shall measure from without the city on the east side two thousand cubits, and on the south side two thousand cubits, and on the west side two thousand cubits, and on the north side two thousand cubits; and the city shall be in the midst: this shall be to them the suburbs of the cities.

Six Levitical cities are appointed as refuges and judicial centers for those accused of capital crimes, besides 42 other Levitical cities

35:6 And among the cities which ye shall give unto the Levites there shall be **six cities for refuge**, which ye shall appoint for the manslayer, that he may flee thither: and to them ye shall add forty and two cities. **35:7** So all the cities which ye shall give to the Levites shall be forty and eight cities: them shall ye give with their suburbs. **35:8** And the cities which ye shall give shall be of the possession of the children of Israel: from them that have many ye shall give many; but from them that have few ye shall give few: every one shall give of his cities unto the Levites according to his inheritance which he inheriteth.

35:9 And the LORD spake unto Moses, saying, **35:10** Speak unto the children of Israel, and say unto them, When ye be come over Jordan into the land of Canaan; **35:11** Then ye shall appoint you cities to be cities of refuge for you; that the slayer may flee thither, which killeth any person at unawares.

35:12 And they shall be unto you cities for refuge from the avenger; that the manslayer die not, until he stand before the congregation in judgment.

35:13 And of these cities which ye shall give six cities shall ye have for refuge.

35:14 Ye shall give three cities on this side Jordan, and three cities shall ye give in the land of Canaan, which shall be cities of refuge.

There were six judicial cities where an accused person could seek judgment at law

35:15 These six cities shall be a refuge, both for the children of Israel, and for the stranger, and for the sojourner among them: that every one that killeth any person unawares may flee thither. **35:16** And if he smite him with an instrument of iron, so that he die, he is a murderer: the murderer shall surely be put to death. **35:17** And if he smite him with throwing a stone, wherewith he may die, and he die, he is a murderer: the murderer shall surely be put to death. **35:18** Or if he smite him with an hand weapon of wood, wherewith he may die, and he die, he is a murderer: the murderer shall surely be put to death.

The court must allow the next of kin of the murdered person to execute the convicted murderer; after a verdict at law declaring that the accused was indeed a murderer and that the death was not accidental.

35:19 The revenger of blood himself shall slay the murderer: when he meeteth him, he shall slay him. **35:20** But if he thrust him of hatred, or hurl at him by laying of wait, that he die; **35:21** Or in enmity smite him with his hand, that he die: he that smote him shall surely be put to death; for he is a murderer: the revenger of blood shall slay the murderer, when he meeteth him.

If the death was ruled accidental

35:22 But if he thrust him suddenly without enmity, or have cast upon him any thing without laying of wait, **35:23** Or with any stone, wherewith a man may die, seeing him not, and cast it upon him, that he die, and was not his enemy, neither sought his harm:

The judgment will decide if the death was an accident or a genuine murder, and the Levitical city's appointed judges must investigate and pronounce sentence.

35:24 Then the congregation shall judge between the slayer and the revenger of blood according to these judgments: **35:25** And the congregation shall deliver the slayer out of the hand of the revenger of blood, and the congregation shall restore him to the city of his refuge, whither he was fled: and he shall abide in it unto the death of the high priest, which was anointed with the holy oil.

35:26 But if the slayer shall at any time come without the border of the city of his refuge, whither he was fled; **35:27** And the revenger of blood find him without the borders of the city of his refuge, and the revenger of blood kill the slayer; he shall not be guilty of blood: **35:28 Because he should have remained in the city of his refuge until the death of the high priest: but after the death of the high priest the slayer shall return into the land of his possession.**

35:29 So these things shall be for a statute of judgment unto you throughout your generations in all your dwellings.

At least two or three witnesses are required to confirm the guilt of the murderer; however some of the witness may be documents etc.

35:30 Whoso killeth any person, the murderer shall be put to death by the mouth of witnesses: but one witness shall not testify against any person to cause him to die.

We are to take no compensation to obtain the release of a willful murderer, the willful murderer must die.

35:31 Moreover ye shall take no satisfaction [no compensation (or bribe) may be paid to save the life of a convicted willful murderer] for the life of a murderer, which is guilty of death: but he shall be surely put to death. **35:32** And ye shall take no satisfaction for him that is fled to the city of his refuge, that he should come again to dwell in the land, until the death of the priest.

35:33 So ye shall not pollute the land wherein ye are: for blood it defileth the land: and the land cannot be cleansed of the blood that is shed therein, but by the blood of him that shed it. **35:34** Defile not therefore the land which ye shall inhabit, wherein I dwell: for I the LORD dwell among the children of Israel.

Numbers 36

A further judgment is requested regarding the inheritance of the daughters of Zelophehad

Numbers 36:1 And the chief fathers of the families of the children of Gilead, the son of Machir, the son of **Manasseh**, of the families of the sons of Joseph, came near, and spake before Moses, and before the princes, the chief fathers of the children of Israel:

The question is put that: If ladies with no brothers inherit land and then marry outside their tribe, their inheritance will go to another tribe breaking up the tribal hegemony over that area.

36:2 And they said, The LORD commanded my lord to give the land for an inheritance by lot to the children of Israel: and my lord was commanded by the LORD to give the inheritance of Zelophehad our brother unto his daughters. **36:3** And if they be married to any of the sons of the other tribes of the children of Israel, then shall their inheritance be taken from the inheritance of our fathers, and shall be put to the inheritance of the tribe whereunto they are received: so shall it be taken from the lot of our inheritance.

36:4 And when the jubile of the children of Israel shall be, then shall their inheritance be put unto the inheritance of the tribe whereunto they are received: so shall their inheritance be taken away from the inheritance of the tribe of our fathers.

Moses renders the judgment of the God Being who later gave up his Godhood to become flesh as Jesus Christ.

36:5 And Moses commanded the children of Israel according to the word of the LORD, saying, The tribe of the sons of Joseph hath said well.

36:6 This is the thing which the LORD doth command concerning the daughters of Zelophehad, saying, **Let them marry to whom they think best; only to the family of the tribe of their father shall they marry.** **36:7** So shall not the inheritance of the children of Israel remove from tribe to tribe: for every one of the children of Israel shall keep himself to the inheritance of the tribe of his fathers.

36:8 And every daughter, that possesseth an inheritance in any tribe of the children of Israel, shall be wife unto one of the family of the tribe of her father, that the children of Israel may enjoy every man the inheritance of his fathers.

36:9 Neither shall the inheritance remove from one tribe to another tribe; but every one of the tribes of the children of Israel shall keep himself to his own inheritance.

Marriage to cousins is the closest allowable marriage possible under the law of God

36:10 Even as the LORD commanded Moses, so did the daughters of Zelophehad: 36:11 For Mahlah, Tirzah, and Hoglah, and Milcah, and Noah, the daughters of Zelophehad, were married unto their father's brothers' sons: 36:12 And they were married into the families of the sons of Manasseh the son of Joseph, and their inheritance remained in the tribe of the family of their father.

36:13 These are the commandments and the judgments, which the LORD commanded by the hand of Moses unto the children of Israel in the plains of Moab by Jordan near Jericho.

Visit our website
theshininglight.info